D1373291

TK 5105.8885 .A34 B74 1999
Brisbin, Shelly
Adobe GoLive 4 for Macintosh and Windows

VISU

A VE 4

FO

She

DATE DUE

WESTERN IOWA TECH-LIBRARY

DEMCO

Visual QuickStart Guide

Adobe GoLive 4 for Macintosh and Windows

Shelly Brisbin

Peachpit Press
1249 Eighth Street
Berkeley, CA 94710
(510) 524-2178
(510) 524-2221 (fax)

Find us on the World Wide Web at:
http://www.peachpit.com

Peachpit Press is a division of Addison Wesley Longman

Copyright © 1999 by Shelly Brisbin

Editor: Corbin Collins
Production Coordinators: Amy Changar, Lisa Brazieal
Copyeditor: Joanna Pearlstein
Compositor: Owen Wolfson
Cover design: The Visual Group

Notice of rights
All rights reserved. No part of this book may be reproduced or transmitted in any form by any means, electronic, mechanical, photocopying, recording, or otherwise, without the prior written permission of the publisher. For information on getting permission for reprints and excerpts, contact Gary-Paul Prince at Peachpit Press.

Trademark Notice
Adobe and GoLive are trademarks of Adobe Systems Incorporated. Visual QuickStart Guide is a registered trademark of Peachpit Press, a division of Addison Wesley Longman.

Notice of liability
The information in this book is distributed on an "As Is" basis, without warranty. While every precaution has been taken in the preparation of the book, neither the author nor Peachpit Press shall have any liability to any person or entity with respect to any loss or damage caused or alleged to be caused directly or indirectly by the instructions contained in this book or by the computer software and hardware products described in it.

ISBN 0-201-35477-2

9 8 7 6 5 4 3

Printed and bound in the United States of America

Printed on recycled paper

For my parents
Emma and Windel Brisbin

WESTERN IOWA TECH-LIBRARY

Acknowledgments

Thanks to my editor, Corbin Collins, for his calm presence and his steady supply of patience, and to the rest of the crew at Peachpit Press.

Thanks to Owen Wolfson for his spiffy and speedy layout services.

Thanks to Joanna Pearlstein for eagle-eyed copy editing.

Thanks to agent extraordinare, Claire Horn.

Thanks to John Kranz, Irv Kanode, Matt Ridley and the collective wisdom of the GoLive team at Adobe Systems for their support and encouragement.

Thanks to Mike Cogliandro for the use of his NanciNet artwork.

Warm fuzzy thanks to Frank Feuerbacher, the kindest person I have ever known.

About the author

Shelly Brisbin has written about technology for thirteen years. Her specialties include the Macintosh, networking, and the Internet. She is the author of four books and hundreds of articles for magazines including *Macworld, MacWeek, NetProfessional, NewMedia* and *WebTechniques.* Currently a freelance writer based in Austin, Texas, Brisbin spent four and a half years as networking editor for *MacUser* magazine. In her free time, she manages a music-related Web site and mailing list.

TABLE OF CONTENTS

INTRODUCTION

Welcome to *Adobe GoLive 4 for Macintosh and Windows: Visual QuickStart Guide.* This book is intended to help you get the most from GoLive and to acquaint you with webtop publishing, generally.

Even if you've used Web authoring tools before, you'll probably find that GoLive is a new experience: a Web authoring tool with a comprehensive approach to page design and site management that isn't available elsewhere.

But I'm not here to sell GoLive to you. You probably own a copy or are considering making it a part of your publishing arsenal. Whatever the case, my goal is to give you the information you need to make the most of the software and to provide a convenient reference as you learn to work with it.

Who should read this book

This book is an introduction to GoLive 4. I cover most features of the product in enough detail to allow you to design Web pages and build Web sites quickly and easily. I've designed it so that you can easily work with GoLive, leaving the book open on your desk as you work, following my step-by-step tutorials.

It is not intended as a comprehensive guide to GoLive, however. Advanced Web authors, particularly those who use animation, QuickTime authoring, and JavaScript actions will find this book a useful introduction but may want to consult other resources for complete, exhaustive coverage of these features (such as *Real World GoLive 4* by Jeff Carlson and Glenn Fleishman, to be published in 1999 by Peachpit Press).

For some readers, this book will serve as an introduction to Web authoring, as well as a GoLive tutorial. Although I do not spend a great deal of time explaining the basics of HTML or the Web, new Web authors need not fear. The step-by-step approach of this book and the visually oriented tools in GoLive make it possible to design increasingly complex pages, even without a knowledge of HTML, the language of the Web.

If you have created Web pages before, dive right in. You won't be bored, even in the early chapters of this book. Though introductory, they relate specifically to GoLive and will be very useful to you as you learn the conventions of both the software and the book.

Whatever your level of Web authoring experience, use this book to jumpstart your adventure with GoLive. You'll be designing cool Web pages and complete sites before you know it.

How this book is organized

The first two chapters of this book introduce you to Web publishing, and to the ways in which it is similar and different from traditional publishing. You'll also find a tour of the GoLive interface and get a glimpse at its most important tools and features.

Chapters 4 through 9 get down to the nuts and bolts of Web page assembly, layout, and design with GoLive. I start with the most basic element of any Web page—text—and move through all the layout tools you have at your disposal with GoLive.

In Chapters 10 through 13, I describe how to use dynamic HTML tools to arrange pages, to position text and graphics, and animate the elements of your Web pages. Chapter 14 takes a look at the source and outline editors and the Web Database.

Finally, Chapters 15 through 17 introduce GoLive's extensive Web site management capabilities, moving Web publishing beyond merely linking a bunch of pages. You'll see how GoLive gives you visual and logical tools to organize and maintain a killer Web site.

QuickStart conventions

The heart of the visual QuickStart guide format is the step-by-step approach taken to teaching GoLive's fundamentals. You'll find instructions and tutorials on all major and most minor GoLive features and functions. Along with each step-by-step example, you'll find screen shots that depict palettes, toolbars, menus, configuration windows, and Web pages as they are created and modified throughout the book.

✔ Tip

- Each chapter contains tips that point out important tricks and suggestions for using GoLive better.

Mac or Windows?

GoLive is available for Macintosh, Windows 98, and Windows NT computers. The tools and interface for each platform are almost identical. Because GoLive began life as a Macintosh application, I've chosen to use mostly Macintosh screenshots. Windows users will find, however, that that the appearance and arrangement of tools is nearly identical on all platforms. In those rare cases where a tool, window or screen differs, I've included an example from each platform.

Windows and Macintosh computers use slightly different keyboard shortcuts and other interface conventions, and GoLive typically follows the rules set down by each operating system. Where there's a difference, I note it within the text like this:

Press Command-Option-O (Mac) or Control-Alt-O (Windows).

In the few cases where a particular feature or tool is available on one platform and not the other, the paragraph or step-by-step section is preceded by an Ⓜ for Macintosh or W for Windows.

1

Learning Your Way Around

GoLive has a lot in common with desktop publishing applications. Both rely on tools and a central layout window, where you create the document you will display on the Web or in print. Like a DTP tool, GoLive uses layout grids and brings text, images, and multimedia files together on the same page. Finally, just as some high-end DTP tools let you organize projects (groups of chapters contained in separate files), GoLive's site management tools let you organize and maintain a Web site in a single window.

GoLive's collection of windows and tools is extensive but compactly organized. You'll also find a number of views that allow you to look at and work with your Web pages in different ways. In this chapter, I'll give you a quick tour of GoLive, touching on the following:

- The GoLive desktop.
- Using views to display Web pages.
- Formatting text with the toolbar.
- Adding content with Palette tools.
- Configuring objects with the Inspector.
- Adding color with the Color Palette.
- Managing sites with site management tools.
- Referring to the Web Database.

The GoLive Desktop

When you open GoLive, you'll see a number of windows that include workspace and tools for creating Web pages.

Figure 1.1 displays the three most important GoLive windows—the Document Window, the Palette, and the Inspector—along with the toolbar. We'll work our way through other GoLive windows in this chapter.

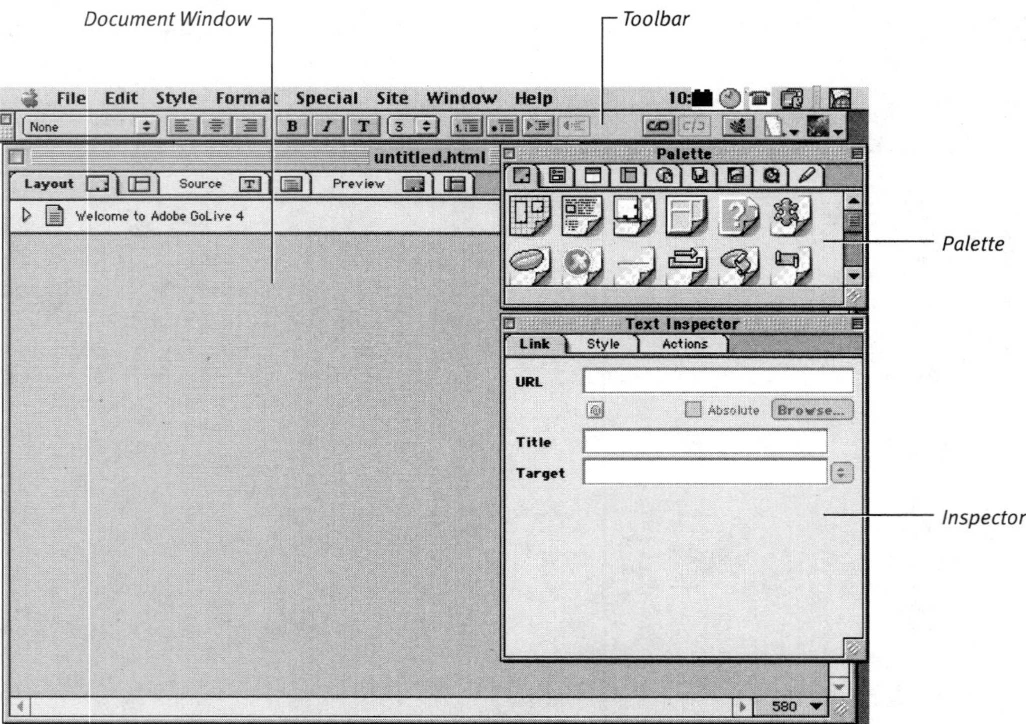

Figure 1.1 The Document Window, Palette and Inspector appear when you open GoLive for the first time.

Figure 1.2 Click on a tab to change views in the Document window.

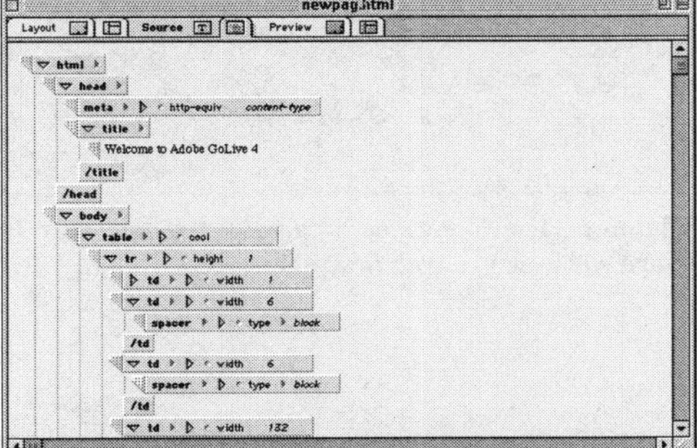

Figure 1.3 GoLive's HTML outline view shows a Web page in a hierarchical view, and it also includes HTML tags.

Page Views

Views allow you to look at and work with the same Web page in six different ways.

Use the tabs at the top of the document window (**Figure 1.2**) to switch among the six views of the current document.

Layout view

In the Layout view, GoLive functions like a frame-oriented desktop publishing application, giving you a WYSIWYG view of your Web pages. You will probably spend most of your time working in the Layout view.

When you launch GoLive and create a new page, or open an existing one, it appears in the Layout view by default. Displaying the page in a different view is as simple as clicking on the corresponding tab at the top of the main window.

Frames view

Use the Frames mode to examine and work on frames-based Web pages. Frames-based pages are actually composites of two or more HTML pages. The Frames view shows frames and icons for each file that makes up the frameset.

HTML Source view

The HTML Source view displays the raw HTML code that makes up your page. If you know HTML, you can use the Source view to check or edit the contents of your page.

The HTML outline view

The HTML outline view displays the HTML tags behind your Web page within a hierarchical structure. Use this view as a reminder of your page's organization and to place new elements at the correct hierarchical location (**Figure 1.3**).

The Layout Preview

In the Preview view, you can see an approximation of how the layout and objects you've created will look and act when viewed from a Web browser. In many cases, the Preview will look very much like the Layout view. It certainly does in **Figure 1.4**. You should not count on the preview for accurate representations or advanced features, like JavaScript or animation.

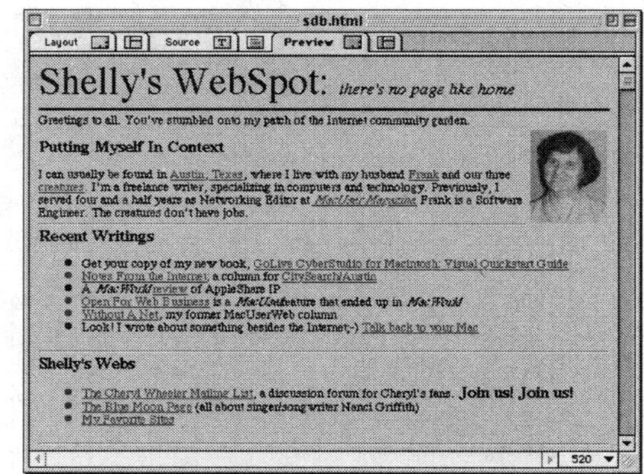

Figure 1.4 The Preview approximates the way your page will look in a Web browser.

The Frames Preview

The Frames Preview assembles the frames that make up a frames-based Web page all together and displays them as they will appear in a Web browser.

The Toolbar

Just like most word processing applications, GoLive's screen is topped by a toolbar. In the Layout view, the toolbar is primarily used to format text (**Figure 1.5**). You can choose a style (head, body text, preformatted, and so on) and apply font size, indent, and more. You can create or break HTML links and create lists in several formats.

The toolbar is context-sensitive. Several GoLive modes, including the Outline view and site management interface, include the toolbar, which changes to match the tools you're working with. I'll explore each set of toolbar options as we move through this book.

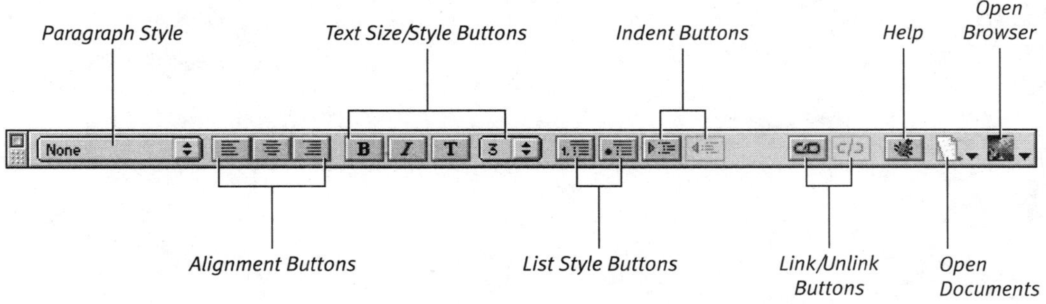

Figure 1.5 The toolbar displays text-formatting options when you display a Web page in the Layout view.

To use the toolbar:

1. Go to the Layout view.
2. Type some text.
3. Select the text.
4. Choose an alignment or formatting item from the toolbar. Your text changes accordingly.

You'll find a few other items on the toolbar, including one that takes you to your favorite Web browser, and another that toggles between open windows in GoLive.

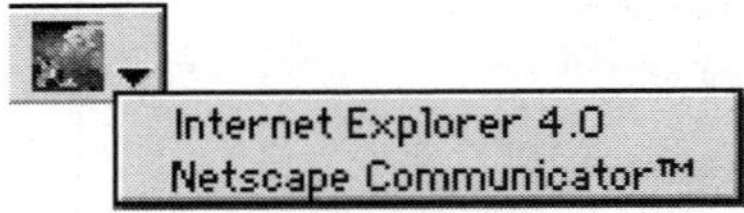

Figure 1.6 The toolbar's browser selection menu.

✔ Tip

- The toolbar includes an item that will switch you to a Web browser, so that you can see how your Web page will look to a visitor using that browser (**Figure 1.6**). To compare the look of your page in several browsers, use GoLive's Preferences command to add as many Web browsers as you like to the toolbar menu.

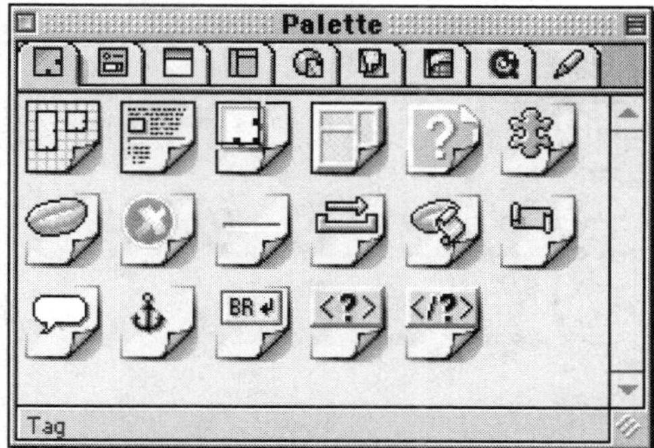

Figure 1.7 The Palette's Basic tab is displayed by default.

Figure 1.8 The Palette's tabs give you access to nine groups of tools.

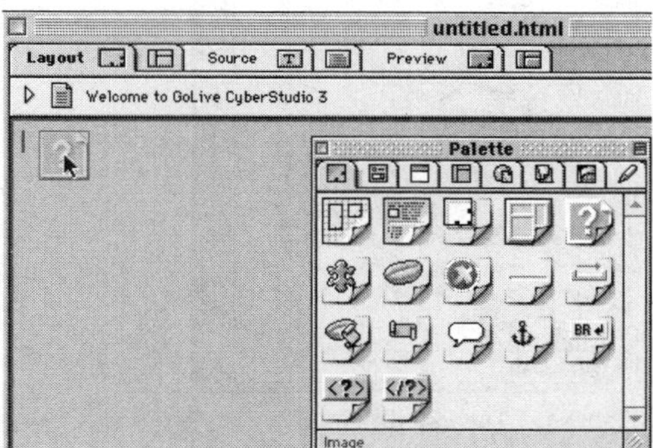

Figure 1.9 You can add images to a Web page by dragging the Image item from the Palette to the document window or by double-clicking the image item.

The Palette

Most of the tools you will use to add items to your Web pages can be found in the Palette (**Figure 1.7**). The Palette is actually composed of nine separate groups of tools, each of which is accessible from tabs at the top of the Palette window (**Figure 1.7**). Similar Palette tools are grouped together under individual tabs. You will learn more about each of the Palette tools in subsequent chapters.

The nine Palette tabs are:

- The Basic tags tab.
- The Forms tab.
- The Head tab.
- The Frames tab.
- The Site tab.
- The Site Extras tab.
- The QuickTime tab.
- The CyberObjects tab.
- The Custom tab.

To use a Palette tool, drag and drop it onto the document window or double-click it. You use Palette tools to add text, layout grids, images, lines, Java applets, and tags that specify most other HTML items. **Figure 1.9** shows an image object being dragged from the Palette to an empty document window.

✔ Tips

- Palette tab labels appear when you move the cursor over the tab. To see labels for individual Palette tools, place your cursor over a Palette tool and notice that its name appears in the lower border of the window (**Figure 1.10**).

Ⓜ Depending on the size of your computer screen, the Palette may overlap the document window, making it hard to get a complete view of your work. You can resize the Palette to get it out of the way, while keeping it available onscreen. Just use your mouse to grab the resizing box at the bottom right corner of the Palette. Drag the box downward and to the left. The Palette objects will fill the narrower window. Now move the Palette to the right, leaving plenty of room for the main Web page window (see **Figure 1.11**).

- You can move the Palette window (and other GoLive tool windows, for that matter) completely out of your way by control-clicking the window's title bar, or by dragging the window all the way to the right side of your screen. GoLive replaces the window with a small tab, visible at the edge of your monitor. Drag the tab back onscreen to bring back the window.

W To move the Palette or Inspector out of your way, drag the window's title bar to the edge of the GoLive window. The Palette or Inspector snaps to the right edge. To cause the window to float again, Control-click the area next to the close box of the item you want.

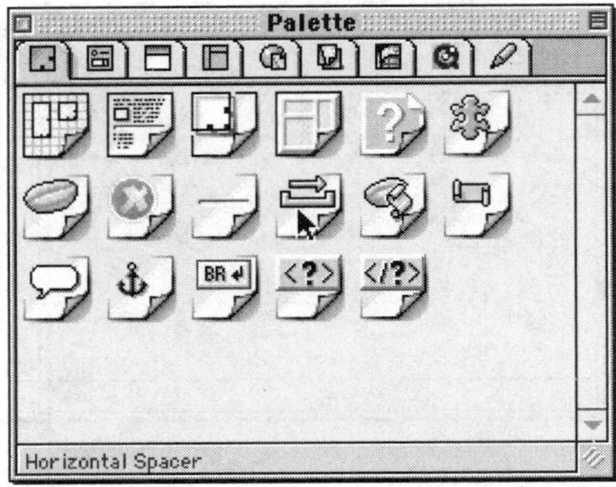

Figure 1.10 When you move the mouse over a Palette tool, its name appears in the lower left corner of the Palette window.

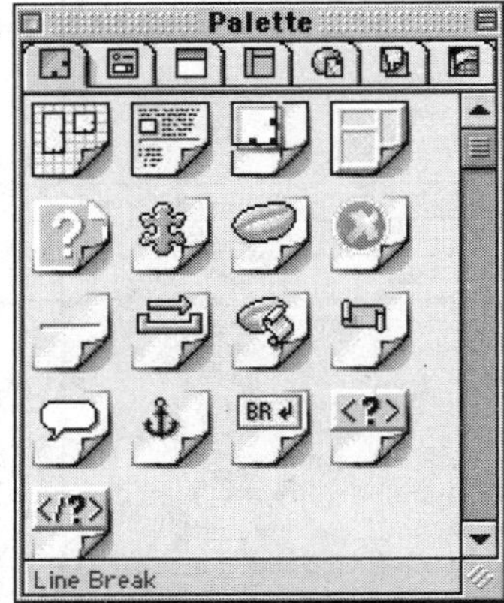

Figure 1.11 The Palette's icons reposition themselves within the window when you use the resizing box to change the window's dimensions.

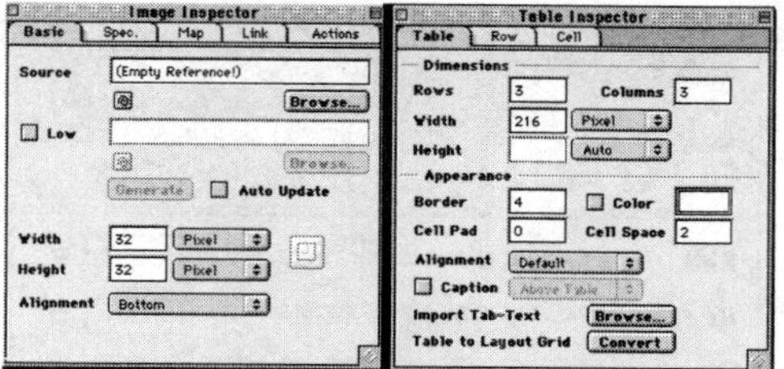

Figure 1.12 Clicking a placholder item in the document window causes the Inspector window's contents to change. Here are the image Inspector (left) and the Table Inspector (right).

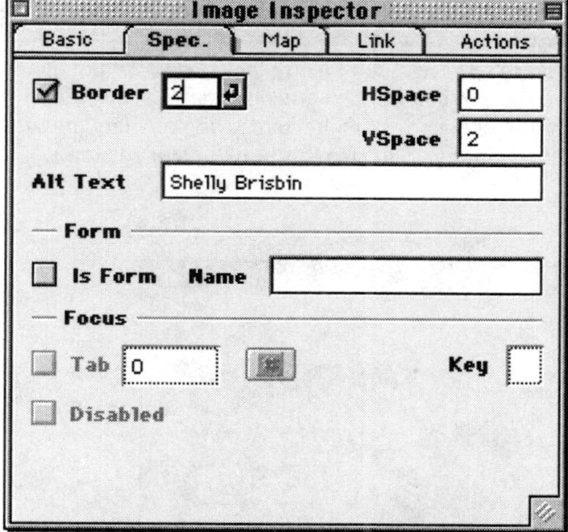

Figure 1.13 Click the Spec. tab within the Image Inspector window to view spacing and border options for an image.

The Inspector

The Palette and the context-sensitive Inspector window work together to give you control over the tools you use to build Web pages. Once you have placed an item (text, image, spacer, applet, or other object) on the page, you can fine-tune its appearance from within the Inspector window. The Inspector window is empty until you select an object in the document window, and its appearance changes depending upon the object you choose.

To use the Inspector:

1. Drag a tool from the Palette into the document window, or click on an object that's already there.

   Notice that the Inspector window is no longer empty, but contains buttons and checkboxes. (If you don't see the Inspector window, choose Inspector from the Windows menu.)

2. Click another object on your Web page and notice that the Inspector window changes again to display the options for the new object.

As you can see in **Figure 1.12**, some Inspector windows have several sets of preferences, organized under tabs. Click on one of the tabs in the Image Inspector to view more options. **Figure 1.13** shows Special preferences for my mug shot.

✔ Tip

- If you need to change an object's preference after you've placed it on a page, just click on the object, and the item's Inspector window returns.

The Color Palette

The Color Palette allows you to add color to elements of your pages. You can color text, background, links—almost any other object GoLive can create. Once you choose a color you like, you can drag and drop it onto objects (or into their Inspector windows' color fields) to change their color.

The Color Palette window appears when you choose it from the Windows menu (Mac) or View menu (Windows). Just like the Palette, the Color Palette contains tabs that organize its tools and color choices (see **Figure 1.14**). Four tabs represent the color types found in image manipulation applications such as Photoshop. The Apple Color and Windows Color palette tabs display colors the same way computer screens do. The HSV tab (Windows only) allows you to choose colors according to the Hue, Saturation, and Value scale (**Figure 1.15**). Two Web color tabs allow you to choose colors that are recognized by most Web browsers.

The nine Color Palette tabs are:

- The RGB tab.
- The CMYK tab.
- The Grayscale tab.
- The Indexed Color tab.
- The Apple/Windows Color palette tab.
- W The HSV Color palette tab.
- The Real Web Colors tab.
- The Web Named Colors tab.
- The Site Colors tab.

To add color to text:

1. With a document open in the main window and the Color Palette visible, choose a color from one of the Color Palette tabs by clicking on it.
2. Click on the Color Palette's Preview pane and drag onto text on your page. The text changes color (**Figure 1.15**).

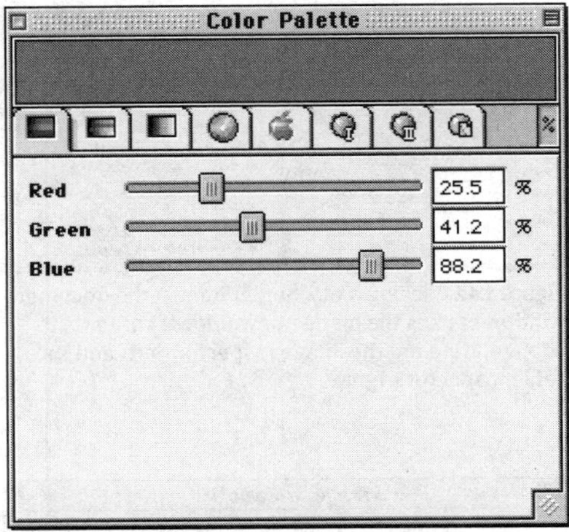

Figure 1.14 The Color Palette includes tools that allow you to add color to text and objects. You can create colors using one of eight color schemes. Here are the RGB options. (See also this book's color section.)

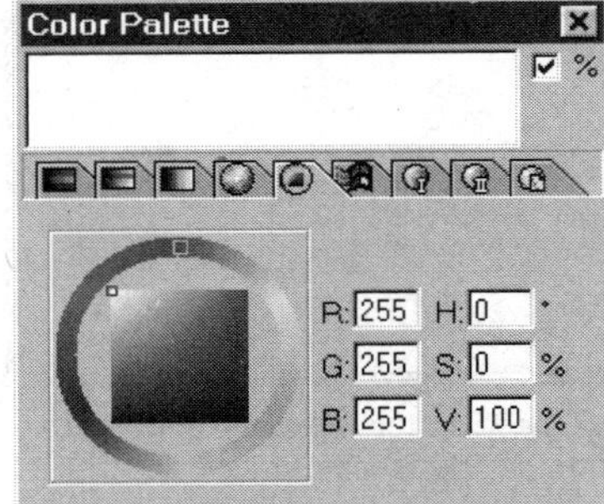

Figure 1.15 GoLive for Windows includes a tab that allows you to choose colors using the HSV scale.

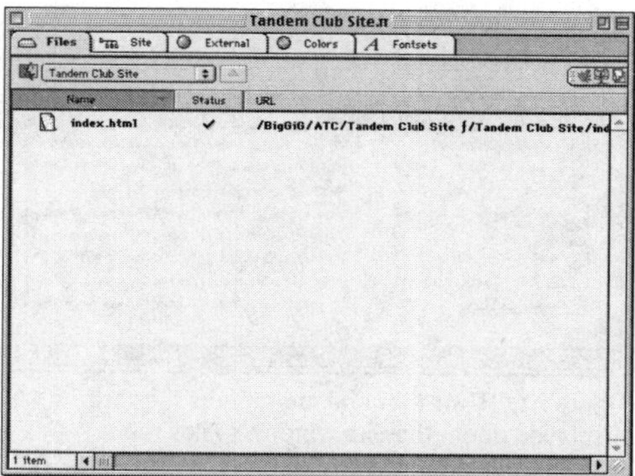

Figure 1.16 A new GoLive Site window displays a blank home page.

Site Management Tools

GoLive includes tools for both creating Web pages and managing complete Web sites. By gathering elements of your Web site, you can make global changes to the site, organize HTML and media files, and verify that all of your links work. You can also use site management tools to view a map of your entire site, either as a collection of linked pages, or as a group of links going to and from a single page. Finally, you can upload your site to a Web server using GoLive's FTP software.

The Site window

The Site window displays the files and other elements that make up a GoLive Web site. Like the Macintosh Finder, or Windows Explorer the Site window displays files and folders that you can open or manipulate when making changes to the site's hierarchy. When you create a new site, GoLive creates a home page for it (called index.html). A new Site window appears as in **Figure 1.16**.

Like the Palette window, the Site window includes a number of tabs. Instead of tools, the Site window stores elements of your Web site. You can drag files into the Site window to add them to your site, or you can create pages from scratch with GoLive.

continues on next page

Behind each Site window tab are the elements of your Web site. You can view each by clicking on a tab at the top of the Site window. Until you add files and resources to your Web site, the Site tabs are empty.

The Site window tabs are:

- Files tab.
- Site tab.
- External tab.
- Colors tab.
- Fontsets tab.

Each Site window tab shows different elements of your site. The Files tab displays your site's component files, while the Site tab provides a graphical view of the site. The other tabs display remote URLs, saved colors, and fontsets, respectively. **Figure 1.17** shows a site with the Files tab selected.

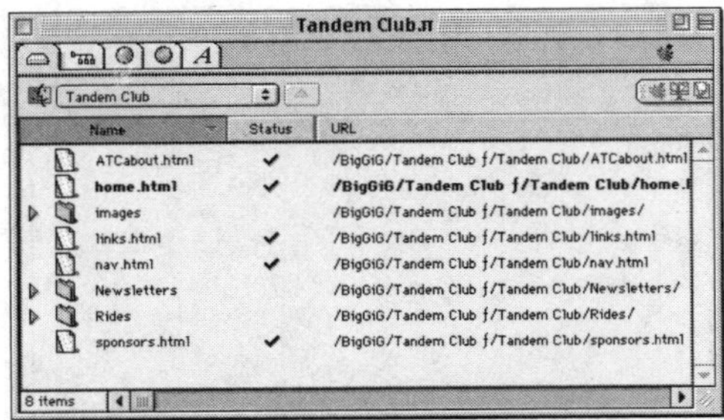

Figure 1.17 HTML files and multimedia files are displayed under the Site window's Files tab.

The Site toolbar

When you create or open a site file, the toolbar (**Figure 1.18**) displays a selection of tools that are specific to site management. You can add and remove files, create new folders, and view your site in different ways.

You'll find drag-and-drop tools for adding new elements to the site in the palette's Site tab.

Figure 1.18 The Site toolbar contains most of the tools you need to make changes to your site.

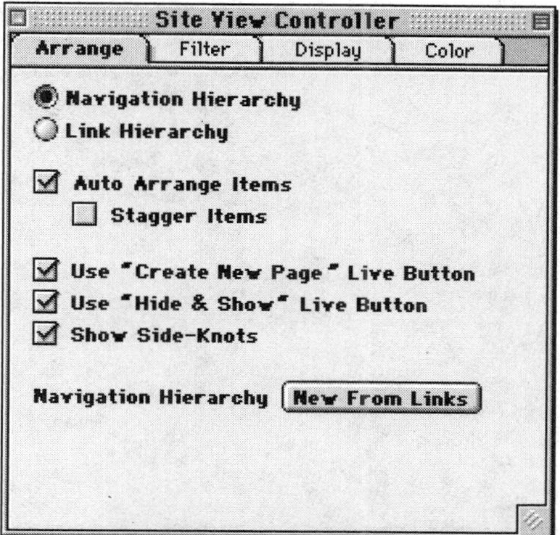

Figure 1.19 The Site View Controller appears in the Inspector window when you click the Site tab in the Site window.

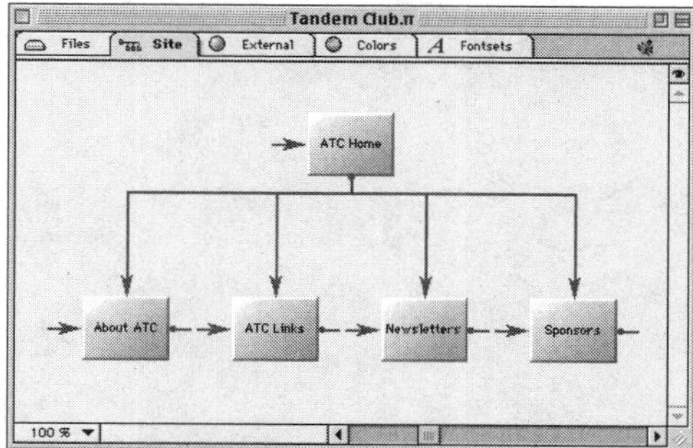

Figure 1.20 When you choose Link Hierarchy in the Site View Controller window, your site appears as a hierarchical tree of files that comprise it.

The Site View

Like any Web site, a GoLive site is a hierarchical grouping of HTML pages and links to other Web sites. The Site View is designed to make it easier for you to visualize and work with your site in these terms. You can even use the Site View to organize your site before you design its individual pages.

To view a site in the Site View:

1. Open a GoLive site file.
2. In the Site window, click the Site tab.
3. If it isn't already visible, choose Inspector from the Windows menu to display the Site View Controller (**Figure 1.19**), an inspector window that lets you set sitewide preferences.
4. Click the Link Hierarchy button. The display in the Site window changes to show a graphical, hierarchical view of your site (**Figure 1.20**).

You can work with files while using the Site View. Clicking once on a file displays its reference Inspector window and highlights the file's relationship to others in the site.

✔ Tip

- Double-clicking a file in the Site View opens it. This applies to both HTML files created in GoLive and image or multimedia files that you add to your site. GoLive will hand off these "foreign" file types to the applications that created them, allowing you to edit the files.

The Link View

Whereas the Site View provides an overhead view of the pages that make up your Web site, the Link View digs one step deeper by displaying links associated with individual page.

To display pages in the Link View:

1. In the Site View, with the Files tab showing, click on a page's icon.
2. Click the Link View button on the Site Toolbar to display the Link View window (**Figure 1.21**).

   The page's icon and name appear near the center of the Link View. Pages that link to the page appear on the left. All items linked from the page appear on the right.

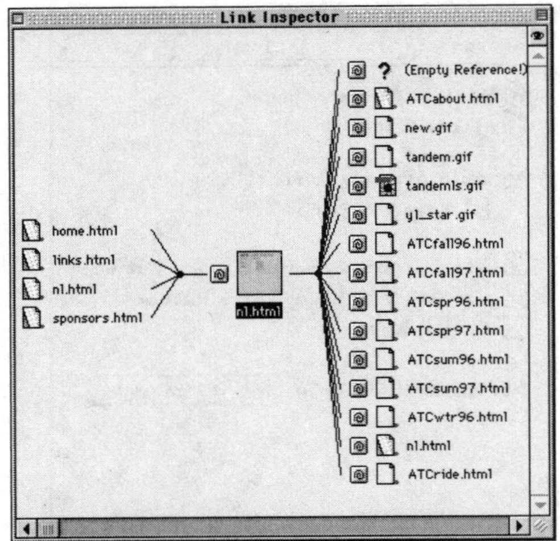

Figure 1.21 The Link View shows a single page with pointers to other pages that link to it (left) and all the local and remote links that appear on that page (right).

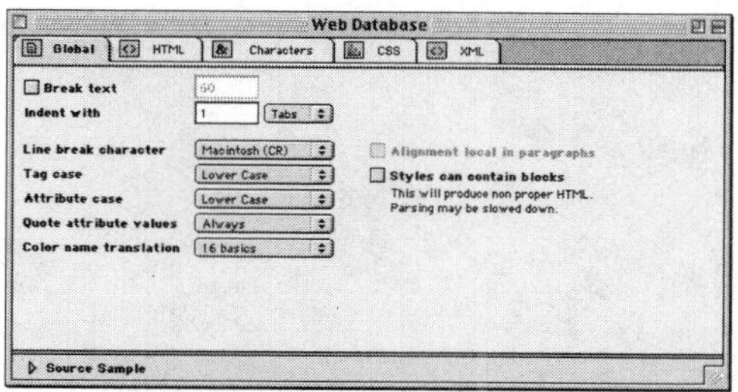

Figure 1.22 The Global tab of the Web Database allows you to specify the way GoLive displays tags and text in the HTML Source view.

The Web Database

Although GoLive's graphical interface means you don't have to know HTML to create a Web site, Adobe has included a handy database of HTML tags and special characters. It's available from the Special menu and includes listings of tags that make up HTML standards. You will also find options that support cascading style sheets and XML. The Web Database also allows you to set preferences for displaying text in the HTML Source View.

You can't use the tags directly in GoLive documents, but you can use the database as a reference when creating or editing your pages. **Figure 1.22** shows the Global tab of the Web Database.

2

YOUR FIRST WEB PAGES

Now that you've had a walking tour of GoLive's important features, it's time to dive right in and make some Web pages. In this chapter, I give a more practical face to the tools introduced in Chapter 1 but keep things fairly simple, leaving the exploration of the full power of GoLive for subsequent chapters.

In this chapter I cover:

- Setting GoLive preferences.
- Setting up a Web page.
- Creating a Web site.

Setting Preferences

You *could* just start typing the text into the document window to create your Web page. If you've used a word processor, you can probably figure out how to create bold text, enlarge it, or center it. But things will go more smoothly if you take the time to set up your GoLive environment before you create your masterpiece.

GoLive's extensive collection of preferences covers everything from controlling page and HTML display to determining how media files are handled. The General Preferences window includes most of the tools I'll cover in this chapter; the rest are specific to topics I'll cover later on.

To open the Preferences window, choose Preferences from the Edit menu. General Preferences appear by default and look like **Figure 2.1**.

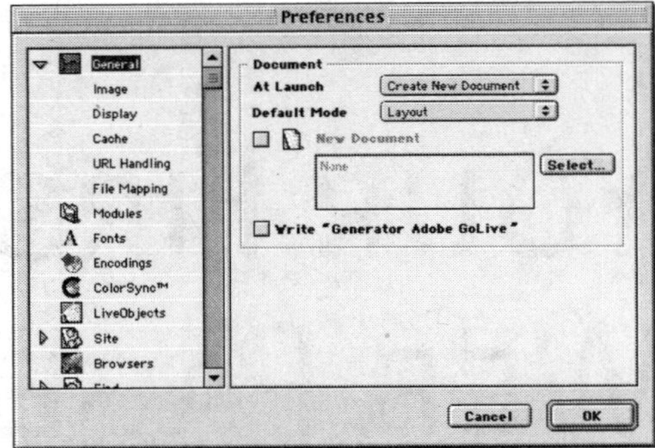

Figure 2.1 The Preferences window is divided into iconized sections, which are further divided by triangles that expand some of the icons to reveal more preferences.

I won't describe each and every option you can choose in the Preferences window but will concentrate on those you might want to set before starting a new site or document. Throughout the book, I'll return to Preferences when they are relevant to the topic at hand.

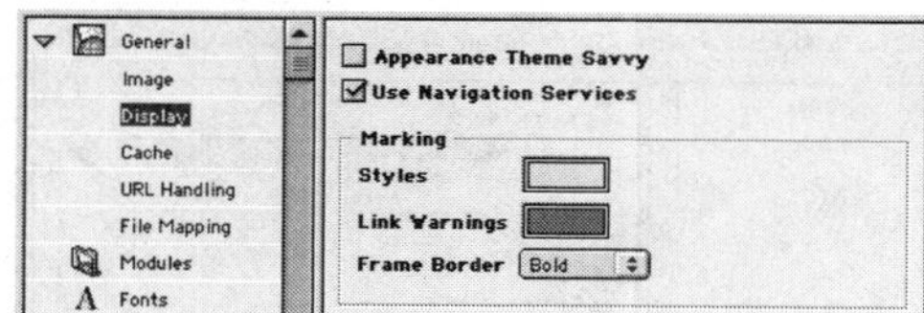

Figure 2.2 Display preferences allow you to use Mac OS 8.5 technologies within GoLive.

Setting startup and appearance preferences

You can tell GoLive how to behave at launch with startup preferences, set in the General Preferences panel. Mac users can also decide whether and how GoLive should support Mac OS options, such as Themes and Navigation Services.

To set startup preferences:

1. Choose Edit > Preferences to open the Preferences window.
2. To tell GoLive to display an Open dialog box at startup, choose Show Open Dialog from the At Launch popup menu. You can also choose to create a new document or do nothing.
3. To choose a page view other than the Layout mode at startup, choose one from the Default Mode popup menu.

Ⓜ To use Mac OS technology:

1. In the Preferences window of GoLive for Mac OS, click the triangle next to the General icon.
2. Click Display. **Figure 2.2** shows display preferences.
3. To use Mac OS 8.5 Themes, click Appearance Themes Savvy. Themes specify the color and pattern of many Mac OS items, including menus, windows, and scroll bars.
4. To use Mac OS Navigation Services (an improved Open and Save dialog box that was introduced in Mac OS 8.5), click Use Navigation Services.

✔ Tip

- You may notice sluggish performance after choosing "Use Navigation Services." If you do, disable the preference.

To assign custom colors:

1. Click the triangle (Mac) or plus sign (Windows) next to the General Preferences item in the Preferences window. The Windows version of this window omits Mac technology options (**Figure 2.3**).
2. Click Display.
3. To choose colors that highlight styles (cascading style sheets) and link warnings (hyperlinks that are broken), click the adjacent color square, and choose from the color wheel.

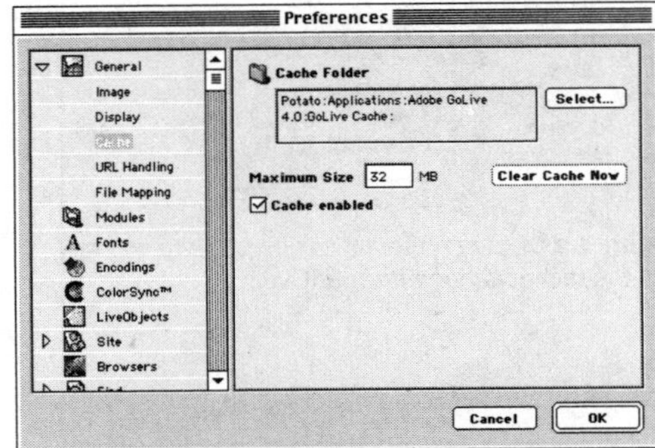

Figure 2.3 Windows display preferences don't include Mac OS technology items. Otherwise, Mac and Windows prefs are the same.

✔ Tip

- Ⓜ In the Mac version of GoLive 4.0 and later, the General preferences tab includes options for setting Cache. Ignore these settings. They are a vestige of previous versions of the software, and have no effect in GoLive 4.0 and later.

Managing GoLive modules

Many of GoLive's functional components, including spell checking, scripting and page views, are controlled by modules—files that are stored in the Modules directory, within the Adobe GoLive folder on your hard drive. You can use Modules preferences to enable or disable modules.

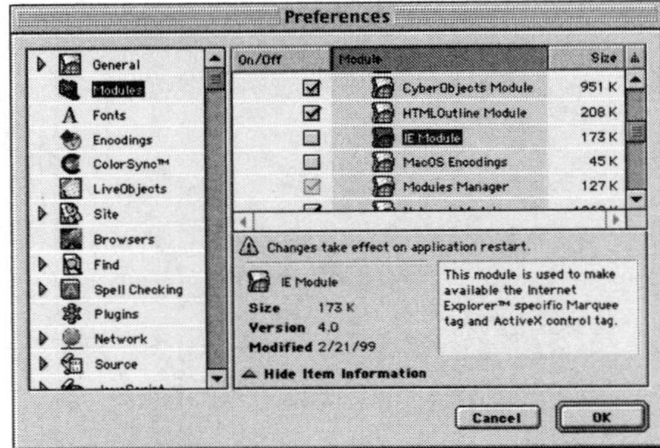

Figure 2.4 Modules preferences allow you to turn GoLive components on and off to save RAM.

To add or remove a module:

1. Click on the Modules item in the Preferences window. The result looks like **Figure 2.4**.
2. GoLive lets you enable and disable certain tools to customize your working environment. GoLive modules can be turned off and on to save memory or disable options you don't want to use. For example, the IE module provides support in GoLive for Internet Explorer-specific HTML tags. If you don't want to use these tags (which

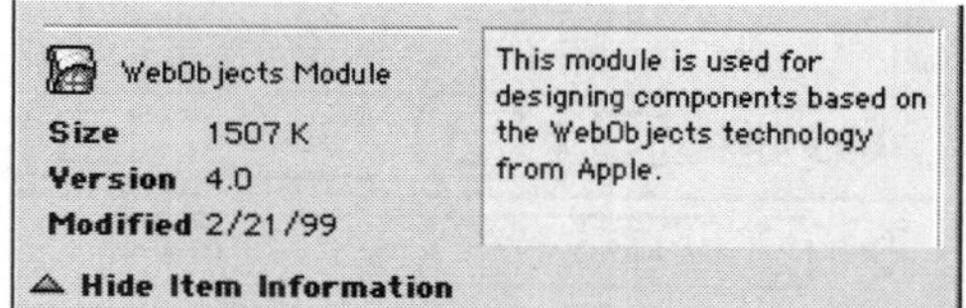

Figure 2.5 Click the triangle in the lower third of the Modules window to view details about the module you've selected.

are not supported in other browsers) you may choose to deactivate them. By default, most of GoLive's modules are enabled, including the IE module. Scroll through the Modules list until you locate the IE Module item.

3. Click the checkbox to disable IE Module. A warning symbol appears below the list of modules.
4. Click the Show Item Information triangle to reveal details about this module (**Figure 2.4**).
5. Click OK to close the Preferences dialog box.
6. Quit GoLive and open it again, so that you can see the effect of adding the IE module.
7. If it isn't already onscreen, open the Palette. Notice that the Scrolling Marquee and ActiveX controls are missing from the Basic tab.

Creating Your First Page

It's a good idea to define a few basic parameters and settings for your Web page before you begin adding text and graphics.

Figure 2.6 Change the title (<TITLE></TITLE>) of a Web page by selecting the default text at the top of a new page.

To give your page a title:

1. Open a new GoLive document.
2. Click anywhere within the title "Welcome to Adobe GoLive." You'll find it at the top of the document window, to the right of the Page icon. See **Figure 2.6**.
3. When you click, notice that the entire title is selected and that there's a box around it. Type a name for your page. Typing that will overwrite the original title.

   The title you type is the text that will identify your Web page when it is added to a Web browser's bookmark list. It's also the text that will appear at the top of a browser window when the page is being viewed. The title should indicate what your Web page is all about in clear, concise terms.

To name your document:

1. Choose Save from the File menu.
2. Give the file a name that conforms to the HTML standard—a page name followed by .html; e.g. index.html.
3. In the Save dialog, create a new folder for your home page and the other documents you'll add to your site.
4. Click Save.

✔ Tip

■ Naming your Web page file in any other format than *name*.html or *name*.htm will prevent you from using it with your Web site. The HTML standard expects pages to include the .html or .htm suffix. That's part of the secret to displaying Web pages

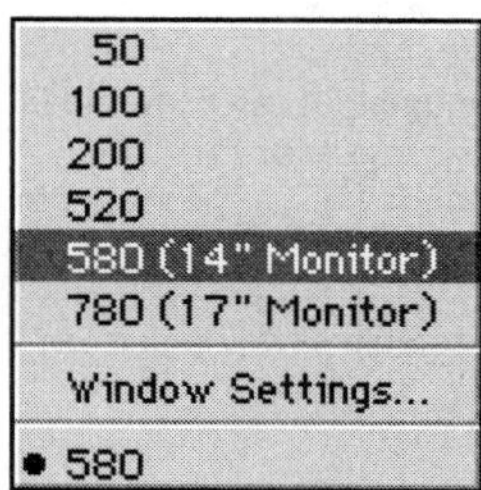

Figure 2.7 Choose a window size from the Page Size popup menu.

on a variety of different computer platforms. Windows and UNIX machines also expect to see filenames with no spaces or slashes (/).

To choose a default page size:

1. Click and hold the Page Size popup menu in the bottom right corner of the main window. **Figure 2.7** shows the popup menu.
2. Choose an appropriate size for your page—the window size for which you want to design the page. GoLive includes sizes that support 14-inch and 17-inch monitors, and some smaller page sizes as well. The 580-pixel (14-inch monitor) and 720-pixel (17-inch monitor) options are probably the safest choice, since most current computer monitors are at least 14 inches. GoLive resizes the main window.

✔ Tip

- Be careful to set the same page size for all of the pages in your site, so that your site's elements display consistently for your visitors.

To add text to a page:

1. Type some text in the document window.
2. Select the text.
3. Choose an item from the toolbar to make the text bold, identify it as a heading, or to add any other typographic property to it.

To add an image to a page:

1. Drag the Image tool (**Figure 2.8**) from the Palette's Basic tags tab to the document window. The Image Inspector appears.
2. Click Browse in the Page Inspector.
3. Navigate to an image you want to add to the page and select it.

✔ Tip

- The preceding steps apply to adding any linked objet (image, Java applet, plug-in file) to a GoLive document.

To create a hyperlink:

1. Select one or two words of text in the document window.
2. Click the New Link icon on the toolbar (**Figure 2.9**). The text you selected turns blue and is underlined. The Text Inspector appears in the Inspector window.
3. Type a URL in the URL field or click the Browse button to navigate to a local file you wish to link to.

Figure 2.8 The Image tool can be found in the Palette's Basic tags tab.

Figure 2.9 Use the toolbar's New Link icon to link selected text.

Figure 2.10 Click the Page icon at the top of a document to view the file's Page Inspector.

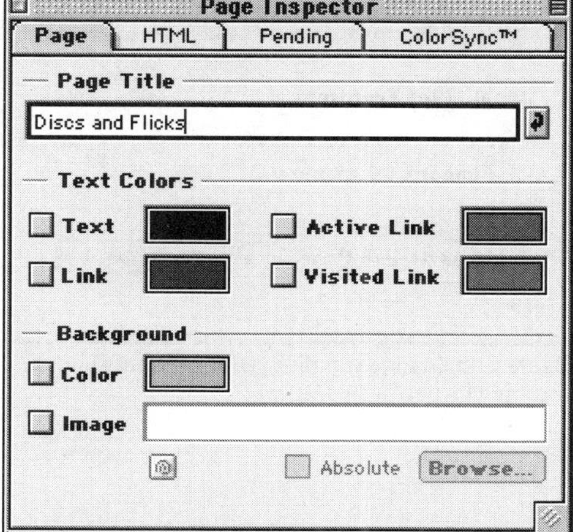

Figure 2.11 You can add a colored background or specify a custom color for text or links in the Page Inspector.

To create page colors:

1. Click on the Page icon in the title bar of the main window. It's shown in **Figure 2.10**.
2. Note that the Inspector window now displays Page settings. If the Inspector window isn't visible, choose Inspector from the Windows menu. The Page Inspector is shown in **Figure 2.11**.
3. To add a background color, click the Color field under the Background heading in the Page Inspector. The Color Palette appears.
4. Select a color and click the Preview pane at the top of the Color Palette. For more information about choosing and applying color, see Chapter 4.
5. Drag from the pane to the Background color field in the Page Inspector. The box changes color, and the checkbox is now selected.

✔ Tip

- If you decide to use custom colors for text, links, or background, use the Preview or a Web browser to check the colors you've chosen.

WESTERN IOWA TECH-LIBRARY

To add a background image:

1. As before, click the Page icon to bring up the Page Inspector window for your document.
2. In the Page Inspector window, click the Image checkbox, below the Background heading.
3. Click Browse.
4. Navigate to the image you want to use as a background for your Web page and click Select. You'll see the image in the main window, and visitors to your Web page will see the image behind the page's other elements.

To specify standing HTML elements:

1. In the Page Inspector, click the HTML tab (**Figure 2.12**).
2. By default, GoLive creates an HTML page framework for each new page you create. You don't see the framework unless you choose the HTML outline or Source view, but it's there just the same. You can remove these defaults by unchecking one or more of the boxes under the HTML tab.

I recommend that you leave all the options checked unless you have a specific reason to remove them. The exception to this rule is if your document is not a Web page, but an HTML fragment—a snippet of HTML code that does not stand on its own as a Web page. Often, HTML fragments are used by other Web pages or by scripts.

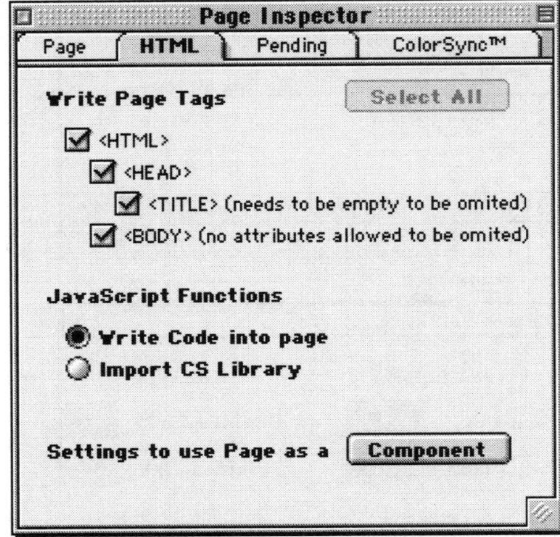

Figure 2.12 Change standing HTML elements under the Page Inspector's HTML tab.

Setting up a Site

Until this point, we've been working with individual Web pages. In many cases, you'll start with a single page or two and then add new items as your needs grow. GoLive supports that way of doing things, but the real power of the software is its ability to create and maintain groups of Web pages and other elements that make up a complete Web site.

When I talk about a GoLive *site*, I mean a group of elements (HTML files, images and other files) that form a Web site, and are managed as a unit and are saved under the umbrella of a single *site file*. The GoLive site file contains pointers to all of the elements of the site. It does not contain the HTML pages and other files themselves; it simply keeps them organized.

In this section, I introduce you to GoLive's site management tools by showing you how to set up a simple site. For a more in-depth look at sites, see Chapter 15.

You can create GoLive Web sites from scratch, or you can import files belonging to an existing Web site into a new GoLive site file. Because we've already created a Web page, albeit an empty one, in this section we'll start a site from scratch and import your current index file into a GoLive site.

To create a new site:

1. With GoLive open, choose New Site:Blank from the File menu (**Figure 2.13**). You can also choose to import an existing site from a folder on your hard drive, or download it from a Web server using FTP. I'll have more to say about using these options in Chapter 15.
2. Select a location on your hard disk in which to store your new site. You can have GoLive create a folder by leaving the Create Folder button checked in the navigation dialog box.
3. Name your site.
4. Click Save.

   The Site window appears (**Figure 2.14**). It contains a single item, a page called index.html. The page name is bold because index.html is the home page for your new site.

With a new site created, the next task is to get your home page up and running. You can either work directly with the home page GoLive has created for you (setting it up just as you did in the first section of this chapter), or you can replace the site's default home page with one you've already worked on.

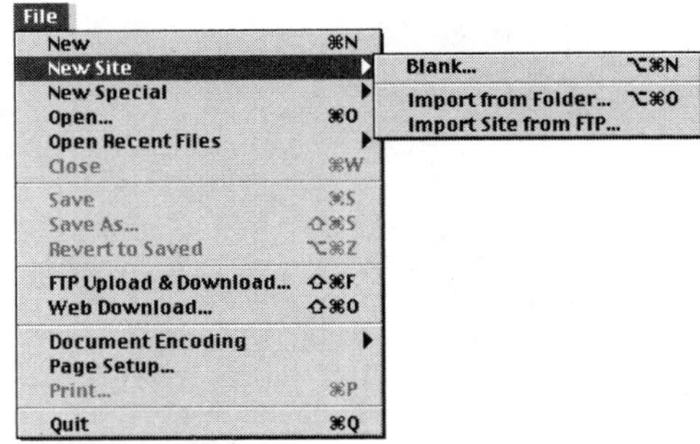

Figure 2.13 Choose File:New Site:Blank to create a GoLive site from scratch.

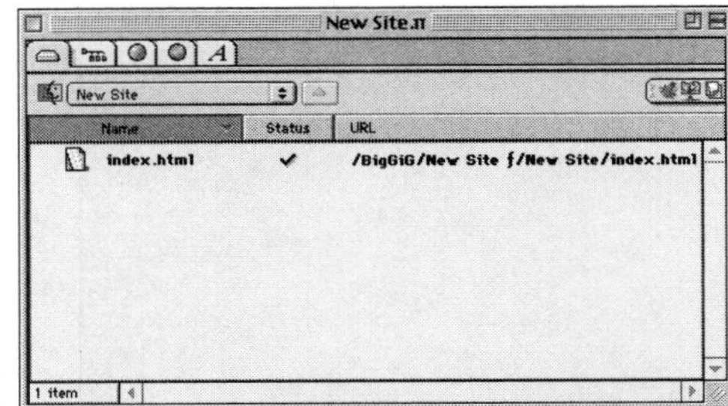

Figure 2.14 When you create a new site, index.html appears in the Site window.

To replace your site's home page:

1. Quit GoLive.
2. In the Finder (Mac) or Windows Explorer (Windows), locate and open the New Site folder you just created. Notice that there are two folders and a file within the New Site folder. The New Site.π (in Windows, the file extension is .site) file is the actual GoLive site file, while the folders hold (or will hold) elements of your Web site.
3. Open the New Site folder (where New Site is the name you gave your site). Notice that the file index.html is stored here.
4. Locate the index.html file you created earlier in this chapter, and drag it into the Open New Site Folder.
5. When asked if you want to replace the existing index.html file, click OK.
6. Open your site by double-clicking on the New Site.π icon. As before, index.html appears in the Site window. If you open it by double-clicking, you'll see that the file has the title and attributes you gave it earlier.

3 Working with Text

GoLive's text handling features are a familiar combination of word processing and desktop publishing tools. You can use the tools to create text in GoLive or import it from elsewhere. From there, you can edit, search, spell check, and manipulate text and text blocks to polish your Web pages.

In this chapter, I cover:

- Adding text to Web pages.
- Formatting text.
- Spellchecking.
- Find & Replace.

Entering Text

You can add text to a GoLive document in several ways. You also have a choice of views in which to add your text. In most cases, you will use the Layout view, either by typing directly into the main window or by using GoLive's layout grid and text frames to place text blocks into a document. You can also use other views to add or edit text—more on that later in this chapter.

Using GoLive text frames and layout grids, you can precisely position text on your Web pages and later move the frames around as you perfect your layout.

To type text directly into a document:

1. Open a new or existing GoLive document. Make sure that the main window is visible.
2. Type some text in the main window.

To add a text frame to a layout:

1. Open a new or existing GoLive document.
2. Drag the Layout Grid tool from the Palette onto the document window (see **Figure 3.1**). Or double-click the Layout Grid tool.
3. Use the mouse to grab the handle at the bottom right-hand corner of the grid you've created and drag the handle to the right, so that the layout grid becomes a horizontal rectangle (see **Figure 3.2**).
4. Drag the Layout Text Box tool (**Figure 3.3**) from the Palette onto the layout grid. Like the grid, the text frame has highlighted handles for resizing the frame (**Figure 3.4**). You'll also notice that the I-beam cursor is positioned within your new frame.

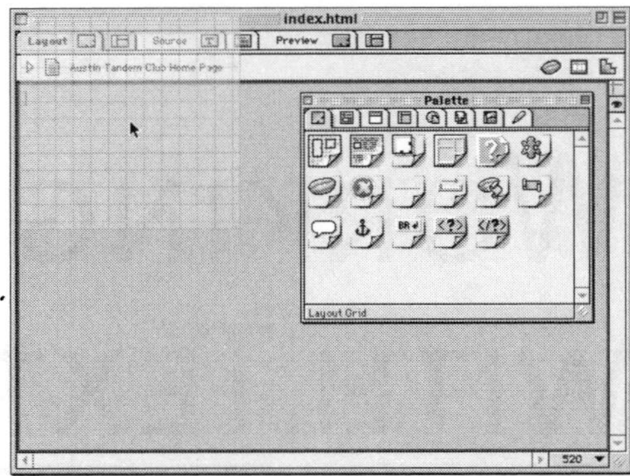

Figure 3.1 When you drag the Layout Grid tool from the Palette to the document window, GoLive creates a grid.

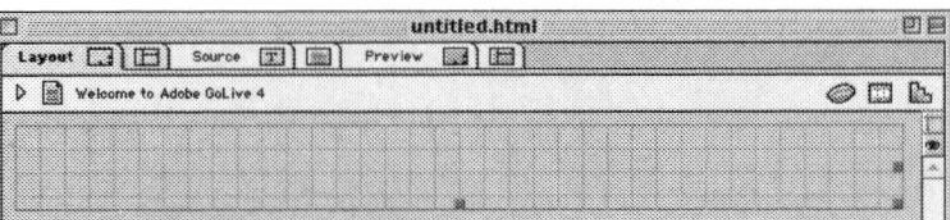

Figure 3.2 To resize a layout grid, grab the handle at the bottom right corner of the grid and drag to change the grid's shape and size.

Figure 3.3 The Layout Text Box tool is on the Basic tags tab of the Palette.

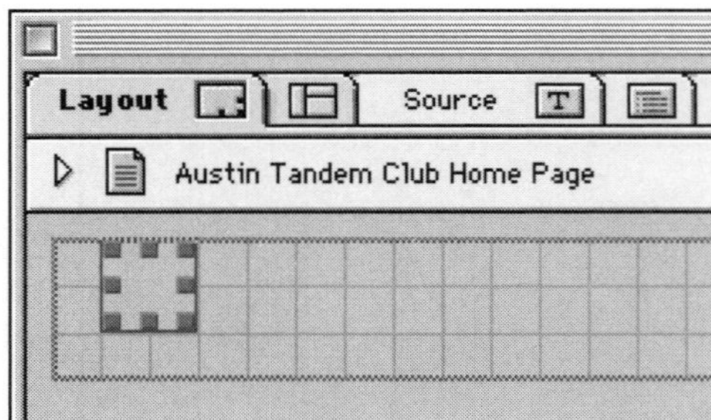

Figure 3.4 When you drag the Layout Text Box from the Palette, a small text frame appears on the layout grid.

Entering Text

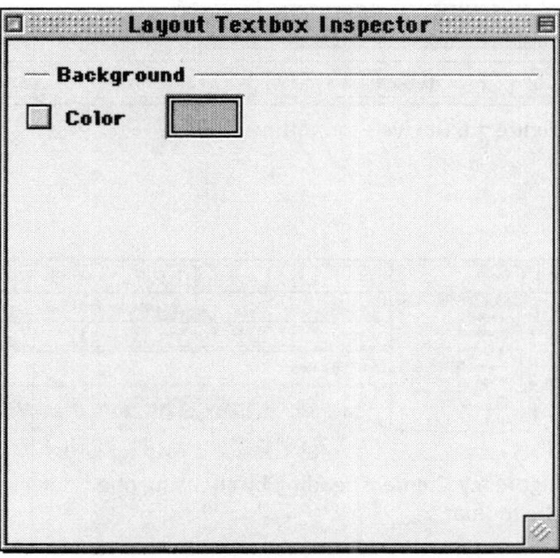

Figure 3.5 The Layout Textbox Inspector allows you to change the background color of a text box.

5. Grab the handle at the bottom right-hand corner of the text frame you've created and drag to the right, so that you'll be able to see what you're about to type.
6. Click within the text frame and type some text.
7. Click on the text block, but not on the text itself. Now you can drag the block to any position within the layout grid.

✔ Tips

- If you type or paste text into a text frame without enlarging the frame first, GoLive expands the frame vertically as text is entered. You can resize the frame after you enter text, but it's easier to size the frame to fit the text first.
- When you click on the text frame, you may notice that the frame is selected but that the handles aren't visible. Without pressing the mouse button, move your cursor over the text frame until it displays a hand icon (when the pointer is on the border of the frame). When you click, you'll see the handles and can move or resize the window.
- Try to use as few text frames as possible, and align them to your layout grid. Each new frame creates a new table (visible in the Source View), and large numbers of tables can cause rendering problems, in some browsers unnecessary frames can cause problems.
- You can change the background color of a layout text box with the Layout Textbox Inspector (**Figure 3.5**). The Inspector appears in the Inspector window when you click on a text frame's border. To change the color of the text, you need to select the text and use the toolbar or menus. I have more to say on that subject later in this chapter.

Formatting Text

Although GoLive uses HTML code to mark text for the Web, you don't need to know HTML to add formatting. GoLive's formatting tools are similar to a word processor's. They are available from the Style and Format menus, and many are repeated on the toolbar (**Figure 3.6**). I've divided GoLive's text formatting tools into four types. They are:

- Paragraph styles.
- Text alignment.
- Text display styles.
- Lists.

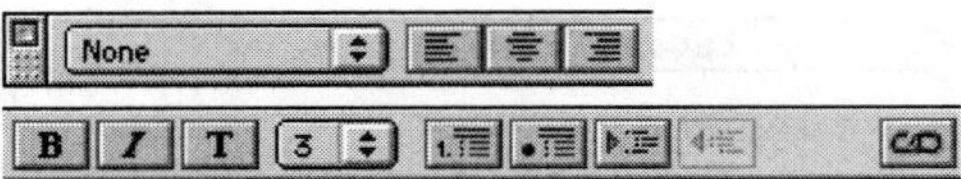

Figure 3.6 GoLive's formatting tools.

Paragraph styles

The items that are called paragraph styles in GoLive's documentation are mostly HTML heading styles. HTML provides for six levels of headings that you can use to call attention to and organize text on the page. Like headlines and subheads in print publishing, HTML headings are larger and bolder than standard Web page text. Heading levels decrease in size, and are bold.

Figure 3.7 Create a heading by choosing one from the toolbar.

To create a heading:

1. Type a new headline or click in a text frame containing text. This text will be the main heading of your Web page.
2. From the toolbar, choose Header 1 (see **Figure 3.7**) by clicking on the Header menu and dragging your cursor down to highlight Header 1. The text is now larger and bold.

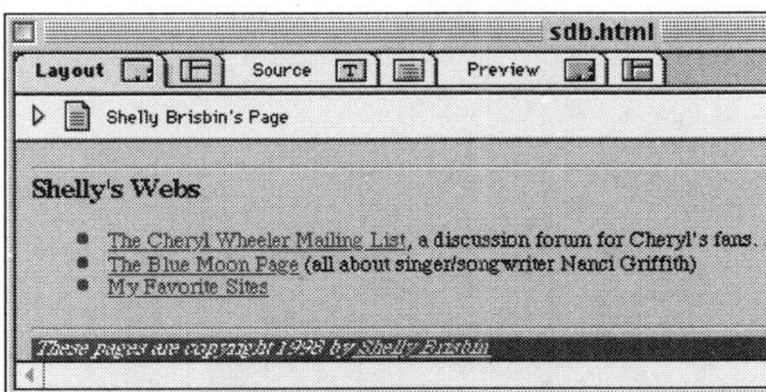

Figure 3.8 The address format italicizes text.

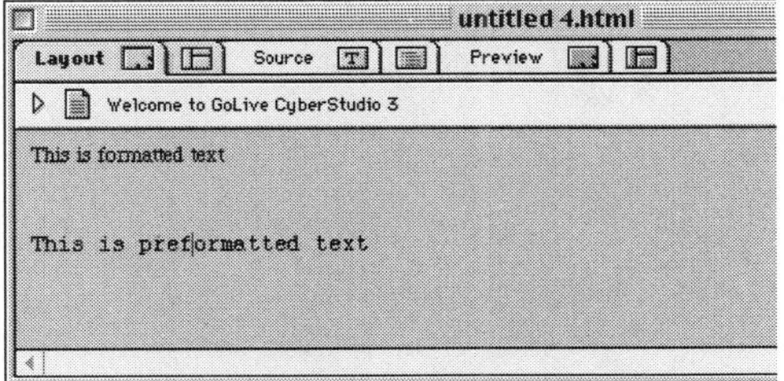

Figure 3.9 Here is an example of formatted versus preformatted text.

Figure 3.10 The text on this page is aligned to the center of the text frame, not to the center of the page or to the layout grid.

More paragraph styles

You'll find two items on the toolbar's Paragraph Styles menu that do not create headings. The styles are Address and Preformatted.

The Address style displays text as address information. This format usually identifies the owner/copyright holder/author of your Web page that is traditionally located at the bottom of a Web page (**Figure 3.8**).

Text that is preformatted does not include the HTML tags that give Web page text its typeset look. Instead, using the preformatted style displays the text exactly as it looks when you type or paste it in. GoLive displays preformatted text using the Courier font (**Figure 3.9**). Web browsers display preformatted text in whatever fixed-width font is specified in the browser. Preformatted text is most often used to display code or from the rest of the page, and to preserve already written text exactly as it appears.

Text alignment

You can align text to the left, center, or right margins, using icons on the toolbar. To align text, select it and choose the Left, Center, or Right icon from the toolbar. In **Figure 3.10**, the text is centered within its text frame.

✔ Tip

- Because text is centered in its frame, you'll have to center the frame on the page to achieve absolutely centered text, unless you have typed text directly into the document window without using a layout grid. If you want to center text over a column, or over a portion of the Web page, first center the text frame, using GoLive's object alignment tools. You can read more about these tools in Chapter 4.

Indenting text

In addition to the alignment options available on the toolbar, the Format menu includes options for increasing or decreasing a text block's indent from the edge of the page or within its text frame (**Figure 3.11**).

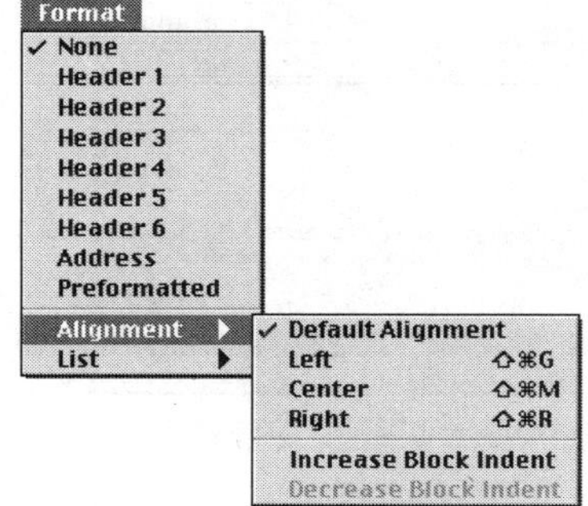

Figure 3.11 You can use the Format menu's Alignment submenu to change alignment and text indents.

To indent text:

1. Select some text in the document window.
2. Choose Alignment:Increase Block Indent from the Format menu. Text is indented from the margin of the document window or text frame.
3. Repeat Step 2 to increase the indent further.

You can remove or decrease text indents with the Decrease Block Indent command.

Text display styles

HTML specifies two types of text display styles: physical and logical. *Physical styles*, such as bold and italic, always look the same, regardless of the Web browser being used to view the page. *Logical styles*, such as strong and emphasis, take their visual marching orders from the user's Web browser. In general, newer browsers do a better job of displaying logical styled text than do older ones.

✔ Tip

- Physical and logical styles should not be confused with cascading style sheets (CSS), which I'll discuss more fully in Chapter 12. Style sheets allow you to specify fonts, type sizes, and other text attributes much the way you do in non-Web applications. To view them, though, a user must have a style sheet-capable browser. Version 4.0 and later versions of Netscape and Microsoft browsers support style sheets.

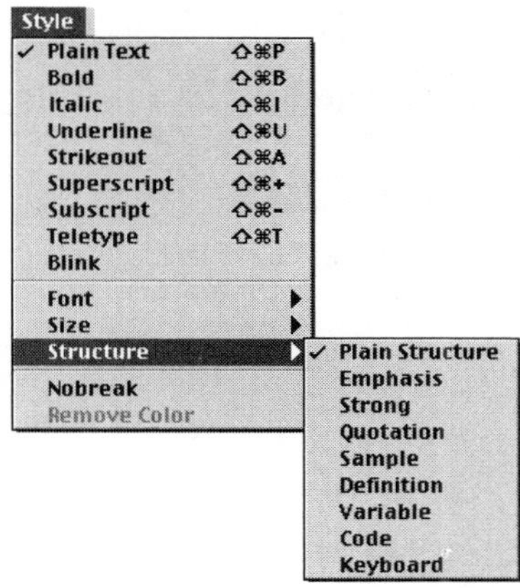

Figure 3.12 The Structure submenu of the Style menu displays logical text styles.

Internet Explorer/Mac	Netscape Navigator/Mac	Netscape Navigator/Windows
Plain Structure	Plain Structure	**Plain Structure**
Emphasis	*Emphasis*	*Emphasis*
Strong	**Strong**	**Strong**
Quotation	*Quotation*	*Quotation*
Sample	Sample	Sample
Definition	Definition	**Definition**
Variables	*Variables*	*Variables*
Code	Code	Code
Keyboard	Keyboard	Keyboard

Figure 3.13 Here are logical styles, as displayed in three different browsers. Note that besides slight differences in type size and display attributes, different browsers use very different vertical spacing attributes

Three physical styles—bold, italic, and teletype—are available from the toolbar. All of the physical styles appear on the Style menu. The rest are:

- Underline.
- Strikeout.
- Superscript.
- Subscript.
- Blink.

✔ Tip

- Blink is a Netscape-only tag. GoLive cannot display the blink tag in either the Layout or Preview view. If you want to use blink to make a Web page's text flash, you'll need to preview it in a Netscape browser.

Logical styles—their HTML description—appear on the Structure submenu of the Style menu. GoLive refers to logical HTML styles as structural styles. **Figure 3.12** shows the Structure submenu.

Because the look of text formatted with a logical style can vary depending on the viewer's browser, it's particularly important to take a look at the page using several browsers, preferably on both the Mac OS and Windows. **Figure 3.13** compares the look of logical styles in three popular browsers—two Macintosh, and one Windows.

Fonts

You can specify typefaces and sizes (commonly called fonts) in GoLive, but there are some HTML-specific barriers that limit your options somewhat and require that you observe a few special rules.

HTML fonts are not expressed in absolute point sizes, as fonts are in most applications. Instead of fixed sizes, fonts are expressed within HTML relative to the default text size or a particular kind of text (body, header 1, header 2, etc.). How large or small text actually appears in a Web browser is determined by the browser and by the user, who can choose to display Web pages with large, medium, or small fonts, depending on the options provided in the browser. HTML fonts come in sizes from 1 to 7—again, these are not point sizes, but HTML measurements that increase in font size steps: 10, 12, 14, 18 points and so on.

It's not essential to specify font sizes to create larger text. If you use HTML header tags, as described earlier in this chapter, HTML and your visitors' Web browsers will specify the tag's size.

If you use the font size menu or toolbar to adjust text size in GoLive, you override the standard size for the text you're styling. For example, selecting a heading, which is already larger than body text, and increasing the font size from 3 to 5 will make the heading text two font sizes larger. Performing the same change on a body text paragraph does not increase your paragraph to heading size but simply adds two font size steps to your body text (see **Figure 3.14**).

Like type sizes, typeface names can either be included or left out of HTML code. If you don't specify a typeface, the user's browser will provide one. If you do want to use a specific typeface, there is still no guarantee that

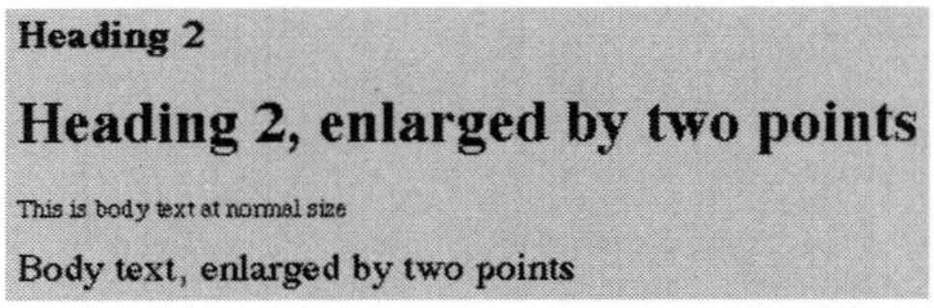

Heading 2

Heading 2, enlarged by two points

This is body text at normal size

Body text, enlarged by two points

Figure 3.14 This sample shows how enlarging the font size of header and body text affects its appearance.

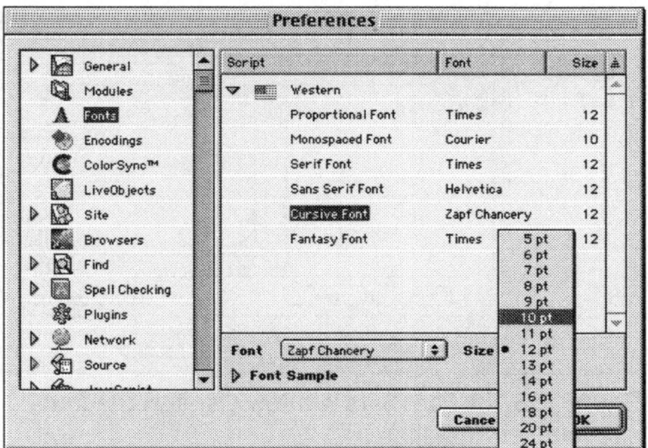

Figure 3.15 You can use global font preferences to modify default typefaces and font sizes.

the user's browser will display it if he or she does not have the font installed. HTML and GoLive allow you to specify several fonts for a single text element: a default font and as many backup fonts as you like. When a user's browser displays an HTML page, it tries to use the specified default font and then the backup fonts in turn, looking for one that is available on the user's system. You can specify alternate font relationships in GoLive with font sets, described below.

GoLive allows you to store and use fonts globally, making them available for all documents you work on, or as page font sets that work with and are saved with individual pages or sites. All of the fonts available to a particular page—whether global, page-specific, or site-specific—appear on the Font submenu of the Style menu.

Using global fonts

An easy way to specify a set of global fonts is with GoLive's Font Preferences. In fact, a set of default fonts is specified when you install GoLive. You can change the existing group of six global font types, if you like.

To change a global font:

1. Choose Edit:Preferences.
2. Click the Fonts icon in the left pane of the window. The window presents a list of font types currently available. Changing one or more of the font types to a font that isn't already displayed will add it to the Font submenu.
3. Click a font type you would like to change.
4. Choose a new font and size from the popup menus in the lower portion of the window (**Figure 3.15**).
5. To see a sample of the new font, click the Font Sample triangle.

Font sets

Not every computer or Web browser uses the same fonts. As a Web author, you run the risk of creating content that doesn't look as you intended within a given browser. Font sets allow you to provide options for the browser by creating a first, second, and even a third choice. If, for example, you create a font set that includes Arial, Helvetica, and Geneva, and then use Arial to produce a page, users who don't have Arial installed can view the text in Helvetica or Geneva, depending on the fonts supported by their system or Web browser.

To edit a font set:

1. Choose Edit Font Sets from the Font submenu of the Style menu.
2. If it isn't already highlighted, click on the Default icon in the left pane of the window. Default fonts are those that GoLive makes available regardless of the document or site you have open.
3. Click New in the middle pane of the Font Sets editor. A new, unnamed font set appears (**Figure 3.16**).
4. Choose a font from the popup menu (**Figure 3.17**). The fonts on this menu are those currently installed in your system.
5. To add another font to the set, click New under Font Names and choose another font from the menu.
6. To create a second font set, click New in the Font Sets pane, and repeat steps 3-5.
7. When you've finished adding fonts and sets, click OK to close the Font Sets window.

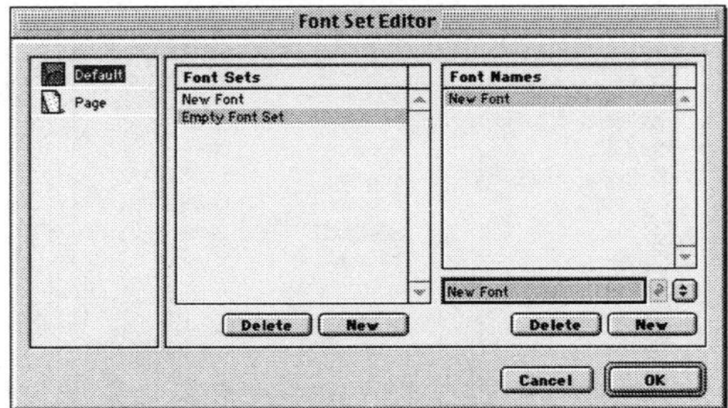

Figure 3.16 The Font Sets window displays the fonts and font sets installed.

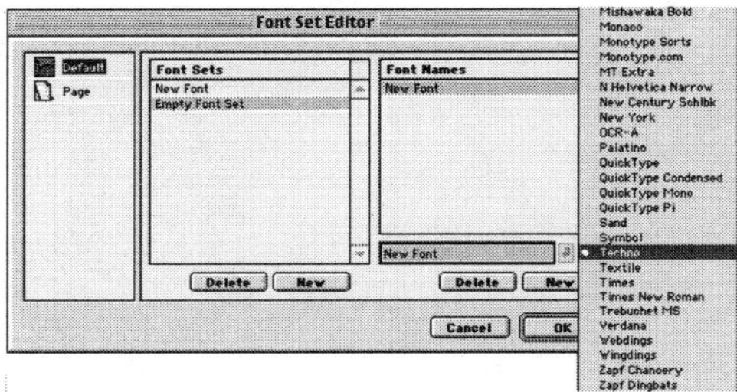

Figure 3.17 Choose a font to add to your font set.

To use a font:

1. Select some text in a document window.
2. Choose a font from the Font submenu of the Style menu.

To create page font sets:

1. To create a font set that is specific to the Web page you're working on, open the page and choose Edit Font Sets from the Font submenu of the Style menu.
2. In the Font Sets editor, click Page.
3. Create the font set and save the page, as described in the previous section. When you open this page in the future, the font sets you have applied will appear on the Font submenu, along with the default fonts.

Lists

Lists are an easy way to organize content on your Web page. Whether you need to create a numbered list of instructions, an outline, or a bulleted list of links, HTML and GoLive provide a list format to cover it.

To create a list:

1. Type the items from your list in a text frame or directly into the document window. After typing each item, press Return.
2. Select the items in the list.
3. Choose a list format from the List submenu of the Format menu. It looks like **Figure 3.18**. The Arabic (numerals) style is shown in **Figure 3.19**.
4. With the text selected, choose a different list format and notice how the appearance of the text changes. **Figure 3.20** shows a bulleted list.

The toolbar includes two list-making options and one tool each for increasing and decreasing the indent of lists. To add a greater indent to your list or to move it back one level, select the Increase List Level and Decrease List Level commands from the List submenu or from the toolbar. To delete all list formatting, decrease the list level until the option is dimmed.

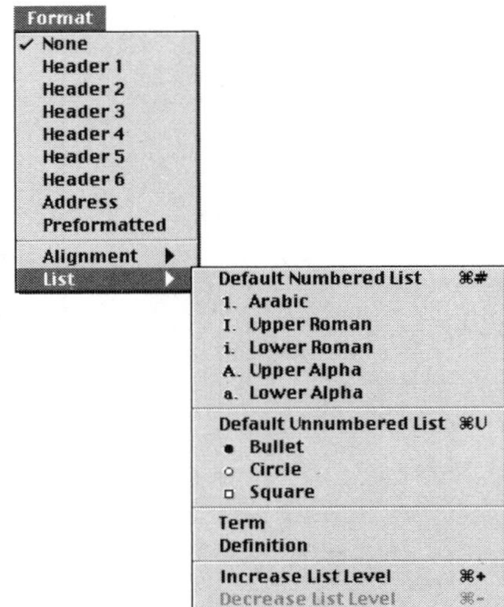

Figure 3.18 You can choose from a number of list types on the List submenu of the Format menu.

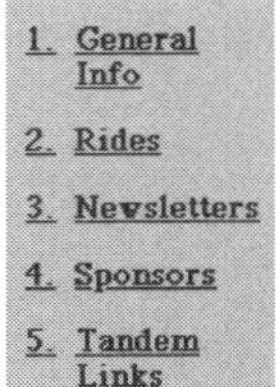

Figure 3.19 Format a list that looks like this by creating a numbered list from the toolbar or List submenu.

Figure 3.20 Change the list to a bulleted one to get this look.

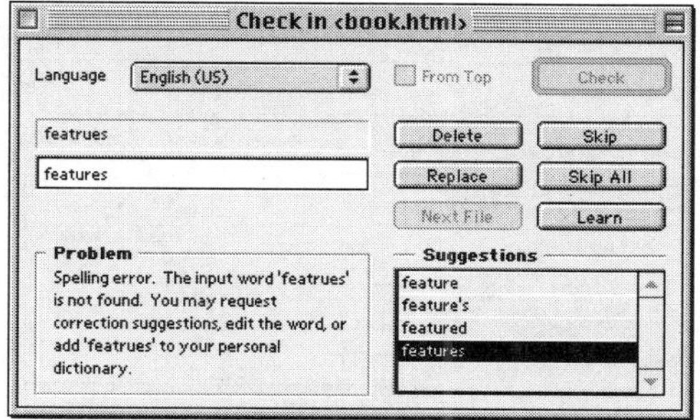

Figure 3.21 The spellchecker makes suggestions when it encounters a word it doesn't recognize.

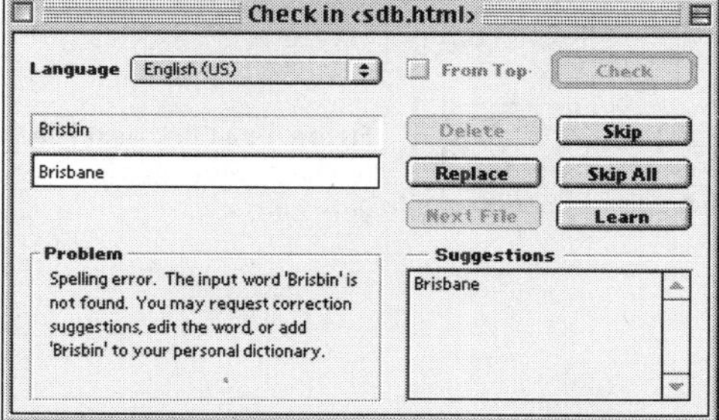

Figure 3.22 Click the Learn button to add an unfamiliar word—such as your own name—to your personal dictionary.

Spellchecking

GoLive's built-in spellchecker can locate spelling errors in a single page or throughout your site. You can use one of several English-language or non-English dictionaries and add your own words to a Personal Dictionary. To use a non-English dictionary, select it when you install GoLive for the first time or run the installer to add the dictionary.

To check spelling:

1. Open a GoLive Document and make sure that you're working in the Layout view.
2. Choose Spellchecking from the Edit menu. The Spellchecking window appears. It looks like **Figure 3.21**.
3. Click Check.
4. The spellchecker locates words that it does not recognize, whether they're misspelled or simply not included in the dictionary.
5. If you would like to use a dictionary other than the default U.S. English dictionary, choose it from the Language popup menu.
6. To correct a spelling mistake, click on one of the suggestions offered and click the Replace button. If you don't see a suggestion you like, type a new spelling in the blank provided.

   You can also tell the spellchecker to simply skip a word that it doesn't know. Skip All passes over all occurrences of the word.
7. If the spellchecker has pointed out a word that should be added to your personal dictionary, click the Learn button (see **Figure 3.22**).
8. Your check is completed when the Spellchecking window displays No Errors. Click the Close box to close the Spellchecking window.

✔ Tip

■ While you have the Spellchecking window open, GoLive highlights questionable words in the document window. You may need to move the Spellchecking window in order to see the highlighting. That's what I did in **Figure 3.23**.

The spellchecker checks all text in a single document, whether it appears in one or more text frames or is simply typed into the main window. If you're working in the Source or Outline view, the spellchecker ignores the HTML code that surrounds your text when performing its check.

To check an entire site's spelling:

1. Open a GoLive site file, so that the Site window is visible.
2. Make certain that the Site window is the front-most window by clicking on the Files tab.
3. Choose Spellchecking from the Edit menu.
4. As before, the Spellchecking window appears and begins to check the first document in your site when you click the Check button.
5. When you've finished checking the first file in the site, click Next File to move on to another document, and so on until all of the files in your site have been checked. See **Figure 3.24**.

   When you click Skip All or Learn, your instructions are carried throughout the current checking session, including all of the files in your site.

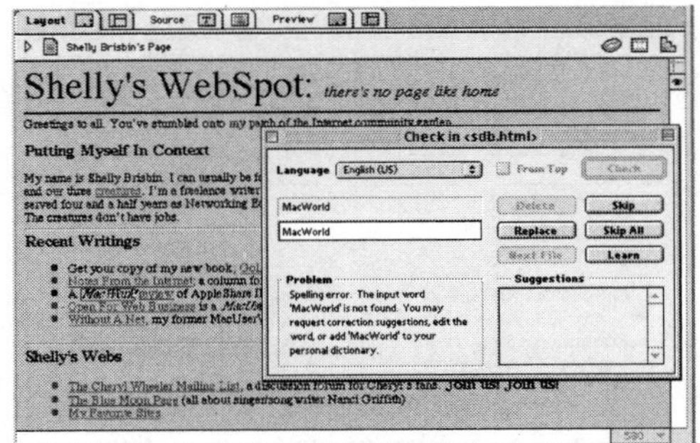

Figure 3.23 Can't find a questioned word in your document? Try moving the Spellchecking window.

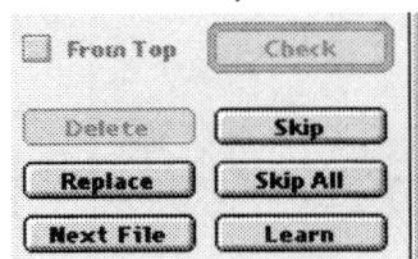

Figure 3.24 Click Next File to check more files in your site.

Figure 3.25 You can enter a word, phrase, or some other string of characters to search for. Choose whether to consider a word's case, and set other options. Click Find to begin.

Find & Replace

You can search one document or a whole site with GoLive's Find & Replace feature. As the name implies, this feature allows you to search text (including Web page content and HTML code) for characters, words, or phrases. Find & Replace works in the Layout, Source, and Outline Views.

GoLive performs three types of Find & Replace functions. They are:

- Local Find & Replace.
- Global Find & Replace.
- Find File.

Both local and global options include the ability to simply search for text and the ability to replace a string of text with something you specify.

Local Find & Replace

Local Find & Replace lets you search for and replace text in a single document. You can use this feature while working within a site, or by simply searching a single open file.

To find text locally:

1. Open a GoLive document and make sure that you are in the Layout, Source, or Outline View.
2. Choose Find from the Edit menu.
3. Type a word that can be found within the document you are searching. **Figure 3.25** shows the Find window ready to search.
4. Click Find.
5. When GoLive finds an instance of the word you've searched for, it is highlighted in the main window. You can click Find Next to look for another instance of the word.

To find and replace text locally:

1. If it's not still visible, open the Find dialog box from the Edit menu.
2. Type some characters to search for.
3. If it is not already visible, open the Replace field by clicking on the triangle near the bottom of the dialog box. **Figure 3.26** shows the fully open dialog.
4. Type some text to replace the characters you're going to find.
5. Click Find. Notice that you have the option to replace the text or to automatically find and replace all occurrences within your document. If you would rather make the decision to replace text on a case by case basis, simply click Replace and then Find to locate another occurrence of your text.

✔ Warning

- While you use Find and Replace to change text in the Source or Outline Views, you may inadvertently destroy links if they contain the text you are replacing.

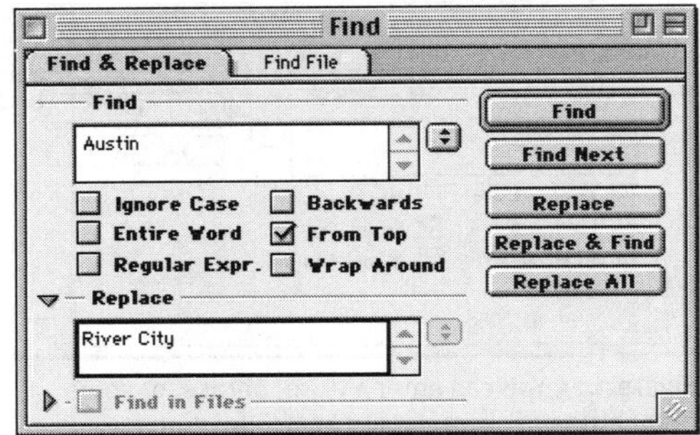

Figure 3.26 The Find window looks like this when you expand the Replace triangle.

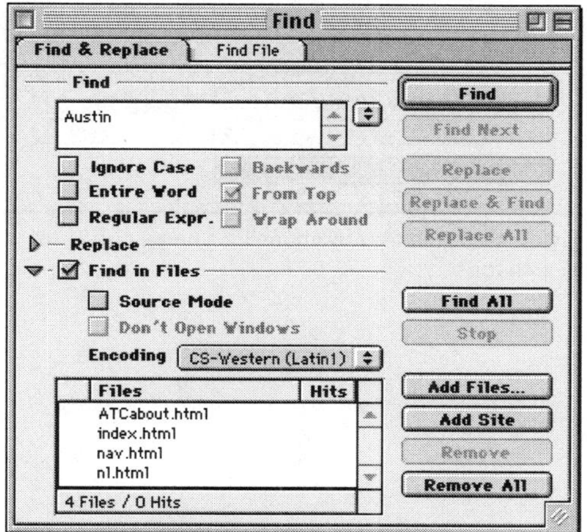

Figure 3.27 Search a site or another group of files with the Find in Files option.

Global Find & Replace

Using Global Find & Replace, you can expand your search for characters, words, phrases, or HTML tags to multiple files within your site. You can even search multiple sites.

To find text globally:

1. Open a GoLive site.
2. With the Site window visible, choose Find from the Edit menu (or type Command-F or Control-F).
3. In the Find window, click the triangle next to the Find in Files label.
4. Click Add Files in the newly revealed pane to add files and/or sites to be searched. A dialog box appears.
5. Navigate to the folder containing the files you want to add.
6. Add files by clicking the Add button. If you want to search all files within your site, open the site's folder and click Add All. The files you add appear in the lower portion of the dialog box.
7. When you have added all of the files you want to search, click done. The Find and Replace window now displays the files you've added to the search. The result looks like **Figure 3.27**. If you want to search for an HTML tag or see your search results within the Source view, click the Source Mode checkbox. Begin your search by clicking Find. When it locates the search string, GoLive opens the file containing the first reference and highlights the text in question.
8. Click Find Next to locate more occurrences of the text.

✔ Tips

- You can search for and replace text globally by opening the Replace pane (click the triangle next to the Replace label) and entering text as described in the local search section of this chapter.
- You can drag files directly from the Site window to the Find in Files box.
- Click the Don't Open Windows checkbox if you expect lots of results. Large numbers of open pages use extra RAM and could cause GoLive to run out of memory.

Finding Files

In addition to locating text within files, you can use Find to locate the files themselves.

To find a file:

1. With a GoLive site open, choose Find from the Edit menu.
2. Type all or part of a filename in your site. If you want to search for a file according to its URL, click the "whose" popup menu to choose a URL. Otherwise, leave the Name item selected.
3. Choose from the next popup, depending on whether you want to find the file's complete name or a portion of the name. My search appears in **Figure 3.28**.
4. Click Find. GoLive highlights the files that match your search in the Site window.
5. To find another file with the name or URL you selected, click Find Next.
6. When you're finished locating files, close the Find & Replace window.

Figure 3.28 Find files by choosing a name or URL to search for.

Layout Tools

In many ways, this is the most important chapter in the entire book. Here I explain how you can use GoLive to construct Web pages and add the elements that almost every Web page has in common: text, graphics, and spacing devices. I'll start with a layout grid and work my way through adding items to the page, fine-tuning each one.

In this chapter, I cover:

- Working with layout grids.
- Using tables.
- Using lines.
- Using browser-specific tags.
- Using multiple objects.
- Working with color.
- Using the Custom tab.

The Layout Grid

GoLive's layout grid is among the application's most useful features. Using the grid, you can precisely place text frames, images, lines, spacers, tables, and plug-in elements on a Web page, and you can use gridlines to arrange and align elements on the page.

Layout grids can also obviate the need for traditional HTML trickery, such as using tables or frames to create multi-column pages. From a designer's point of view, a GoLive layout grid acts just like a traditional publishing application's grid. Underneath the visual grid, though, GoLive actually generates HTML tables. It uses tables to display free-standing elements or multiple columns on a Web page. Finally, because the grid itself is customizable, you can choose settings and spacing that match the page you're working on.

I introduced the layout grid in Chapter 3. In this chapter, I make fuller use of grids and customize them for different applications.

To create a layout grid:

1. Open a new GoLive document.
2. Drag the Layout Grid tool (**Figure 4.1**) from the Palette onto the document window, or double-click the tool. A square layout grid appears (**Figure 4.2**).
3. Click on the grid to display the Layout Grid Inspector (**Figure 4.3**). In the Layout Grid Inspector window, you can resize the entire grid, set a color for the grid, and align it to either side of the page.
4. With the Inspector visible, click in the Horizontal field under the Grid label. Type 12, replacing the default value of 16.
5. Press Tab. The Vertical field is now selected. Notice that the horizontal gridlines are now closer together. They are 12 points apart.

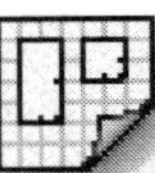

Figure 4.1 The Layout Grid tool.

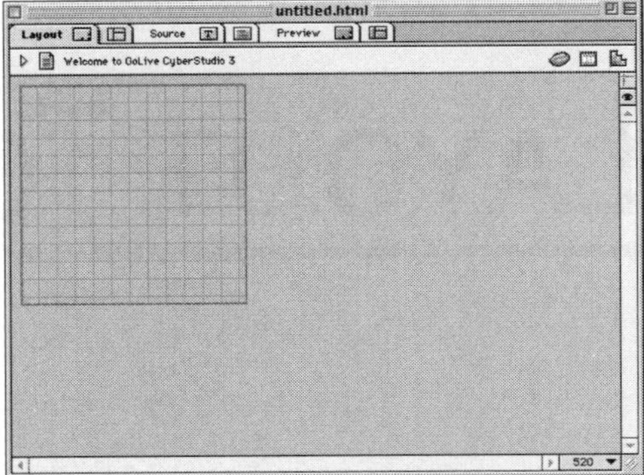

Figure 4.2 Here is a newly placed layout grid.

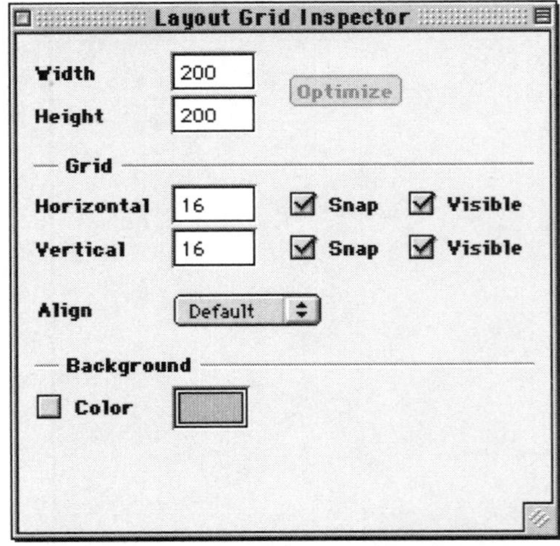

Figure 4.3 The Layout Grid Inspector controls the appearance of layout grids.

6. Type 12 in the Vertical field and press Tab to finish the newly denser grid.

   Closer grid spacing can be useful if you want to place a number of objects close together on a page. Likewise, adding space between gridlines keeps objects further apart on the page.

✔ Tips

- By default, the horizontal and vertical Snap checkboxes are selected in the Layout Grid Inspector. With Snap turned on, objects you drag onto a layout grid automatically snap to the nearest gridlines.
- Turninzg off the Visible checkbox hides the grid from view but doesn't prevent it from snapping objects into place. Hiding the grid can make previewing pages in the Layout view a bit easier.

Positioning a layout grid

You can use a single layout grid for an entire Web page, or you can divide the page into multiple grids. A single grid forms a consistent background for the entire document and is usually a good choice if your Web page contains lots of items that should appear relative to one another, and/or will be aligned with one another. If your page is modular with distinct sections that might be moved or copied to other pages—such as a navigation bar or logo section—a grid for each section is the best choice. In the following example, I create two grids to accommodate a modular layout.

To size a layout grid:

1. Click on the grid to select it.
2. Click on the border of the grid to display the grid's handles.

continues on next page

3. Drag the handle at the bottom right-hand corner of the grid downward and to the right until the grid extends to the bottom and right edge of the window. The result appears in **Figure 4.4**.
4. From the Page Size popup menu at the bottom right-hand corner of the document window, choose 580 (for a 14-inch monitor). This will enlarge your main window a bit.
5. Select the layout grid and drag the bottom right handle of the grid to the edge of the window

   or

   Type 580 in the Layout Grid Inspector's Width field.
6. Save your work. We will be using this grid in the next section.

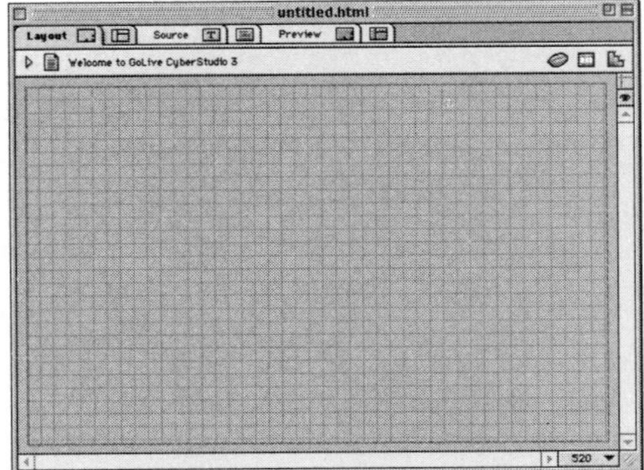

Figure 4.4 Resize the layout grid to fill the document window.

✔ Tip

- As you resize the grid, the horizontal and vertical measurements in the Layout Grid Inspector change. You can use the Inspector to resize your grid precisely if you prefer.

Using multiple layout grids

Many Web sites use a navigation bar, logo, or other standing elements to unify all the pages within a site. You can easily design individual pages around these standing elements by adding layout grids to your Web pages, using them as placeholders. Even better, you can save the entire grid under the Palette's Custom tab and add the grid, along with its contents, to pages where you want the standing element to appear.

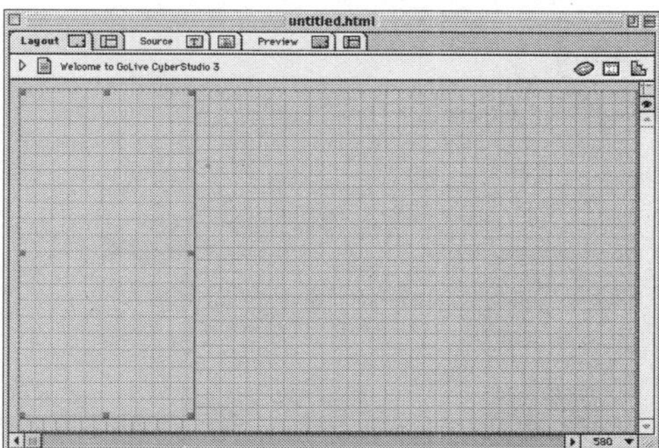

Figure 4.5 Add a second layout grid to the page by dragging the layout grid tool from the Palette, and drag the grid's border to fill the document window, vertically.

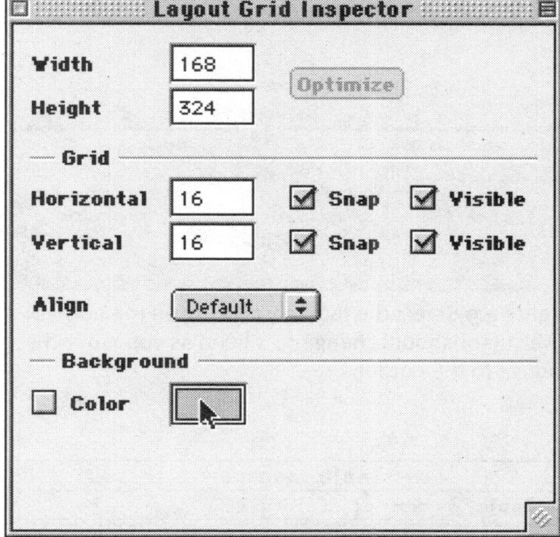

Figure 4.6 Choose a background color for the new grid in the Layout Grid Inspector.

✔ Tip

- Grids *can* be placed next to one another, but problems with alignment, especially when browser windows are resized, make it tough to keep several grids in place. One way to use grids effectively is to confine them to a distinct portion of the page, say the top or bottom. Vertically placed grids don't cause as many alignment problems, and offer an easy way to separate banners, logos or other header and footer information from the page as a whole.

To add a second layout grid:

1. Open the document you created earlier in this chapter. Make sure that you fill the document window with a layout grid.
2. Drag the Layout Grid tool from the Palette onto the main window. The grid will snap to the top left-hand corner of the underlying grid.
3. Drag the lower right handle of the new grid down and to the left a bit, so that it looks like **Figure 4.5**. This will contain your Web site's table of contents.
4. With the new grid selected, click on the Layout Grid Inspector window.
5. Change the gridline settings, if you like.
6. Click on the Color box in the lower part of the Inspector window. **Figure 4.6** points to it.
7. When the Color Palette window appears, choose a color for your layout grid and drag it onto the Layout Grid Inspector's Color field. (You will find more details about choosing colors and using the Color Palette later in this chapter.)
8. Save your work.

Tables

Tables are a versatile HTML feature that you can use to create grid-like page elements such as spreadsheets, calendars, or other items that use columns and rows. In many HTML editing applications, tables are also an important design tool because they allow you to "fake" multi-column layouts in HTML. GoLive employs this fakery but hides it under every layout grid. In fact, a layout grid is actually a table, whose cells form the grid.

The GoLive documentation goes so far as to suggest that you can use layout grids instead of tables. You can use grids to create columns or simulate frames, but conventional HTML tables allow you to create and manage a large number of columns and rows simultaneously.

To create a table:

1. With a document open, double-click or drag the Table tool (**Figure 4.7**) from the Palette to the document window. You can drag the table tool directly into the window or onto a layout grid. A three-by-three cell table appears in the document window (**Figure 4.8**).
2. Select the table. When you drag the Table tool onto the document window, the resulting table is selected, displaying the Table Inspector. If you deselected the table after you created it, place your cursor on the top, left, or right border of the table—the cursor will change into a two-headed arrow on the right border, or into a hand (**Figure 4.9**) on the top or left border. Click the border to view the Table Inspector (**Figure 4.10**).
3. Type 4 in the Rows field.
4. Press Tab. The table expands downward to add a new row.

Figure 4.7 The Table tool.

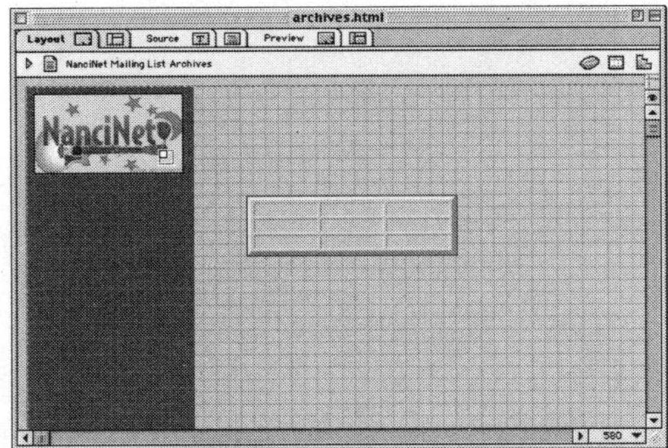

Figure 4.8 Dragging the Table tool into the Layout view creates a three-by-three table.

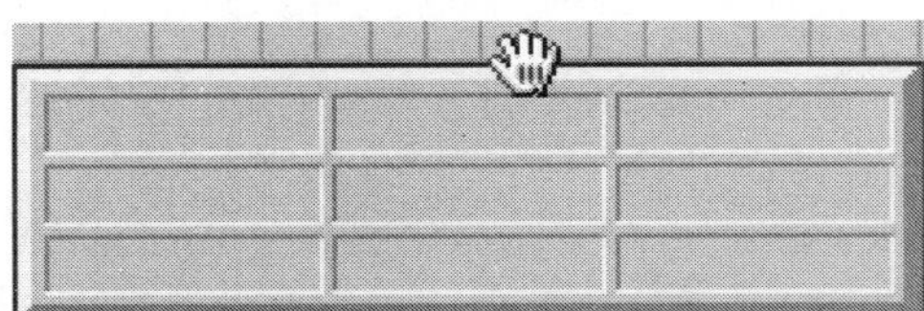

Figure 4.9 Select the table by clicking on the border. The cursor should change to a hand as you move the mouse to the border.

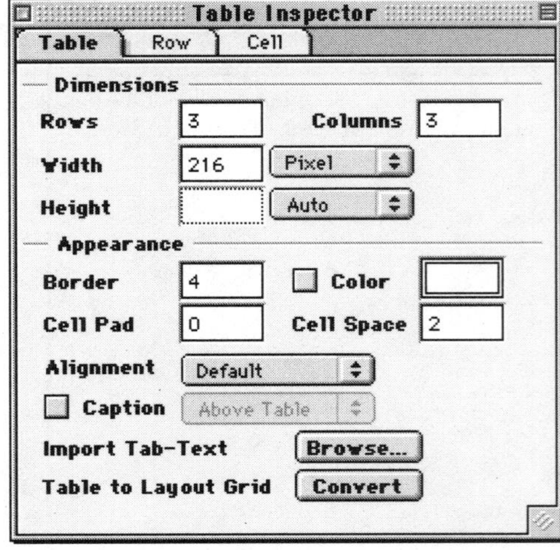

Figure 4.10 The Table Inspector.

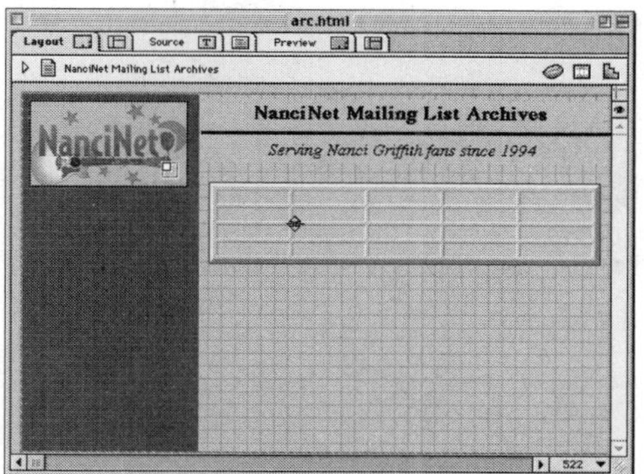

Figure 4.11 Adding columns and rows in the Table Inspector enlarges the entire table, leaving each row or column with the same dimensions it had before you made the change.

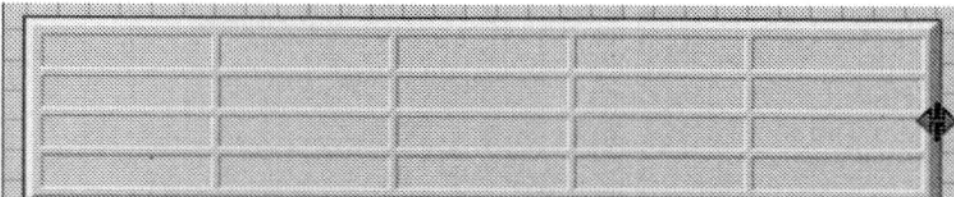

Figure 4.12 The two-sided arrow cursor indicates that you are dragging the table's border.

5. Type 5 in the Columns field.
6. Press Tab. The table expands to the right, adding two columns (**Figure 4.11**).

✔ Tips

- If adding rows and columns has changed the table's position relative to other items on the page, you can relocate the table by moving your cursor to the left or top border of the table. When the cursor changes to a hand, click and drag the border to move the table to the desired location.
- Clicking on the top or left border is also the quickest way to delete an entire table. Click and then press the Delete key.

Resizing tables

You can resize table cells, rows, and columns, and even the table itself by dragging table gridlines or by typing values into the appropriate fields in the Table Inspector.

✔ Tip

- If you plan to add rows and columns to a table, it's a good idea to do so *before* resizing the table, because placing new cells will expand the table on the page, possibly shifting other elements of your layout out of their proper positions. You can fix that, of course, but it's better to plan your tables and their dimensions from the start.

To resize a table horizontally:

1. Move the cursor to the right edge of the table. The cursor changes to a dark blue, two-sided arrow (**Figure 4.12**).
2. Drag the border to the left to shrink the table horizontally. All of the cells decrease in size proportionally.

To resize a table vertically:

1. Move the cursor to the lower border of the table and hold down the Option (Mac) or Alt (Windows) key. The cursor changes to a blue, two-headed arrow (**Figure 4.13**).
2. With the Option (Mac) or Alt (Windows) key held down, drag the border downward to expand the table vertically. The cells increase in size proportionally.

Figure 4.13 The blue, two-headed cursor appears when you hold down the Option (Mac) or Alt (Windows) key and move the cursor onto the table's border.

✔ Tips

- You can also resize the table using the Inspector. With the table selected, be sure that the Table tab is visible and type values (in pixels) in the Width and Height fields.
- By default, the Inspector displays the width of a table in pixels. The first time you drag the table's border to resize the table vertically, the Inspector's Height measurement changes from Auto to Pixel and allows you to edit the table height from the Inspector.
- When the table's height is measured in pixels, you need not hold down the Option (Mac) or Alt (Windows) key to change its dimensions. Using the Option (Mac) or Alt (Windows) key the first time you resize the table resets the measurement scheme to pixels.

To resize a column:

1. Place your cursor on the right border of an interior cell of the table. Hold down the Option (Mac) or Alt (Windows) key. The cursor changes to a two-sided arrow (**Figure 4.14**).
2. Drag the border to the left to shrink the table cell and its column. Unlike resizing the table, resizing columns does not affect adjacent columns, although it does narrow the table as a whole.

Figure 4.14 With the Option (Mac) or Alt (Windows) key held down, the cursor changes to a two-sided arrow. You can now drag cell borders right or left to change the dimensions of columns.

Figure 4.15 Placing the cursor on a cell's border and holding down the Option key displays the light blue, two-headed resizing cursor.

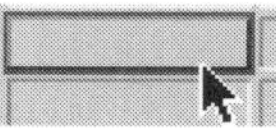

Figure 4.16 When you click on the border of a table cell, a marquee appears, indicating that the cell is selected.

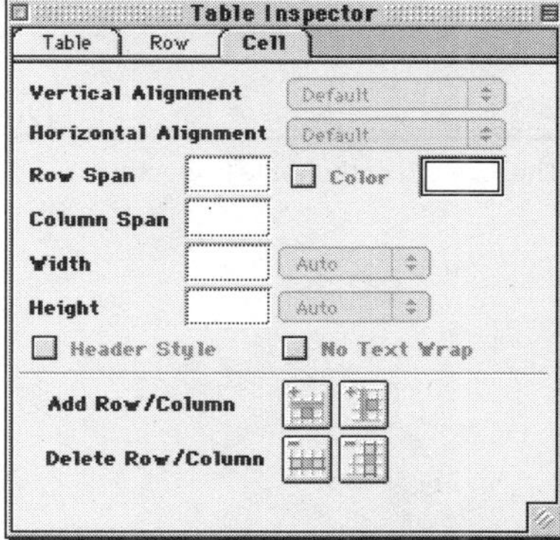

Figure 4.17 The Table Inspector's Cell tab appears when you select an individual cell.

1994				December
1995	January	February	March	April
	May	June	July	August
	September	October	November	December

Figure 4.18 The leftmost column in this table has a row span of 3.

1994				December
1995	January	February	March	April
	May	June	July	August
	September	October	November	December

Figure 4.19 A column span of 3 looks like this.

1994	**Digests began in December 1994**			December
1995	January	February	March	April
	May	June	July	August
	September	October	November	December

Figure 4.20 Table headers are centered, and appear in bold type.

To resize a row:

1. Place the cursor on the lower border of a cell within the table. Hold down the Option (Mac) or Alt (Windows) key. The cursor changes to a two-headed arrow (**Figure 4.15**).
2. Drag the border downward to expand the row. Unlike resizing the table, resizing a row does not affect adjacent rows.

To customize a cell:

1. Click on the bottom or right border of a cell you want to customize. A marquee appears within the cell (**Figure 4.16**), and the Table Inspector displays the Cell tab (**Figure 4.17**).
2. To align text to the cell vertically, choose Top, Bottom, or Middle from the Vertical Alignment menu.
3. To align text to the cell horizontally, choose Left, Right, or Center from the Horizontal Alignment menu.
4. To cause the selected cell to span several rows, enter 3 in the Row Span field. The result appears in **Figure 4.18**.
5. To cause a cell to span multiple columns, enter 3 in the Column Span field. The result appears in **Figure 4.19**.
6. To color the cell, click the Color checkbox and make a choice from the Color Palette.
7. Click the Header Style checkbox to center cell text and make it bold (see **Figure 4.20**).
8. Click No Text Wrap if you want to prevent text from wrapping at the end of a line.

✔ Tips

- It is usually easiest to resize cells by dragging their borders, as described in the previous section. But if you want a precise measurement, use the Width and Height fields to resize them. First choose Pixels from the appropriate popup menu, and then enter a value.
- You can format multiple table cells at once by selecting them together. First, select a cell. With the Shift key held down, select another cell. Now you can format the cells together, using options in the Table Inspector's Cell tab.

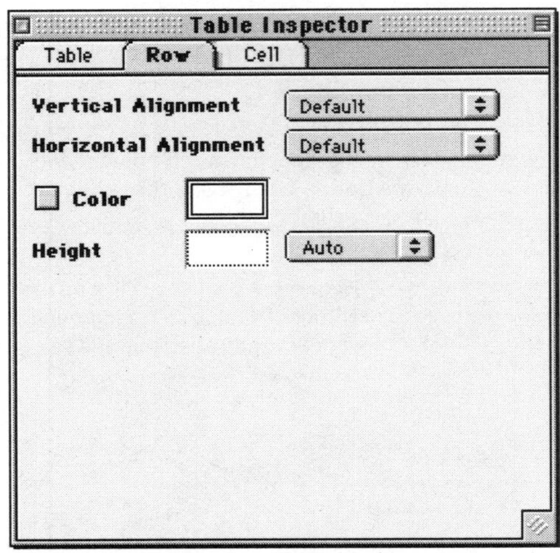

Figure 4.21 The Row tab of the Table Inspector.

To customize a row:

1. Shift-click the left border of a row to select the row.
2. In the Table Inspector, choose the Row tab (**Figure 4.21**).
3. Choose an alignment for the row from the Vertical Alignment popup menu. You can align text within the selected row to the top, middle, or bottom of the cells.
4. Choose an alignment from the Horizontal Alignment popup menu. You can align text within the selected row to the left, right, or center of the cells.
5. Click the Color field to view the Color Picker. Choose a color and drag it to the Color field within the Table Inspector.
6. Choose a custom height for the selected row by selecting Pixels from the Height popup and then typing the height measurement you want.

✔ Tip

- To select all items in a row or column except the currently selected item, Shift-click the left border (row) or top border (column). The previous selection is deselected.

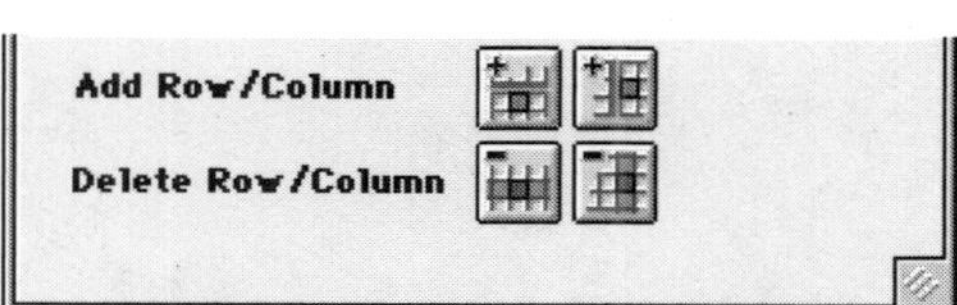

Figure 4.22 You can add or remove individual rows and columns with these buttons found under the Cell tab of the Table Inspector.

To customize a column:

1. Select a column by Shift-clicking on the top border of a column.
2. In the Cell tab of the Inspector, choose an alignment for the column from the Horizontal Alignment popup menu. You can align text within the selected row to the left, center, or right edge of the cells.
3. Choose an alignment from the Horizontal Alignment popup menu. You can align text within the selected column to the left, right or center of the cells.
4. Click the Color field to view the Color Palette. Choose a color and drag it to the Color field of the Table Inspector.
5. Click the Header Style box if you want the column's text to be bold.
6. Click the No Text Wrap checkbox if you want to keep column text on a single line. This option increases the width of the column as text is added.

✔ Tip

- It's a good idea to click outside a table you've been working on before you select an entire row or column. Because Shift-clicking a cell or group of cells inverts any previous selections, it's possible that Shift-clicking will cause cells outside your target row or column to be affected by changes you make in the Table Inspector. Clicking outside the table before you Shift-click will prevent this possible effect.

To add a row:

1. Select a table cell that lies below the position your new row will occupy.
2. In the Cell tab of the Table Inspector, click the Add Row button (**Figure 4.22**). A new row appears above the selected cell.

To add a column:

1. Select a table cell that lies to the right of the position the new column will occupy.
2. In the Cell tab of the Table Inspector, click the Add Column button. A new column appears to the left of the selected cell.

Adding cells to the bottom or right edge of a table

When you use the Add Rows/Columns buttons to add cells to a table, the new cells appear above or to the left of existing cells. You can add cells to the bottom or right edge of the table by adding rows or columns in the Table tab of the Table Inspector. First select the table, or a cell, and switch to the Table tab of the Inspector. Add the number of rows or columns you want to add to the current number and type the result in the Rows or Columns field.

Adding content to a table

HTML tables can include any element you can put on a Web page, including text, images, and multimedia objects. You can type directly into the table, use the Palette to add objects, or drag and drop items into a table.

To add text:

1. Click in one of the table's cells—not on the border.
2. Type the text.
3. Press Tab. The insertion point moves to the next horizontal cell. Tabbing from the last cell in a row moves the insertion point to the first cell in the text row.

Figure 4.23 A heavy border gives the table a 3-D look.

1994	Digests began in December 1994			December
	January	February	March	April
1995	May	June	July	August
	September	October	November	December
	January	February	March	April
1996	May	June	July	August
	September	October	November	December
	January	February	March	April
1997	May	June	July	August
	September	October	November	December
	January	February	March	April
1998	May	June	July	August
	September	October	November	December

Figure 4.24 Even a small amount of padding adds a large amount of white space to table cells.

✔ Tips

- When you type text into a table cell, and the text exceeds the visible boundaries of the cell, the cell grows downward to accommodate the text. So, if you're typing the contents of your table from scratch, you should complete the typing before you finish sizing the table cells.
- When you add an image to a table (either by drag-and-drop or by using the Image Inspector to place the image) the table cell grows to accommodate the image. If you resize the image, the cell's size changes too, though not in direct proportion to the image.

To change the appearance of a table:

1. Select the table by clicking on the top or left border.
2. In the Table Inspector window (under the Table tab), type a value (in pixels) in the Border field. **Figure 4.23** shows the table with a six-pixel border.
3. Click the Color checkbox and then the Color field to bring up the Color Picker. Choose a color for the table and drag it from the Color Picker into the Color field.
4. Type 2 in the Cell Pad field to create extra vertical space within each cell. **Figure 4.24** shows the table we've been working on, with a two-pixel pad in each cell. The Cell Space field controls the amount of space between cells. By default, tables use a pad of two spaces.
5. If you are not using a layout grid, choose an option from the Alignment menu to place the table, relative to the page you're working on. You can align the table to the left or right or leave it unaligned.

To add a caption:

1. Click on the Caption checkbox within the Table Inspector (under the Table tab).
2. Use the adjacent popup menu to place the caption above or below the table.
3. Type a caption in the space created above or below the table (**Figure 4.25**).

Importing table content

You can add content to a table by typing or by importing the contents of a tab-delimited text file into your GoLive document. The fields (which will become table cells) in your file must be separated by tabs, and each record (row) must include a carriage return at the end.

To import table content:

1. Drag the table tool from the Palette into the document window to create a new table.
2. In the Table Inspector, click the Import Tab-Text button.
3. Locate a tab-delimited file in the dialog box that appears. When you click Open, the file's contents appear in the table (**Figure 4.26**).
4. Resize the table, its rows and columns so that the data fits correctly on the page.

Click on a month link to see a list of daily digest files				
1994				December
1995	January	February	March	April
	May	June	July	August
	September	October	November	December
1996	January	February	March	April
	May	June	July	August
	September	October	November	December
1997	January	February	March	April
	May	June	July	August
	September	October	November	December
1998	January	February	March	April
	May	June	July	August
	September	October	November	December

Figure 4.25 A caption is a cell that spans the full width of a table.

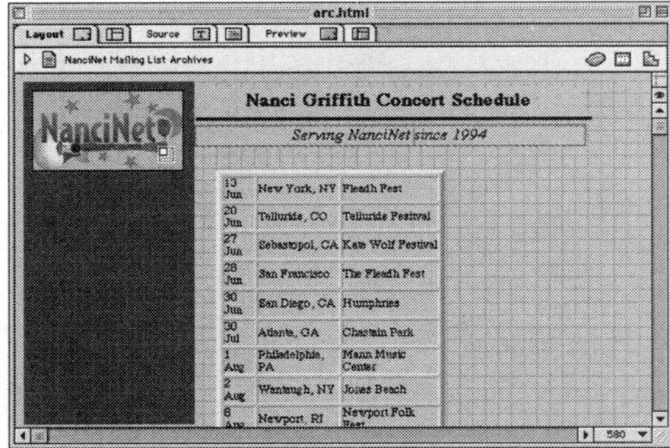

Figure 4.26 When you import text into a new table, chances are that it won't look the way you want it to. The newly populated table (and its rows and columns) needs to be resized.

Converting tables to layout grids

GoLive allows you to break tables out into text frames, within a layout grid. This feature allows you to redesign a page by moving its tabular content around freely.

To convert a table to a layout grid:

1. Select a table.
2. In the Table tab of the Inspector, click the Convert button. The table is replaced onscreen by a layout grid. Each former cell is now a text frame.

Lines

You can use lines to divide your Web page into sections, or simply to give the text and graphics elements a little breathing room. Like most page elements, lines work best when you use a layout grid to position them, although you can work without a grid.

You can vary the appearance of lines by thickness and color.

Figure 4.27 The Line Tool.

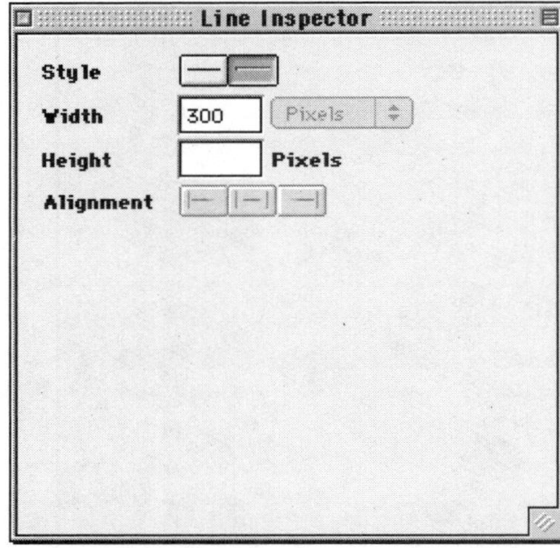

Figure 4.28 The Line Inspector.

To insert a horizontal line:

1. With a GoLive document open to the Layout view, add, or locate a text frame to which you want to add a line. If you are not using a layout grid, you can drag the line directly into the document window.
2. Drag the Line tool from the Palette to the document window. **Figure 4.27** shows the Line tool.
3. When you add a horizontal line, the Inspector window displays the Line Inspector (**Figure 4.28**). By default the Hollow Line icon is highlighted.

✔ Tips

- You can shorten or lengthen a line by dragging one of its handles or by changing the value in the Line Inspector's Width field.
- When using layout grids, you can fit a line within a grid or text frame by dragging the line tool into the desired grid or frame. The line will snap to the width of the grid or frame.
- If you want to align a line, you must drag it into a text frame or into the document window. Alignment doesn't work when the line appears directly on a layout grid.

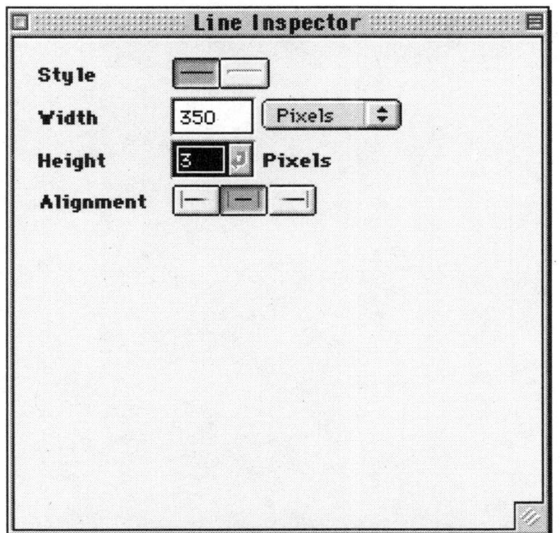

Figure 4.29 The Left, Center, and Right buttons in the Line Inspector align lines to the document window, and are enabled only when you are not using a layout grid.

- Even if you're not using grids, you can create lines that drop easily into place. To create a line next to an image, for example, place the image first and drag the line tool into place next to the image. The line is drawn to fill the available space.

To configure a line:

1. Click on a line you've created to select it. The Line Inspector appears.
2. To change the line from hollow to solid, click the Style button in the Line Inspector that matches your choice.
3. Note the measurement (it's in pixels) in the Width field and type a new one to shorten or lengthen the line, if you like.
4. In the Height field, type a number (in pixels) to change the thickness of the line.
5. If the line is located within a text frame, or you're not using a layout grid, choose one of the alignment buttons (**Figure 4.29**). The line will be aligned to the left, center, or right side of the document window.

Browser-Specific Tags

Both Netscape and Microsoft have tinkered with standard HTML, creating nifty new tags that either add features to your Web page or gum up the works, depending on your point of view. GoLive supports some browser-specific tags. Using them means either that your Web pages will not be compatible with both major browsers, or that you will need to create versions of the page for each. The choice you make depends on how important the browser-specific option is to your design. You may also find that there's way to achieve the same effect without using a browser-specific tag.

Spacers

A spacer is a Netscape-only tag that must be viewed with a Navigator 3.0 or later browser. Spacers create room between elements on the page, making it easier to combine text and objects or to create desired text effects. Unlike alignment tags, which position items relative to other items, spacers enforce absolute boundaries. Spacers are especially useful when you work without a layout grid.

But because spacers are a Netscape-only tag, consider alternatives. If absolute positioning of text or objects is important to your layout, consider using Cascading Style Sheets, which are discussed in Chapter 12. Style sheets, like spacers, don't work with all browsers; your visitors will need at least a 4.0 browser, either Navigator or Internet Explorer.

GoLive can create three types of spacers: horizontal, vertical, and block spacers.

- *Horizontal spacers* are most useful in formatting lines of text. Insert one at the beginning or end of a line to precisely control line breaks or the width of an area of white space.

Figure 4.30 Despite its name, the Horizontal Spacer tool is used to create vertical and block spacers, too.

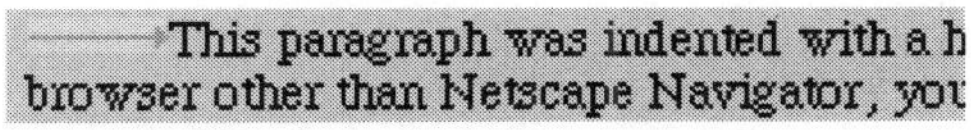

This paragraph was indented with a h
browser other than Netscape Navigator, you

Figure 4.31 Use a horizontal spacer to indent a paragraph.

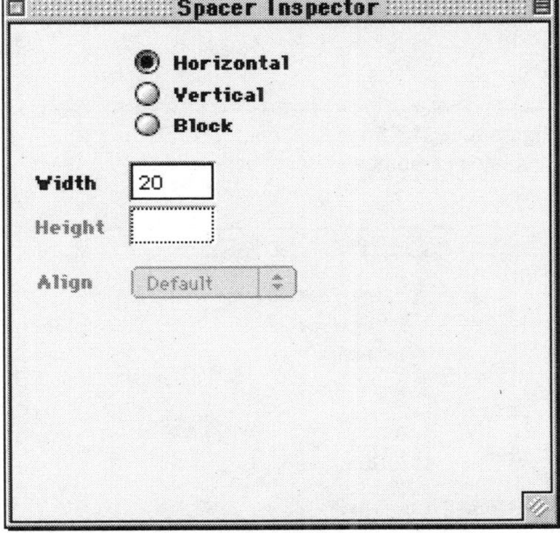

Figure 4.32 The Spacer Inspector

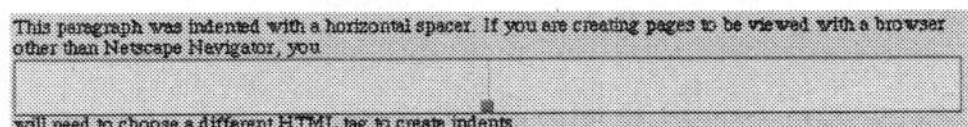

Figure 4.33 A vertical spacer creates space between lines of text.

- *Vertical spacers* can work like line breaks to divide text blocks, or they can be used to correctly position images relative to the text above or below them.
- *Block spacers* are two-dimensional, meaning that you can create a square or rectangle to separate items on your page. Use a block spacer to create indents (when you're not using a layout grid or when you want to position text without using list tags to create indents).

To insert a horizontal spacer:

1. With a document open to the Layout view, drag the Horizontal Spacer tool (**Figure 4.30**) from the Palette to the document window.
2. Position the spacer between words in a paragraph or headline. The text moves to accommodate the spacer (**Figure 4.31**).
3. Click on the spacer to select it. The Inspector window changes to display the Spacer Inspector (**Figure 4.32**).
4. Lengthen the spacer by typing a number (in pixels) in the Width field of the Inspector window or by dragging one of the spacer's handles.

To insert a vertical spacer:

1. With a document open to the Layout View, drag the Spacer tool from the Palette to the document window.
2. Click the Vertical radio button in the Spacer Inspector.
3. Position the spacer between two lines of text that you want to separate. By default, the vertical spacer is 32 pixels in height (**Figure 4.33**).

continues on next page

4. Click on the spacer to select it. The Spacer Inspector is displayed. This time the Vertical button is selected, and the Height field is editable (**Figure 4.34**).
5. Resize the spacer by typing a number (in pixels) in the Height field of the Inspector or by dragging the spacer's handle.

To insert a block spacer:

1. With the vertical spacer you've just created selected, click the Block button in the Spacer Inspector. The Width, Height, and Align fields are now editable (**Figure 4.35**), and the vertical spacer has changed to a small block.
2. Move the spacer to the beginning of the text block. The result appears in **Figure 4.36**.
3. Change the spacer's dimensions by using the Width and Height fields or by dragging the spacer's handles.
4. Align the block spacer to the left edge of the text by choosing Left from the Align menu in the Inspector. The block spacer now indents the entire paragraph, as shown in **Figure 4.37**.

✔ Tip

- Block spacers can be aligned according to the same rules that apply to images, and other two-dimensional HTML elements. For a complete explanation of the alignment options available, see Chapter 5.

Scrolling marquees

Microsoft invented the scrolling marquee tag and, you guessed it, Netscape doesn't support it, but Internet Explorer does. WebTV also supports scrolling marquees.

Unlike the other layout tools we've worked with in this chapter, marquees do not just sit

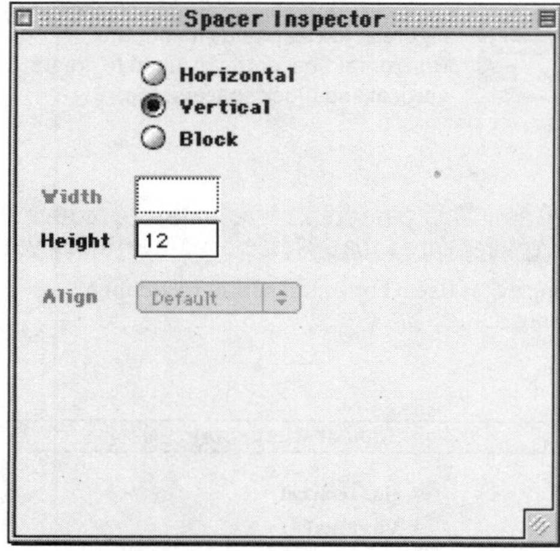

Figure 4.34 The Spacer Inspector configured to display a 12-point vertical spacer.

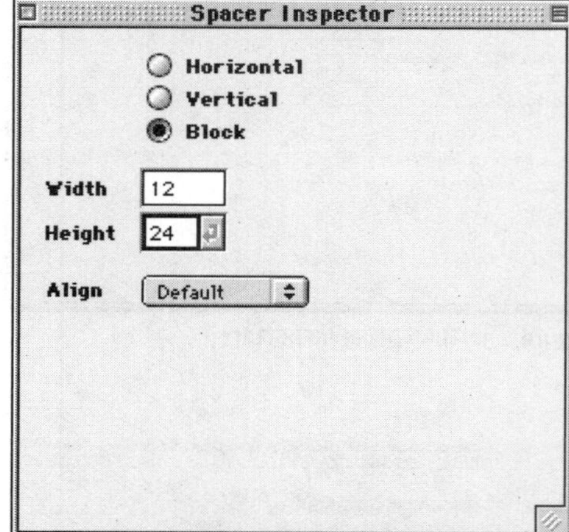

Figure 4.35 Choosing the Block Spacer button in the Spacer Inspector activates the alignment fields.

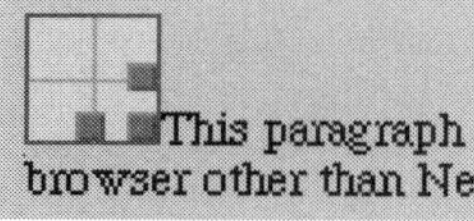

Figure 4.36 Block spacers create both horizontal and vertical space around the text they adjoin.

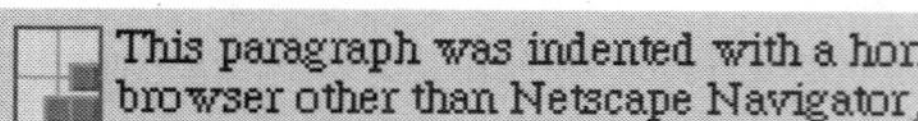

Figure 4.37 Align a block spacer to the left edge of text to create an indent for all lines in a paragraph.

Figure 4.38 The Scrolling Marquee tool.

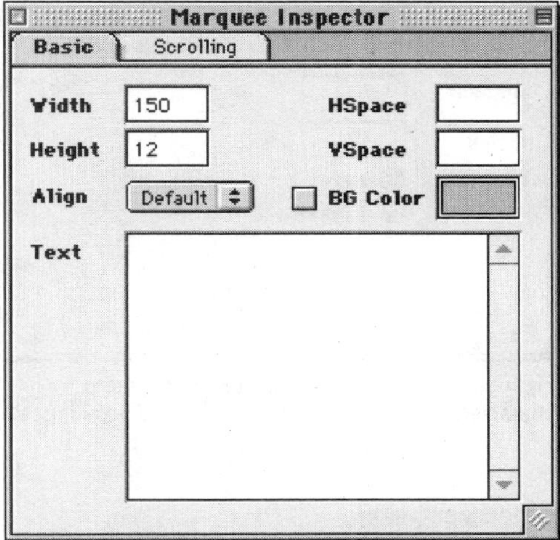

Figure 4.39 Edit the properties of a scrolling marquee in the Marquee Inspector.

Read the most recent edition of the NanciNet

Figure 4.40 Text appears in the document window as you type it into the Marquee Inspector.

there on your Web page. Scrolling marquees actually move. A scrolling marquee is a line of text that scrolls horizontally—à la the famous *New York Times* sign in Times Square—across your Web page.

To create a scrolling marquee:

1. Drag the Marquee tool from the Palette to the document window (**Figure 4.38**). You can place it on a layout grid or directly in the window. The Marquee Inspector appears (**Figure 4.39**).
2. With the marquee selected, click on the Inspector window to bring it forward.
3. Type some text into the Text field of the Marquee Inspector. The text becomes visible in the marquee (**Figure 4.40**).
4. To resize the marquee, drag one of its handles or type values (in pixels) into the Width and Height fields in the Inspector window.

✔ Tips

- Because text will be scrolling across the screen, it isn't necessary that the marquee be large enough to display the full line of text. Size the marquee so that it displays the number of words you'd like to be visible at any given time.
- If a marquee is inserted into a text frame, you can align the surrounding text to the top, middle, or bottom of the marquee. Choose one of these options from the Align popup menu in the Marquee Inspector.
- Use the HSpace and VSpace fields to add horizontal and vertical space, respectively, around the marquee.

To set a marquee's scrolling pattern:

1. Select the marquee in the document window.
2. Click on the Marquee Inspector window's Scrolling tab (**Figure 4.41**).
3. Choose a scrolling method for the marquee from the Behavior popup menu (**Figure 4.42**). *Scroll* moves the text across the page continuously. *Slide* moves the text into the marquee box and leaves it there. *Alternate* moves the text into the marquee and bounces it from side to side.
4. Choose the number of loops you want the marquee to scroll through. You can also click the Forever checkbox to continue scrolling indefinitely. Loops are only available when you choose the Scroll or Alternate pattern.
5. Set scrolling speed by typing a value in the Amount field.
6. Type a value in the Delay field to set the time between loops.
7. Choose a direction to scroll by pressing the Left or Right button.
8. Click on the Preview tab at the top of the document window to view your scrolling marquee in action. To change marquee settings, return to the Layout View, select the marquee and open the Marquee Inspector.

✔ Tips

- If you choose Alternate scrolling, make sure the marquee is wide enough to display the full line of text. Alternate bounces text from one side of the marquee to the other—it won't display text that won't fit in the visible marquee.
- Try several marquee settings to determine which one best fits your needs. As you set up the marquee, use the Preview View to watch its scrolling method and speed. You should also preview the marquee in one or more Web browsers.

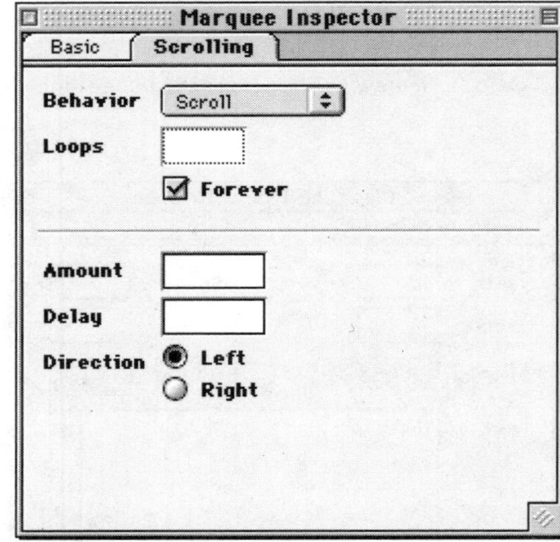

Figure 4.41 Determine a marquee's movement characteristics in the Marquee Inspector's Scrolling tab.

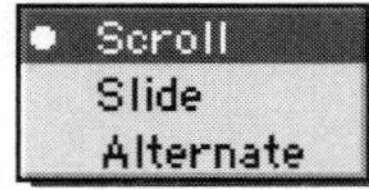

Figure 4.42 The Behavior popup menu.

Figure 4.43 Shift-click several items on a layout grid to select them.

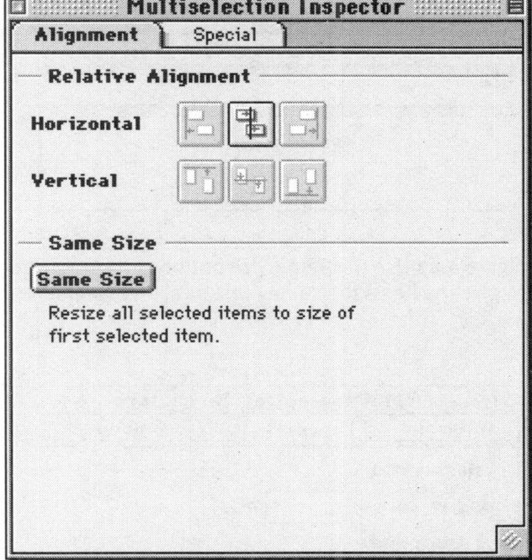

Figure 4.44 The Multiselection Inspector includes tools that establish relationships between selected objects.

Figure 4.45 Align objects to the layout grid itself with tools from the layout toolbar.

Working with Multiple Objects

Like most drawing programs, GoLive allows you to align and distribute objects in relation to one another and group them so that you can work with them together.

To work with multiple objects:

1. Open a document that includes several objects on a single layout grid.
2. Select an object.
3. Select a second and third object by holding down the Shift key while you click on each. Just as you would when selecting any object on a layout grid, be sure that the cursor has changed to a hand before you click on an object.

   With multiple objects selected (**Figure 4.43**) the layout grid toolbar takes the place of the formatting toolbar and the Multiselection Inspector appears.
4. Use the Relative Alignment buttons in the Multiselection Inspector (**Figure 4.44**) to align the left, center, or right edges of selected objects horizontally.
5. Use the top, middle, and bottom buttons in the Inspector to align objects vertically.
6. If you want to align the selected objects to the layout grid, use the alignment tools on the toolbar (**Figure 4.45**). You can also use the toolbar to align objects to one another.

✔ Tips

- If you select objects and find that an alignment choice is dimmed and not usable, it is either because the two objects cannot be aligned with that choice, or because they are already aligned.
- If you align objects and don't like the results, choose Undo from the Edit menu before you do anything else and the objects will return to their original position.

To resize aligned objects

1. Choose a group of objects that you want to align and that should also be the same size. This option is useful when you are creating lines, form elements or other objects that form part of a larger layout.
2. Select the object whose size you want the other objects to take on.
3. With the Shift key held down, select more objects and align them in the Multiselection Inspector. **Figure 4.46** shows a set of objects at their original size. Note that they are aligned but have different widths.
4. Click the Same Size button in the Inspector window. The horizontally aligned objects are now the same length (**Figure 4.47**).

To distribute or set objects off from one another:

1. Choose several objects to work with.
2. Click the Special tab of the Multiselection Inspector. It looks like **Figure 4.48**.
3. Click the Offset button under the Vertical label.

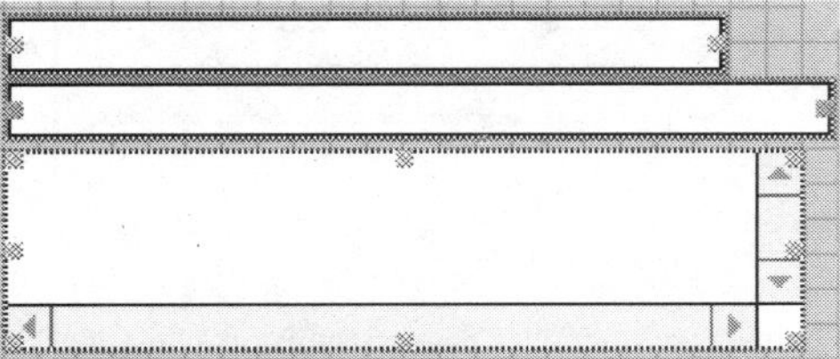

Figure 4.46 The selected objects are aligned, but have different widths.

Figure 4.47 Use the Same Size button in the Inspector to give the items the same horizontal measurement.

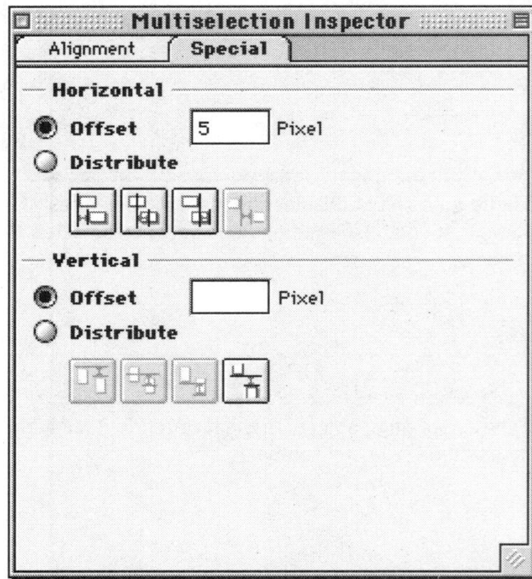

Figure 4.48 Create an offset or distribute objects in the Multiselection Inspector's Special tab.

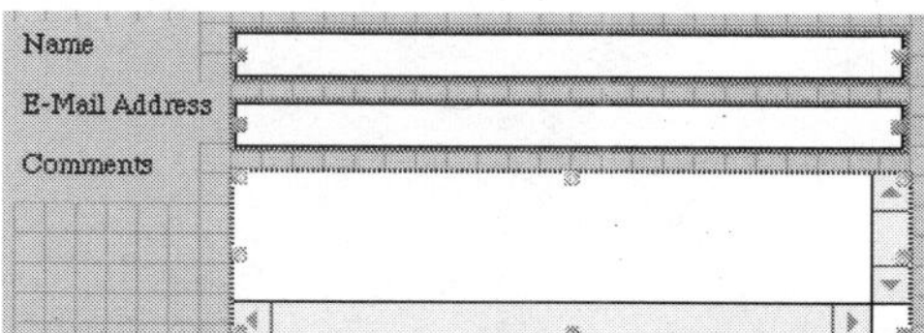

Figure 4.49 An offset adds space between or around selected objects.

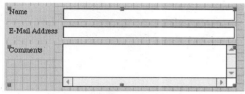

Figure 4.50 When objects are grouped, they move as one, and have a single set of selection handles.

4. Enter a number (in pixels). Entering 6 creates 6 pixels of space between the form fields (**Figure 4.49**).
5. Select the labels and enter the same offset, so that labels and fields remain even with one another. Because you cannot arrange objects vertically that have a horizontal relationship (and vice versa), you need to offset the field labels separately from the fields themselves.

To group objects:

1. Select several objects and align or distribute them as you like.
2. Click the Group button on the toolbar. The objects' individual selection handles become one large set of handles surrounding the newly grouped object (**Figure 4.50**).
3. Drag the grouped object. All the elements move together, allowing you to position the complete set of objects.
4. When you create a group, the Inspector changes to the Group Inspector. Here, you can choose to lock the group so that its elements will continue to move together.
5. To break up a group, choose Ungroup from the toolbar.

Adding Color

Adding color to a Web page is tricky. Actually, placing color on the page is easy, but making sure that the colors you choose or create in the Color Palette actually work presents some challenges.

Because Web pages are viewed on many kinds of computers, employing different color-handling conventions, the developers of HTML (with additions by the folks at Netscape) created a standard for Web color that makes it possible for all Web users with color-capable browsers and computers to see the same colors. Of course, creating that standard meant that many of the colors available on the Macintosh, for example, are not supported by Web browsers on other platforms.

Whatever development platform they prefer, it's important that Web designers use "Web-safe" colors on their Web pages. Using GoLive's Color Palette and the Site window, you can use and store a collection of Web-safe colors for your Web page. And if you want to create a more colorful version of your site, just for those users fortunate enough to have browsers and computers that support a wider color palette, there are plenty of "dangerous" colors to pick from on the RGB and CMYK color palettes.

Color tabs

The Color Palette's nine color tabs each deal with color composition in a different way, mirroring palettes familiar to print publishers (RGB, CMYK, Grayscale, Indexed, and HSV), to computer users (Apple Color or Windows Color), and to Web developers (Real Web and Web Named).

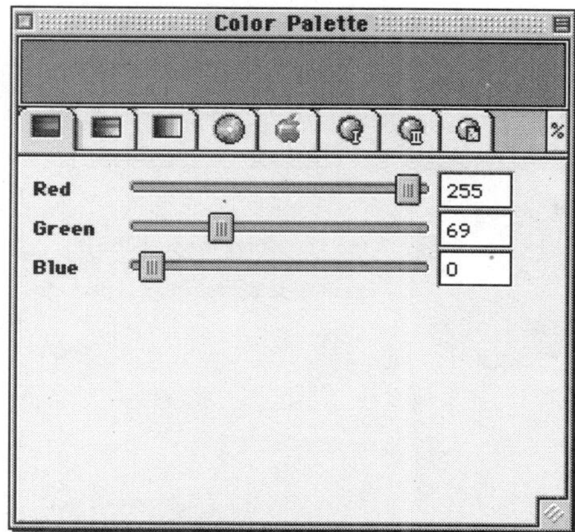

Figure 4.51 The RGB tab.

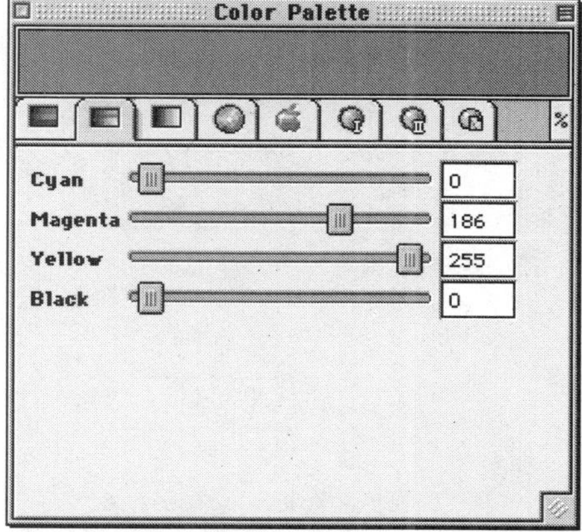

Figure 4.52 The CMYK tab.

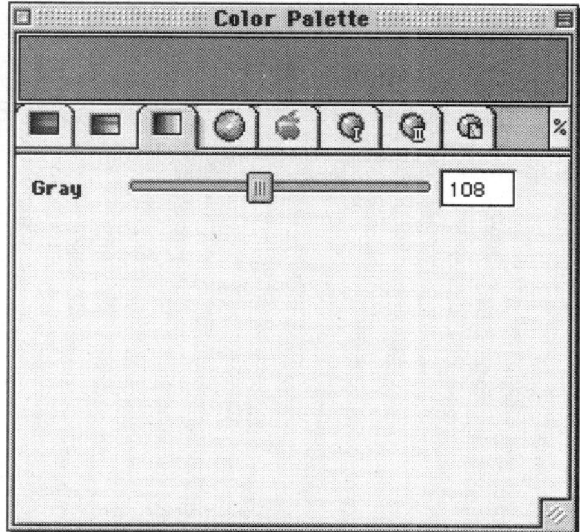

Figure 4.53 The Grayscale tab.

To use the RGB tab:

1. Choose Color Palette from the Windows menu (Mac) or the View (Windows).
2. If the RGB tab isn't displayed, click on it to display it (see **Figure 4.51**).
3. To choose a color, move one of the sliders left or right to change the color percentage. Each of the three sliders represents a color (red, green and blue) of the RGB spectrum. The color in the preview pane changes as you adjust the sliders. RGB is most often associated with video and computer imaging.

To use the CMYK tab:

1. Click on the CMYK tab in the Color Palette (**Figure 4.52**).
2. Use the Cyan, Magenta, Yellow and Black sliders to create a color. CMYK is most often associated with printed publishing, rather than the Web.

To use the Grayscale tab:

1. Click on the Grayscale tab in the Color Palette (**Figure 4.53**).
2. Use the slider to choose a grayscale percentage. 0% gray is white, and 100% gray is black. Like CMYK, grayscale is most often used in printing.

To use the Indexed Color tab:

1. Click on the Indexed Color tab in the Color Palette (**Figure 4.54**).
2. Click on the Color Wheel to select a color.
3. Use the Brightness slider to adjust the color's brightness.

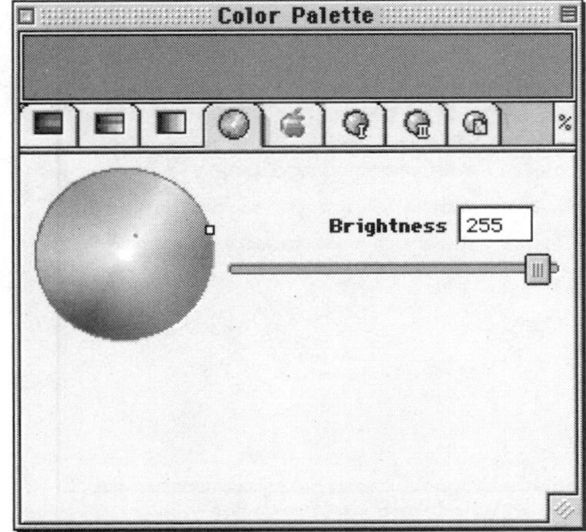

Figure 4.54 The Indexed Color tab.

W To use the HSV color tab:

1. Click on the HSV tab in GoLive for Windows. At this writing, the Macintosh version of GoLive does not include this tab (**Figure 4.55**). HSV stands for Hue, Saturation, and Value.
2. To choose a hue, click on the outer ring.
3. To pick a saturation level, click in the inner square, moving the cursor along the horizontal access to adjust the saturation level.
4. To choose a value, click in the HSV tab's square, and move along the vertical access to adjust the value.

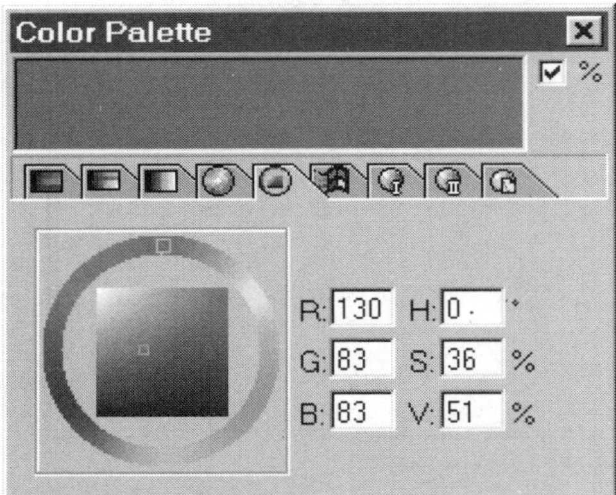

Figure 4.55 The HSV tab.

✔ Tip

- You can choose colors under the HSV tab by entering RGB and HSV values in the fields provided.

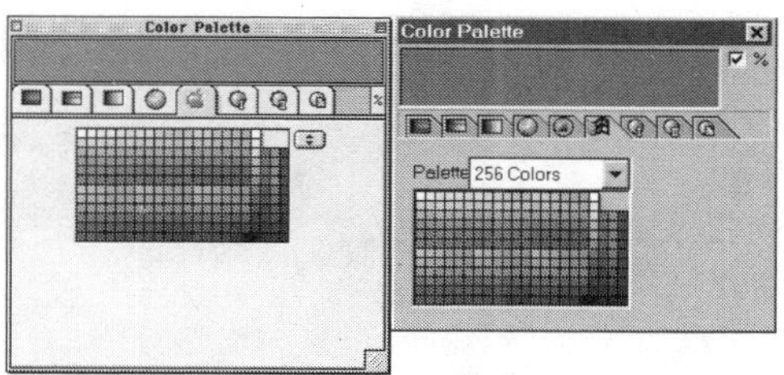

Figure 4.56 The OS color tabs give you access to Macintosh and Windows screen color palettes.

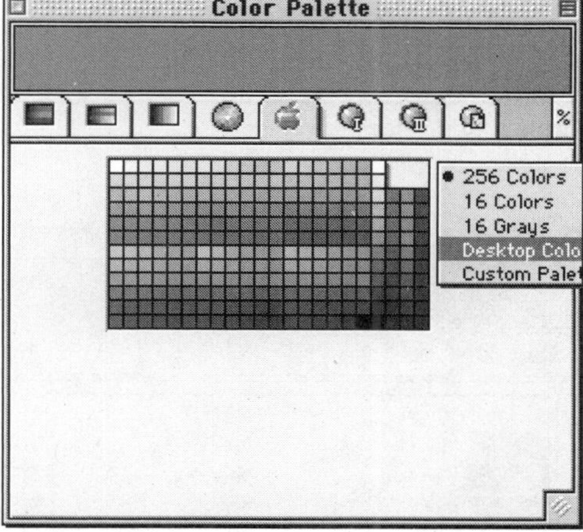

Figure 4.57 Use the popup menu to choose the portion of the OS color palette you want to work with.

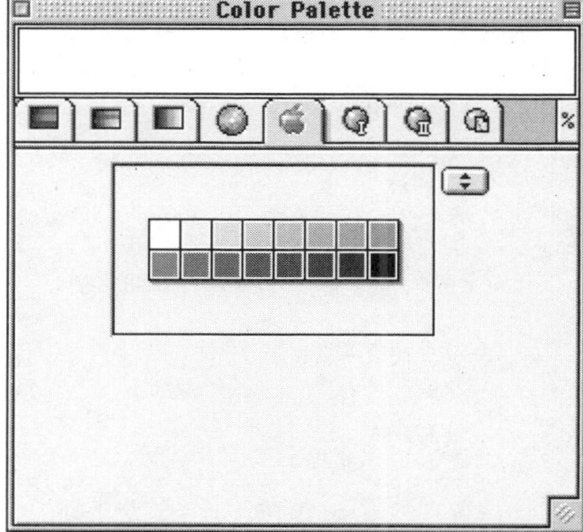

Figure 4.58 The 16-color palette in the Apple color tab.

To use the OS color tab:

1. Click on the Apple Color tab (Mac) or Windows Color tab (Windows) in the Color Palette (**Figure 4.56**).
2. Choose a color palette from the popup menu (**Figure 4.57**).
3. Colors in the Macintosh-supported Apple palette are expressed in terms of the number of colors visible onscreen. The palette squares represent all the available colors.
4. Select a color by clicking on a square within the palette (**Figure 4.58**).

To use the Real Web Colors tab:

1. Click on the Real Web Colors tab in the Color Palette (**Figure 4.59**).
2. Choose a color from the scrolling list on the right, or by clicking in the spectrum window on the left. The color value is entered in the field at the bottom of the Color Palette. It includes an RGB, decimal, and hexadecimal value. This value appears in the HTML code representing your chosen color.

✔ Tip

- Real Web colors are the best choice for creating Web pages, because they translate properly, no matter what browser or computer your site's visitors use. Other color options, including Web Named colors, may not look right in all browsers.

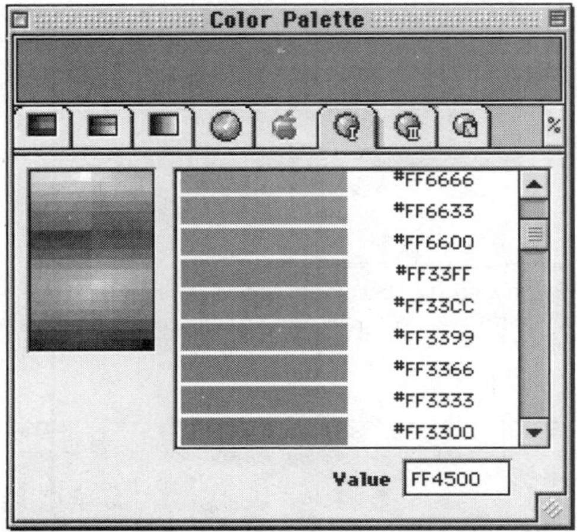

Figure 4.59 The Real Web Colors tab.

To use the Web Named Colors tab:

1. Click on the Web Named Colors tab in the Color Palette (**Figure 4.60**).
2. Choose a color from the list. The color names and values are recognizable by Web browsers that support color.

Figure 4.60 The Web Named Color tab.

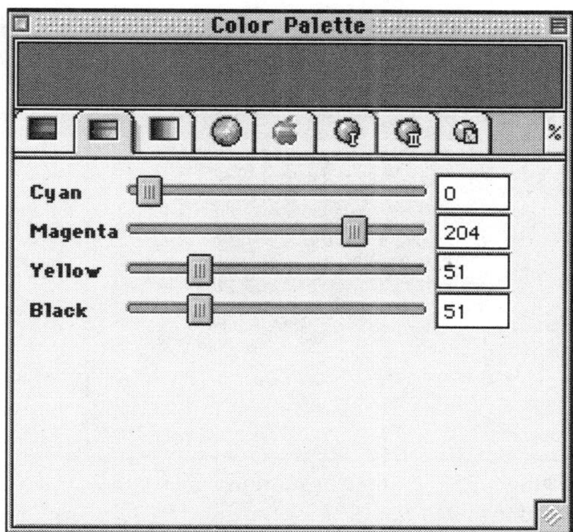

Figure 4.61 Here is a color as it appears in the CMYK tab...

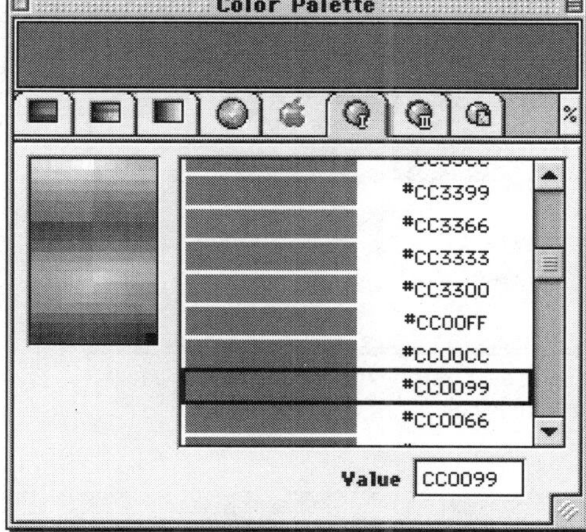

...and Real Web Colors tab.

✔ Tips

- If you want to use Web-safe colors but prefer to work with CMYK or another print-friendly (and, perhaps, more familiar) color palette, you can usually do it. Start by creating a color you like in the spectrum of your choice. Then click the Real Web or Web Named tab. GoLive duplicates or approximates the color you chose. Click to confirm the safe color. **Figure 4.61** shows a CMYK color and its Web-safe sibling.
- If you are using GoLive's site management features, you can save colors that you create within the Site window and determine whether your colors are Web-safe. Create a color while working in a site, and then drag it to the Site window's color tab to save it. If the color is not Web-safe, a bullet appears in the Site window.

Site Colors

The final tab in the Color Palette is the Site Colors tab. When you are working in a GoLive site, you can use the tab to store colors you use throughout the site. The items in the Site Colors tab are the same as those under the Colors tab of the Site window, and vice versa. The Site Colors tab is just another way to access frequently used colors. You can add or delete colors from either the Site window or Site Colors tab.

Using colors

In most cases, you access colors from the Inspector window: When you click on objects that support color, the resulting Inspector usually includes a color field. Simply click the color field to call up the Color Palette, choose a color and drag it from the preview pane to the Inspector's color field. You can also reverse the process. By matching colors on a Web page with the Color Palette, you can apply existing color to new objects.

To match colors:

1. Open a document containing a color you would like to use, as well as the Color Palette.
2. In the Color Palette, click on the Apple Color tab to display it (**Figure 4.62**).
3. Click on any color square, and hold down the mouse button. The cursor changes to a pipette (**Figure 4.63**).
4. Without letting go of the mouse button, drag into the document window and over the text or object with the color you want to match.
5. Let go of the mouse button when the Color Palette preview pane displays the color you want (**Figure 4.64**).
6. Open the document or site where you want to use the color you've chosen.

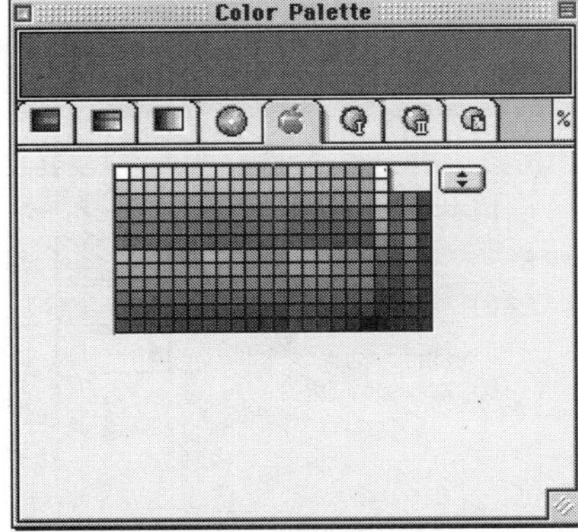

Figure 4.62 The Apple or Windows Color tab is used to match colors.

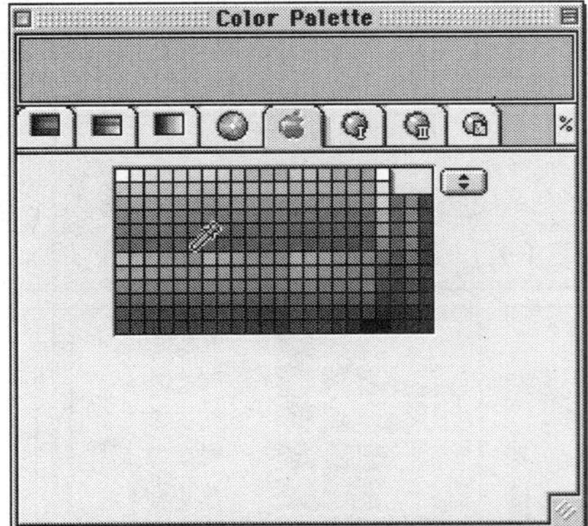

Figure 4.63 Getting the eyedropper for use in matching colors.

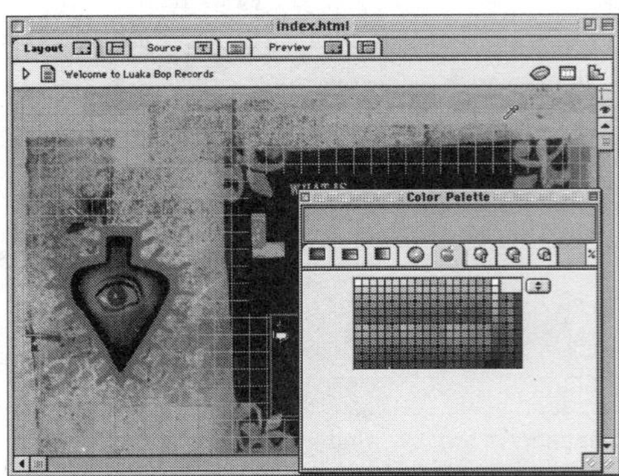

Figure 4.64 Copying a color from a Web page to the Color Palette.

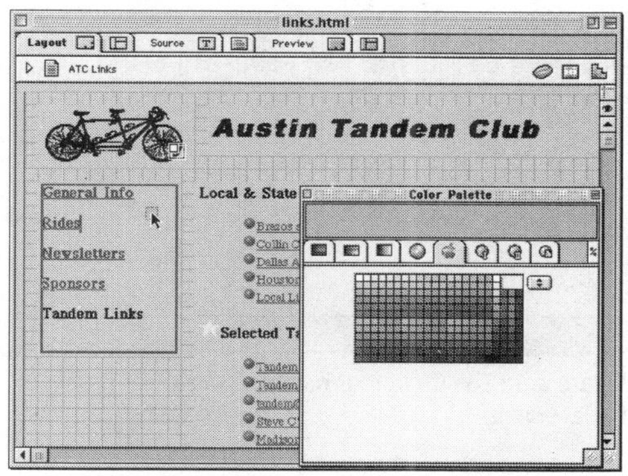

Figure 4.65 Adding a matched color to a Web page.

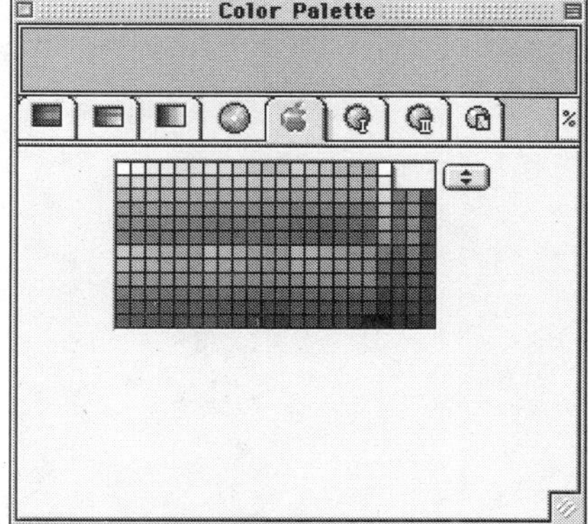

Figure 4.66 The newly added color...

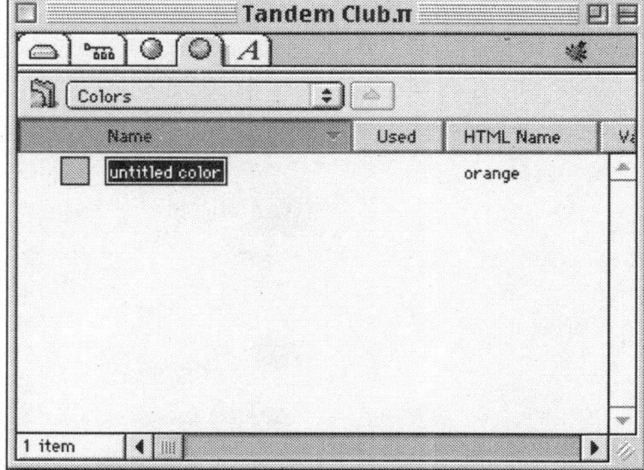

...appears in the Site window's Colors tab.

7. Drag the color from the preview pane to the object you want to color (**Figure 4.65**) or into the Site window's Colors tab (**Figure 4.66**), where the color will be saved for future use.
8. In the Site window, name your new color.
9. In the Color Palette, click on the Site Colors tab. Your new color is there, too.

✔ Tip

- You can also match colors with the Web Safe tab by Option-clicking (Mac) or Alt-clicking (Windows) the Palette and dragging over the Web page color you want to use.

Recycling Page Elements

Web sites and pages often contain common elements—headers, navigation elements, etc. You can replicate common elements more quickly if you save them under the Palette's Custom tab. You can use the Custom tab to store layout grids—and their contents—and other Web page elements that you want to be able to reuse. When you create a new page, just drag the saved element to the new page, and add the page's unique content.

You can also use dynamic components to repeat page content throughout your site. For more, see Chapter 13.

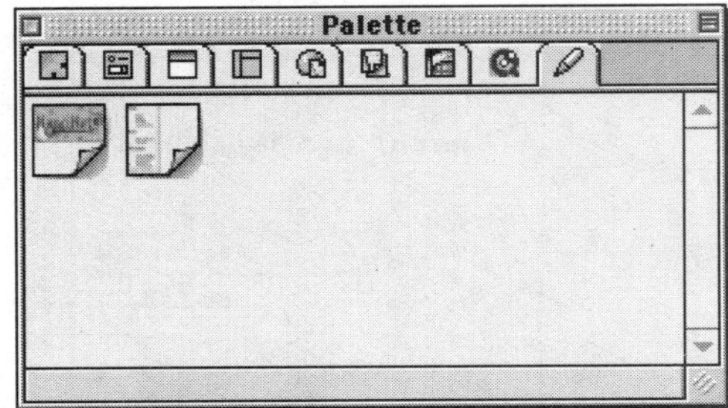

Figure 4.67 The Custom tab, with several items saved for later use.

To add an item to the Custom tab:

1. In the Palette, click on the Custom tab to make it visible (**Figure 4.67**).
2. In the document window, locate an item or items you want to save.
3. Drag the item(s) into the Palette window. An icon representing the item you've chosen appears under the Custom tab.

✔ Tips

- Saving templates in the Custom tab is another great reason to use several layout grids. Add all your standing elements to one grid, move it to the Favorites tab and reuse it when you like.
- When dragging a layout grid containing lots of items, you may have to click and hold the mouse button for a second or two before the grid begins to move.

To use items under the Custom tab:

1. Open a document where you want to use the saved material.
2. Click the Custom tab of the Palette.
3. Drag an icon for the desired item from the Palette into the document window.

5

Working with Images

Images bring Web pages to life. They may be pictures that accompany text, buttons, or navigation elements. They may even be animated.

Unlike text that exists as part of a Web page, images are external files that are connected to a Web page via hyperlinks. HTML and GoLive allow you to specify a number of image attributes that change the appearance of pictures or alter their relationship with surrounding elements.

In this chapter, I cover:

- Adding images.
- Modifying image attributes.
- Creating image maps.

✔ Tip

- You can use script-based actions to manipulate images, and create animated effects. I'll have more to say about actions and images in Chapter 11.

Adding Images

The two most common image types on the Web are GIF (Graphics Interchange Format) and JPEG (Joint Photographic Expert Group). GIF and JPEG account for almost all of the still images on the Web. All browsers support both formats. You can also use the newer PNG (Portable Network Graphics) format, which is supported by current versions of Internet Explorer and some versions of Netscape Communicator. Other file formats, such as QuickTime and PDF (Portable Document Format) are viewed with Web browser plug-ins. I discuss them more fully in Chapter 9.

GoLive can import image formats that are not HTML-friendly and converts graphics files when you drag them onto a GoLive document. You can also edit images in other applications by double-clicking their icons within the GoLive Site window.

To add an image to a Web page:

1. Open a new or existing GoLive document. Be sure that the Layout View is visible.
2. Drag the Image tool (**Figure 5.1**) from the Palette onto the document window. An image placeholder appears, and the Inspector window displays the Image Inspector. It looks like **Figure 5.2**.

   or

   Double-click the Image tool.
3. In the Inspector window, click the Browse button.
4. Locate a GIF or JPEG image file that you would like to add to the Web page, and select it. The image appears in the GoLive window at full size, as shown in **Figure 5.3**.

Figure 5.1 The Image tool.

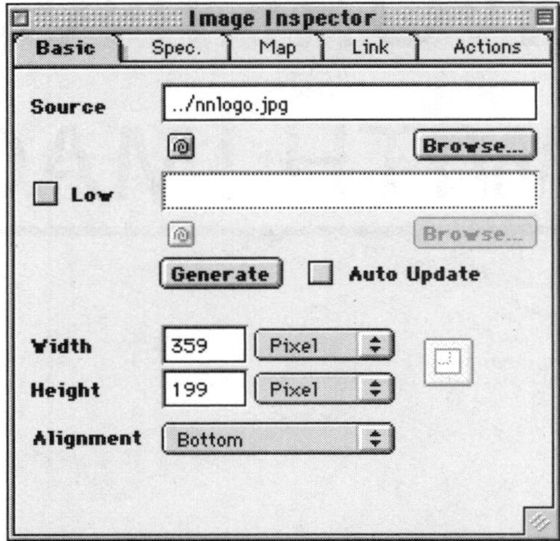

Figure 5.2 When you add an image to a page, the Image Inspector's Basic tab appears.

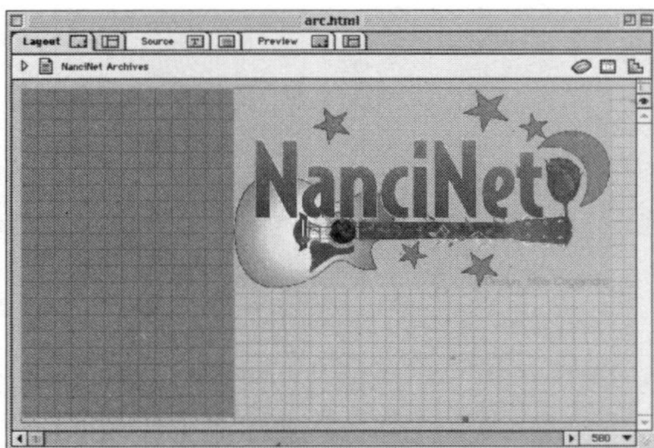

Figure 5.3 The JPEG image I imported is much larger than it needs to be.

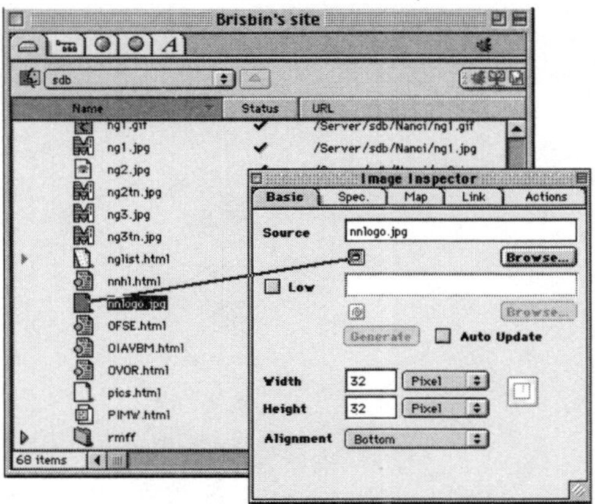

Figure 5.4 Point and shoot from the Image Inspector to the Site window to link an image to a page.

✔ Tip

- Even though I plan to place the logo on the table of contents grid, I dropped it on the main grid to preserve the dimensions of the smaller grid. When you add an image to a grid that is smaller than the image, the grid expands. In this case, I'll resize the image before I place it on the small grid, avoiding an unwanted expansion of the small grid.

To add an image with Point & Shoot:

1. If you have created a GoLive site, open it and then open the Web page where you want to add an image.
2. Double-click the Image tool on the Palette.
3. In the Image Inspector, click the Point & Shoot button and drag the resulting line to the Site window's Files tab.
4. Choose an image by dragging the line over its icon (**Figure 5.4**). When you release the mouse button, the image appears in the main window.

Importing images

You can use images other than GIF, JPEG, and PNG, provided you have enabled the PNG module in GoLive. You should also keep in mind that imported images are not high-quality graphics, but approximations of the originals. To ensure that your images are of the highest quality, edit them in a graphics application and save or convert them to the GIF or JPEG format.

GoLive converts PICT (a Macintosh format), BMP, or TIFF images to Web-friendly GIF and JPEG formats.

To enable PNG image import:

1. Choose Edit:Preferences.
2. In the Preferences window, click the Modules Icon.
3. Scroll to the PNG Module item on the right, and click the checkbox if it is not already selected.
4. Close the Preferences window and quit GoLive.
5. Restart GoLive to enable the PNG image module.

When you import an image, it is saved in a directory called Import Images within the GoLive application directory. GoLive creates a low-quality GIF version of the imported file. I'll have more to say about this in the section "Setting Image Import Preferences" later in this chapter.

Resizing an image

The Image Inspector provides three ways of measuring an image. You can set image width and height by typing numbers in the corresponding fields. Image sizes can be measured by:

- *Pixel*—the image's size in pixels.
- *Percent*—the image's size as a percentage of the size of the document window.
- *Image*—automatically sets the width or height measurement to that of the original image.

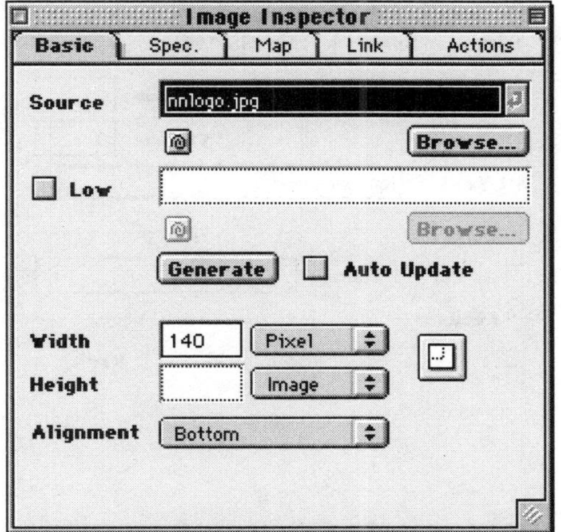

Figure 5.5 Use the Image Inspector's height and width controls to adjust the size of a graphic.

Pixel is the default measuring system. To use the percent or image option, make the appropriate choice from the Width or Height popup menu.

To resize an image:

1. Click on the image to be resized. The Image Inspector displays parameters including the current height and width of the image.
2. To resize the image proportionally, change the unit of measure in the Height popup menu to Image.
3. Type a number of pixels in the Width box with the Pixel option still selected, as shown in **Figure 5.5**. The image resizes proportionally.
4. To return the image to its original size, click the Size button next to the Height and Width fields in the Image Inspector.
5. If necessary, drag the image you have resized into its proper location on the layout grid.

✔ Tips

- The best way to ensure that your image is the proper size is to set its width and height in the graphics program you used to create it. Besides saving you a step in GoLive, inserting a correctly sized image ensures a faster download. Images resized in GoLive maintain their original file size.
- It's easy to move from GoLive to an image-editing program. If, say, you add an image to your Web page and realize that it needs a tweak, just double-click the image. If you have configured File Mapping preferences in the Preferences window, the image you click will open in the appropriate graphics program.

Adding alternative text

Some Web browsers, such as Lynx, do not support images. In addition, visually impaired users often have difficulty navigating Web pages with images included, especially if they use screen reading software to speak the contents of Web pages. To get around this problem, you can add alternative (alt) text to an image reference—just a word or two. Text-only Web browsers display these alternative tags where the image would otherwise be.

To add alternative text to an image:

1. Click on the image, making the Image Inspector visible.
2. Click the Special tab at the top of the window. The result looks like **Figure 5.6**.
3. Type a one or two word description of the image in the Alt. field.

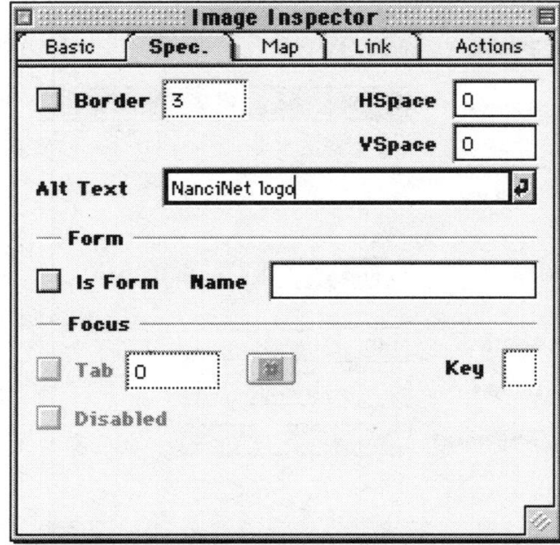

Figure 5.6 Type a description of the image in the Alt Text field.

To add a border to an image:

1. Click on an image.
2. Click the Spec. tab at the top of the Inspector window.
3. Click on the border checkbox. Type 3 in the border field. You can see the result in **Figure 5.7**. You can choose a border that matches your image. If you uncheck the Border checkbox, the border disappears.

Figure 5.7 Here is our image with a three-pixel border.

✔ Tip

- If you choose not to use a layout grid to construct your Web page, you can use the HSpace and VSpace fields of the Image Inspector to add space (in pixels) between an image and text. If you do use a layout grid, you can use gridlines to properly position images relative to text.

Aligning images

In HTML parlance, aligning an image means aligning it to adjacent text. It's not necessary to align an image to text unless you want the text and image to move together. In other words, if you want text to wrap around an image or to maintain a certain position relative to the image, you need to use the alignment tools. With a layout grid, you need to insert the image into the text frame. Image alignment also works (and is almost essential) if you're designing pages without a layout grid.

You can align images vertically or horizontally in one of several ways. It's simple enough to apply an alignment to an image, but it's trickier to know just which alignment to choose because many of the choices have similar properties.

To align an image to adjacent text:

1. Add a new text frame to your layout grid. If you aren't using a grid, begin with step 2.
2. Drag the Image tool from the Palette into the text frame.

   or

   If you're not using a layout grid, just place the image anywhere on the page.
1. With the image icon selected, locate an image with Point & Shoot or by browsing through the Inspector.
2. Resize the image if necessary.
3. Select the text frame by clicking on the border of the frame.
4. Enlarge the frame a bit by dragging one of the handles to the right.

continues on next page

5. Type some text into the frame; a sentence should do. If you're not using a text frame, type directly into the document window, right next to the image.
6. Click on the image to select it.
7. In the Inspector window, choose an alignment from the Alignment popup menu (shown in **Figure 5.8**). **Figure 5.9** shows the effect of aligning images to text, using the nine available options.

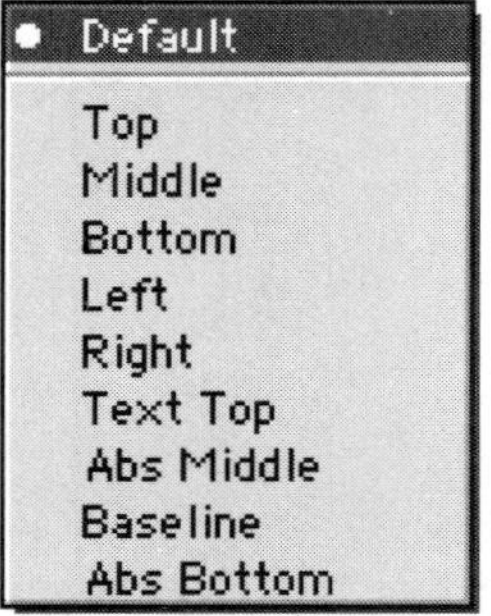

Figure 5.8 Choose from nine alignment options. You'll find the menu on the Basic tab of the Image Inspector.

Using an image as a link

Like hyperlinked text, images can be used to connect one Web page to another with just a click.

To link from an image:

1. Click on an image you want to link.
2. Choose the Link tab in the Inspector window. It looks like **Figure 5.10**.
3. Type a URL if you want the image to link to a remote Web site. Or, if you are linking to a location within your site, click Point & Shoot to locate the appropriate HTML file.

You can give your site's visitors something to look at while large images load by adding a low-resolution version of the image to your site. This image is displayed while the high-quality graphic is downloaded to the user's computer.

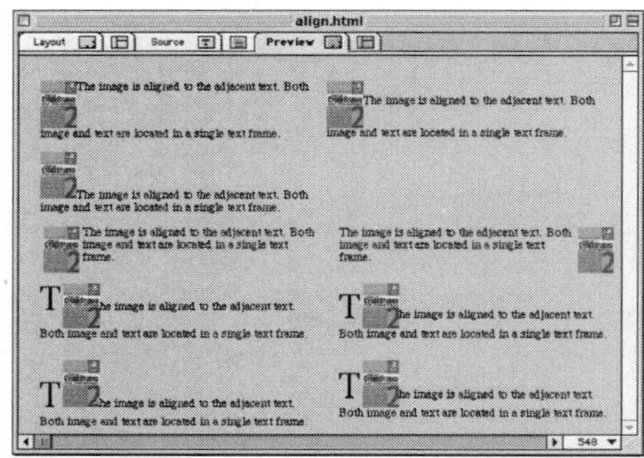

Figure 5.9 The nine alignment options appear in this screenshot. In each case, the image is inside a text frame. The first three images show an image aligned vertically to the text. The next two frames align images horizontally to text. The final four frames show images aligned to the large T character.

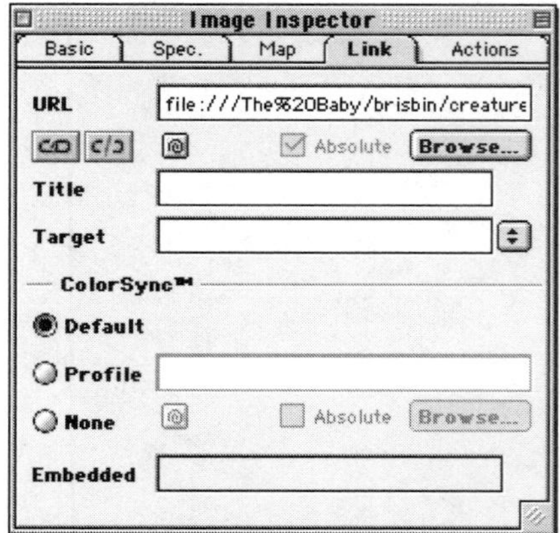

Figure 5.10 The Image Inspector's Link tab allows you to use an image as a hyperlink.

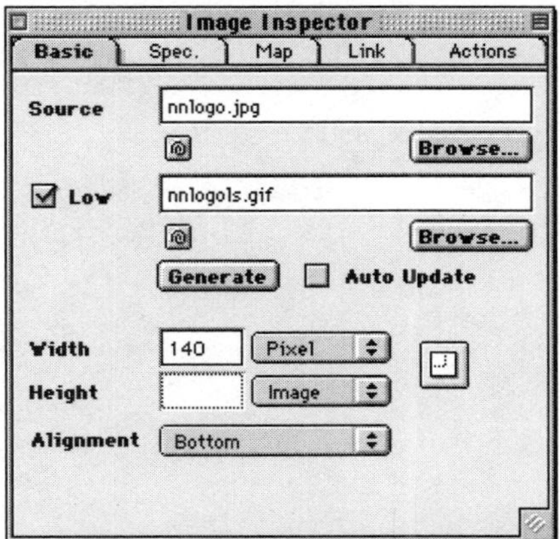

Figure 5.11 Choose a low-resolution version of your image by checking Low and locating an image.

To add a low-resolution image:

1. Under the Image Inspector's Basic tab, click the Generate button. GoLive creates a low-resolution version of the image you're working with. The file name appears in the Low field.
2. If you would rather create your own low-res image, use Adobe Photoshop, GraphicConverter, or an image manipulation program of your choice to save a low-resolution version of your original image. Be sure to save the new image as a GIF or JPEG file.
3. Give the low-resolution image a name similar to that of the original (e.g. imagel.gif) and store it in the same folder as the original.
4. In GoLive, click on a high-quality image that you have already placed.
5. Under the Basic tab of the Image Inspector window, click the Low checkbox.
6. Click the Browse button next to the checkbox. (See **Figure 5.11**.)
7. Find the low-resolution image you created earlier and click Open.

Setting Image Import Preferences

The Preference windowís image options refer to the way GoLive handles imported images.

To configure image import:

1. In the Preferences window, click the triangle (Mac) or plus sign (Windows) next to the General Preferences label.
2. Click the Image item.
3. Click Browse to choose an image import folder, or leave the default folder selected.
4. Click the Ask User button to have GoLive ssk where to store imported images, and what file format imported files should use. Otherwise, choose a file format from the popup menu.
5. Under the low source label, choose options for creating a low-resolution version of the imported image.
6. With these options configured, you can drag an image PICT, TIFF, PNG or BMP) from its native application into a GoLive document. If you have chosen the Ask User option, GoLive will present a dialog box allowing you to locate an imported version of the file, choose a file format, and rename the file, if you want to.

✔ Tip

- When you use the Import Images feature, GoLive makes sure that all images have a three-character extension (.gif, .tif, and so on). When you add images to your pages, be sure that they include extensions in this format. Be sure that JPEG images use the .jpg suffix.

Clickable Image Maps

We've seen that you can use an image not only as decoration for your site, but also as a link to another location on the Web. Actually, you can include several links within a single image. That arrangement is called a *clickable image map,* and the locations your site's visitors will click on are called hot spots. Some site designers use image maps to add *hot spots* to logos or other large Web graphics. A picture of a car, for example, might include hot spots on the tires, doors, and hood, indicating that the user can get more information about these parts of the car by clicking on the appropriate hot spot.

You can invoke image maps in two ways. The first way is from the Web server, using a CGI (Common Gateway Interface) application to support the image map. The second, simpler way is to create *client-side* image maps, which are configured entirely within your Web pages. When you use a client-side image map, neither you as the page designer nor a user clicking on an image map needs to have any interaction with the Web server beyond the usual downloading HTML files and images. Client-side maps, as you can imagine, are easier to work with. GoLive allows you to create client-side maps.

There are two steps to creating a client-side image map: setting up the map and linking hot spots.

To set up a clickable image map:

1. Choose an image with which you will create an image map. The image you choose should be large enough to accommodate several hot spots and should include distinct sections that lend themselves to the image map treatment.

continues on next page

2. Add the image to a GoLive document.
3. Using the tools I've described in this chapter, make any necessary changes to the image.
4. Click on the image.
5. In the Inspector window, choose the Map tab.
6. Click the Map checkbox to activate the Map tools. The result looks like **Figure 5.12**.
7. Type a name for the image map in the Name field.

   The Image Map toolbar contains the tools you need to create and modify image map hot spots. Refer to **Figure 5.13** for an illustration of all of the available tools.
8. Choose one of the three region tools (rectangle, circle, or polygon) that best matches the hot spot shape you want to create.

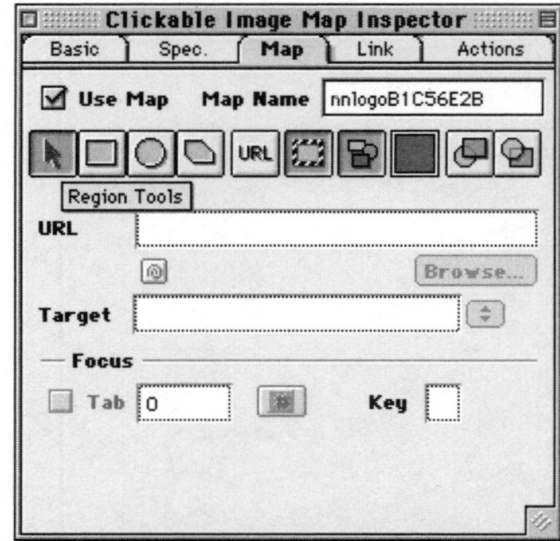

Figure 5.12 Open the Map tab and click Map to activate the image map tools.

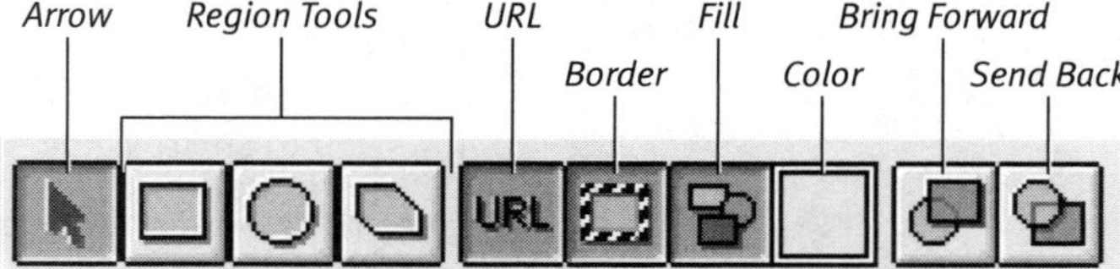

Figure 5.13 The Map Toolbar includes the tools illustrated here.

Figure 5.14 Create a circular image map by clicking on the circle tool and drawing on your image. You can adjust the hot spot's size with the handles on the sides and corners.

Figure 5.15 Add a border to your hot spot with the border tool.

Figure 5.16 Change the hot spot's color with the Color tool.

Figure 5.17 Display a URL in the hot spot with the URL tool.

9. Draw the hot spot on your image. Handles appear at the sides and corners (**Figure 5.14**), so that you can adjust the size of the hot spot if you need to.
10. With the hot spot selected, type a URL for it in the Inspector window's URL field or click the Browse button and choose a local file to link to.
11. Repeat steps 8-10 for each hot spot you want to create.

To enhance the display of hot spots:

1. With a hot spot selected, click on the Border icon of the Image Inspector Map tab. A border appears around the hot spot, as shown in **Figure 5.15**.
2. Click on the Map tab's Color icon to add color to the hot spot (**Figure 5.16**). This option is a convenience for the Web author. Hot spot colors do not appear within a user's browser.
3. To use a different color, click the Select Color icon. The Color Palette appears, allowing you to choose a new color and drag it onto the Color icon.
4. To display a URL on the hot spot, click the URL icon (**Figure 5.17**).
5. To remove a border, color, or URL, click the appropriate Map tab icon to toggle it off. You can use any combination of border, color, and URL with your image map.

You can use the Arrow icon to resize or move hot spots and the Bring Forward or Send to Back items to work with hot spots that overlap one another.

6 Working with Links

Hyperlinks are as essential to the World Wide Web as PostScript is to modern desktop publishing or phone numbers are to telecommunication. Links between Web pages make it possible to jump instantly (surf) from place to place on the Internet.

Using links effectively is also an integral part of building a useful Web site. You use links to move visitors from page to page and to provide points of reference (in the form of navigation bars and tables of contents) for your site.

GoLive provides several ways to create links, and it supports the various kinds of links that are standard parts of HTML. In this chapter, I describe how to create text links. Other chapters focus on linking to images and multimedia files. The process of creating these links is quite similar, however.

In this chapter, I cover:

- How links work.
- Creating links.
- Editing links.
- Named anchors.
- Link warnings.

How Links Work

An HTML link is a pointer from a Web page to another item (Web page, FTP server, newsgroup, or e-mail address, for example) on the Internet. Links can be words or images. Text links are usually designated visually on the page by underlining and by color, usually blue. Links have two parts: a URL (Universal Resource Locator) and a label or image that is visible in a browser. When a visitor clicks on a link's label, the Web browser locates the desired item. The browser then displays, downloads, or connects to it.

Links can point to other pages within your site, to a remote Web site, or to non-Web resources, such as FTP servers, newsgroups, and e-mail addresses.

Anatomy of a URL

URLs contain all the information needed to turn a link into a means of transportation from one page to another. All URLs have the same structure:

```
Protocol://server.domain/page.html
```

See **Table 6.1**.

Absolute and relative links

Links to remote sites always appear in the URL format described above. These are *absolute* links. URLs that point to files or other objects within the same Web site as the referring page may be absolute (with fully spelled out URLs), or they may be relative—using only the portion of the URL that's needed.

For example, a relative URL from your home page to a product catalog page within your site might have the URL `/catalog.html`, or even `/products/catalog.html`, if the file resides within a different directory of your site. The full URL is not needed because when relative URLs are used, Web servers are smart

Table 6.1

URL Anatomy

Element	Description
Protocol	The type of link. Links to Web pages use the http protocol,http:, while FTP links begin with ftp:. E-mail addresses use mailto:.
Server	Most Web URLs include "www" here, though others don't use it. Non-Web URLs may include a server names, too, but they're not required.
Domain	The name of the site (often a version of the company's or organization's name) followed by the domain type, such as .com or .edu.
Page	The name of the individual page to which the URL points. In most cases, entering a URL without a specified page takes you to the site's home page. If the link leads to a subsidiary page within a site, the page's name will appear, preceded by a slash (/) and followed by an extension (.htm or .html). Links to pages stored within directories include the directory name (/directory/page.html).

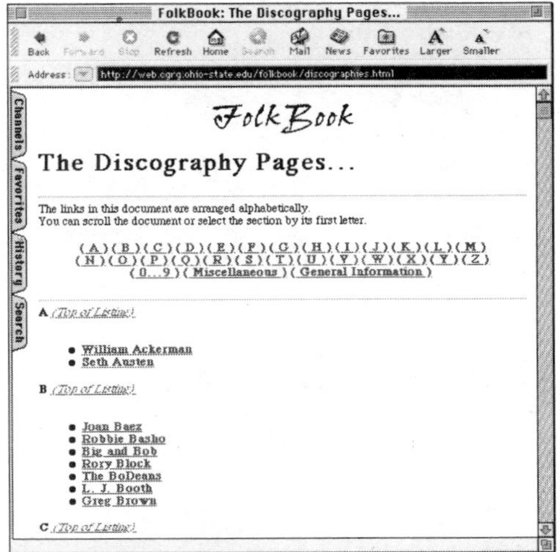

Figure 6.1 The alphabet at the top of the Folk Book Artists' Page consists of anchors that connect to lettered links further down the page.

enough to look first within their own site for requested pages.

Relative URLs can point to any object within the same site, whether it's in the same directory or in a directory that is above or below the source file. You can also create links that point to locations on the same page as the link; these links are called *anchors* and are used to make it easier to navigate through long documents (see **Figure 6.1**).

Using relative links is often simpler than typing a long, absolute URL, and it also makes things go a lot more smoothly when you need to add or change links within your site, or when you move your site from one server to another, either for testing or production purposes. By default, the links you create in GoLive will all be relative, unless you specifically choose to use absolute links. To do so, you'll need to set the "Make new links absolute" option in URL Handling Preferences in GoLive's Preferences window.

Creating Links

You can add links to your GoLive pages by using the toolbar and Inspector to type and configure them, or by using GoLive tools to create links to items stored within a GoLive site. Either way, you can link to files in your site, or to remote sites, e-mail addresses, and FTP servers.

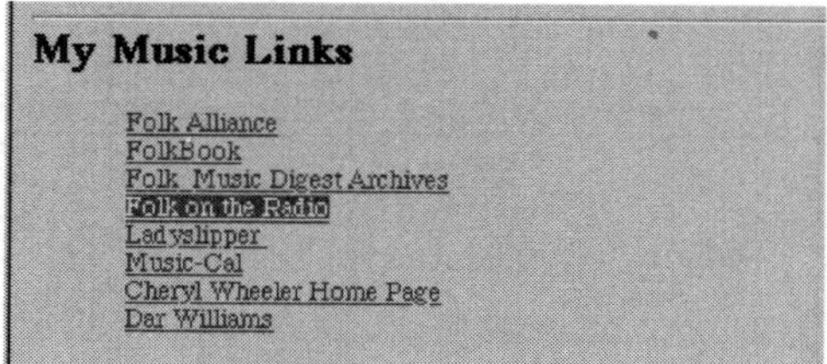

Figure 6.2 Text links should be short, but descriptive.

Figure 6.3 Use the toolbar's Link icon to create a link.

To link text to a remote URL:

1. In the Layout view, select some text (a single word or short phrase) or an object that you would like to link to a remote resource (**Figure 6.2**).
2. Click on the Link icon on the toolbar (**Figure 6.3**). The Text Inspector window becomes visible (**Figure 6.4**) and displays the link tab. Or Type Command-L (Mac) or Control-L (Windows).
3. Type a complete URL in the URL field of the Inspector window. Be sure that the URL includes the correct protocol i.e. http:// or ftp://

   or

   If you are working with a GoLive site, Point & Shoot to the item in the Site window that you wish to link to.
4. Optionally, you can type the title of the item you are linking to in the Title field.

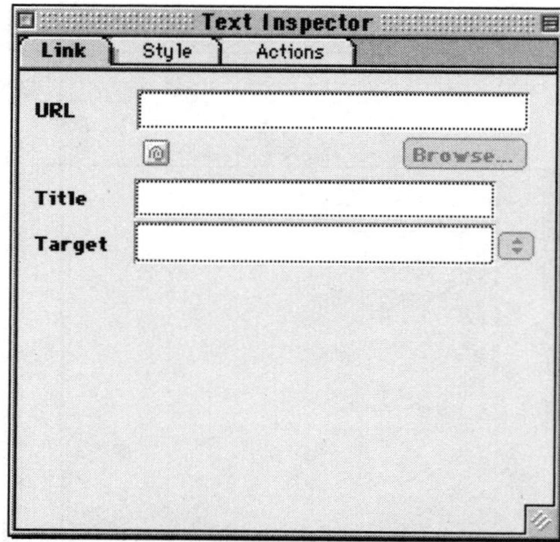

Figure 6.4 Enter your link's URL in the Text Inspector.

✔ Tip

- With text selected, you can move between the text and the Inspector with keyboard shortcuts: select the text, then type Command-. (period) (Mac) or Control-. (Windows). The URL field in the Inspector becomes active. Type Command-; (Semicolon) (Mac) or Control-; (Windows) to select the text again.

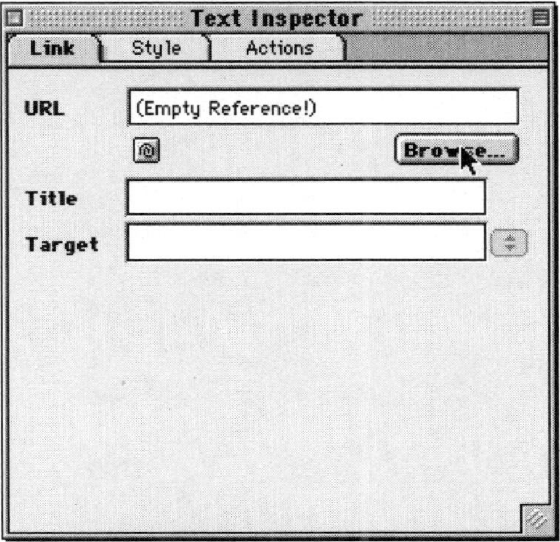

Figure 6.5 Click the Browse button to navigate to files within your Web site.

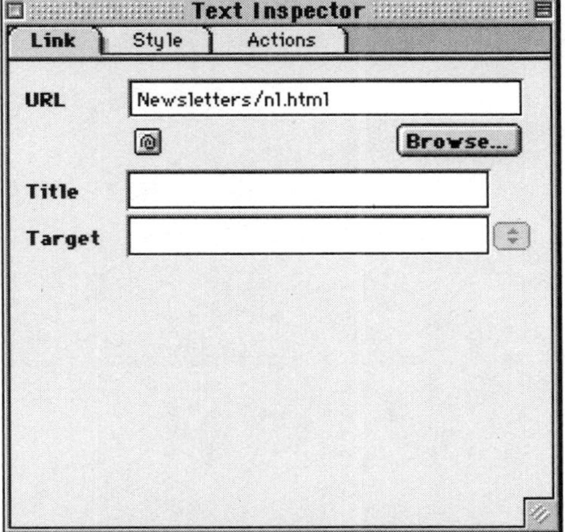

Figure 6.6 When you've chosen a URL to link to, the relative URL appears in the Inspector's URL field.

To link to a local file with the toolbar:

1. In the document window, select some text that you would like to link to another file in your Web site.
2. Choose the Link icon from the toolbar. An underline appears under the selected text, and the dimmed fields of the Text Inspector's Link tab light up.
3. In the Inspector window, click the Browse button (**Figure 6.5**).
4. In the dialog box that appears, locate the file you want to link to, and press Open. The relative URL appears in the URL field of the Inspector window (**Figure 6.6**), and the linked text is underlined in the document window.

✔ Tips

- When you link to a file stored on your hard disk, the URL will appear in the Inspector in the format: `file://drive/folder/page.html`. Don't be concerned. The actual URL that appears in the GoLive pages you will upload to a Web server do not contain this local path information, but the proper relative URL. The relative URL will work as long as you do not change the relationship between a document and an item you've linked it to.
- You can use this method to link to files that are part of a local Web site, whether you use GoLive to manage the site or not, as long as the directories and file locations are exactly as they will appear when you upload your site to a Web server.

To link to a site file with Point & Shoot:

1. Open a GoLive site.
2. Open a document by double-clicking its icon in the Site window.
3. If the file you want to link to is not already part of your site, add it by dragging it into the Site window before proceeding to step 4.
4. In the Site window, click on the Files tab to display pages within your site.
5. In the document window, select some text or an object that you would like to link.
6. Command-click (Mac) or Control-click (Windows) the text.
7. While holding down the mouse button, drag into the Site window, creating a line as you drag. If the Site window is covered by other windows, it will be brought to the front as you drag over it.
8. Stop dragging when your cursor is over the file you want to link to, and let go of the mouse button to finish the link. You can verify that the link is complete in the Link Inspector.

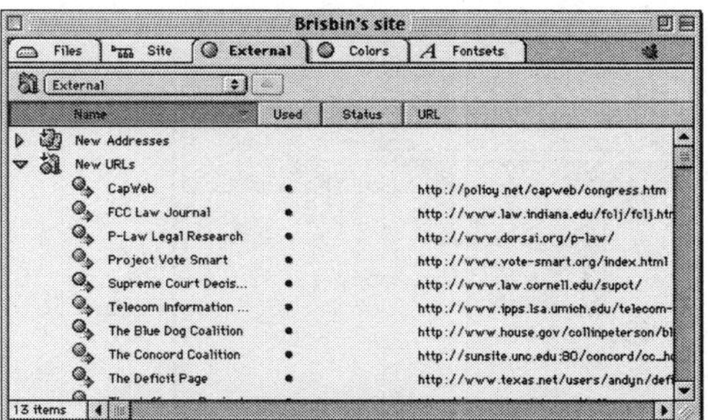

Figure 6.7 Bookmarks for remote Web sites, FTP servers, and other resources are stored under the External tab of the Site window.

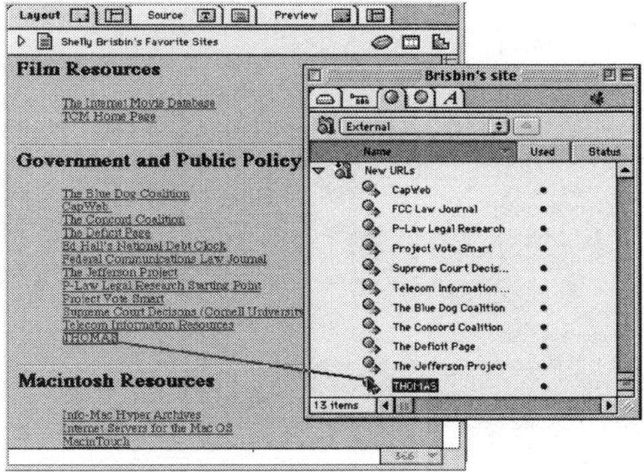

Figure 6.8 Point and shoot from your link to an external resource in the Site window.

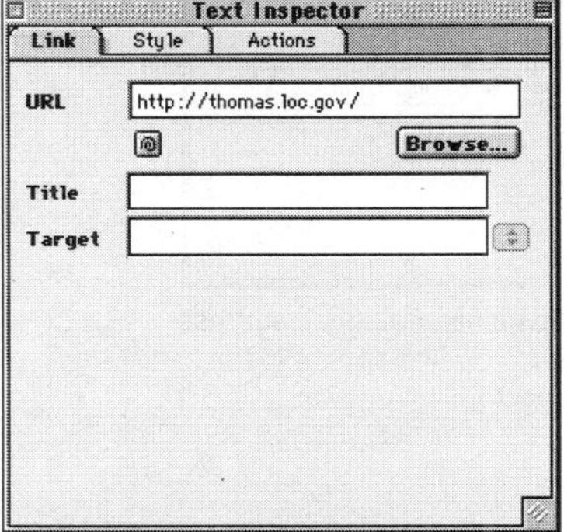

Figure 6.9 When your cursor appears within the new link you've created, the URL appears in the Inspector.

Linking to site resources

GoLive sites can manage not only HTML files and images, but also bookmarks that contain URLs for remote resources. You can store the remote resources your site points to within the site file and point and shoot your way to them whenever you need to add a link.

To link to a stored URL:

1. Open a GoLive site file.
2. Open a document by double-clicking it in the Files tab of the Site window.
3. In the Site window, click on the External tab to display external resources that you have stored there (**Figure 6.7**).
4. If there is a URLs folder under the External tab, open it by clicking the triangle (Mac) or plus sign (Windows) on the left.
5. In the document window, select the text or object that you want to link.
6. Command-click (Mac) or Control-click (Windows) the selection and drag the resulting line to the Site window.
7. Stop dragging when your cursor is over the URL you want to link, and let go of the mouse button (**Figure 6.8**).
8. Verify that the link is complete in the Link tab of the Text Inspector (**Figure 6.9**).

Linking to an e-mail address

You can create a link between a Web page and an e-mail address with Point & Shoot, if the address is stored within your site. You can also type e-mail links into the Inspector, using the format, `mailto:user@domain`. When an e-mail link is clicked, the user's browser opens an e-mail application, assuming that the user's system is configured to do so.

To link an e-mail address with Point & Shoot:

1. Follow steps 1–3 in the "To link to a stored URL" section.
2. If there is an Addresses folder under the External tab, open it (see **Figure 6.10**).
3. In the document window, select the text or object you want to link.
4. Command-click (Mac) or Control-click (Windows) the selection and drag the resulting line to the Site window.

   or

   Drag and drop an e-mail address from the Site window to the link text.
5. Stop dragging when your cursor is over the address you want to link to and let go of the mouse button (**Figure 6.11**).
6. Verify that the link is complete in the Link Inspector (**Figure 6.12**).

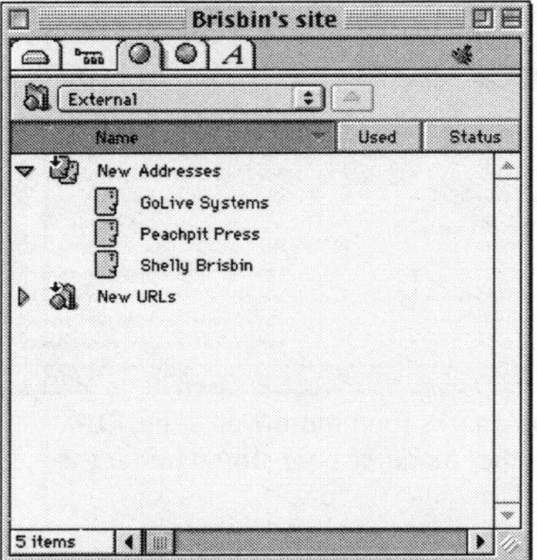

Figure 6.10 E-mail addressees are stored under the External tab of the Site window.

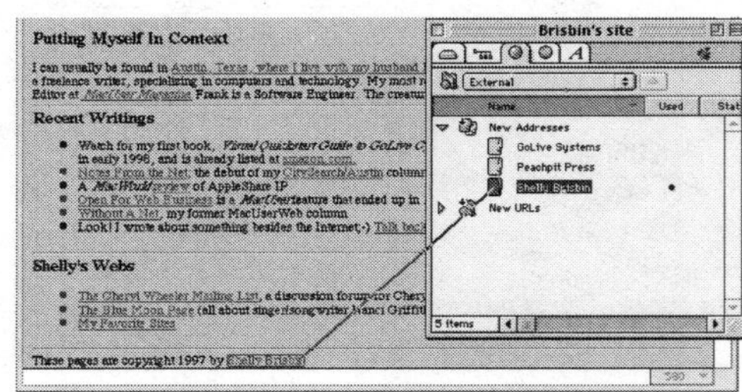

Figure 6.11 Point & Shoot from an e-mail address on your Web page to a stored address in the Site window.

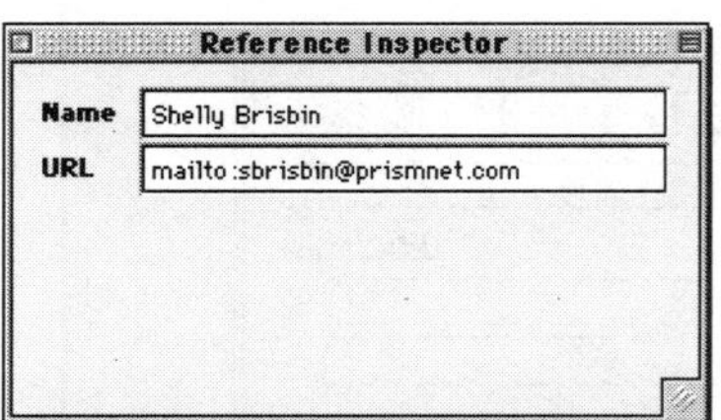

Figure 6.12 The name and e-mail address included in your new link appear in the Reference Inspector.

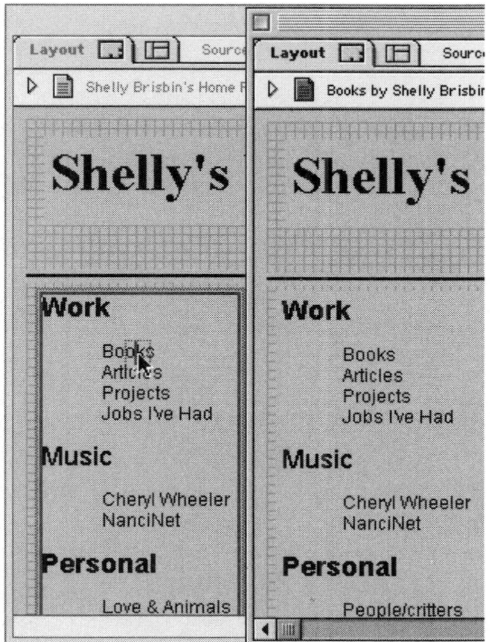

Figure 6.13 Select some text in one document, and link to a second open document by dragging its Page icon over the text you are linking.

Linking open documents

You can use the GoLive Page icon to create links between open documents, whether or not they are part of a GoLive site.

To create a link with the Page icon:

1. With a document open, select some text or an object that you would like to link.
2. Open another document.
3. Position the new document onscreen so that you can see the portion of the first document that contains the selected text or object.
4. Drag the Page icon at the top of the new document's window onto the selected text or object in your destination document (**Figure 6.13**). The link is complete.

✔ Tip

- You can use the Page icon method whether you're working within a site or just constructing individual pages. If you're working with a site, using Point & Shoot is an easier way to link.

Editing Links

Once you've established links, it may be necessary to change them. A remote URL may change; you might rename a directory, or update an e-mail address. In any case, you can edit any link in the Inspector, or with Point & Shoot.

To edit a link with the Inspector:

1. Open the file containing the link you want to change.
2. Click on the link. The appropriate Inspector window is now visible, with the link's URL and other information displayed.
3. Type the new absolute (full) URL, or relative URL in the URL field.

   or

   If the link is to a new or renamed file within your site, click Browse. Locate the new file you want to link to, and click Open. The new link is complete.

To edit a link within a site:

If you rename or move a page within your site, you will need to relink items that point to it.

1. Open your GoLive site, if it isn't already open.
2. Open the file containing the link you want to change.
3. If you are linking to an external URL or an e-mail address, click on the External tab in the Site window. Otherwise, proceed to step 4.
4. In the document window, Command-click (Mac) or Control-click (Windows) on the link.
5. Drag the resulting line to the Site window.
6. Let go of the mouse button when the line connects with the new link point. The new link is complete.

✔ Tip

- You can use GoLive's site management tools to update all occurrences of a link within your site at the same time. The Site window's error icons also let you know which pages contain broken links.

To delete a link:

1. In the document window, click on a link, so that the insertion point is within the text of the link, or the linked object is selected.
2. From the toolbar, choose the Unlink icon. The link is deleted.

Named Anchors

Named Anchors are a special kind of link. Rather than linking one page to another, named anchors are used to navigate within a single page—linking a list of headings at the top of a page to subsequent sections of the document, for example—or to link to a location in the middle of a different page. Clicking on a named anchor link scrolls the browser to the appropriate point on the page or opens another page in the middle, displaying the specified anchor point.

You can begin by creating links, then making named anchors to go with them, or you can set up the anchors first. The first method works best if you're creating a single link that connects to a single anchor. Creating the anchor or anchors first works best if you plan to create several links that point to a single anchor point, or if you are designing a navigation scheme or table of contents that goes with an existing document.

To create a named anchor on the current page:

1. With a document open to the Layout view, select the text or object you want to link from.
2. Command-click (Mac) or Control-click (Windows) the text or object and drag the resulting line through the document until you reach the point where you would like the anchor to appear (**Figure 6.14**).
3. Release the mouse button. An anchor icon appears (**Figure 6.15**). The Link Inspector is now visible and displays a unique anchor name.

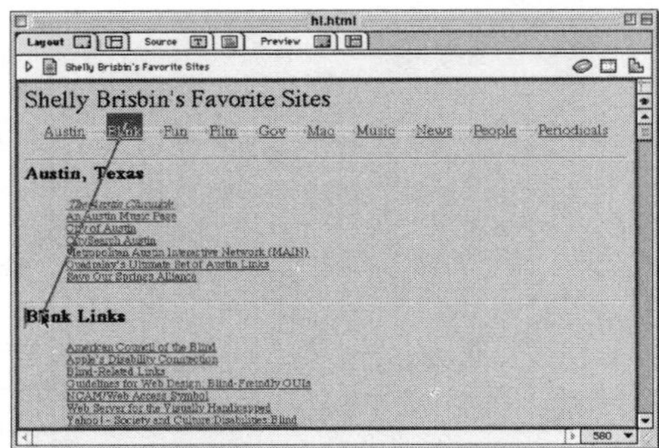

Figure 6.14 Command-click on the item you want to link, and drag to the location where you want the anchor to appear.

⚓ **Blink Links**

Figure 6.15 The anchor icon appears when your anchor is complete.

✔ Tips

- Not all browsers place anchors properly. For best results in GoLive, position the anchor point in a text frame or within a table, rather than on a bare layout grid.
- Anchors work best when they appear at the left margin of a window.
- As always, it's a good idea to check your work by previewing it. For best results, open your document in a Web browser rather than GoLive's Preview mode, then click the link you've created to see whether it properly moves to the anchor point.

To create anchors before linking them:

1. With a document open, drag the Anchor (**Figure 6.16**) tool from the Palette to the document window. An anchor icon appears where you stop dragging, and the Anchor Inspector appears (**Figure 6.17**).
2. In the Anchor Inspector window, type a unique, one-word name for the anchor.
3. Create more anchors within your document.
4. Locate some text or an object (in the current document or in any other document) that you would like to link to one of the anchors you just created.
5. Select the text or object and Command-click (Mac) or Control-click (Windows) the selection.
6. Drag the resulting line to the anchor you created earlier and release the mouse button (**Figure 6.18**). The link is now complete.
7. Repeat steps 3 and 4 to add links to the anchor you've created.

When a Web page visitor clicks on the new link, the anchor point comes into view. If the anchor appears in a different document, that document opens and displays the anchor location.

✔ Tip

- You can create as many links to a single anchor as you like, from any number of documents. Just Point & Shoot from each link to the anchor.

Figure 6.16 The Anchor tool is available from the Palette's basic tab.

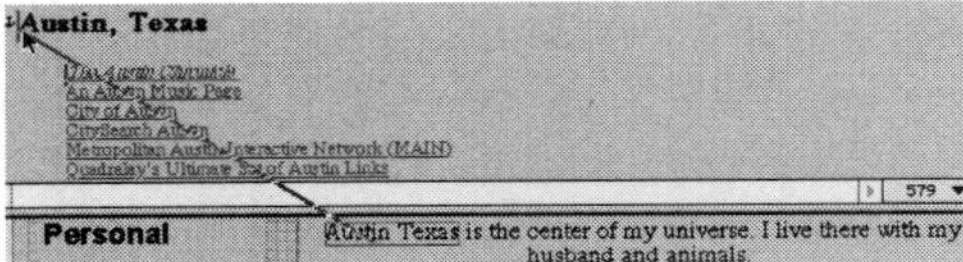

Figure 6.17 Point and shoot from a new link to an anchor icon, to create a named anchor.

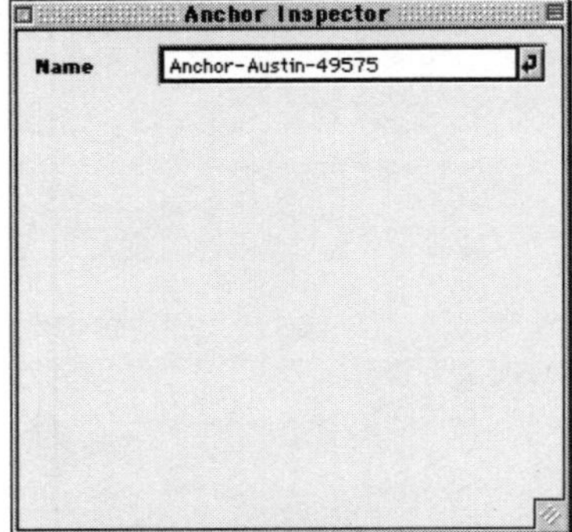

Figure 6.18 The Anchor Inspector appears when you add an anchor by dragging the Anchor tool to the document window.

To move an anchor:

In the document window, click on the anchor's icon and drag it to its new location on the page. Any links you've created will now point to the new location.

To delete an anchor:

1. Click on an anchor icon to select it.
2. Press the Delete key to remove the anchor.
   Now, you need to remove links to the anchor you've just deleted.
3. Locate a link you have created and click on it, so that the insertion point is within the text or the object is selected.
4. Click the Unlink icon in the toolbar. The link is removed.

✔ Tip

- Removing a link does not delete the text or object you previously linked. It simply deletes the pointer between that item and those items.

Link Warnings

GoLive can alert you to broken links using a variety of link warnings. You can turn link warnings on and off to determine the status of your links. By default, problem links are highlighted in red. You can change the color in the Preference window's General:Display Preferences, if you like.

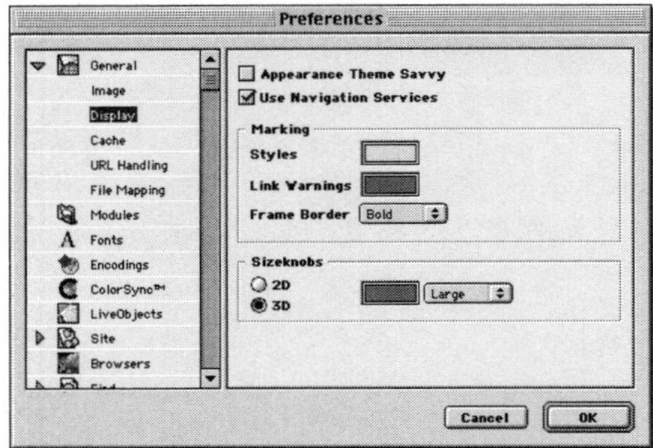

Figure 6.19 Change the color of Link Warnings under Display, within the General preferences window.

To change the color of link warnings:

1. Choose Preferences from the Edit menu.
2. Click the triangle (Mac)or plus sign (Windows) next to the General label in the left side of the Preferences window to view more options.
3. Click the Display label. The resulting screen (**Figure 6.19**) includes a color box for changing the appearance of link warnings.
4. Click on the color box. A color picker appears (**Figure 6.20**).
5. Choose a color from one of the panels. If you need help with the color picker, see your system's Help feature.
6. Click OK. The new color appears in the Link Warnings color box.
7. Click OK again, to close the Preferences dialog box.

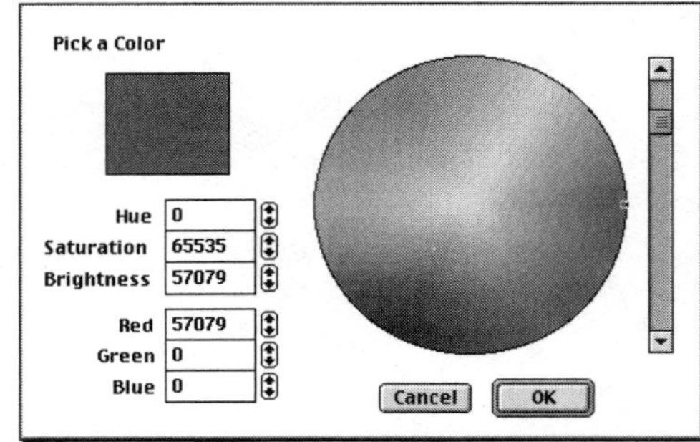

Figure 6.20 Pick a link warning color from the Mac OS Color Picker.

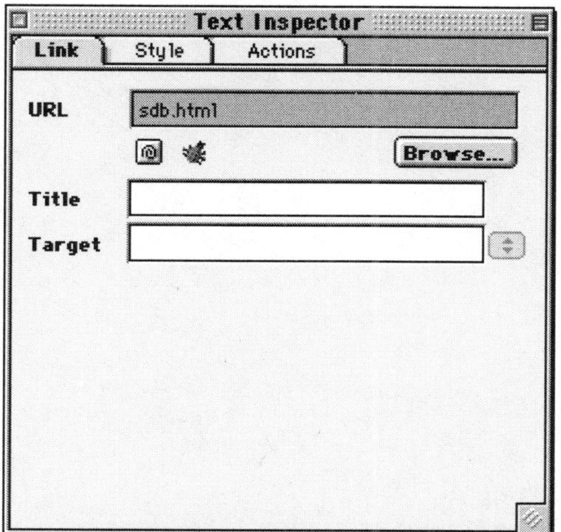

Figure 6.21 The Text Inspector displays the link and the bug icon that indicates a problem with the link.

To locate errors with link warnings:

1. Choose Show Link Warnings from the Edit menu. If the Edit menu command says "Hide Link Warnings" instead, link warnings are already available. Proceed to the next step.
2. Scroll through your document to locate links that are highlighted (in the color you chose when you set Link Warnings preferences).
3. When you locate a broken link click on it to place your cursor within the link. The Text Inspector appears, displaying the broken link and the bug symbol that alerts you to the problem (**Figure 6.21**).
4. Repair the link.

✔ Tip

- GoLive will display link warnings for images and multimedia files, too. The procedure for finding and fixing broken links is exactly the same. When an image or media file link is broken, you'll see a red (or whatever color you want to use for link warnings) border around the image box. Of course, you'll also notice that the image itself is missing, since its link is no longer in place. To locate the source of the break, you may need to examine all of tabs of the appropriate Inspector.

7

Working with Forms

Forms add interactivity. Guest books, search engines, and product ordering systems are just a few of the applications that use forms.

Basically, a form is a Web page component that allows a user to send information to the owner of the page. A form can contain one or more elements—text fields, checkboxes, radio buttons, or popup menus—that allow user input. Web servers accept the input and return information or confirmation to the Web site visitor.

In this chapter, I cover:

- How forms work.
- Creating and configuring forms.
- Basic and special form elements.
- HTML 4.0 form elements.
- HTML 4.0 form features.

✔ Tip

- In order to use forms with your Web site, your Web server (run by your company or an ISP) must have a CGI (Common Gateway Interface) application installed that supports the forms you create. Before you design any forms, be sure that you will be able to actually *use* them with your Web server. If not, you can skip this chapter.

How Forms Work

To a Web site visitor and, perhaps, to a Web page designer, forms look and behave just like any other Web page element. Most forms are integrated with text and graphics, and their appearance is usually designed to complement the overall look of the page.

What differentiates forms is how they work behind the scenes. When a user enters text in a form, clicks a checkbox, and hits the Submit button, the form's work is done. From that point on, the Web server takes over.

As I pointed out, a Web server must be running a script or CGI application designed to process the information Web site visitors submit. The CGI application transfers data entered into a Web page form into a database on the Web server. If, for example, the site visitor is using a form to reach a search engine, the database sends the search result to the server, which sends it back to the user via the CGI application. The result is an HTML page containing search engine hits.

When you create a form page, you have two tasks: designing the form so that it looks the way you want it to, and creating the hooks that allow your form to work with a Web server and CGI application.

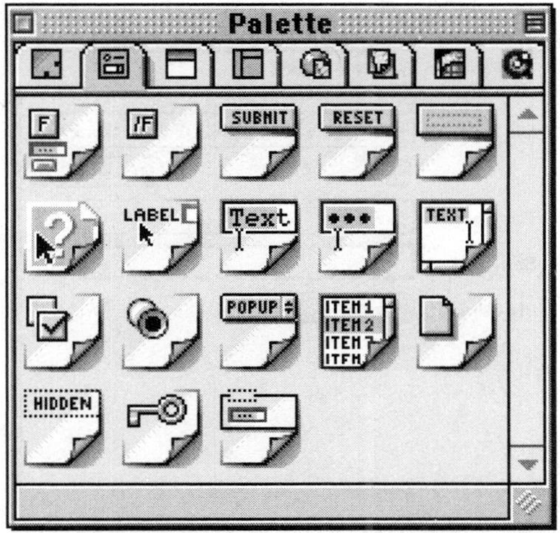

Figure 7.1 The Palette's Forms tab.

Figure 7.2 The Form tool.

Figure 7.3 The Form tab.

Creating Forms

Like other HTML elements, GoLive supports forms through a set of Palette tools. They are stored under the Palette's Forms tab (**Figure 7.1**).

Each tool is linked to a context-sensitive Inspector, where you configure the form to work with your Web page and the script or CGI that processes your form's input, which comes from users.

To create a functional form, you need to precede the elements that comprise it with a *form tag* and configure it, as well as the individual fields and buttons that make up the form.

To create a form element:

1. Plan your form. Based on its size and location within the Web page you're working on, create or add to a table to contain the elements of your form. Use the table cells to align fields and labels to one another.
2. Click the Palette's Form tab to display the form-creation tools.
3. Drag the Form tool (see **Figure 7.2**) onto the layout grid. GoLive creates a small square containing an F, as shown in **Figure 7.3**.

Because the Form tag is the first of several elements you'll be adding to your form, position it on the page so that there is plenty of room to the right and below the Form icon. The tag need not be immediately adjacent to the form fields.

The Inspector window allows you to configure your new form. In order for the form to work, you must connect it to a CGI program on your Web server and provide the server with other information about how to work with the data that will be transferred from the form.

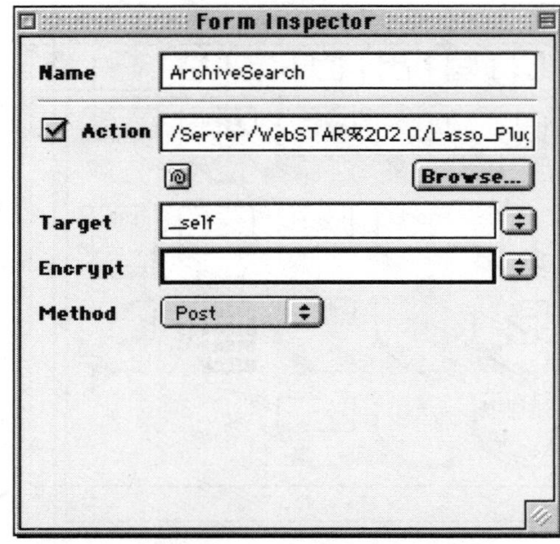

Figure 7.4 Use the Form Inspector to connect a form to a CGI application on your Web server.

To configure the form:

1. Click the Form item, to make the Form Inspector (**Figure 7.4**) visible.
2. Type a unique name for the form into the name field.
3. In the Action field, type the directory or URL of the CGI application that will process data entered into the form.
4. To specify the target window for your form's output, choose a target. By default, the form's results will appear in the current browser window.
5. Choose an encryption method from the popup menu if you are creating forms for a secure server. If you are not the Webmaster for your site, check with the person who manages the server before applying an encryption method.
6. The Method field specifies the way the form's output will be returned to the user. From the Method popup menu, choose Post or Get. Post is usually the better choice.

✔ Tips

- The quickest way to specify scripts for your forms is to set each script you use as an external item within your site. With the pointer to your CGI stored in the Site window, you can Point & Shoot from the Form tag Inspector to the External tab to reach the CGI you need. For more information about creating references to external URLs in a GoLive site, see Chapter 15.
- The Post method returns form responses (such as search results) separately from the rest of the Web page, pasting the data into the page that's generated for the user. Get, on the other hand, appends the form response to the URL of the results page, making the URL long and cumbersome.

You've just linked your form to the Web server, making it possible for the form to send and receive information. You've also set up a container for all the elements that will become part of your form. In order for your form to be useful, you now need to add fields, buttons, and other elements with which your Web page visitors can interact.

Basic Form Elements

Think of the form tag you just created as a container; it encloses the rest of the items that make up your Web page form and includes instructions (the Method and Action elements) that indicate how the form's input and output should be handled.

Every element of the form must fall between the <FORM> and </FORM> HTML tags. You'll see these tags only if you examine your page with GoLive's Outline View or Source View. When you add form elements in the Layout View, be sure that they appear between the Form tags.

Text and password fields

Text fields allow users to enter a line of text into a form. Text fields can contain names, addresses, search engine queries, or just about anything else that can be expressed in a single line of text. If you need to accommodate multiple lines of text, use the Text Area field, described later in this chapter. The Password Field element is identical to the Text Field except that it supports password entry, which conceals text as it is entered.

To create a Text or Password Field:

1. With a Form tag in place and configured as discussed earlier in this chapter, drag the Text Field tool (**Figure 7.5a**) from the Palette to the document window, or double-click the tool and move the field into place.
2. The field is displayed in the document window, and the Inspector window changes so that you can configure the Text field element. (**Figure 7.5b**).
3. Type a name in the Name field.

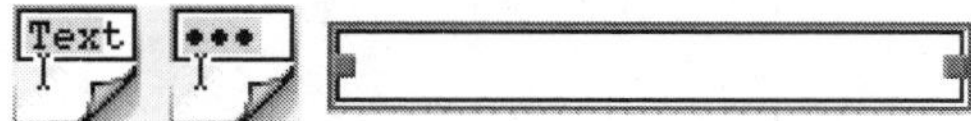

Figure 7.5a The Text Field and Password Field tools, and a text field.

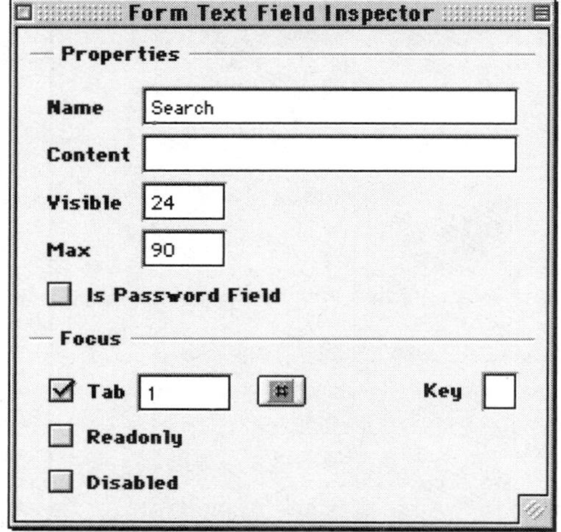

Figure 7.5b The Text Field Inspector.

4. If you want the field to contain default text (such as "Type Your Search Request Here"), enter it in the Content field. If not, leave the Content field blank.

5. In the Visible field, enter the number of characters you want to be visible to the user. The field may actually contain more characters. The field's visible contents will scroll as a user types beyond the number you've chosen to make visible.

6. Enter a larger number in the Maximum field if you want to give the user more room to type but don't want the entire field to be visible.

7. Leave the "Is Password Field" checkbox unchecked unless you're creating a password field.

✔ Tips

- When you choose a name for your field and other form elements, keep in mind that the field names are used by your Web server's CGI application to connect the form to the underlying database. Your field names should match the field names of your database and be intuitively linked to the form you're working with.

- You create a password field using exactly the same procedure you used to make the Text field. When you add the Password field tool into the document window, the Inspector selects "Is Password Field." Password fields require a connection to a CGI script that passes passwords to the Web server.

You have two choices when designing Web page forms: to label or not to label. To give each form element (such as a text field) a label, you'll need to create a text frame for it and leave room in your page for the label. Alternatively, you can use the Content and Value fields found in most form elements to label the fields internally.

You can resize a text field by dragging one of the field's two handles. As you drag, the value in the Inspector window's Visible field changes.

Text areas

A text fields contain a single line, but text *areas* allow you to provide multiple lines in which a user can enter information. You can use text areas to provide comments on your site, for example.

To create a text area:

1. Drag the Text Area tool from the Palette to the document window (**Figure 7.6a**). The Inspector window displays the Text Area Inspector. (**Figure 7.6b**).
2. Name the text area.
3. If you want to change the default size of the text area, do so by raising or lowering the values in the Columns and Rows boxes or dragging the text area's handles to alter the field's size.
4. Use the Wrap popup menu to tell the form whether or not to wrap the text at the end of each line—usually a good idea.

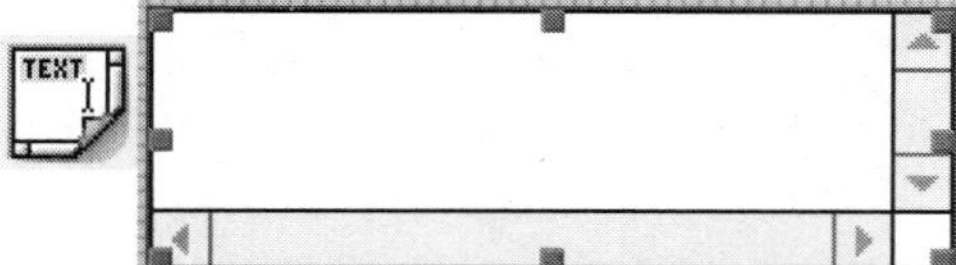

Figure 7.6a The Text Area tool and a text area.

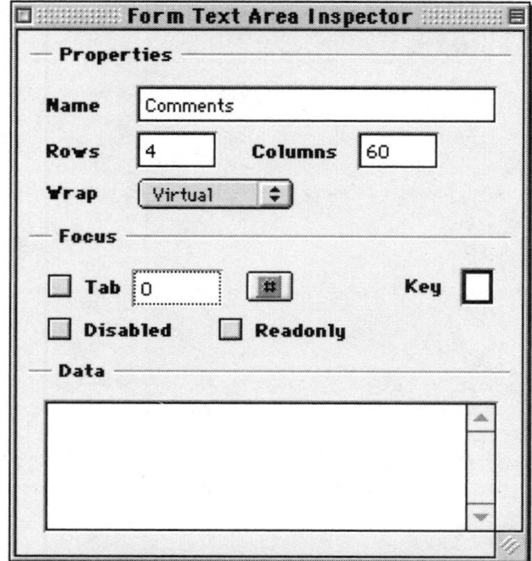

Figure 7.6b The Text Area Inspector.

Figure 7.7a The Checkbox Tool and a checkbox.

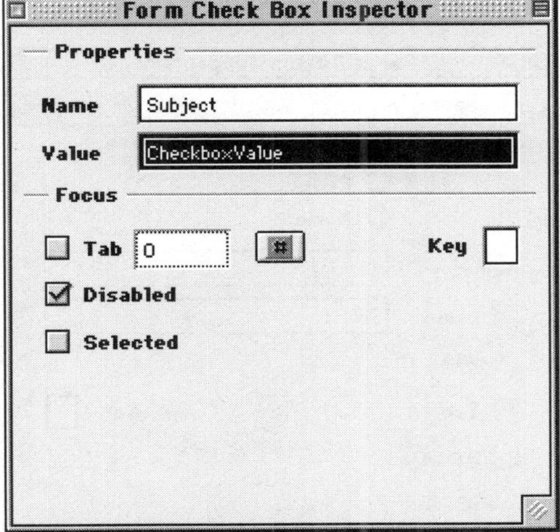

Figure 7.7b The Checkbox Inspector.

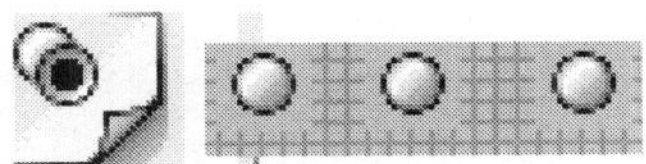

Figure 7.8a The Radio Button tool and three radio buttons.

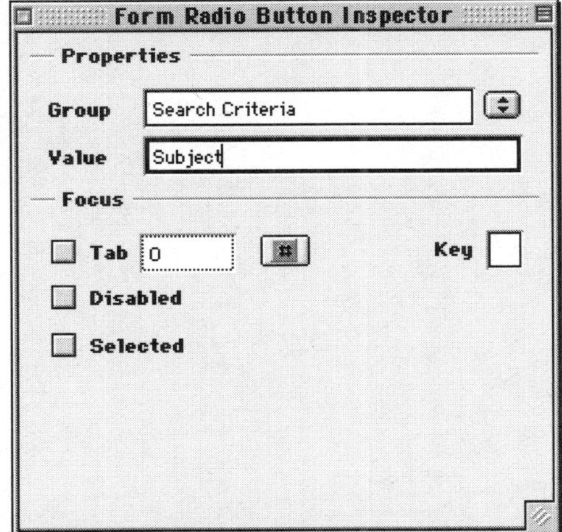

Figure 7.8b The Radio Button Inspector.

Checkboxes and radio buttons

Adding a set of checkboxes or radio buttons to your form provides a way for site visitors to choose from a number of options. Radio buttons allow users to choose an option from a group of several options. Checkboxes allow the user to pick one or more items from a group.

To create a checkbox:

1. Drag the checkbox tool from the Palette to the document window. A checkbox appears (**Figure 7.7a**).
2. In the Checkbox Inspector (**Figure 7.7b**), type a name for the checkbox.
3. Enter an optional descriptive name for the checkbox in the Value field.
4. If you want the box checked by default, click the Is Selected checkbox.

To create a set of radio buttons:

1. Drag several radio buttons from the Palette to the document window (**Figure 7.8a**).
2. Instead of a name for a single checkbox or field, the Radio Button Inspector window (**Figure 7.8b**) asks for a group name, which represents all the radio buttons you will use as part of this series. Type a group name.
3. Type a descriptive name for this button in the Value field, if you like.
4. Repeat steps 2 and 3 for each button you created, choosing the group name that applies to all of them from the popup menu as you go.

Submit and Reset buttons

The Submit and Reset buttons make your forms truly interactive. After filling out a form, the user clicks the Submit button, sending the information off to the server. A Reset button clears the form, which is useful if the site visitor decides to erase the data he or she has entered.

To create a Submit or Reset button:

1. Drag the Submit button tool from the Palette to the document window **(Figure 7.9a)**.
2. In the Inspector window (**Figure 7.9b**), choose a name for the button.
3. If you want the button text to say something other than "Submit Query," click the Label checkbox and type your new label.

   Because you used the Submit Button tool, GoLive has chosen Submit as your button's type. Leave it unchanged.

✔ Tip

■ You create a Reset button using exactly the same procedure you did to make the Submit button. When you drag the button onto the document window, the Inspector selects Reset, rather than Submit, as the button type.

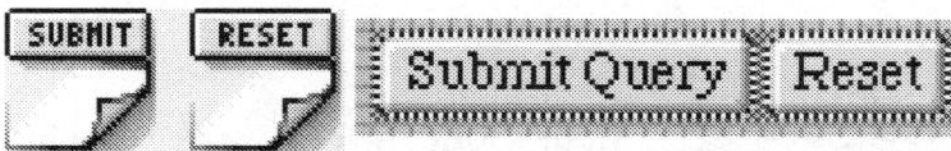

Figure 7.9a The Submit and Reset button tools, and the buttons they create.

Figure 7.9b The Button Inspector.

Popups and list boxes

You can display a list of choices within your form using a popup menu or a list box. They perform the same basic function but look a bit different from each other.

✔ Tip

■ Popups and list boxes can be used like checkboxes and radio buttons, but they're much easier to configure as a group. They also take up less space on the page—a design bonus or drawback, depending on the look you're trying to achieve.

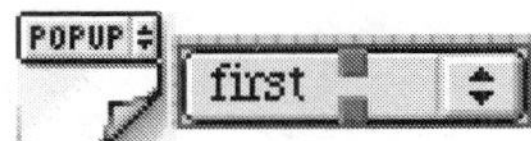

Figure 7.10a The Popup tool and a popup menu.

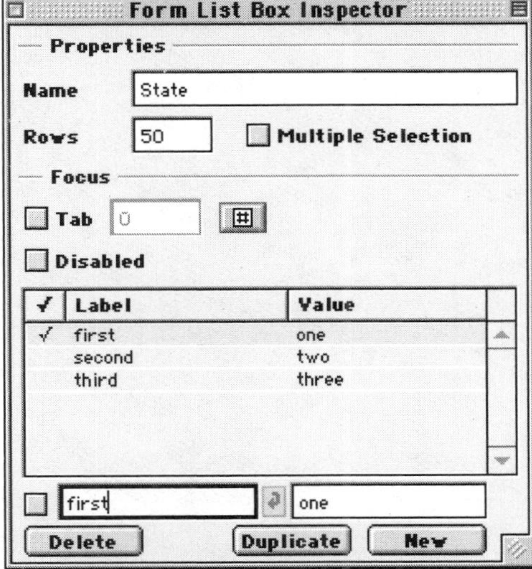

Figure 7.10b The Popup Inspector.

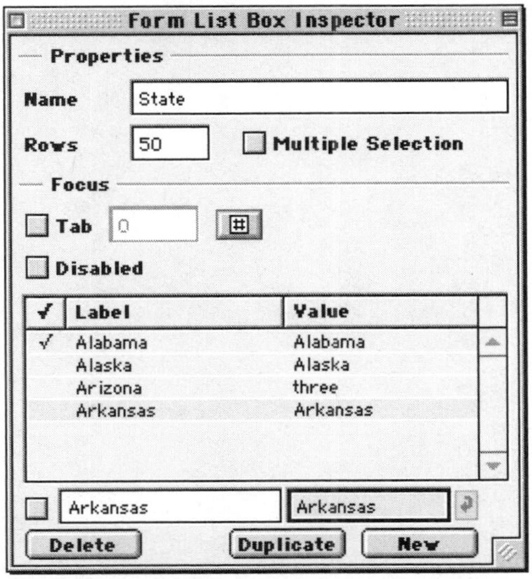

Figure 7.11 Change and add labels and values in the Inspector, to customize popup menus. Click New to add an item, Delete to remove one.

A popup menu looks just like a Macintosh popup menu. (Windows users call them drop-down menus.) Only a small rectangle is visible until you click on it to pull down the menu. List boxes, on the other hand, display more of their contents on the Web page. Simply clicking on an item from the list box selects it.

Configuring the two form elements is similar, too.

To create a popup menu:

1. Drag the Popup tool from the Palette to the main window (**Figure 7.10a**).
2. Name the popup in the Form Popup Inspector (**Figure 7.10b**).
3. If you want site visitors to see more than one popup item, enter that number in the Rows box.

   Note that making multiple rows visible makes your popup identical to a list box and defeats the purpose of having a popup. The same goes for the Multiple Items checkbox, which lets users select more than one item from the popup.
4. By default, the Inspector shows three items that you can edit and include in a popup menu. You modify them, add items, or delete items. To modify an item, first select it.
5. Notice in **Figure 7.11** that the Name and Value of the item are now visible in boxes at the bottom of the window. Rename the labels and values with names you want to appear in the popup menu.
6. To select the item by default, click the checkbox to the left of the Label name at the bottom.

continues on next page

7. To add new items to the popup, click New and type the new item's name and value in the appropriate fields.

To create a list box:

1. Follow steps 1-3 of the Popup section, above.
2. Because the whole idea of a list box is to view several options, use the Rows box to enter the number of items you want to be visible on the list.
3. Click "Multiple Selections" if you want the user to be able to pick several options from the list.
4. Follow steps 4-7 of the "Popup" section, above.

✔ Tips

- List boxes have scroll bars, allowing you to display some rows and make others available by scrolling. Choose the number of rows you think will both look best on the page and also display the items you think will be most popular, saving most site visitors the trouble of scrolling down the entire list.
- You can change the number of visible rows either by using the Inspector or by dragging the handle on the list box downward.

Special Form Elements

The form elements in Table 7.1 are not supported in all forms-friendly browsers, but they will work in Netscape and Microsoft browser versions 3.0 and later.

Table 7.1

Special Form Elements

Element Type	Palette Tool	Form Icon	Description
Input Image			Substitute an image for the standard Submit or Reset button
Hidden Element			Hidden elements are not a visible part of a form. Instead of holding information entered by a form user, hidden elements store information that is being transferred between the browser and Web server by the CGI.
Key Generator		Key Gener...	Key generators insert an encryption key into the transaction between Web site visitor and Web site owner. Keys are often used when forms contain financial transactions or personal information. When a site visitor submits a form, the Web server sends a dialog box to the visitor, asking the visitor to accept or decline the key so that the transaction can be completed.
File Browser		Browse...	The File Browser element lets you open a window to the FTP directory on your Web site. Using a File Browser, site visitors can look for and download files, provided that the Web server has a CGI application that supports this.

HTML 4.0 Forms

The latest version of the HTML specification includes several new form tags and a couple of new form features that will help users navigate your forms. The catch is that your Web site's visitors' must use a 4.0 browser to view and use the new tags and features.

Button

An HTML 4.0 button is like the Submit and Reset buttons I described earlier in this chapter, except that you can customize its appearance and function with the Text Inspector.

To create an HTML 4.0 button:

1. Drag the Button tool from the Palette to the document window (**Figure 7.12a**).
2. Drag your cursor over the button until it changes from a hand to an I-beam. You can now type text in the button and customize that text just as you would any other text in your document. If you click on the text, notice that the Inspector window displays the Text Inspector, allowing you to add a link or other attribute of your choice.
3. Click on the border of the button to select the entire button. The Button Inspector appears.
4. In the Inspector window (**Figure 7.12b**), choose a name and value for the button.

Figure 7.12a The HTML 4.0 Button tool and a button.

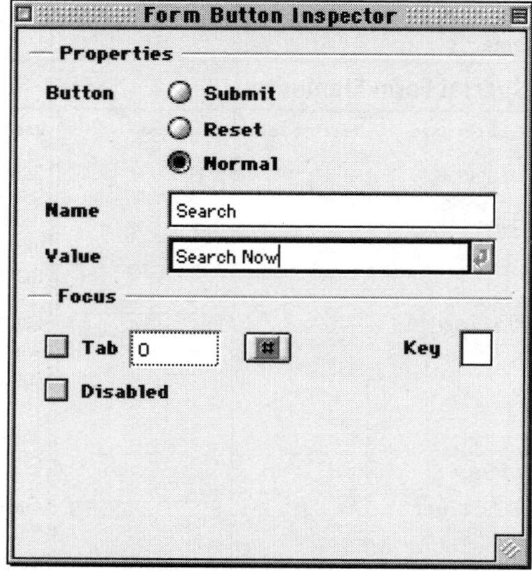

Figure 7.12b The Button Inspector.

Figure 7.13a The Label tool and a label.

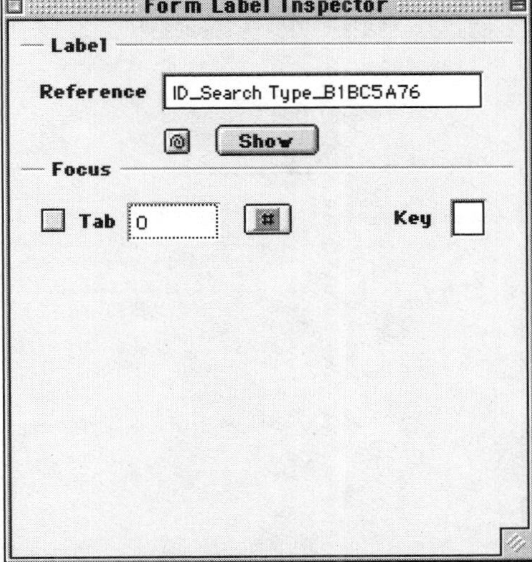

Figure 7.13b The Label Inspector.

Label

It seems like a pretty simple matter to create a text label for a form element such as a radio button or checkbox. HTML 4.0's Label form element is a nifty way of connecting a label with a button or a box, though, because clicking on the label activates the other form element, much as clicking on a label in the GoLive Inspector activates the button or box associated with it.

To create a label element:

1. Create or locate a checkbox, radio button, or any other form element you would like to label. Make sure that you have configured your form elements before trying to create a label.
2. Drag or double-click the Label item (**Figure 7.13a**) from the Palette to the document window.
3. Double-click the label to select the text and type the label.
4. Position the label element near the item you want to connect it to.
5. Command-click (Mac) or Control-click (Windows) the label (not the text inside it) and Point & Shoot the resulting line to the box, button, or other element you want to link to. Note that the Label Inspector window becomes visible (**Figure 7.13b**), and that it now displays an ID number that connects your label to the form element.

✔ Tip

- Just like an HTML 4.0 button tag, you can format label text when it (not the label) is selected. Formatting makes it easier to ensure that the labels you create fit into your page layout.

Fieldset

The Fieldset element provides a physical grouping for other form elements. You can work with and move a group of buttons, checkboxes, or radio buttons around together once they've been added to a Fieldset. The legend option allows you to label the group.

To create a fieldset:

1. Drag the Fieldset item (**Figure 7.14a**) from the Palette to the document window.
2. In the Fieldset Inspector (**Figure 7.14b**), choose an alignment for the Fieldset legend or uncheck the Legend box to disable this feature.
3. If you plan to use a legend, click the word Legend in the main window and change the word Legend to a title of your choice.
4. Drag a table (either one you've worked on already or a new one from the Palette) into the Fieldset box you just created. The Fieldset box expands to hold the table.
5. Drag some checkboxes into the Fieldset box and table. Add labels to the table.

✔ Tip

- Fieldsets display very differently on different browsers. Netscape browsers do not fully support this form element.

Figure 7.14a The Fieldset tool and a fieldset.

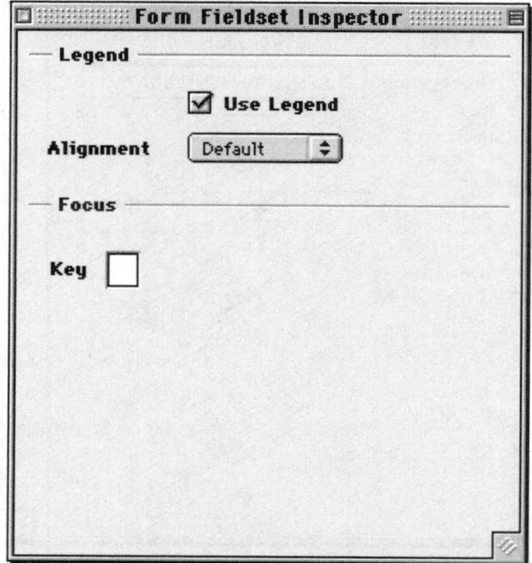

Figure 7.14b The Fieldset Inspector.

HTML 4.0 form features

Filling out a long online form is much easier if you can move from one field to the next using the Tab key. GoLive and HTML 4.0 give you a way to create and control the order in which users move from field to field.

You may have noticed several items under the Focus label of many form element inspector windows. These items specify the 4.0-specific features I'll cover in this section.

HTML 4.0 form features supported in GoLive are:

- Tab chains.
- Access keys.
- Read-only elements.
- Disabled elements.

✔ Tip

- The navigation method covered in this section is currently available only to users of the Windows version of Internet Explorer.

Form elements that support tab chains are:

- Text and password fields.
- Text areas.
- Submit and Reset buttons.
- Checkboxes and radio buttons.
- Popup menus and list boxes.
- Labels.

To create a tab chain:

1. Open a document that contains fields that require the user to make a text entry, such as a text field, password field, or text area.

continues on next page

2. Choose Start Tabulator Indexing from the Special menu. Small yellow boxes with numbers appear next to the indexable fields in your form.
3. Click the boxes in the order you want the tabs to appear. The numbers change to reflect your clicks.
4. Choose Stop Tabulator Indexing from the Special menu.

✔ Tip

- You may have noticed a checkbox and a field labeled Tab in the Inspector window of some form elements. You can check on or change the tab order of fields within your forms in this Inspector field.

Access keys

Defining an access key within a form element allows the user to activate the element or field by typing a certain character.

Form elements that support access keys are:

- Text and password fields.
- Text areas.
- Submit and Reset buttons.
- Checkboxes and radio buttons.
- Labels.
- Legends.

To create an access key:

1. Choose a supported element. If it's not already placed within a form, drag it to the document window and configure it.
2. In the Inspector, type an alphanumeric character in the Key field.
3. Test your new key in a browser that supports access keys, such as Internet Explorer for Windows.

✔ Tip

- It's a good idea to include some sort of label or other visual cue on the page, so that your visitors will know that the form field includes an access key.

Read-only elements

You can use read-only elements to prevent visitors from editing the contents of a form field. If, for example, you want to limit the visitor to submitting a pre-defined text string, you could create a field that includes it.

Form elements that support read-only elements are:

- Text and password fields.
- Text areas.
- Submit and Reset buttons.
- Checkboxes and radio buttons.
- Popup menus and list boxes.

To create a read-only element:

1. Select the element you want to make read-only in your document.
2. Add text that you would like to appear in the field.
3. In the Inspector, click the Read-Only checkbox.

Disabled elements

You can disable any form element. While it may seem silly to create an element only to disable it, you can use scripts to bring disabled elements to life conditionally—the item will be disabled unless a script activates it. You could, for example, disable order form fields until your e-commerce system has verified a credit card number. Once the affirmative result is returned to the Web server, a script re-enables the form fields, and your customer can complete the order.

To disable a form element:

1. Choose the form element you wish to disable.
2. Write or edit a script (CGI, JavaScript, AppleScript or other script supported by your Web server) to provide for enabling the element, when appropriate.
3. Select the element in the document window.
4. In the Inspector, click the Disabled checkbox.

8

Working with Frames

Think of frames as multi-paned windows to your Web site. Instead of a single, scrollable page full of text and images, framed pages display two or more pages within the same browser window. Usually, framed pages (*frame sets*, in HTML-speak) contain a main pane and one or more smaller ones. Panes may include scroll bars that move you through the frame independently of the other elements on the page. Some frames remain stationary in the browser as you click through other pages within a Web site.

Many Web designers use frames as navigation tools. A frame can display a table of contents for the entire site alongside each individual page. Other sites use frames to force visitors to view advertisements or other banner content.

In this chapter, I cover:

- How frames work.
- Creating frames.
- Adding content to frames.
- Adding frames and frame sets.

How Frames Work

Most Web pages consist of a single HTML file. Frame-based Web pages, on the other hand, actually display several HTML documents at once, each in its own pane of the browser window. **Figures 8.1a** and **8.1b** are examples of the variety of design choices available using frames.

To use frames, you'll need to create and link several files into a frame set. Although the files you need will vary based on the arrangement of your frames, these are the most basic ones:

- A frame set document.
- A navigation document.
- A main page document.

The frame set document contains instructions on how the browser window and its panes should look by default, and how they are positioned on the page. Whatever frame setup you choose, the frame set document is required. The frame set document does not contain HTML that is displayed. It forms the structure for your framed page.

The file I'm calling the navigation document provides a table of contents (including links) of pages that can be make up your Web site, and it will appear in the main pane when you click.

The main page document is a placeholder for HTML content that will appear in the main pane of the browser window.

You can add advertising banners, message boxes, or other items using additional frame documents. Like basic navigation and content frames, you specify these frames' size and appearance within the frame set document.

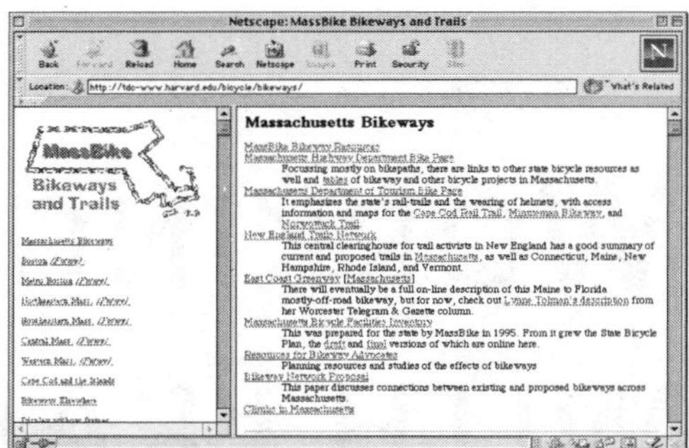

Figure 8.1a The MassBike links page uses two frames: a table of contents on the left and a body frame containing individual links.

Figure 8.1b *MacAddict* magazine uses a navigation frame on the left and a bottom frame for advertising.

Frame caveats

Frames are not really a full-fledged part of the HTML standard. Netscape Communications introduced frame tags as an extension to HTML At this writing, only Netscape browsers (Navigator and Communicator) and Microsoft Internet Explorer support frames. Although browser software from Netscape and Microsoft dominates the marketplace, Webmasters who use frames run the risk of creating pages that users of other browsers cannot view. The solution for some is to create both frame-filled and no-frames versions of their Web sites.

Even when site visitors use browsers that support them, frames can be a challenge to Web site visitors. Although frames make it possible to look at more of your site at once, they also limit the user's ability to use the mouse and cursor to move freely. For example, if you're used to using the Page Down key to scroll through a Web page, you'll find that impossible to do in some framed pages unless you first click in the frame you want to navigate.

Frames also decrease the amount of screen space available to display Web site content. Contents areas and navigation frames leave less room for the main pane. To be fair, though, the same is true of other templated site design methods that use tables to create fixed navigation elements on the side or top of the browser window. The challenge is to leave as much space as possible in the main frame while retaining readability within smaller frames.

Creating Frames

Once you've decided what portions of your Web site belong in frames, you can create a page with one or more *frame sets*. Frame sets specify the way a group of frames on the page will look and interact.

All the tools you need to create and customize frame-based pages can be found under the Frames tab of the Palette.

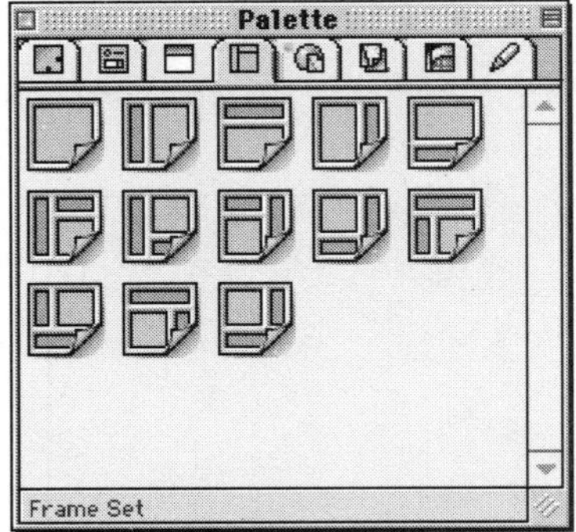

Figure 8.2 The Palette's Frames tab contains tools you can use to create a variety of frame sets.

To locate the Frames tab:

1. Make sure that the Palette is visible. If it's not, choose Palette from the Windows menu.
2. Click on the Frames tab at the top of the Palette. It's the fourth tab. **Figure 8.2** shows the Palette with the Frames tab selected.

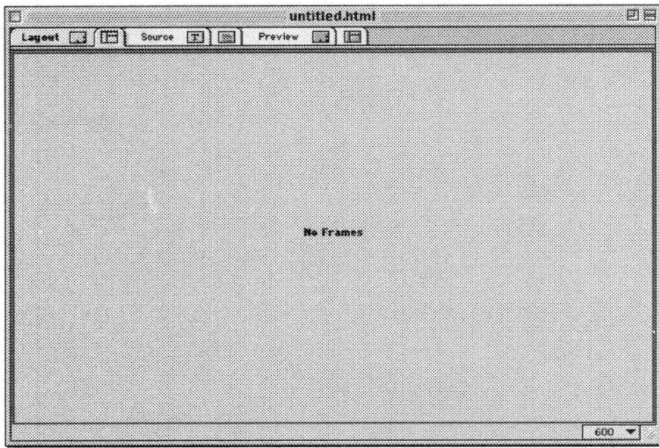

Figure 8.3 The Frame view displays the structure of a frame set page. It's blank when no frames are present.

To create a frame document:

1. Open a new GoLive document.
2. Switch from the Layout view to the Frames view by clicking on the Frames tab in the document windows. The result looks like **Figure 8.3**.
3. Choose the Frame tab from the Palette.
4. Drag a frame set icon (all but the upper, leftmost icon are frame sets) from the Palette onto the main window.

   The configuration I chose as an example is displayed in **Figure 8.4**, along with the corresponding frame set icon from the Palette.

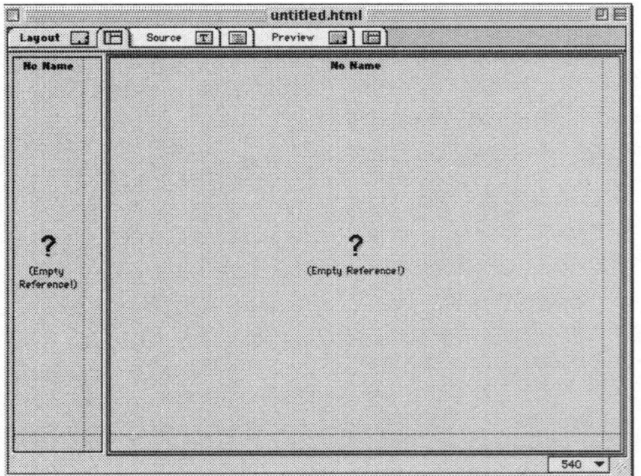

Figure 8.4 Here's a simple frame set, displayed in the Frame view.

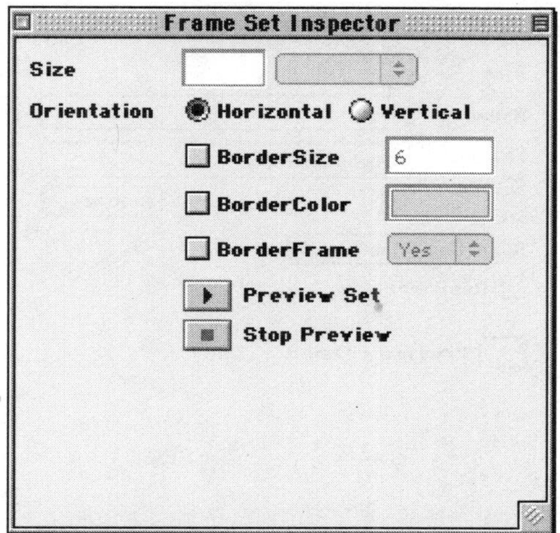

Figure 8.5 The Frame Set Inspector sets all preferences for frames in a set. You probably won't spend much time here.

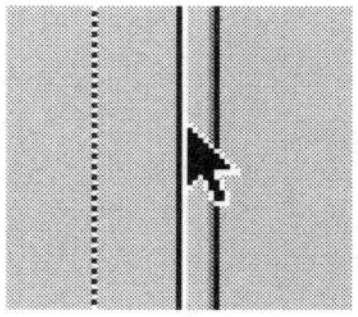

Figure 8.6 When you attempt to resize a frame, be sure that your cursor is positioned on the border between frames, rather than within one of them.

5. Click on the border between the two frames to bring up the Frame Set Inspector in the Inspector window (**Figure 8.5**). If you don't see the Inspector window, choose Inspector from the Windows menu.

Options you choose here apply to all frames within the frame set. You can change the set's orientation, specify the thickness of the border, the border color, and whether there should be a border frame. You can also tell GoLive whether or not to allow frame previewing within the Frame view.

To arrange frames:

1. Click and hold the mouse button inside the leftmost frame on your page and drag to the right, across the document window. When the frame you've selected reaches the other frame onscreen, the two change places. Drag the frame to the left to return it to its original position.
2. By default, the smaller frame, sometimes called a sidebar, is very narrow. To widen it, click and drag the border of the frame to the right. I'll need the extra space, because I'm going to use the frame as a table of contents for a Web site.

✔ Tip

- Be careful to position your cursor on the border of the frame, as shown in **Figure 8.6**, rather than the outline of the scroll bar (to the left of the cursor). As we've seen, dragging from inside a frame moves the entire frame. All you want to do at this point is resize it.

To configure frames:

1. Click within a frame. The Inspector window now displays the Frame Inspector (**Figure 8.7**).
2. Type a name for the frame in the Name field.

   Give your frames simple and descriptive names. The name will be used to identify the frame later on, as you build connections to items within your Web site. I'll name the sidebar frame contents.html.
3. Choose Yes or No in the scrolling popup menu to determine whether your contents frame will have scroll bars, or leave Auto selected to allow the browser to add bars only when the content is long enough to warrant them. In this example, I'll turn off scrolling because the table of contents won't be long enough to require scrolling. Leaving off the scroll bars also conserves valuable screen real estate.
4. Save your frame document. Again, give it a descriptive name, one that conforms to the HTML naming convention i.e. name.html. Because this example Web site uses only one frame set configuration, I'll call the file frame.html. Remember that this document won't contain any content, just instructions for the display of framed pages.

I named the page frame.html so that it would be obvious which document we were working with. Chances are, though, that you'll want to use a different name if your new, framed look will be the home page of your site.

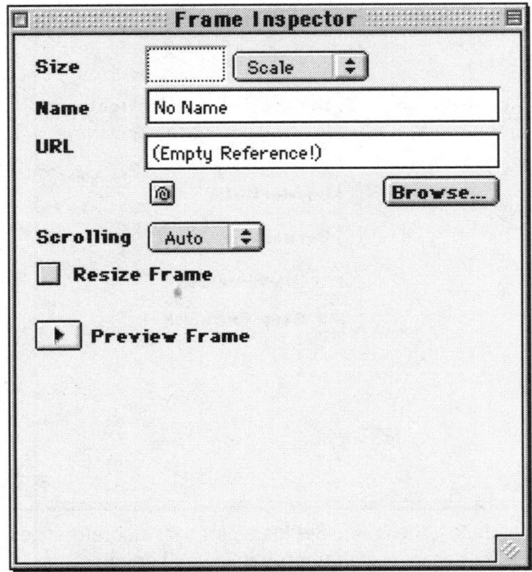

Figure 8.7 Name and configure individual frames in the Frame Inspector.

✔ Tips

- If you want to use a frames-based page as your home page, name it index.html, home.html or some other name that your Web server recognizes as your default Web page.
- Even if your server doesn't care how your page is named, Webmasters redesigning existing sites will want to preserve their previous home page URLs by giving the frame page the same name as the previous home page.
- Some Webmasters avoid this naming headache (as well as problems caused for people whose Web browsers don't support frames) by offering framed and non-framed versions of home pages and sites. In that case, create a page that offers that choice, and name it index.html and let site visitors click on the version of their choice. In that case, you can name your framed document anything you like and can link to it from your index page.

Adding Content to Frames

With your framework in place (pun intended), it's time to dress up those window panes with some content. Although frames can simply provide windows to individual Web pages, they are much more powerful when used as a navigation tool for your entire site. The example frame structure I'm using in this chapter does that. The contents frame offers a list of available pages within our site, and the larger frame (I'll call it the body frame) displays a page your site visitors request from the table of contents.

Like the frame document itself, the body frame is a container for information. The contents of the body frame change depend on the hyperlink a user selects.

To add a body page to your frame set:

1. Open a new document.
2. Click on the title bar (currently labeled "Welcome to Adobe GoLive 4") and change the title to "body."
3. Save your document as body.html.
4. Open the frame.html document you created in the preceding section. Switch to the Frame view.
5. Click in the larger of the two frames (on the right) to select it.
6. Click the Browse button in the Frame Inspector and locate and select the file you want to appear in the body frame by default. This is probably your home page

   or

   Locate a file in the Site window and use Point & Shoot to link it to the body frame

   or

   Drag a file from the Site window or from the Finder (Mac) or from Windows

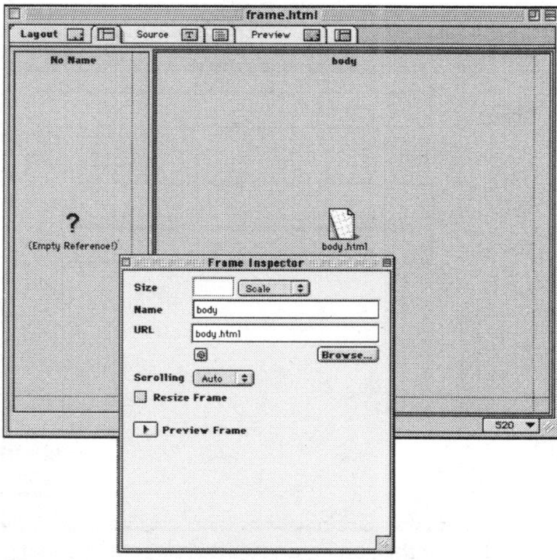

Figure 8.8 With the body frame's Inspector completed, the question mark in the body frame changes to a page icon, and the frame's name appears at the top of the page.

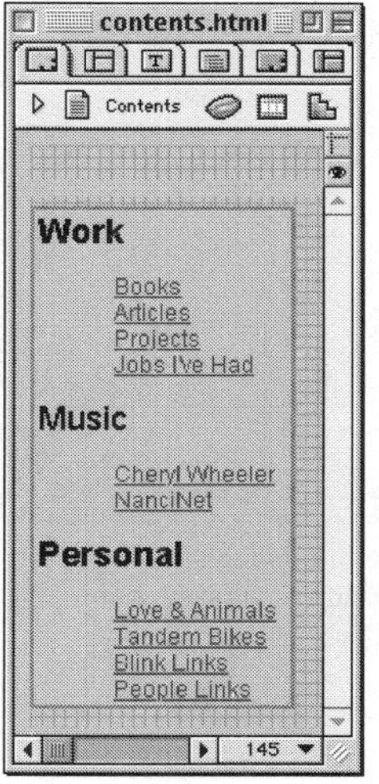

Figure 8.9 The contents.html page will appear as a navigation frame on each page of my Web site. I narrowed the window so that it would be easier to work with.

Explorer or the desktop (Windows) into the body frame.

7. In the Frame Inspector, name the frame "body." If you want to add scroll bars to the frame, choose that option. **Figure 8.8** shows the completed body frame Inspector window and the frame itself.

   If you check Resize Frame, those who view your page will be able to shrink or enlarge the frame in their browser windows. Otherwise, the frame is always the same size you created it.

The contents frame contains a fixed HTML page, usually including links that activate the body frame. You can also add text, graphics, or any other element you'd like to appear in the navigation frame. The contents of the body frame vary based upon the link a site visitor activates. Site designers often set the body frame to default to your site's home page, as described in the next section.

✔ Tip

- When you're designing your contents frame, remember that it will probably be quite narrow. Limit your text elements to headings and listings, and keep logos and graphics small. Of course, you *can* make your contents frame as wide as you like, but you'll be sacrificing valuable body frame screen space with every expansion of the contents frame.

To add a contents frame:

1. Open a new GoLive document.
2. Title your document "contents" and save it as contents.html.
3. Type the text for your table of contents. **Figure 8.9** shows my contents page.

I included several elements: headings, listings (including links to individual pages), and spacers. Your next task is to create hyperlinks that connect the listed items to the body frame. Although connecting frames together is very much like creating links or anchors for a normal page, it comes with one added wrinkle: the target.

Targets tell the Web browser where a link should be displayed: in a new window, at the top of a page, or, in this case, in a frame that is part of the current frame set.

To create targeted links:

1. Open contents.html. Be sure that frame.html is also open.
2. In contents.html, select an item from your table of contents list.
3. Choose Link from the toolbar and type a URL in the Inspector window to complete the link.

   or

   Point and shoot from the Site window to link a file within your site.
4. Connect the new link to the main frame (body) of your frame set (frame.html) by filling in the Target field of the Inspector. Because this is the first frame link you've created, you need to type the word body (the name you gave to your main frame) in the Target field. The completed Inspector window looks like **Figure 8.10**.
5. Save the contents.html document.
6. Bring frame.html to the front.
7. In the main window, choose the Frames preview tab. You should see the contents document in the left frame and an empty pane on the right (**Figure 8.11**).

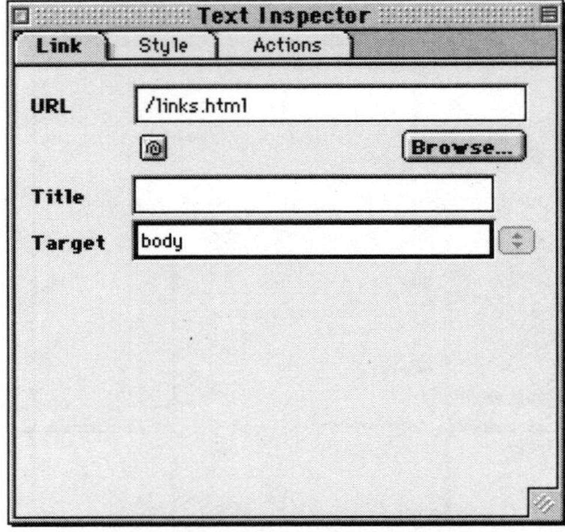

Figure 8.10 In the Inspector, you can target links that appear in the navigation frame to the body frame, so that the links will appear there when clicked by site visitors.

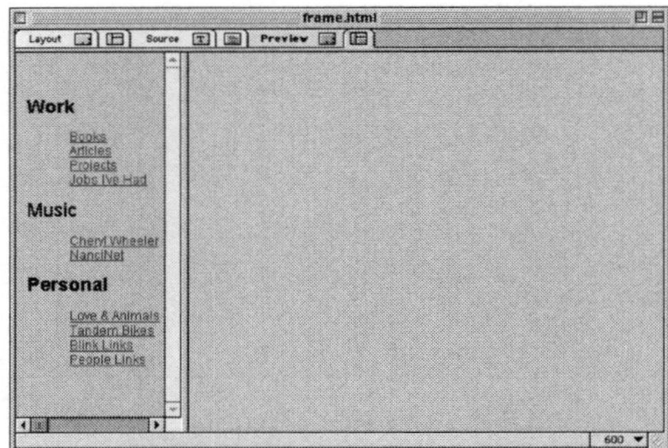

Figure 8.11 With the contents.html file linked to frame.html, you can preview the navigation bar in the Frame Preview mode.

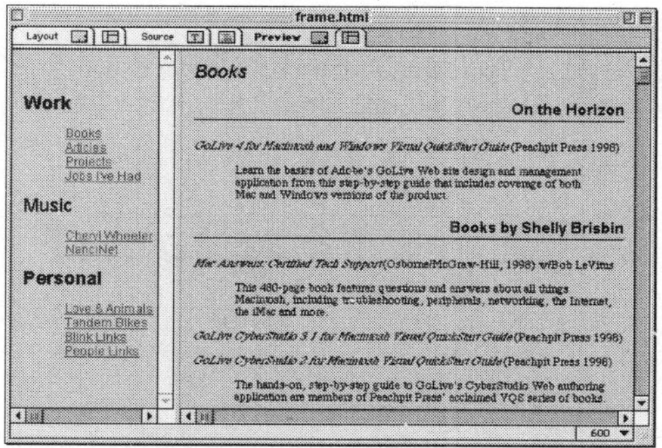

Figure 8.12 In the Frame Preview mode, clicking on the properly configured link in the contents frame displays the requested page in the body frame.

8. Click on the link you just created in the contents frame. The page you've linked appears in the body frame (**Figure 8.12**).

9. Repeat steps 2-5 for each table of contents element you'd like to connect to a document that will appear in the main frame.

✔ Tip

- When you choose targets in the Link Inspector, use the popup menu. Once you create the first link you'll notice that the target menu now includes the word *body*. Creating the first body target added this item to the menu. This shortcut does not work, however, unless the frame set document (frame.html) is open.

Does the contents frame look right to you in Preview mode, and/or in your Web browser? Do the line breaks occur where you want them to? If not, you can adjust the contents frame's width in the Frames view. Here's how.

To tweak the contents frame:

1. Open frame.html and choose the Frames view.

2. Click on the contents frame.

3. In the Frame Inspector window, click the Preview Frame button. Contents.html pops into the contents frame.

4. To adjust the width of the frame, drag the border to the left or right (depending on whether you think the contents frame is too wide or too narrow), and note the impact the movement has on line breaks and available space within the body frame.

5. For that extra measure of accuracy, click the Frame Preview tab and verify the look of your frames.

Adding Frames and Frame Sets

GoLive allows you to create frame sets in a wide variety of configurations. The Frames tab of the Palette suggests a number of options, including the simple two-frame arrangement I've been using in this chapter. You can also modify existing frame sets by adding new frames, one at a time. You can even use multiple frame sets on the same page, creating *nested frame sets.*

To add a single frame:

1. Open the frame.html document you've been working with and switch to the Frames view.
2. Drag the Frame item (**Figure 8.13**) from the Palette to the main window, dropping it into the body frame. A new frame appears.
3. Click on the new frame and drag it upward so that it switches places with the body frame, as shown in **Figure 8.14**. I'm going to use this frame as a banner.
4. Click on the new frame. Now you can use the Frame Inspector to resize it.
5. In the Size popup of the Frame Inspector, note that the default setting is Scale. Choose Percent from the menu. You can now enter a number (try 25) that states the frame's size as a percentage of the available vertical space. The upper frame shrinks. Now you're ready to add content to your new frame by dragging an HTML file into it.

Figure 8.13 Add a single frame to your frame set with the Palette's Frame tool.

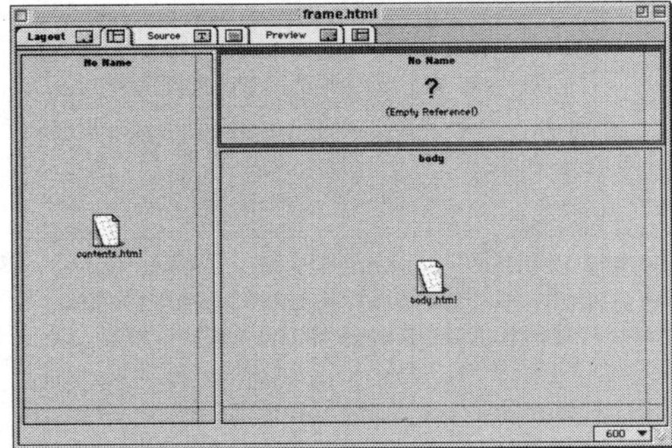

Figure 8.14 Dragging the frame icon onto an existing frame set creates a frame that is the same size as the one you drag it onto.

✔ Tips

- If you'd rather use the mouse than the keyboard, you can resize the frame by dragging its border, so long as either Pixel or Percent are chosen in the Frame Inspector's Size popup menu.
- If you want to add a group of frames to an existing frame-based page, simply drag a frame set from the Palette to the main window. Each frame set on a page operates as a separate entity, meaning that the preferences you set for one frame set do not apply to other sets on the same page.

Special Cases

You can create options for users without frames-friendly browsers, and add an inline frame to a page, giving it a scrollable "window."

Adding Noframes Content

Not all Web browsers support frames: 2.0 versions of Netscape Navigator and Microsoft Internet Explorer don't, and neither do text-only browsers like Lynx. Using the <noframes> tag, you can design your pages so that browsers that don't support frames will display a version of your page. The <noframes> tag encloses HTML that is displayed when a non-frames browser accesses the page. You can create a complete, frameless version of the page, or a simple message directing the user to a non-frames version of your site, or to a frames-capable browser.

Adding a <noframes> element to a frame set in GoLive requires you to work with HTML source code; you can't do it in the Layout view of the Frames view.

To add a noframes element:

1. Create a page that you would like to greet visitors who use browsers that do not support frames. You may create one from scratch, or copy and paste the contents of your framed pages into the new page.
2. Save the page.
3. Open a GoLive document containing a frame set.
4. Switch to the Source view by clicking the Source tab at the top of the document window.
5. Locate the opening <frameset> tag, and type <noframes> after the frameset tag.

continues on next page

6. Return to the page you created in Step 1, and switch to the Source view.
7. Locate the opening <body> tag and copy everything below it and above the closing </body> tag to the clipboard.
8. In the frameset document, paste your noframes content into the Source view, following the <noframes> tag.
9. Type **</noframes>** to finish the tag.
10. Save and preview the page in both a frames-capable browser and a browser that does not support frames.

✔ Tips

- If you include a full copy of a Web page within <noframes> tags, you'll have to update two copies of the page whenever a change is needed. And because the <noframes> items are invisible in GoLive's Layout view, you must perform these updates in the Source view. If you update your pages frequently, consider creating a simple message in the <noframes> section that asks users to upgrade to a frames-capable browser.
- It's very important to remove head and HTML tags from documents you copy into <noframes> tags. A Web page must only have one set of these tags. GoLive creates the tags at the beginning and end of all HTML documents , including the frameset document that contains the <noframes> element.

Inline frames

Standard frames always have at least one edge along the browser window's margin. *Inline frames*, also called floating frames, are not constrained in this way, but can "float" in the middle of a page. Inline frames are a Microsoft addition to the HTML standard, and are compatible only with Internet Explorer browsers. You can create inline frames in GoLive, but you must use Internet Explorer to preview them.

Unlike standard frames, inline frames can appear within any HTML page. You don't need to create a frameset, or use other frames with an inline frame. Inline frames have many of the same attributes as image tags do. Like images, inline frames take a position on a Web page relative to other items on the page.

To add an inline frame:

1. Open a GoLive document to which you would like to add an inline frame.
2. Switch to the Source view.
3. At the location on your page where the inline frame should appear, type **<iframe SRC="filename.html">** where filename.html is the name of the document that will appear in the frame.
4. Set any additional attributes, such as size or background color, just as you would when setting up an image.
5. Type **</iframe>** to close the inline frame element.
6. Save the GoLive document.
7. View the document with Internet Explorer. You can do this by choosing IE from the toolbar's browser menu (if you've configured this option in GoLive Preferences), or by opening Internet Explorer and then opening the document that includes the inline frame.

9

WORKING WITH MULTIMEDIA

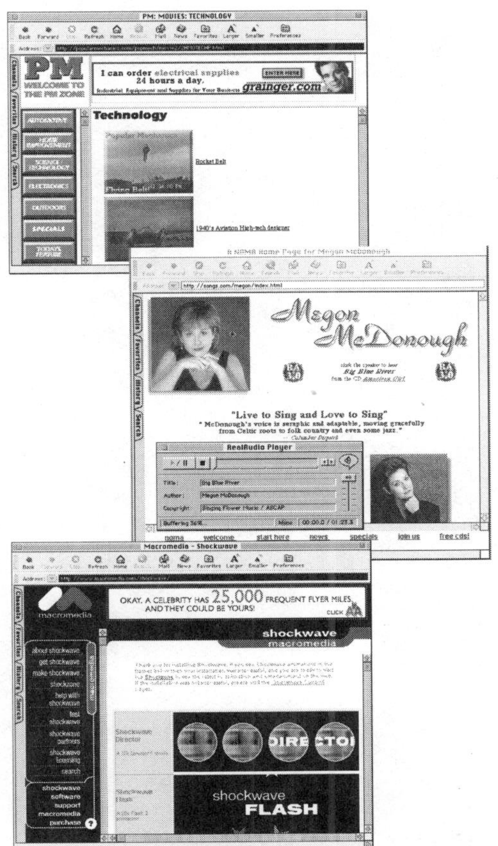

Figure 9.1 Here are (top) a QuickTime movie from Popular Mechanics, (middle) a RealAudio sound clip from the National Online Music Alliance, and (bottom) Shockwave animation from Macromedia.

You can add multimedia to your Web site in much the same way you add GIF or JPEG images. Like images, some multimedia files are displayed *inline*—as part of the Web page. Others are displayed in their own windows.

Multimedia formats supported on the Web include QuickTime video, QuickTime VR, RealAudio, and a number of other sound, video, animation, and publishing formats. GoLive also displays Java applets, JavaScripts, and ActiveX controls. In order for the user to view multimedia files, Web browsers must either directly support the appropriate format or support *plugins*. Plugins are software that is automatically activated when a multimedia file is called for and which can play or display the files. **Figure 9.1** shows three Web pages that include plugin items.

GoLive allows you to add plugin-based content and to configure the files' appearance and behavior within a Web page. In the case of JavaScript and QuickTime, you can create or edit your own content within GoLive.
In this chapter, I describe the QuickTime authoring interface. Chapter 11 shows you how to create JavaScript to modify the behavior of Web content.

In this chapter, I cover:

- Setting up plugins.
- Setting plugin preferences.
- QuickTime authoring.
- Java applets.
- JavaScript (configuring existing).
- ActiveX controls.

Figure 9.2 The Plugin tool.

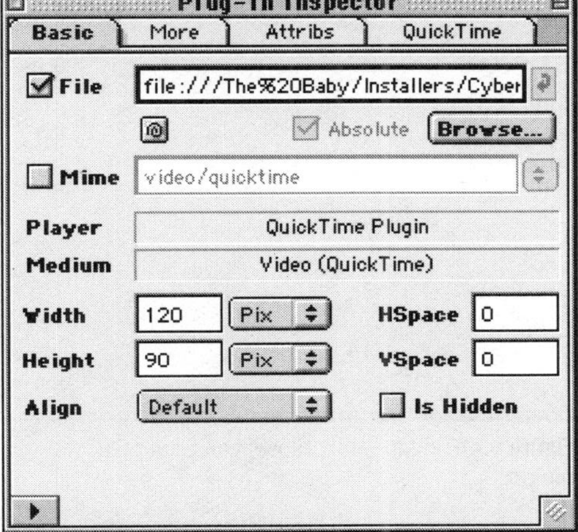

Figure 9.3 The Plugin Inspector.

Figure 9.4 The name of the plugin file appears within the placeholder when you have finished linking it.

Setting Up Plugins

GoLive supports a variety of plugins. QuickTime plays a number of audio and video formats, including standard QuickTime movies and QuickTime VR movies. Like a Web browser, GoLive can display new plugins once you have installed plugin software in the GoLive Plugin folder. Just drop the plugin into the Plugins folder, inside the GoLive folder.

Adding plugin content

Adding a plugin file to a Web page is much like adding an image. The differences between plugins and static images, and between different types of plugins, become clear as you configure them.

To add a plugin file to a Web page:

1. Open a GoLive document.
2. Drag (or double-click) the Plugin tool (**Figure 9.2**) from the Palette to the document window. A plugin icon with a question mark appears, and the Plugin Inspector appears in the Inspector window (**Figure 9.3**).
3. In the Inspector, point and shoot to a plugin file stored within your GoLive site

   or

   Click Browse and navigate to a media file that you want to use and click Open to select it. The plugin placeholder in the document window now shows the name of the media file (**Figure 9.4**).

To configure a plugin file:

1. If it isn't selected, click on a plugin placeholder to select it. The Plugin Inspector appears.
2. Resize the plugin placeholder by dragging one of its handles or by typing new height and width values in the corresponding Plugin Inspector fields.
3. If you are not using a layout grid, add horizontal and vertical spaces between the plugin and other items on your Web page by entering values (in pixels) in the Plugin Inspector's HSpace and VSpace fields.
4. Align the plugin placeholder to Web page text with the Alignment popup menu. The same rules that govern the alignment of images to text apply when using plugins. For a full description of alignment options, see Chapter 5. Like the spacing options, alignment choices are only available when a plugin is outside a layout grid or when the plugin is inside a text frame.
5. Name the plugin by clicking on the More tab in the Inspector window (**Figure 9.5**) and typing a unique name in the Name field.

✔ Tip

- You can play or display a media file at any time while you are configuring it by clicking the Play button at the bottom of the Plugin Inspector window (**Figure 9.6**). Click the button again to stop playback.

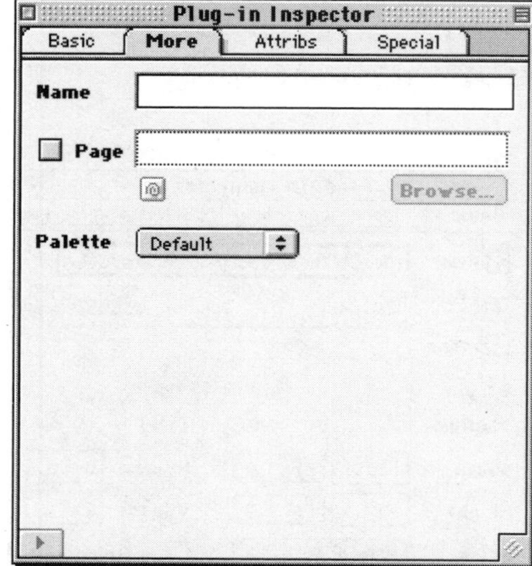

Figure 9.5 The More tab allows you to name the plugin.

Figure 9.6 Click the Play button in the Plugin Inspector to play the movie, audio file, or other plugin content. The button appears under all tabs of the Plugin Inspector.

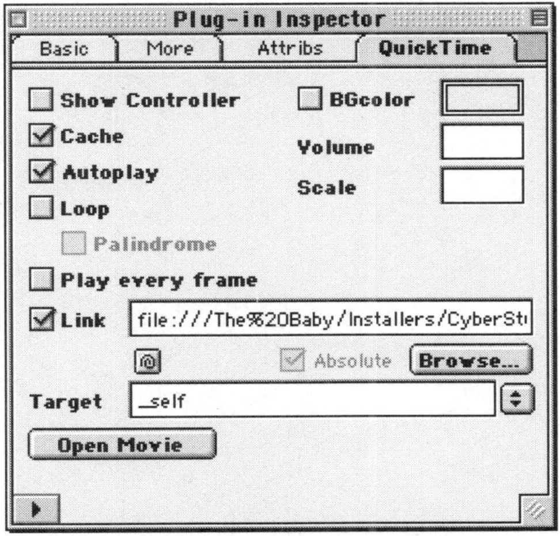

Figure 9.7 The QuickTime tab of the Plugin Inspector.

Configuring specific plugin types

GoLive has built-in support for a number of popular plugin formats, including QuickTime, QuickTime VR, and audio. When you link a supported media file to a plugin placeholder, the Plugin Inspector displays not only generic plugin configuration tools but also a tab that supports the file's specific attributes and options. If you link a media file that isn't supported, the tab is simply labeled Special and is empty. Later in this chapter, I'll describe how to configure plugins that GoLive doesn't know about using the Plugin Inspector's Special tab.

To configure a QuickTime file:

1. In the document window, select a plugin placeholder for a QuickTime file.
2. Click the QuickTime tab in the Plugin Inspector (**Figure 9.7**).
3. Choose the Show Controller checkbox to display the QuickTime audio/video controls at the bottom of the movie as it plays on screen.
4. Choose the Cache checkbox to tell the browser to cache the movie in RAM.
5. Leave the AutoPlay checkbox selected if you want the movie to play automatically when the page is opened. Otherwise, uncheck the box.
6. Click the Loop checkbox to play the movie continuously. If you choose a loop, checking the Palindrome option will play the move in reverse on every other loop.
7. Click the BGColor checkbox, and choose a color from the Color Palette if you want the movie to have a background color. (For details on using the Color Palette, see Chapter 5).

continues on next page

8. Type a value (as a percentage of 100) in the volume field to change the movie's sound level. Leave the field blank to use the default value.

9. Type a value (as a percentage of the movie's current size) in the Scale field to shrink or enlarge the movie's play area. Leaving the field blank displays the movie at its original size.

10. Click Play Every Frame to prevent the browser from dropping frames. Frames are dropped to improve playback speed.

✔ Tip

- GoLive includes QuickTime movie authoring tools, which allow you to modify and add effects to movies within GoLive. I have more to say about editing movies later in this chapter.

Flattening QuickTime movies

In order for QuickTime movies to play correctly on the Web, the movies must be *flattened*—saved in a format that Web browsers can accept and that can play correctly at the typical speed of an Internet connection. You can flatten movies before or after you've configured them within GoLive, by using the built-in QuickTime editor.

To flatten a QuickTime movie:

1. Create or edit a QuickTime movie using GoLive's QuickTime Editor.
2. Choose Save from the File menu.
3. In the dialog box, click Flatten. GoLive saves the new movie as a separate file, and compresses it for display on the Web.

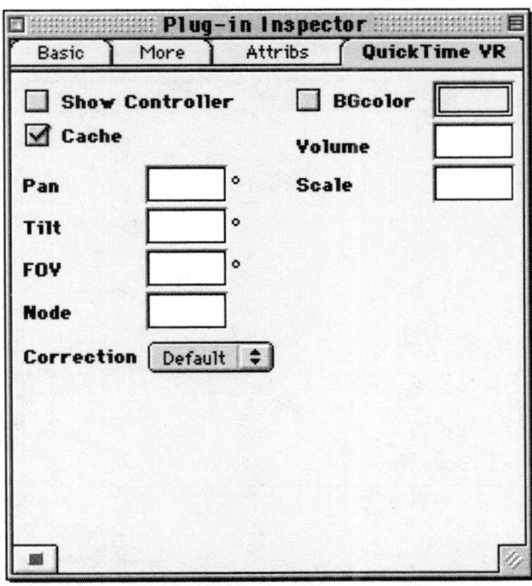

Figure 9.8 The QuickTime VR tab of the Plugin Inspector.

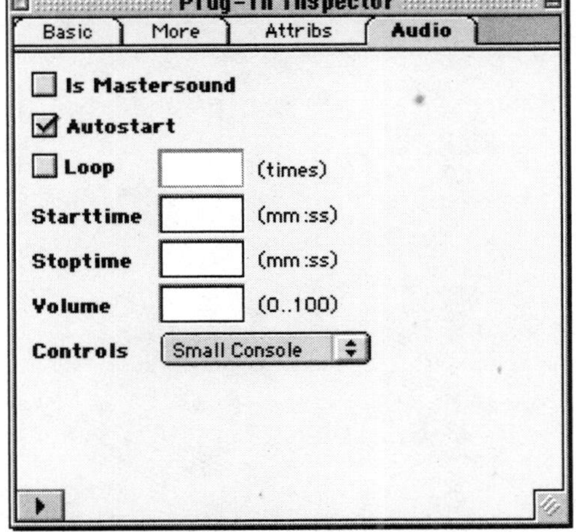

Figure 9.9 The Audio tab of the Plugin Inspector.

To configure a QuickTime VR file:

1. In the Layout View, select the QuickTime VR file that you have already placed.
2. Click the QuickTime VR tab in the Plugin Inspector window (**Figure 9.8**).
3. Click Show Controller to display a QuickTime VR console within the displayed image.
4. Choose the Cache checkbox to tell the browser to cache the movie.
5. Enter a percentage in the Volume box if the VR movie has sound.
6. Scale the movie (as a percent of 100) to resize it onscreen.
7. Enter values (in degrees) in the Pan, Tilt, and FOV fields to change the way a VR image moves when a Web site visitor manipulates it.
8. Choose a Node value.
9. Make a choice from the Correction popup menu to affect the amount of correction applied to the VR movie as it is manipulated.

To configure an audio file:

1. Use the Plugin Palette tool to add an audio file to a Web page.
2. Configure spacing and other attributes in the Plugin Inspector.
3. To configure audio-specific attributes, click the Inspector's Audio tab (**Figure 9.9**).
4. If you plan to call the audio file with a script (supported by Netscape browsers and the LiveAudio plugin), click the Is Mastersound checkbox and give the audio file a name in the More tab.

continues on next page

5. If you do not want the sound to play when the Web page containing it loads in a browser, uncheck AutoStart.
6. To cause the sound to repeat automatically, click loop, and enter the number of repeats in the adjacent field.
7. To specify start and stop times for the audio file, enter them in minutes and seconds in the Starttime and Stoptime fields.
8. Choose a volume level (as a percentage of 100) for playback.
9. Choose how and whether to display a controller for the sound from the Controls menu. A controller, if you choose to display one, can include start, stop, and pause buttons, as well as a volume control.

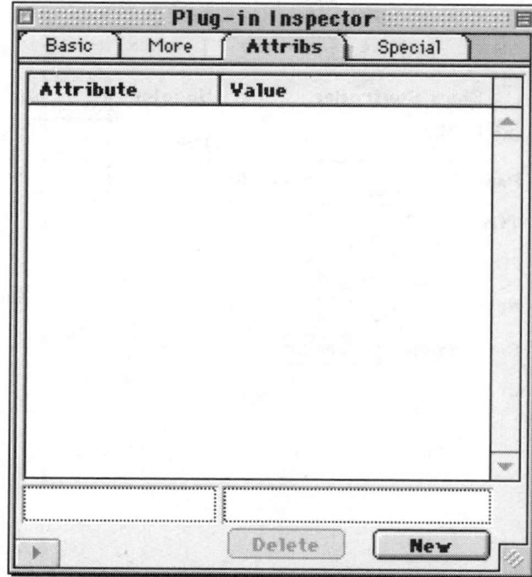

Figure 9.10 The empty Attribs tab of the Plugin Inspector.

Adding plugin attributes manually

Many plugin formats have attributes similar to those specified in the plugin-specific definitions I've described. You can add these attributes manually, using the Plugin Inspector's Attribs tab. The plugin has its own set of attributes, which you will need to know before you can configure it. Attribute information is usually available from the Web site of the company whose plugin file you want to add. In the following example, I will add some of the same attributes we just used to configure an audio file.

To add attributes manually:

1. Select a plugin placeholder pointing to a media file that you have already placed.
2. In the Plugin Inspector window, click on the Attribs tab (**Figure 9.10**).
3. Click the New button to set up a new attribute. A pair of fields appears in the Attribs window. The Attribute field is selected.

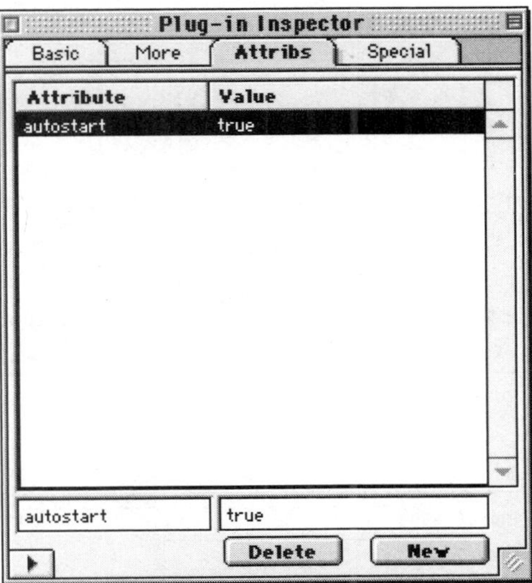

Figure 9.11 The Attribs tab with a new attribute configured.

4. Type **autostart** in the Attribute field and press Tab.
5. Type **true** in the Value field and press Enter. The attribute is complete and it appears in the upper portion of the window (**Figure 9.11**). The new autostart attribute tells a Web browser to play the content associated with this plugin when the page is loaded.
6. Click the New button again.
7. Type **loop** and **three** in the Attributes and Value field, respectively. Adding a loop attribute means that the sound plays continuously. I chose to play it only three times, so as not to annoy the site's visitors. If you had typed **true** instead of **three**, the sound would play continuously.

✔ Tips

- Microsoft's Internet Explorer browser supports a few IE-specific plugin attributes. To learn about these, check out Microsoft's Authors and Developers' site at http://www.microsoft.com/ie/authors/.
- GoLive includes a feature that enables you to create interfaces to new plugins as they become available. Once you create and save the definition for a user-defined interface, the Plugin Inspector's Special tab includes the interface attributes. You will need to study each new plugin's requirements and attributes before you can create these custom interfaces.

Setting plugin preferences

Most Web browsers that support plugin playback allow you not only to use plugins but also to choose which file formats are read by each plugin. Like a Web browser, GoLive uses plugins to play multimedia files. Some of these choices are automatic. Besides movies, the QuickTime 2.0 plugin (the current version at this writing, and the one included with GoLive) supports a variety of sound files that are listed in GoLive's plugin preferences window. GoLive automatically associates a plugin with each file format it knows about, and vice versa. Adjusting plugin preferences in GoLive does not affect plugin viewing in a user's browser.

You can change these relationships if you would rather use different plugins to play files of a given format. You can also tell GoLive not to play the media files at all, if you choose.

To change plugin/media relationships:

1. Choose Preferences from the Edit menu.
2. Click the Plugin Preferences icon. Scroll through the window to find it, if necessary. The Plugin Preferences panel **(Figure 9.12)** shows media formats, the plugin used to play them, and the file extension associated with each format.
3. Select a media type from the list. Editable fields light up in the lower portion of the window (**Figure 9.13**). You can edit the media type, subtype, and extension; delete the selected item; or create a new one. If the media type you chose can be read by multiple installed plugins, the plugin menu will include several options.
4. Leave the Play/Don't Play menu alone so that file files can play when you open a Web page that contains them.

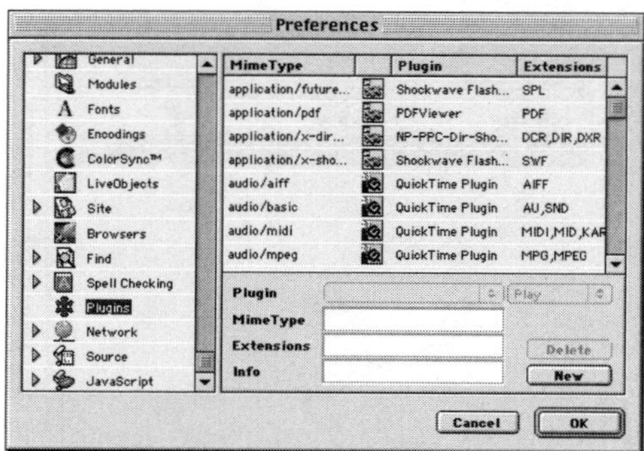

Figure 9.12 The Plugin Preferences window.

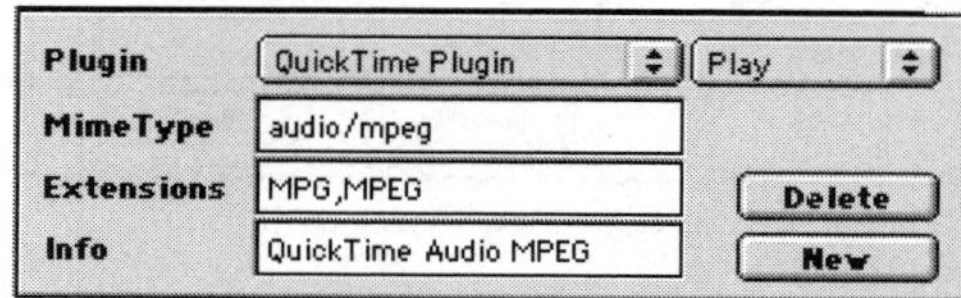

Figure 9.13 View or edit a media type by selecting it in the Plugin Preferences window.

✔ Tips

- All the formats listed in the Plugin Preferences window were entered there automatically by the plugins stored in the GoLive Plugins folder. To use a plugin with GoLive, you either need to store a plugin or its alias there.
- You can use the Plugin Preferences window to create entries for new media formats, but that is usually not necessary. When you add a new plugin to the Plugins folder and launch GoLive, the plugin software registers the media formats it supports and displays them under Plugin Preferences.
- The Plugin popup menu in the Preferences window is a good way to remember which plugins support which formats. When you select a format and click on the menu, only those plugins that support the format you've selected are available.
- The QuickTime plugin supports a large number of audio and video formats. You may be able to reduce the number of different plugins you use by selecting QuickTime whenever it is available.

QuickTime Authoring

The built-in QuickTime movie editor makes it possible to edit movies and add effects to them within GoLive. When you're finished creating your movie masterpiece, you can prepare it for the Web with GoLive, as described in the previous section, and upload it to a Web server along with your HTML documents.

QuickTime authoring tools

GoLive's QuickTime authoring tools are the Movie Viewer and the Track Editor. The viewer allows you to play and control movies, while the Track Editor controls the tracks and sequencing that comprise the movie. The Palette's QuickTime tab includes tools that allow you to add tracks and effects to the Track Editor. Finally, like most other GoLive elements, you will use the Inspector to configure movies and their components. **Figure 9.14** shows the elements of the movie-editing interface.

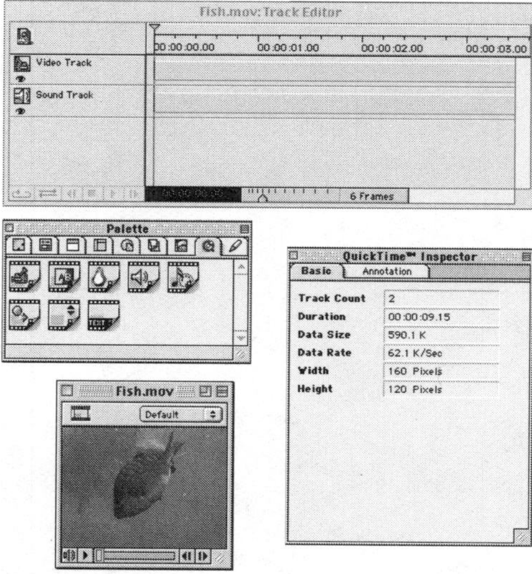

Figure 9.14 GoLive's QuickTime editing tools include the Track Editor, QuickTime Inspector, and QuickTime Palette tab.

Opening and editing QuickTime movies

You can open a QuickTime movie that you have already placed within a GoLive document or you can simply open the movie by itself. You can also create a new QuickTime movie file and add tracks and effects to it to complete the movie. Though you can view placeholders for and play movies within the document window, you need to open them in the Movie Viewer to edit them.

To open a previously placed QuickTime movie:

1. Open a document containing a movie and select the movie.

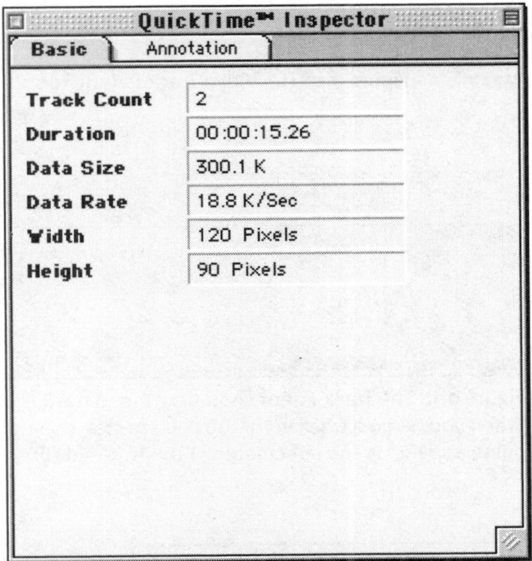

Figure 9.15 The QuickTime Inspector displays specifications for the selected movie.

Figure 9.16 Click the button to view the QuickTime Track Editor.

2. Double-click the movie to open it in the Movie Viewer

   or

   Select the movie, click on the QuickTime tab in the Plugin Inspector, and click Open Movie. The movie opens in the Movie Viewer, and the QuickTime Inspector (**Figure 9.15**) appears.

To open a new QuickTime movie:

1. Under the File menu, choose New Special:New QuickTime Movie.
2. In the navigation dialog that appears, name the movie. Be sure to leave the .mov suffix intact. An empty movie window appears.
3. Add content (tracks) to the movie by pasting or importing them into the Movie Viewer window.
4. To view the Track Editor, click the Open Track Editor button (**Figure 9.16**).

To copy content from another movie:

1. In GoLive, open the movie from which you want to copy a track.
2. Open the Track Editor.
3. Click on the track you want to copy, to select it.
4. Choose Edit:Copy, Command-C (Mac), or Control-C (Windows) to copy the track.
5. Open the movie to which you want to add the copied track, and then open its Track Editor.
6. Paste the track by typing Command-V (Mac) or Control-V (Windows) into the track editor.
7. Use the Track Inspector to configure the new track, or integrate it into the existing movie, if necessary.

QuickTime tracks

QuickTime movies are composed of one or more *tracks* of information. The most basic type is the video track. You can also add sound or music tracks, as well as several types of effects tracks that filter, distort, enhance, or otherwise manipulate other tracks. Text tracks allow you to attach a URL or titles to a movie.

Track types supported by GoLive are:

- Video tracks.
- Audio tracks.
- Effects tracks.
- Sprite tracks.
- HREF tracks.
- Chapter tracks.
- Text tracks.

Video tracks

Just as you might imagine, a video track contains moving video images. You can work with the video track of existing movie or import frames and complete tracks from other movies.

To import and configure a video track:

1. Open a new movie in the Movie Viewer and then open the Track Editor.
2. Drag the Video Track tool (**Figure 9.17**) into the Track Editor window. A selection dialog appears.
3. Locate and select a movie. The new video track appears in the Track Editor **(Figure 9.18**), the first frame appears in the Movie Viewer window, and the Video Track Inspector **(Figure 9.19)** appears.

Figure 9.17 The Video Track Palette tool

Figure 9.18 The Track Editor contains a video track. When you name a track in the Track Inspector, the name appears in the left column of the Track Editor.

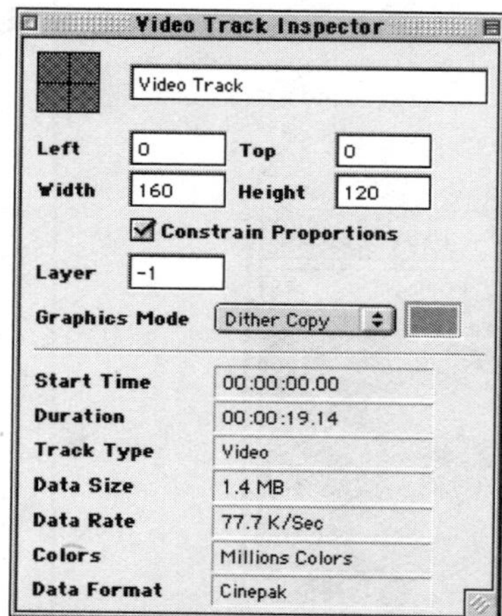

Figure 9.19 The Video Track Inspector.

4. In the Inspector, give the new track a name.
5. To change the location of the track within the movie frame, type pixel values in the Left and Top fields.
6. To change the track's display size, type new pixel values in the Width and Height fields. Leave the Constrain Properties box checked so that the movie will resize proportionally when you change the width or height value.
7. You can choose a layer for the track, giving it priority or subordinating it to other tracks. The lower the number you choose, the closer to the front of the movie the track appears.
8. Choose an option from the Graphic Mode popup menu if you want GoLive to do something other than dither the video image so that it looks better in a Web browser. Dithering attempts to compensate for differences in browser display characteristics. I'll have more to say about the Graphics Mode options in the Inspector when I explain effects in subsequent sections of this chapter.

Video effects tracks

QuickTime video effects allow you to animate movies, create transitions, and otherwise enhance the look of the video image. GoLive supports a variety of effects, all of which can be added and configured with an effects track in the Track Editor. *Filter effects* are applied to the video track as a whole, and they change the appearance of the complete image. *Transition effects* bridge the gap between two video tracks, creating a visual effect that starts as one track ends and the next begins. *Generic effects* do not depend upon the presence of video tracks. Filter tracks are referred to as single-source tracks, because they apply to a single video track. Transition tracks are dual-source—they link multiple tracks. **Table 9.1** lists all of GoLive's video effects.

Figure 9.20 The Filter Track Palette tool.

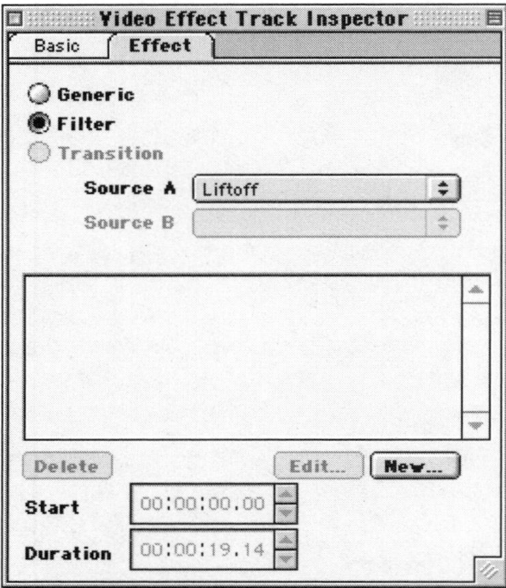

Figure 9.21 The Video Effect Track Inspector.

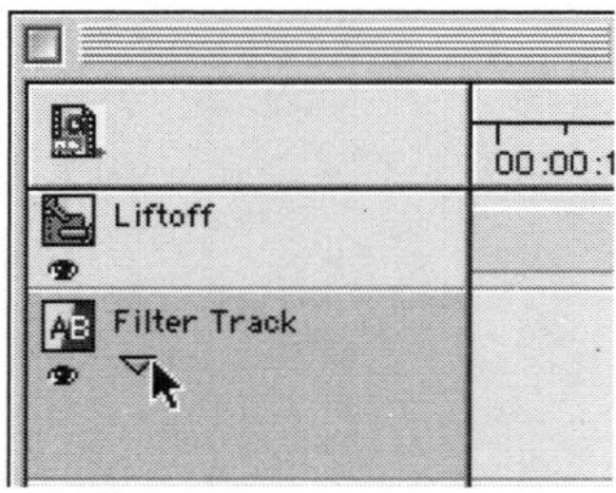

Figure 9.22 Before you add effects to a new track, click the triangle below the name of a new effects track in the Track Editor.

Adding a filter effect:

1. Open a movie in the Movie Viewer, and then the Track Editor.
2. Drag the Filter Track tool (**Figure 9.20**) from the QuickTime tab of the Palette to the Track Editor. The new track is inserted, and the Video Effect Track Inspector (**Figure 9.21**) appears, with the Effect tab showing. Note that the Filter radio button is selected, indicating that you're creating a filter effect.
3. In the Track Editor, click the triangle immediately below the label for the Video Effect track you just added, as shown in **Figure 9.22**.
4. Click the Basic tab in the Inspector, to view positioning and sizing options. Name the filter track. Like the Video Track Inspector, the Basic Tab here includes options for positioning, sizing, and displaying the filter track. In general, these options should match the ones that are

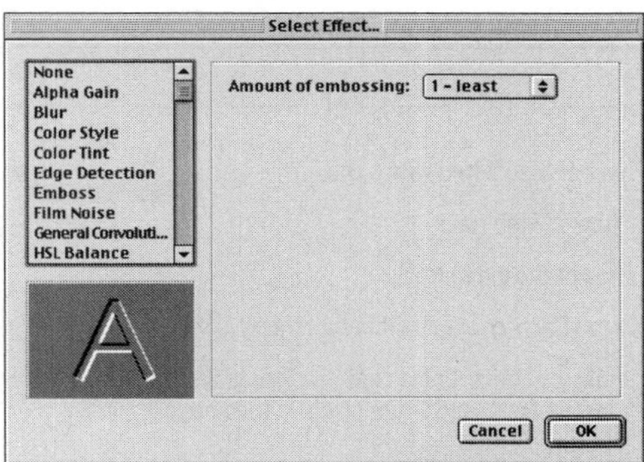

Figure 9.23 Choose an effect from the list, view the preview at left, and configure the new effect.

applied to the video track related to this effect. These values should be entered by default, if the movie already contains a video track.

5. Return to the Effect tab of the Inspector by clicking it.
6. If your movie contains multiple video tracks, select one from the Source A popup menu. If you have only one video track, it's already selected.
7. Click the New button to add a new effect. A dialog box presents your options.
8. Choose an effect from the list at left. GoLive applies your choice to the sample image in the dialog, and displays controls for the effect (**Figure 9.23**).
9. Adjust the effect using the controls.
10. Click OK to finish the effect. Its listing appears in the Video Track Effect Inspector and in the Track Editor.
11. Add additional effects by repeating steps 7-10.

Table 9.1

Video Effects in GoLive

Effect Type	Effect Name	Description
Filter	Alpha Gain	Controls the alpha channel associated with a track.
	Blur	Blurs the image on a single video track.
	Brightness/Contrast	Controls the illumination of the video track.
	Color Style	Allows two color change effects to exist within one track.
	Color Tint	Creates a two-color image by converting a color track to grayscale, then substituting one color each for the black and white pixels in the image.
	Edge Detection	Adds an edge to shapes within an image.
	Emboss	Causes image surfaces to appear raised (in relief).
	Film Noise	Simulates the hairs and scratches that are visible in aged or distressed film.
	General Convolution	Provides access to the pixel grid by assigning values to each pixel in a 3x3 matrix.
	HSL Balance	Adjusts the hue, saturation, and lightness channels of a single track.
	Lens Flare	Adds colored highlights, as if there were a solar flare.
	RGB Balance	Adjusts the red, green, and blue channels of a single track.
	Sharpen	Applies sharpness to an image at one of seven levels.
Transition Effects	Alpha Compositor	Blends two tracks at the alpha channel level.
	Chroma Key	Replaces pixels of a specified key color within the first track with a specified color with corresponding pixels from the second track, allowing the second track to show through.
	Cross Fade	Dissolves one track into another with an alpha channel blend.
	Explode	Causes the second track to appear from a central point within the first track, gradually increasing in size until it replaces the first track.
	Gradient Wipe	Imposes an image over the first track, then wipes it away to reveal the second track.
	Implode	The first track collapses to a central point, revealing the second track.
	Iris	Creates a cut-out over the first track, in which the second track appears.
	Matrix Wipe	Splits the first track with a wipe pattern, revealing the second track.
	Push	The second track moves onto the screen as the first track is pushed out of view.
	Radial	Second track rotates into view as the effect moves around the first track in a clock-like pattern.
	Slide	The second track moves over the first track, covering it as it proceeds.
	Wipe	Like a slide effect, a wipe can cover one track with another. Other options allow you to change the angle and direction of the wipe.
	Zoom	One track (you choose which one) zooms into the other one.
Generic	Cloud	Applies a fluffy, cloud-like structure, which rotates within the movie.
	Fire	Adds a bonfire across the bottom of the movie.
	Ripple	Creates a rippling water effect.

Generic video effects

Unlike filters and transitions, generic effects do not depend upon the presence of a video track within the movie. You add generic effects just as you do filter tracks. Adding and opening an effect with the Filter Effect tool will display the Video Effects Track Inspector with the Generic option selected. There are three generic effects available: fire, cloud, and ripple.

Sprite tracks

Like video tracks, sprite tracks contain images that form movies. But instead of continuous video, sprite tracks consist of images, sequenced and animated, to create the effect of movement. A sprite is typically a static image that moves through a movie in a certain way.

Creating sprites requires several steps: first, you need to create the sprite track within a movie. Next, you must import graphics into an image gallery, from which you will draw when you create and animate individual sprites.

Sound and music tracks

GoLive supports most common audio types, including AIFF, WAV, Mac OS system sounds, and MIDI. All but MIDI are imported as a sound track, while MIDI files are imported as music tracks. The process of adding and setting up sound and music tracks is identical.

✔ Tips

- Ⓜ You can add tracks from audio CDs into QuickTime movies using the QuickTime Player, or you can use MoviePlayer to convert them to a usable format. Insert an audio CD and then open a track in QuickTime Player. Name the track and save it to your hard disk. Finally, add the CD track as a sound track in GoLive's QuickTime movie editing interface.

- Remember to observe copyright laws when you copy CD audio tracks. If the audio CD contains copyrighted material and you don't own it, distributing the audio material with your movie on the Web is illegal.

HREF tracks

HREF tracks are among the most often-used track types, and GoLive is an elegant way to add them. An HREF track embeds a URL within a movie. The URL can be activated automatically when the movie plays or with user input, such as a click. The HREF's contents appear in the movie window as it plays.

To add an HREF track:

1. With a movie open and the Track Editor visible, drag the HREF Track tool (**Figure 9.24**) from the Palette's QuickTime tab to the Track Editor. The HREF Track Inspector (**Figure 9.25**) appears.
2. Name the HREF track in the Basic tab of the HREF Track Inspector.
3. Click the "eye" icon in the Track Editor to make the HREF track invisible (**Figure 9.26**).
4. Choose left and top coordinates for the HREF track. The track will look best at the top or bottom of the movie, where its text will not obstruct the video track. To position the HREF track above the movie, leave the top dimension at zero. To position the HREF track below the movie, position it one pixel below the video track. You can locate the video track's dimensions by clicking on it in the Track Editor and noting the dimensions in the Inspector.
5. Choose width and height measurements for the track. These measurements define the visible box that surrounds the HREF text.

Figure 9.24 The HREF Track Palette tool.

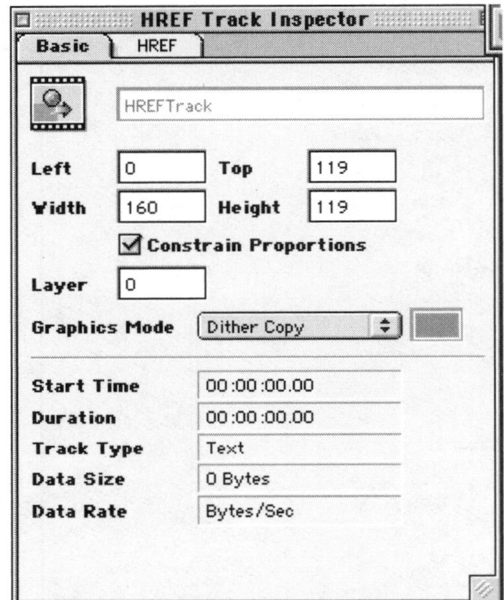

Figure 9.25 The HREF Track Inspector's Basic tab.

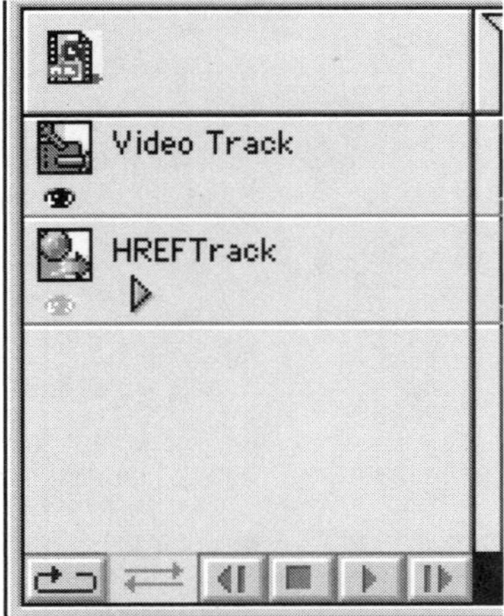

Figure 9.26 Click the "eye" icon to make an HREF track invisible. If you see the eye in the Track Editor, the track will appear over the video track.

QuickTime Authoring

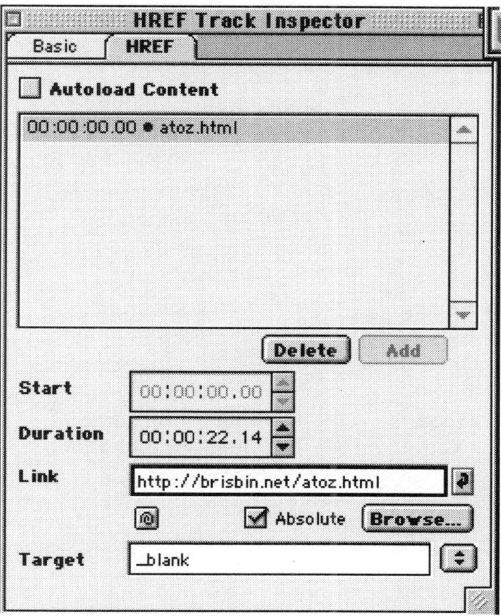

Figure 9.27 The HREF Inspector's HREF tab, with one new HREF segment visible.

6. Click the HREF tab in the Inspector.
7. Enter the URL for the HREF track or use Point & Shoot to locate a file or URL within a GoLive site.
8. Choose a target from the popup menu to control where (new window, new frame, etc.) the track's URL will be displayed.
9. Click Add to create an HREF track segment. A new item appears in the Inspector (**Figure 9.27**). With only one segment in place, the HREF track will appear throughout the movie.
10. With the new segment selected, adjust the duration of the track using the up and down arrows next to the Duration field.
11. To adjust the start time of the track, click and drag the HREF track within the Track Editor window. To time its start more precisely, use the up and down arrows near the start field after you have selected the track in the Track Editor.

✔ Tips

- If your HREF track links to a file within your site using a relative URL, be sure to click the Absolute checkbox in the HREF Track Inspector's HREF tab to display the full URL to visitors. Check the URL to be sure that it displays correctly.
- The width and height of an HREF track are related. If you change one dimension, the other adjusts proportionally. The best way to achieve the correct balance is trial and error, keeping one eye on the Movie Viewer window as you adjust the HREF track's dimensions.

Chapter tracks

Like HREF tracks, chapter tracks are text additions to QuickTime movies. Chapter tracks provide a way to segment movies for users, who can choose "chapters" from a popup menu at the bottom of the movie frame. Creating and configuring chapter tracks is almost identical to building an HREF track.

Text tracks

Text tracks add text to a movie window. From a configuration point of view, a text track is a hybrid of the HREF and chapter tracks. Like an HREF track, the position of a text track must be carefully set, so that the text track is visible above or below the movie image. Like a chapter track, a text track can consist of multiple segments, timed to replace one another as the movie plays.

JavaScript

Netscape originally created JavaScript as a scripting language to enhance Web pages. JavaScript can be used to give life to a Web page with moving banners, animation, and other decorative touches. JavaScript can also be used to give instructions to Java applets or link multiple applets together.

The most common and powerful use of JavaScript these days is the manipulation of HTML pages and elements with scripted *actions*. Actions can create image effects or invoke dynamic HTML (DHTML) functions. Unlike Java, JavaScripts are composed of code within your Web page or stored with it. Java applets are actually programs that are downloaded to and run on a Web browser.

GoLive provides tools that allow you to embed JavaScripts within a document, and it includes tools that allow you to create and edit scripts yourself.

✔ Tip

- In this section, I introduce you to GoLive's JavaScript editing tools. To use them effectively, you'll need to learn JavaScript's language and syntax. This level of detail is beyond the scope of this book. Fortunately, there are plenty of good JavaScript resources available, both in print and online. Start with *JavaScript for the World Wide Web: Visual QuickStart Guide*, by Tom Negrino and Dori Smith. On the Web, check out Netscape's JavaScript documentation at http://developer.netscape.com/docs/manuals/javascript.html.

To add an existing JavaScript to a Web page:

1. Open a GoLive document to the Layout View.
2. Double-click, or drag the JavaScript tool (**Figure 9.28**) from the Palette to the document window. A JavaScript placeholder and the Body Script Inspector (**Figure 9.29**) appear.
3. Name the script.
4. Choose a language (based on the target browser you want to support) from the Language popup menu. GoLive enters a JavaScript dialect to match your choice in the dialect field.
5. Click the Source checkbox to activate the Reference field and Browse button.
6. Point & Shoot to locate a JavaScript.

Figure 9.28 The JavaScript Palette tool.

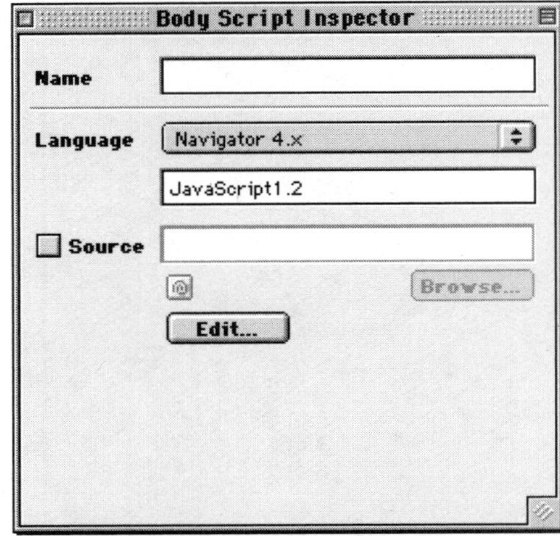

Figure 9.29 The Body Script Inspector configures JavaScripts.

✔ Tips

- To ensure the highest possible browser compatibility for your JavaScript, choose an older browser version from the Language popup menu in the Body Script Inspector. The tradeoff, of course, is that older browsers and script dialects don't include all of the features of newer offerings. At this writing, I recommend choosing Navigator 3.x (JavaScript1.1) if you want to be conservative. Use Netscape 4.x if you want to use the most advanced JavaScript features.
- If you want to use a later version of JavaScript, consider creating a page that supports older browsers or doesn't use JavaScript at all as an alternative for older browsers. You can implement this either by detecting the user's browser (with a DHTML browser switch action) or simply by asking the user to click to reach a non-JavaScript page.

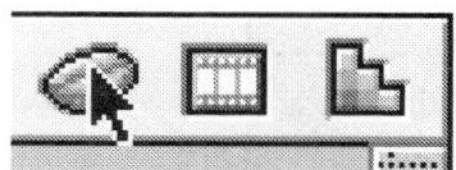

Figure 9.30 Open the JavaScript Editor by clicking the Java Bean at the upper right corner of the document window.

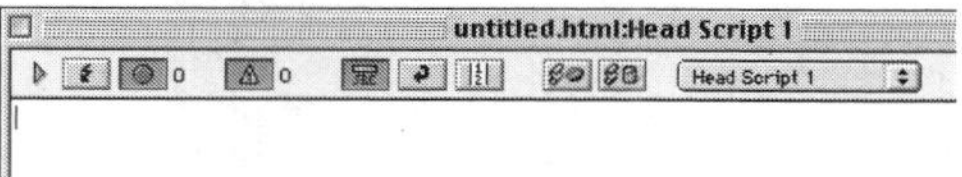

Figure 9.31 The JavaScript Editor is a text editor that includes controls for managing and checking JavaScripts.

Figure 9.32 Start building a script by clicking the New Script button on the JavaScript Editor toolbar.

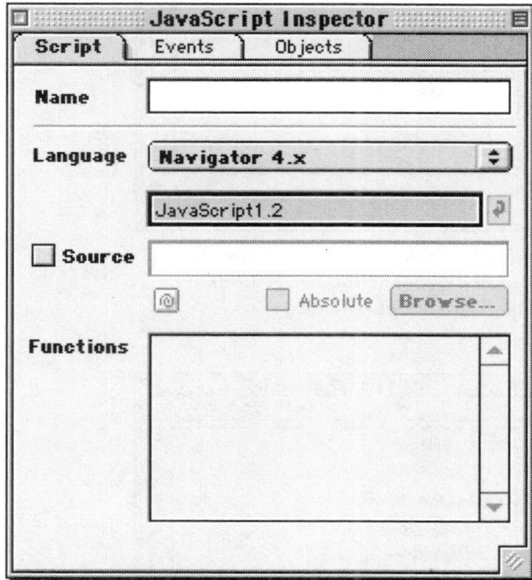

Figure 9.33 Configure a new script in the JavaScript Inspector window.

Creating JavaScripts

GoLive includes a full-fledge JavaScript editor, where you can write your own scripts. The editor includes a variety of drag-and-drop tools and selectors for creating the script.

There are three ways to reach the JavaScript editor:

- Drag the JavaScript item from the Palette to the document window and double-click the placeholder.
- With a JavaScript item selected in the document window, click the Edit button in the Body Script Inspector.
- Click the Java Bean icon in the document window. Lest you get confused, the Java Bean button opens the JavaScript editor. It *does not* add a Java applet to your page.

I'll use the Java Bean.

To begin a JavaScript:

1. Click on the Java Bean, near the upper-right corner of the document window (**Figure 9.30**). The JavaScript Editor (**Figure 9.31**) and JavaScript Inspector appear.
2. Click the New Script Item on the toolbar in the JavaScript Editor (**Figure 9.32**).
3. In the JavaScript Inspector (**Figure 9.33**), name the script and choose a language, as described in the previous section. When you do, the JavaScript version supported by the chosen browser appears in the field below the popup menu.
4. Type a script in the Script Editor window.

The JavaScript Inspector window contains events and objects you can use in your JavaScripts. By dragging these items into the script window, you can assemble a JavaScript without having to type the whole script. You will need to enter the script's variables, however.

To add script items with the JavaScript Inspector:

1. In the document window, create a hyperlink.
2. Open the JavaScript Editor window.
3. Click the Events tab of the JavaScript Inspector (**Figure 9.34**). The tab lists items (windows and documents) that can support events. Under each heading are the events themselves.
4. Click the triangle (Mac) or plus sign (Windows) next to the Document item.
5. Locate the event that corresponds to the hyperlink you created earlier, and drag it into the Script Editor window.
6. Click the Objects tab of the JavaScript Inspector (**Figure 9.35**). Window, Document, and Other objects are available for inclusion in JavaScripts.
7. Expand the headings to view subcategories and then individual objects.
8. Click on an object in the window. It is highlighted, and a description appears at the bottom of the Inspector window (**Figure 9.36**).
9. To add events and objects to your script, drag and drop individual items into the JavaScript editor window.
10. Add HTML code or variables to the script.
11. When you've finished adding items, save the script.
12. View the HTML page on which the script appears, using a JavaScript-capable Web browser. You can't preview JavaScripts within GoLive's preview window.

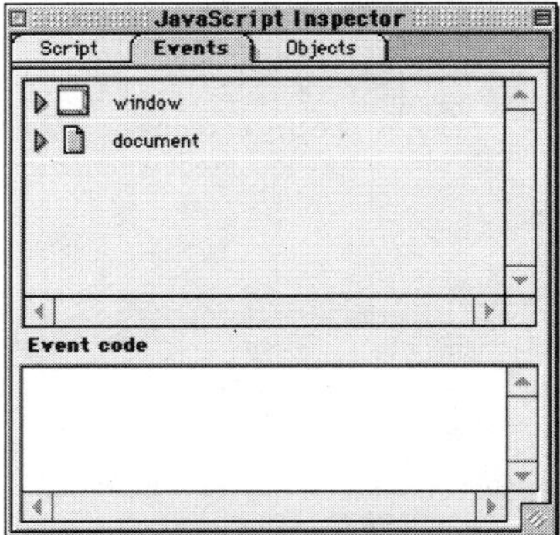

Figure 9.34 Add events to JavaScripts by dragging them from the Events tab of the JavaScript Inspector.

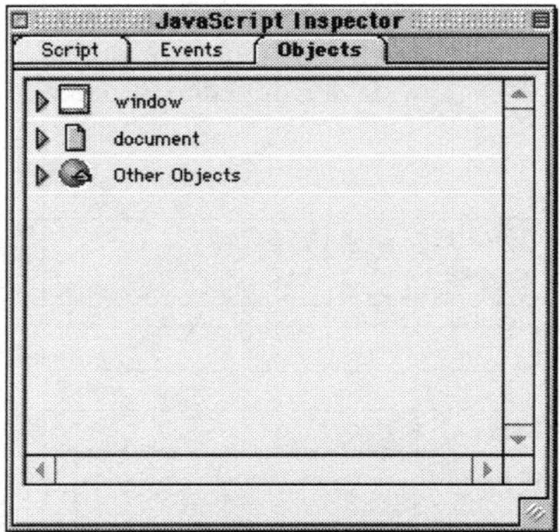

Figure 9.35 Drag items from the Objects tab of the JavaScript Inspector to add them to a script.

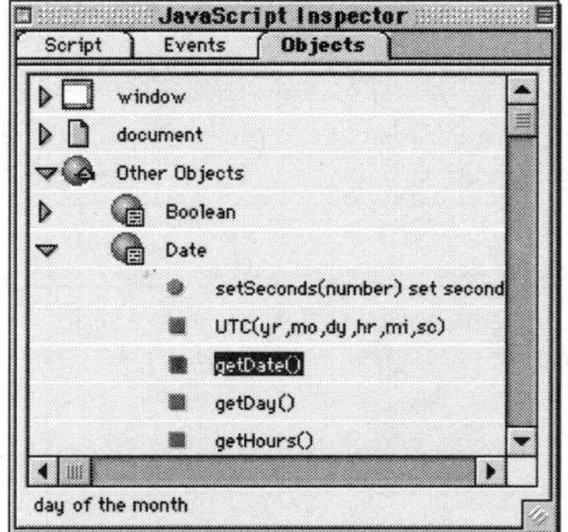

Figure 9.36 When you select a JavaScript object or heading in the Inspector, a description appears at the bottom of the window.

JAVASCRIPT

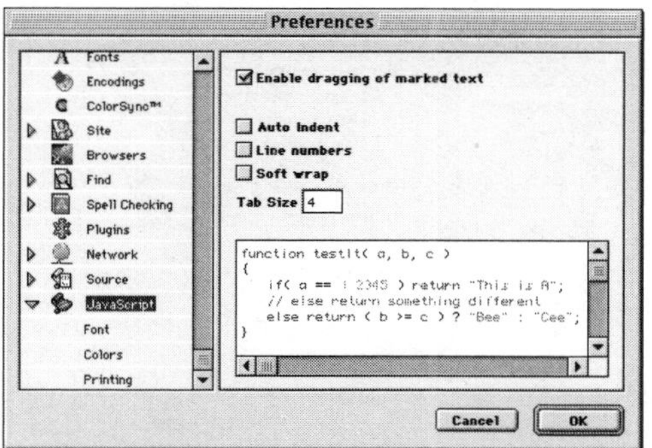

Figure 9.37 JavaScript preferences are organized under the JavaScript tab. General preferences allow you to customize the appearance of text in the JavaScript Editor.

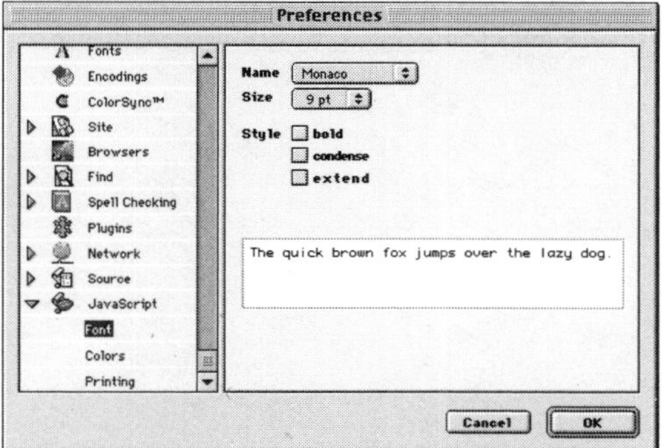

Figure 9.38 Choose type options for the JavaScript Editor in the JavaScript Font Preferences window.

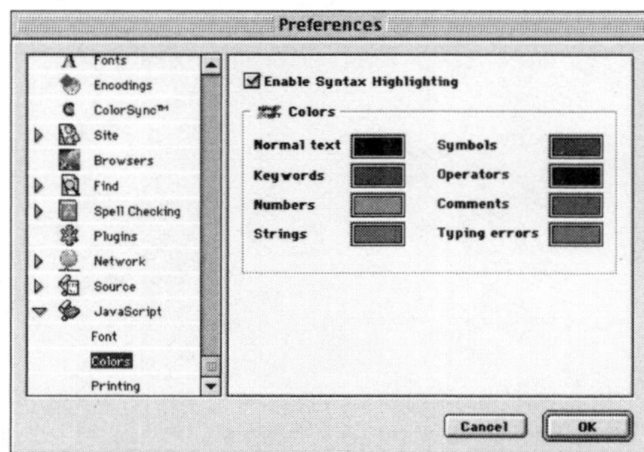

Figure 9.39 Apply custom colors to different code types in the JavaScript Color Preferences window.

To set general JavaScript preferences:

1. Choose Preferences from the Edit menu.
2. Click the JavaScript item. Scroll through the window to find it, if necessary. JavaScript preferences appear in (**Figure 9.37**).
3. Leave the "Enable dragging of marked text" box checked to support drag-and-drop within the Script Editor.
4. Leave "Auto-Indenting" checked if you want lower-level tags indented by default.
5. Check "Soft Wrap" to cause JavaScript code to wrap to subsequent lines.

To set JavaScript font preferences:

1. Click the triangle (Mac) or plus sign (Windows) to the left of the JavaScript item to reveal more preferences.
2. Click the Font item in the JavaScript Preferences window (**Figure 9.38**).
3. Choose a typeface, size, and style. Your choices affect the fonts in the JavaScript Editor only.

To set JavaScript color preferences:

1. Click the Colors label in the JavaScript Preferences window (**Figure 9.39**).
2. Leave the "Syntax Highlighting" box checked to use colors to highlight elements and errors in your scripts.
3. Click a color field to apply color to a specific type of script code. A color panel appears.
4. Choose a color and click OK to apply it.

To set JavaScript printing preferences:

1. Click the Printing item under the JavaScript Preferences label (**Figure 9.40**).
2. Click "Printer specific settings" to light up several choices that relate to display of items when you print scripts.
3. Click "Use special font for printing" to choose font, style, and size options.

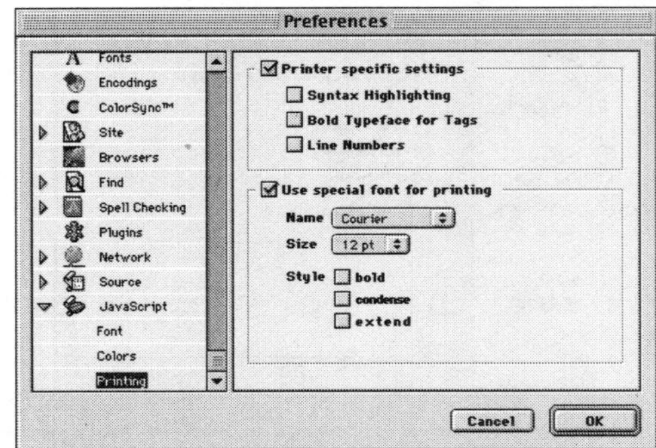

Figure 9.40 Choose printing options under the Printing Preference option.

Checking a script for errors

With JavaScript color preferences set, you can use colors to display syntax and errors within a script.

Figure 9.41 Click the Check Syntax button on the JavaScript Editor toolbar to locate errors within the current script.

To check a script:

1. With a script visible in the JavaScript Editor, click the Syntax Highlighting button on the toolbar (**Figure 9.41**). GoLive highlights any syntax errors found within your script.
2. Click the Display Errors button and/or the Display Warnings button to list the number of errors in your script.
3. If errors in your script were highlighted, click the triangle next to the Syntax Highlighting button to view errors in a pane of their own. When you correct the errors, they are removed from the panel.

Figure 9.42 The Java Applet Palette tool.

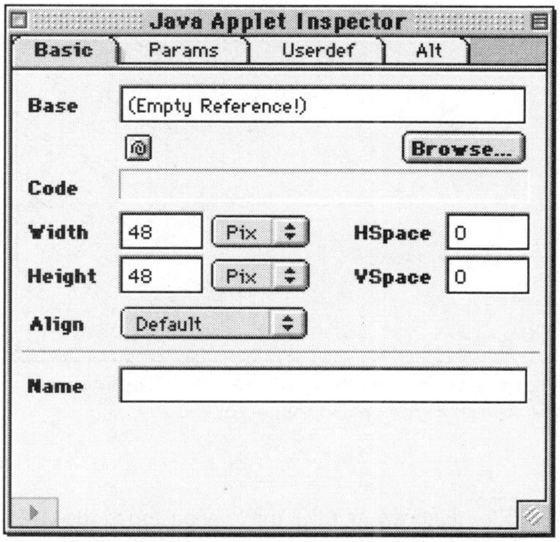

Figure 9.43 Name and save the applet in the Java Applet Inspector.

Java Applets

Despite the similarity of their names, JavaScripts and Java applets are not the same thing at all. As I pointed out earlier, JavaScripts are usually fairly simple pieces of code that are embedded in a Web page's HTML code. Java applets, on the other hand, are complete programs, written in the Java language, that are called by and may even appear within a Web page but are not part of that page. Java applets can be database interfaces, games, or any number of other applications.

You don't write Java applets in GoLive. For that, you'll need Java development tools and enough knowledge of the Java language to create applets. You connect existing applets to GoLive pages, specifying the appearance of the applet primarily within the applet itself. HTML (and GoLive) allows you to specify basic size, spacing, and alignment options, but the rest is up to the applet developer. You can preview applets in GoLive because, like newer Web browsers, GoLive supports Java.

To add a Java applet to a document:

1. Open a GoLive document.
2. Double-click or drag the Java Applet tool (**Figure 9.42**) from the Palette to the document window. The Java Applet Inspector appears (**Figure 9.43**).
3. Use the browse button or Point & Shoot to locate a Java applet. The applet's location (Base) and Code appear in the Inspector window.
4. Resize the applet if you like, either by dragging the placeholder's handles in the document window or by typing new dimensions in the Inspector's Width and Height fields (in pixels).

5. If the applet is not on a layout grid or if it is within a text frame, you can add horizontal and vertical space between the applet and adjacent text with the Hspace and Vspace fields. You can also use the Align popup menu to align the applet to adjacent text.
6. Name the applet by typing a unique name (one that's not being used by any other applet on the page) in the Name field.
7. To add alternative text or HTML that will be displayed by browsers that support Java but whose Java option is disabled, click on the Alt tab of the Java Applet Inspector (**Figure 9.44**).
8. Type the alternative text in the Alt Text field.
9. If you want to display an HTML object in browsers that do not support Java, click the "Show Alternative HTML" box.
10. Return to the document window and click on the Java applet placeholder. Drag the Palette tool of your choice into the placeholder and configure the HTML object (text, image, plugin, etc.) you want to appear when Java is unavailable.

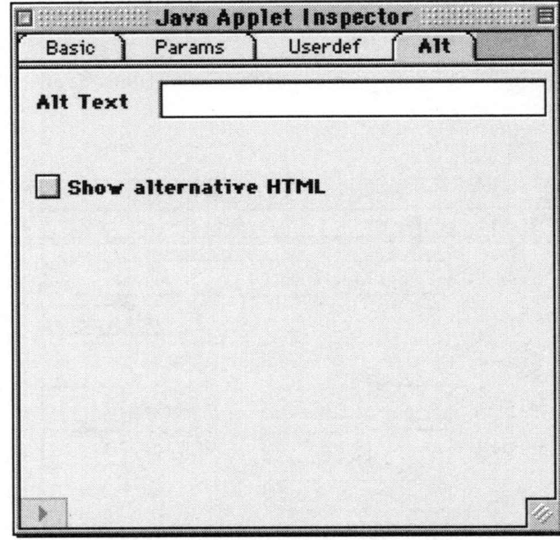

Figure 9.44 Create alternative text or HTML links in the Alt tab of the applet Inspector.

Figure 9.45 Click the Play button in the Java Applet Inspector to preview the applet within GoLive.

✔ Tip

- You can view the contents and action of a Java applet in two ways: click the Play button in the Java Applet Inspector (**Figure 9.45**) or view your document with the Preview View.

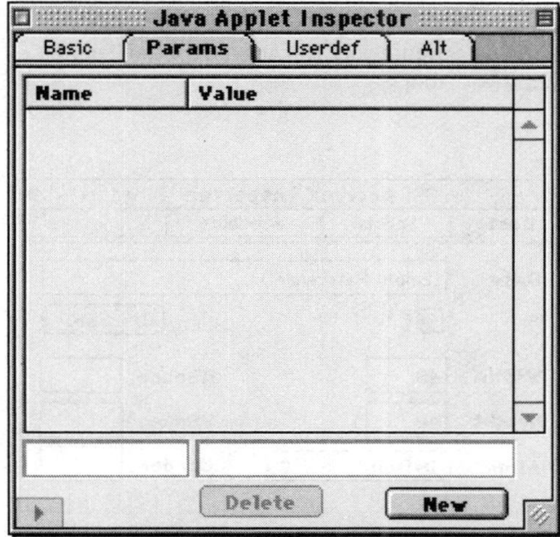

Figure 9.46 Add parameters under the Params tab of the Java Applet Inspector.

To add Java parameters:

1. Select a Java applet in the document window.
2. In the Java Applet Inspector, click the Params tab. The Params window appears (**Figure 9.46**). Parameters are applet-specific attributes.
3. Click New to set up a new parameter.
4. Type the name of the parameter in the Param field when it appears. Press Tab.
5. Type a value for the parameter in the value field. Press Return to confirm your entry. The new parameter appears in the window above.

ActiveX

Microsoft's ActiveX is often thought of as an alternative to Sun's Java language, as an improvement on current plugin technology, and as a way to add interactivity to Web sites. Unlike Java, ActiveX is not platform-independent. It's a proprietary technology that is supported primarily by Windows versions of the Internet Explorer browser.

You can add ActiveX *controls*—the equivalent of plugins, or applets—to a Web page in all versions of GoLive, but you won't be able to view them in the Mac version. GoLive's Windows version includes more ActiveX configuration options than the Mac offering. On the Mac, you can link to a control, but that's about all.

✔ Tip

- If the ActiveX control tool doesn't appear in the Palette's Basic tab, make sure that the ID module is active. To do this, choose Edit:Preferences, click the Modules label, and scroll to the IE module.

To add an ActiveX control to a Web page:

1. With a document open in the Layout View, double-click, or drag the ActiveX Control tool (**Figure 9.47**) from the Palette to the document window. The ActiveX Inspector appears in the Inspector window (**Figure 9.48**).
2. Locate an ActiveX control on your hard disk with the Browse button or Point & Shoot. The control's location (Base) appears in the Inspector window.

Figure 9.47 The ActiveX control Palette tool.

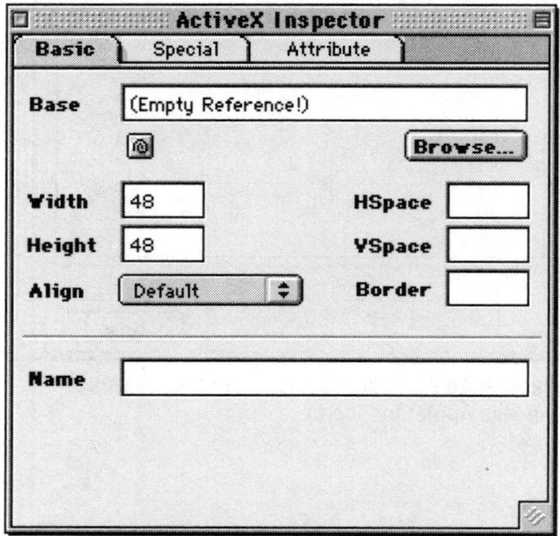

Figure 9.48 The ActiveX Inspector.

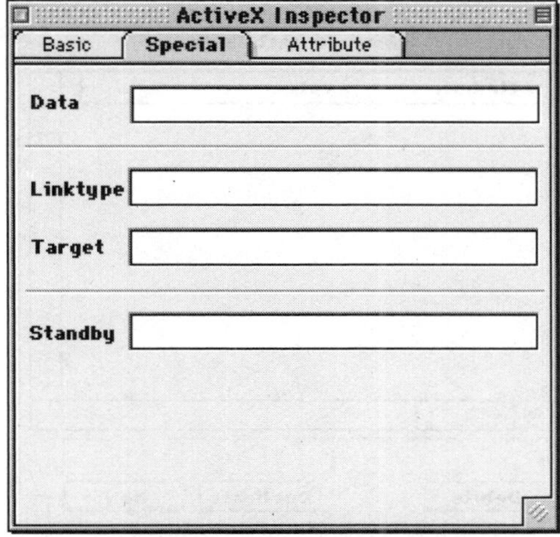

Figure 9.49 Link the ActiveX control in the Special tab of the ActiveX Inspector.

3. Resize the control if you want, either by dragging the placeholder's handles in the document window or by typing new dimensions in the Inspector's Width and Height fields.
4. If the control is not on a layout grid, or if it is within a text frame, you can add horizontal and vertical space between the control and adjacent text with the Hspace and Vspace fields. You can also use the Align popup menu to align the control to adjacent text.
5. Name the control by typing a unique name (one that isn't being used by any other control on that page) in the Name field.
6. Click the Special tab in the ActiveX Control Inspector window (**Figure 9.49**).
7. In the Data field, enter the URL for a resource to be used when the ActiveX is activated. Press Tab.
8. In the Linktype field, type the link that the control should use to transfer data to the target location. Press Tab.
9. The Target is the page where ActiveX control data will appear. Type the name of the file or application to receive ActiveX control data. Press Tab.
10. Type a message in the Standby field if you want a message to appear on the page as the ActiveX control loads.

To add ActiveX attributes:

1. With an ActiveX control selected, click the Attribute tab in the ActiveX Inspector to display the Attributes window (**Figure 9.50**).
2. To create a new attribute, click New.
3. Type the attribute's name in the Name field and press Tab.
4. Type a default value for the attribute in the Value field. Press Return to confirm the attribute.
5. Repeat steps 2–4 to add additional attributes.

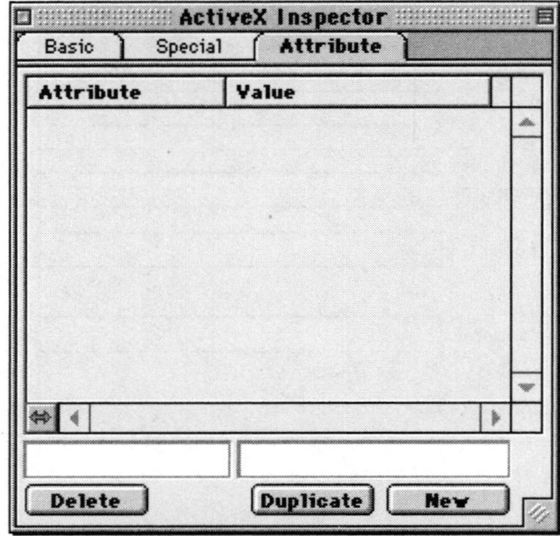

Figure 9.50 The Attribute tab of the ActiveX Inspector.

10

Advanced Layout with DHTML

HTML can be frustrating for those who want to place text or images precisely on a page, complete with pixel measurements and unchangeable relationships between one element and another. The language's latest evolution makes it possible to control positioning of Web page content much more precisely than traditional HTML allows.

It's all done with DHTML (Dynamic HTML). DHTML is an extension to HTML that makes it possible to animate, position, and layer content on a page, creating a variety of effects as well as offering flexible layout options.

In this chapter, I concentrate on the layout properties of DHTML. Chapters 11, 12, and 13 round out my coverage of DHTML, with discussions on how to modify the behavior of items on a page, using cascading style sheets, and adding animation.

In this chapter, I cover:

- How layers work.
- Floating boxes.
- Style sheet-based positioning.

How Layers Work

DHTML layers add two important capabilities to your Web page layout toolbox: discrete positioning of elements at a specific location on the page, and stacking—the ability to arrange and move groups of HTML elements around on a page.

You can use layers on a page much the way you would a GoLive layout grid or a table, dividing the page into functional sections. Layers have the advantage of allowing you to position items exactly, as measured by pixels, and lack the overhead of grids, which are composed of many table cells. Although layers can be, and often are, multi-level schemes that overlap on a page, you can use the technique to create page sections that appear adjacent to one another but do not overlap.

Aside from their visual attributes, layers make it possible to confine the effects of alignment, style sheets, scripts, and other attributes to the area defined by a layer. You can use layers over all or part of a page, combining them with tables and grids or leaving the non-layered portion of a page to be displayed as it would with no layout boundaries imposed.

The downside to using layers is that not all browsers support them. The layer element made its first appearance in Netscape's 4.0 generation of browsers, and older browsers from all vendors do not necessarily display them correctly. The <DIV> tag, which makes the GoLive floating box element possible, is available to browsers that support HTML 3.2 (all version 3 browsers), allowing you to create but not overlap layers.

The use of multiple overlapping layers has advantages beyond the ability to blend HTML elements; you can use layers to move items around the page and create other animated effects. I have more to say about this aspect of layering in Chapter 13.

Figure 10.1 The Floating Box Palette tool.

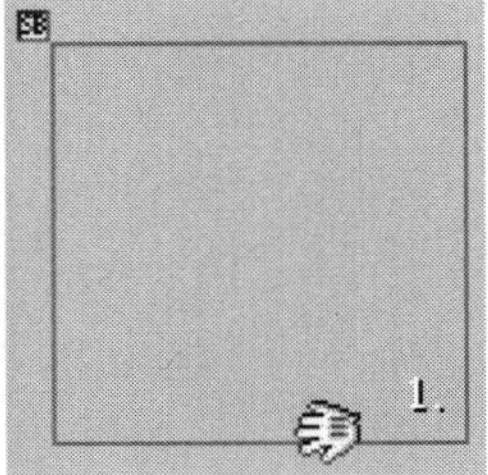

Figure 10.2 Select a floating box by moving the cursor to the border of the box, where it changes to a hand.

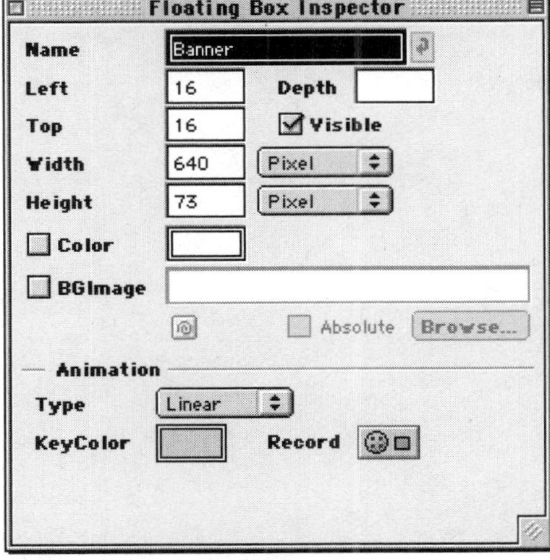

Figure 10.3 The Floating Box Inspector.

Floating Boxes

The floating box is the basic layer tool used in GoLive. The HTML tag associated with a GoLive floating box is <DIV>, which encloses the HTML content that forms the box. Everything within the <DIV> tag and displayed in the floating box in the Layout View is bounded by the box and can be aligned to it, rather than a grid, table, or the page as a whole. When you move a floating box, its contents come along.

To create a floating box:

1. With a document open in the Layout View, double-click or drag the Floating Box tool (**Figure 10.1**) from the Basic tab of the Palette to the document window. A floating box appears.
2. Without clicking, move the cursor over the bottom or top border of the floating box until the I-beam changes to a hand, as shown in **Figure 10.2**.
3. Click and drag the box to a new location, if desired. Unlike most other elements, you can drag a floating box around the Layout View, even if the page does not contain a layout grid or table.
4. Change the size of the box by dragging handles on the sides and corners of the box.

To configure a floating box:

1. With a floating box selected (move the cursor over the box until the hand pointer appears and click), set options in the Floating Box Inspector (**Figure 10.3**).
2. Type a name for the floating box (layer) in the name field. The name will become more useful to you if you use and stack multiple floating boxes.

continues on next page

3. Fine-tune the position of the box, relative to the edge of the page, using the Top and Left fields. Measurements are in pixels.
4. Choose the box's location, relative to other layers you have or will create in the Depth field. The lower the number, the lower the layer appears in the stacking order.
5. Adjust the Width and Height of the box (measured in pixels, percent, or Auto).
6. Click the Color field to display the Color Palette, and choose a color for the box.
7. Point and shoot or browse to locate a background image, if desired.

Adding content to a floating box

Think of a floating box as a miniature Web page. You can type text directly into the box or add images and other elements that constrain the text. You can even place tables within the box. The boundaries of the box constrain everything within it, regardless of what's on the outside. To add content, use Palette tools or any other method that can be used in the Layout view.

✔ Tips

- Though it is sometimes useful to add a table to a floating box, it's not a good idea to include layout grids. Remember that a grid is actually a densely populated table. That density can make trouble when displaying a floating box in some browsers. Some suggest that even a table is overkill in a floating box. Remember that you can use boxes in the same way you use grids or tables—to segment the page. In other words, avoid tables and grids if you can.
- To minimize table-related problems within a floating box, set the box's depth to a value greater than zero (the default is empty), and set the table's width to Auto.

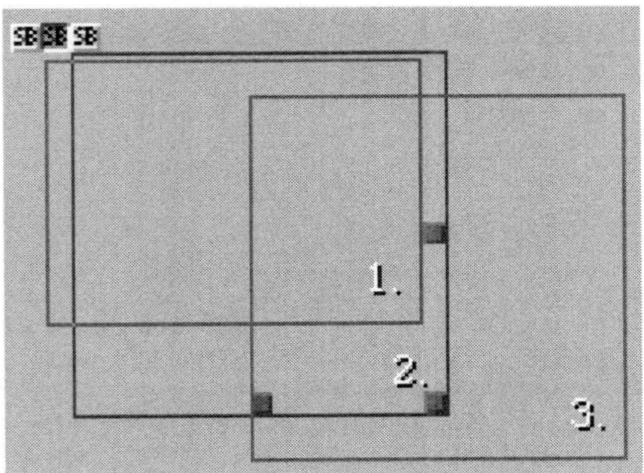

Figure 10.4 Three floating boxes display their z-indexes. Notice that layer 3 appears to be in front of the other two.

A word about positioning types

As I mentioned earlier, GoLive floating boxes (layers) are defined by the <DIV> tag. DIV creates a layer with an absolute position, relative to the top of the parent element—usually, the page itself. That means that floating boxes, like their contents, do not interact with the rest of the page, whose content flows above, through, and below the layer.

You can create boxes (layers) that form a boundary around their content but which are themselves part of the flow of the page. Text wraps around such a layer and you can align the box to text, just as you can an image of media item. For more on positioning, see the "Style Sheet-Based Positioning" section in this chapter.

Boxes as layers

Floating boxes can be used to layer content on a Web page. The ability to stack floating boxes makes it possible to create a wide variety of visual effects. You can stack floating boxes so that they overlap one another as much or as little as you like.

Web browsers keep track of layers with an attribute called the z-index. Each layer is assigned a number, which corresponds to its position within the layer hierarchy. The higher the z-index, the closer the layer is to the top of the stack. X and y indexes, by the way, correspond to the Left and Top measurements that determine a layer's distance from the origin. A layer's z-index appears in the lower right corner of the layer (**Figure 10.4**) and can be changed in the Floating Box Inspector's Depth field.

Managing multiple floating boxes

If you use floating boxes merely as a way to organize a Web page and do not overlap them, manipulating them is fairly easy. Simply select and configure the box or move it as needed. If, on the other hand, you group and stack layers, you will probably appreciate the Floating Box Controller, a window which allows you to easily select one of several layers.

You can also use the Floating Box Controller to hide or lock individual layers in any combination. Adjustments you make to a layer's visibility and editability only affect the look of the page during the current editing session. They don't change the HTML code or affect layer display within a browser.

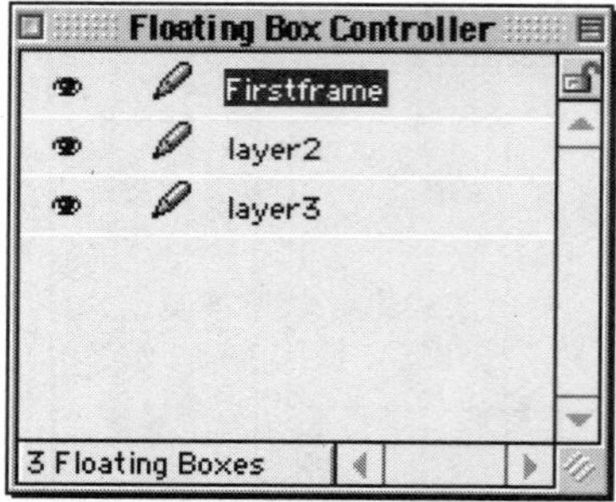

Figure 10.5 The Floating Box Controller contains listings for three layers.

Managing layers with the floating box controller:

1. Add two or more floating boxes to a Web page by dragging the Floating Box tool from the Palette.
2. Position each box on the page and change its z-index (Depth, in the Floating Box Inspector) if desired.
3. Choose Window:Floating Box Controller. The controller appears (**Figure 10.5**).
4. Click once to select a layer in the controller window. The Floating Box Inspector appears and the selected box moves to the front of the stacking order. At this point, you can add content or change the configuration of the box. The new position in the stack is temporary, and it won't be changed for good unless you change the box's z-index.
5. If you haven't already done so, name the selected layer. The Floating Box Controller is updated.
6. In the Floating Box Controller, click the eye symbol. The content of the selected layer is now hidden, and the eye is grayed out (**Figure 10.6**).
7. Click the eye again to make the box's content visible again.

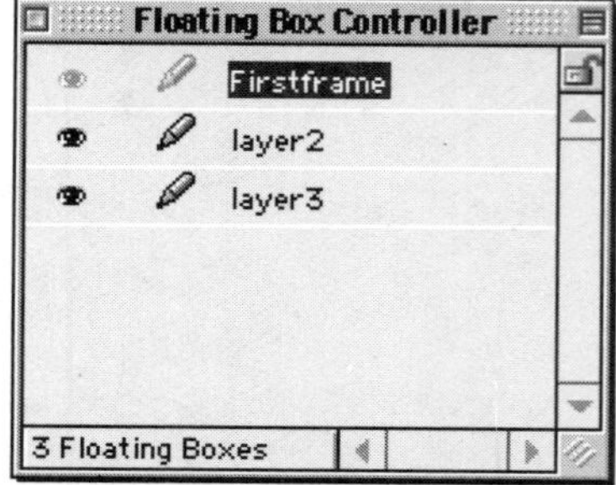

Figure 10.6 The grayed eye symbol next to the Firstframe layer indicates that the layer's content is hidden.

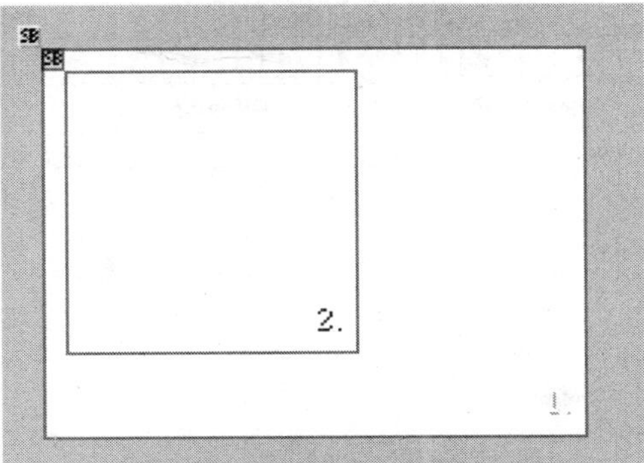

Figure 10.7 Nesting a layer inside another layer by first clicking in the first layer, then adding a second one. The second layer is now a child of the first.

8. Click the Pen icon next to a layer to lock the layer, so that it cannot be moved. The Pen is also a toggle.

✔ Tip

- To hide a layer for real—when the page loads in a browser—select the Layer and uncheck Visible in the Floating Box Inspector.

Nesting layers

You may remember that I wrote earlier in this chapter that you could include a table within a layer to format text or other elements. That's true, but you can also nest layers within other layers. This is useful if your positioning needs are either more precise or if you want to avoid the potential hassles associated with using tables *and* layers in some browsers.

To nest a layer within a layer:

1. Add a layer to a document.
2. Enlarge it by a few pixels so that it can easily hold another layer at the default size.
3. Click within the floating box so that an insertion point appears.
4. Double-click the Floating Box tool in the Palette. A new layer appears in the first one (**Figure 10.7**). Notice that the floating box icon for the new layer appears inside the first — not at the top of the window as it would if the layers were independent.

Style Sheet-Based Positioning

Floating boxes can be used to organize HTML elements or animation. If precise positioning of text is your goal, cascading style sheets (supported by browsers that support layers) are the way to go.

Style sheets make it possible to format and display text precisely, rather than leaving its appearance to the user's browser. Most style sheets allow you to choose fonts borders, colors, and other text properties. I have more to say about style sheets in Chapter 12. In this section, I cover style sheet positioning properties that allow you to do with text what you can do with a layer—put it exactly where you want it.

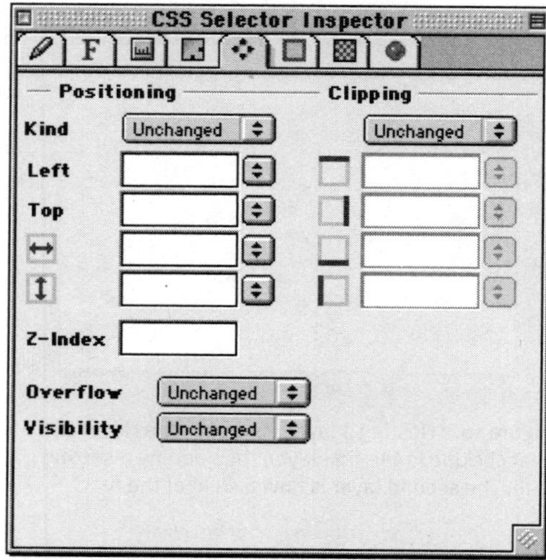

Figure 10.8 The Positioning Properties tab of the CSS Selector Inspector.

✔ Tip

- Before reading the following section, you may get more out of it if you first read about creating style sheets in Chapter 12.

To add positioning properties to a style sheet:

1. Create an internal style sheet by clicking on the Style Sheet button in the upper-right corner of the document window. The Style Sheet Selector Inspector appears.
2. Create a new selector by choosing an option from the toolbar.
3. With the new selector highlighted, enter a name for the selector in the Name field.
4. Click the Positioning Properties tab in the Inspector (**Figure 10.8**).
5. Choose a type of positioning from the Kind menu. Like the <DIV> element that creates a floating box, absolute positioning relates the styled element to the left and top edges of the page. Static positioning keeps the styled element

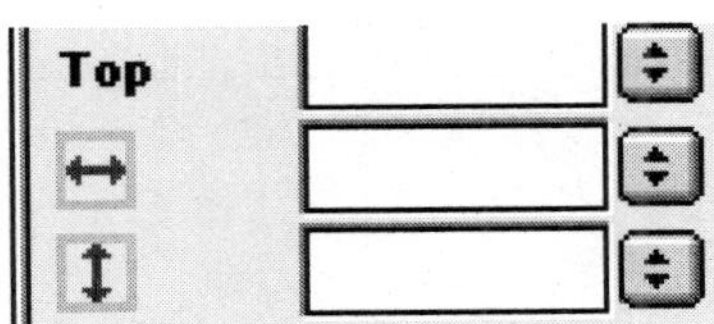

Figure 10.9 Choose Width and Height values from the fields with the arrow labels.

within the flow of text. Relative positioning acts like a <DIV> tag, relating the styled element to its parent element.

6. Enter Left and Top coordinates to determine the element's distance from the corner of the page or parent element.
7. Choose Height and Width values to specify the size of a styled element. The fields are labeled with arrows, as shown in **Figure 10.9**.
8. If the element is one of several layers, choose a z-index that determines the element's place in the stacking order.
9. Choose a clipping method. Auto allows the visitor's browser to define the clipping area. Rect lets you set the clipping area on each side of the element.
10. If you chose a Rect clipping area, enter its dimensions in the fields below.
11. Choose an item from the Overflow popup menu to tell the browser how to display content that does not fit within the defined boundaries of the styled element.
12. Choose whether and how the element will be visible on the page.

✔ Tip

■ GoLive does not directly offer a tool for creating the <SPAN> tag. A <SPAN> tag creates a layer that's positioned relative to other elements on the page, while a <DIV> element (created by a floating box) creates a layer that's aligned to the origin of the page. Style sheets are an easy way to create a layer with a <SPAN> tag. Create a style sheet selector, as described above, and choose Relative from the Kind popup menu. Next, choose Width and Height dimensions to create the box that constrains the element. Finally, apply the new style sheet to a document, as described in Chapter 12.

MODIFYING BEHAVIOR WITH DHTML

11

DHTML makes it possible to script Web pages so that they can generate effects, interact with one another, or respond to a user's action in the browser. You've already seen how DHTML makes precise item positioning possible, and the next two chapters address text formatting with cascading style sheets and object animation. I concentrate on using DHTML tools and scripted actions to modify the behavior of a page or element on the page.

GoLive includes DHTML tools—CyberObjects and pre-built actions—that shield you from the coding process. If you really want to roll your sleeves up and dig into scripting, GoLive supports your efforts with the Source Editor, JavaScript Editor, and Web Database.

It's important to note that DHTML features will only be visible to users of 4.0-compatible browsers, such as Netscape Communicator and Microsoft Internet Explorer 4.0 and later. While it is safe to say that modern browsers gain more users every day, developers who make extensive use of DHTML will inevitably leave some users behind.

In this chapter, I cover:

- Behavior modification tools.
- Using pre-built DHTML objects.
- Working with Actions.

DHTML Tools

GoLive tools available for customizing the behavior of Web page elements include:

- The CyberObjects Palette tab.
- The Inspector's Actions tab.
- The JavaScript editor.

The CyberObjects Palette tab

GoLive includes several pre-built DHTML objects, available simply by dragging a Palette tool from the CyberObjects tab (**Figure 11.1**) onto a Web page.

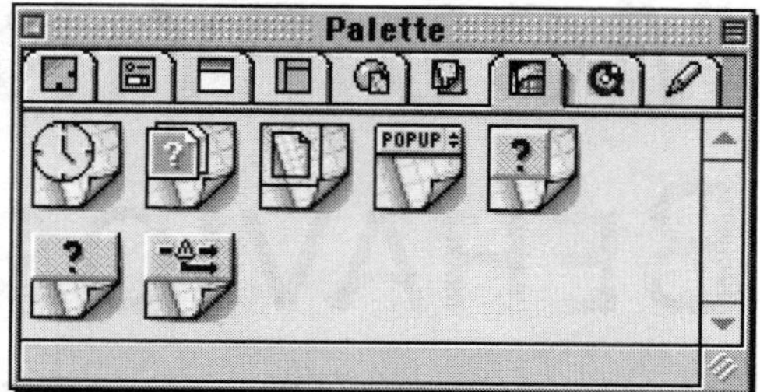

Figure 11.1 The Palette's CyberObject's tab.

CyberObjects Inspectors

Each CyberObjects tool is paired with an Inspector window. The Inspectors differ from object to object.

The Actions tab

You can apply DHTML actions to text, buttons, and images. You configure DHTML actions in the Actions tab (**Figure 11.2**) of the Inspector associated with the object. You add actions to animation in the Actions track of the timeline editor. I have more to say about animation in Chapter 13.

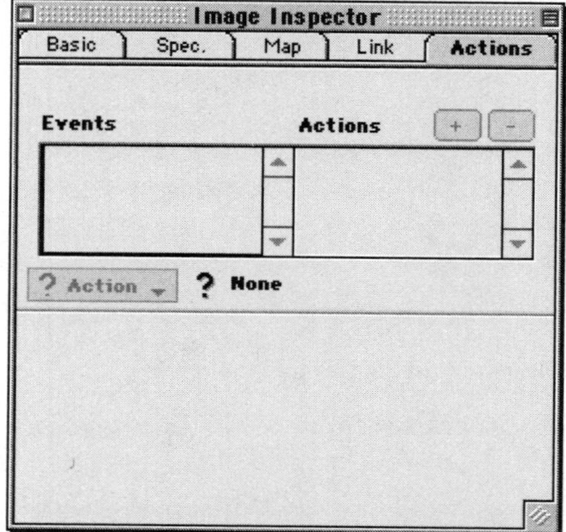

Figure 11.2 The Actions tab of the Image Inspector.

The JavaScript Editor

GoLive includes a JavaScript Editor where you can create or edit your own JavaScript actions. If you use Adobe's included set of actions or add actions created by others, you may never need the Editor. You'll find a description of the Editor, how to use it, and where to find information about JavaScript authoring in Chapter 9.

Figure 11.3 The Date & Time Palette tool.

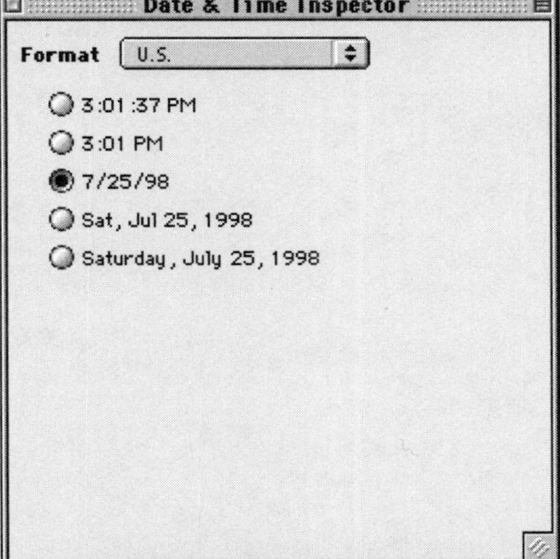

Figure 11.4 The Date & Time Inspector.

Using CyberObjects

You'll find several ready-to-use objects under the CyberObjects tab of the Palette. Each uses DHTML to add a feature to your Web page. Drag one onto your page, configure it with the associated Inspector window, and you've added DHTML to your Web site. The items available from the CyberObjects tab are:

- Date and time stamp.
- Button image.
- Dynamic component.
- URL popup.
- Inline action.
- Action head item.
- Browser switch head item.

Date and time stamps

A date & time stamp adds the current date and time to your Web page. "Current" means the date and time at which the page was saved.

To add a date & time stamp:

1. With a document open in the Layout view, locate the position where you want to add a date and/or time stamp. You can embed the stamp within a block of text, or set it apart on the page. If you want to display both the date and time, you need to create a stamp for each.
2. Click the CyberObjects tab in the Palette.
3. Double-click, or drag the Date & Time tool (**Figure 11.3**) from the Palette. A date and time stamp appears.
4. In the Date & Time Inspector (**Figure 11.4**), choose a display format by clicking on one of the radio buttons.

5. To change the language of your stamp, choose one from the Language popup menu in the Inspector window. When you alter the language or format of the stamp, the sample in the document window changes, too.

6. In the document window, select the stamp as if it were text by clicking and dragging across it. You can edit the stamp's appearance, just as you would any text item, with the toolbar or the Text Inspector, which appears when you select the contents of the stamp.

7. To add a second stamp, repeat the preceding steps and choose a time format if your first stamp included the date, or vice versa.

✔ Tips

- You can use a date & time stamp just as you would any other HTML element: drag it onto a layout grid or into a text box in order to relate it to other items on your page.
- Many Web page authors create date & time stamps that display the current date and time when a user visits the page. To do this, the Web server must be running a CGI that supports that function, and the Web page must contain code that links to the CGI.

Mouseovers

A button image is probably the easiest form of animation to create. With a button image, you can cause a button to change its appearance when a visitor moves the mouse over the button, or clicks on it—that's commonly referred to as a *mouseover* or *rollover.*

Before you can add the animated image to your page, decide how the image should change when your visitors mouse over it and when they click it. You will probably choose to create slightly different versions of a single

Figure 11.5 The Button Image tool.

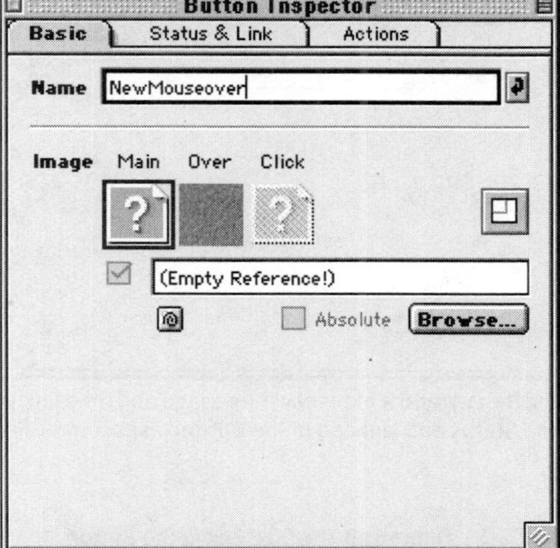

Figure 11.6 The Button Inspector.

image, though you might decide to display a completely different one when the user moves across it.

If you decide to use a variant of one image, you will need to create the variants using an image editor, such as Adobe Photoshop. Start with the original image and edit it, saving each version at the same size and resolution as the first image to make the transitions look smooth. When you have three images (the original, the version that appears when a user mouses over it, and a final one that appears when the user clicks on the image), you're ready to animate it with the GoLive button image tool.

To set up a mouseover:

1. With a document open in the Layout view, double-click or drag the Button Image tool (**Figure 11.5**) from the CyberObjects tab. The image tag that appears looks like a standard image placeholder.
2. In the Button Inspector, name the button.
3. Click on the box marked Main (**Figure 11.6**).
4. Browse or Point & Shoot to locate an image.
5. When you have finished placing the first image, click the box labeled Over. The checkbox next to the Image Path field is enabled.
6. Browse or Point & Shoot to the image you want users to see when their mouse moves over the first image you created.
7. With the second image in place, repeat steps 4 and 5 with the Click box to place an image that will replace the original when a visitor clicks on it.

continues on next page

8. To use the image as a link, click on the Status & Link tab in the Button Inspector. You can link an image to a file or URL, even if you're also displaying a new version of the image when a user clicks it.

9. Click the URL checkbox to enable the adjacent field (**Figure 11.7**).

10. Browse or Point & Shoot to a page you want to link to or type a complete URL.

11. You can target the link to a new location (window, frame, etc.) with the Target popup menu.

12. You can cause a message to appear when a visitor mouses over the link by clicking on the Status checkbox and typing in a short message.

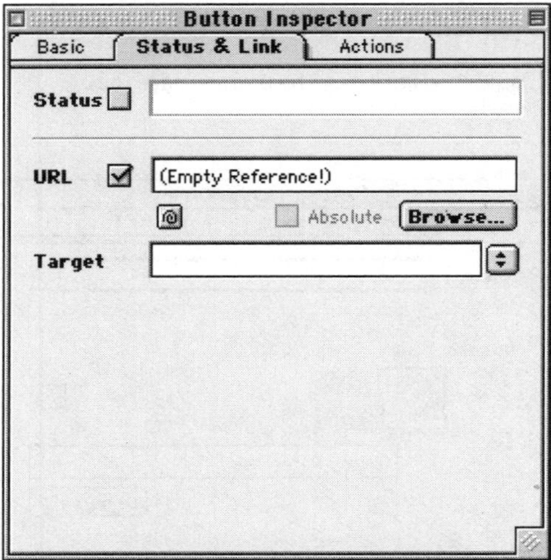

Figure 11.7 Add a mouseover message and/or a link in the Status and Link tab of the Button Inspector.

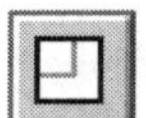
Figure 11.8 The Size Box in the Button Inspector window allows you to view all button images at the size of the image you've selected.

✔ Tips

- If you want to add button image properties to an image that already appears on your Web page, do so by dragging the Button Image tool over the image. Then configure the button as described in steps 5-11.
- You don't have to create both a mouseover image and a click image. You can use one or both options with your button.
- If you decide to use completely different images for the three elements of button animation, you must at least make sure the images are the same size. If they aren't the same size when you create them, they may be stretched or "smooshed" to fit into the image placeholder you've created for them in your document. If you want to try to reach a happy medium when working with images that are different sizes, you can experiment using the Size box in the Button Inspector (**Figure 11.8**). With your two or three images placed and configured, click on the one whose size most closely matches the

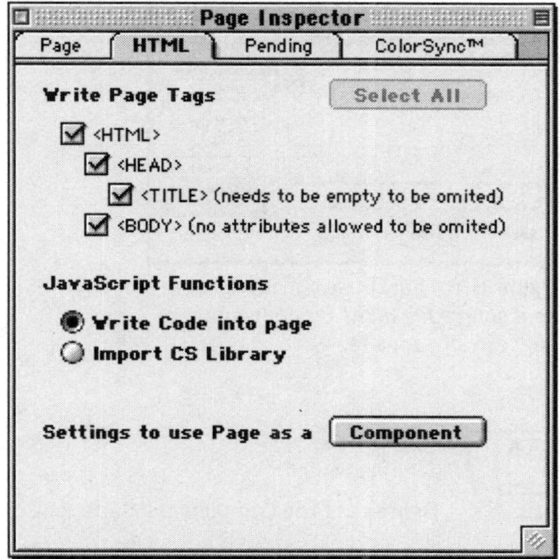

Figure 11.9 The HTML tab of the Page Inspector.

image size you have in mind. Then click the Size box. The placeholder box changes to fit the image you've selected. See how everything looks by clicking the Preview tab. Mouse over your image and then click on it. If an image is out of proportion, go back and fix it in your graphics software.

Dynamic components

Dynamic components are a lot like master elements in desktop publishing: You can use a component throughout a site to provide a header, footer, logo, or other standing element. Unlike other methods of creating standard elements in GoLive, such as storing a layout grid full of text and images in the Custom tab of the Palette, components allow you to make changes to one source file and have those changes apply to all files that use the component. Components work by inserting HTML fragments into other documents, and keeping the fragments updated automatically whenever you edit the original. If you look at the Source code for a file that includes a component, you'll see the HTML fragment within the file.

To use components, you must create the source file and then add component objects to each file that will use the component. Although you can use components outside GoLive's site metaphor, the Site window does offer special support for components, as you'll see.

To create a component source file:

1. Open a GoLive site.
2. Begin a new document and create the content you want to use as a component. Click the Page icon at the top of the document window.
3. In the Page Inspector, switch to the HTML tab (**Figure 11.9**).

continues on next page

4. Click the Component button. The button dims, and the document is ready to be saved as a component source file.
5. Save the file to the Components folder within the Site.data folder directory of your site. You can reach the Components folder quickly by clicking on the popup menu near the upper right corner of the Save dialog box (**Figure 11.10**) if you're using a Mac. The popup is at the lower right corner in Windows.

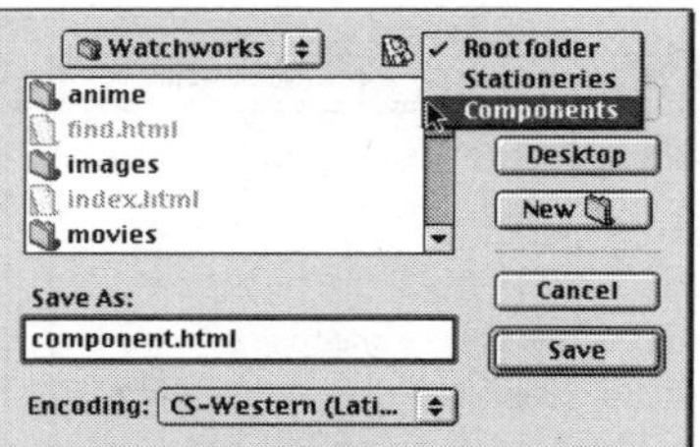

Figure 11.10 Quickly save a new component source file in the Components directory of your site.

To apply a component:

1. Open a new document or locate an existing document in which you would like to use a component.
2. Drag the Component tool (**Figure 11.11**) from the Palette to the document window. A large, horizontal rectangle appears, and the Component Inspector (**Figure 11.12**) appears.

Figure 11.11 The Component Palette tool.

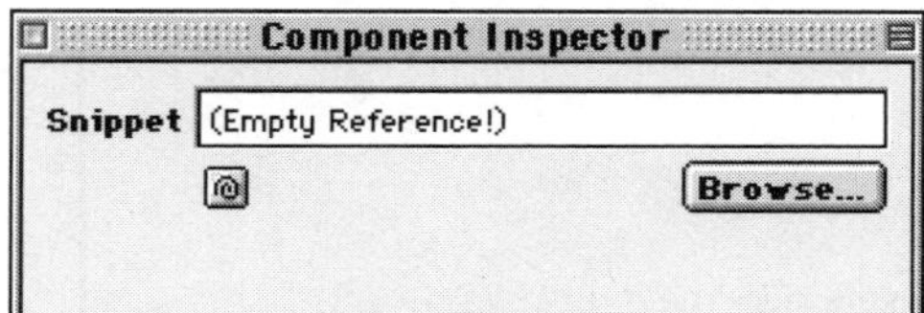

Figure 11.12 The Component Inspector.

3. Browse or Point & Shoot to the component file you want to use. The component appears in your document.

   Though it's easier to browse to a component, you can Point & Shoot to the Site window's right-hand pane. Open it by clicking the button on the right side of the Site window (**Figure 11.13**). When you drag the Point & Shoot line into the Site window, move it over the Extra tab on the right side of the window and onto the Components directory. When it opens, connect to the file you want, as shown in **Figure 11.14**.

Figure 11.13 Click the button at the upper right corner of the Site window to view the pane containing site directories.

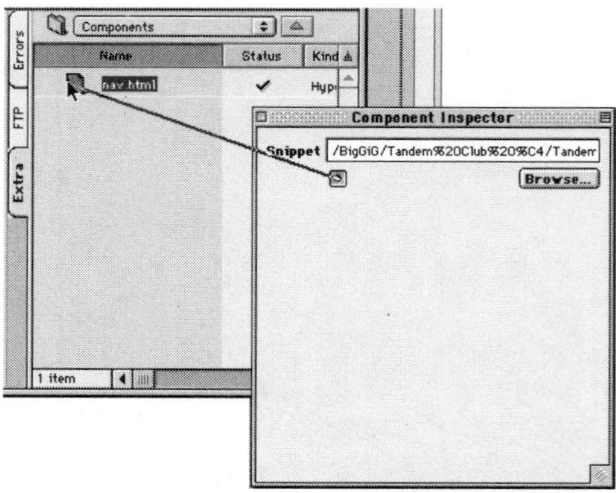

Figure 11.14 Point & Shoot from the Component Inspector to the Components directory of your site.

✔ Tips

- Once you've created and saved components in the Components directory of your site, each component appears in the Site Extras tab of the Palette. To locate components, click on the tab and then choose the Components item from the

Figure 11.15 The URL Popup Palette tool.

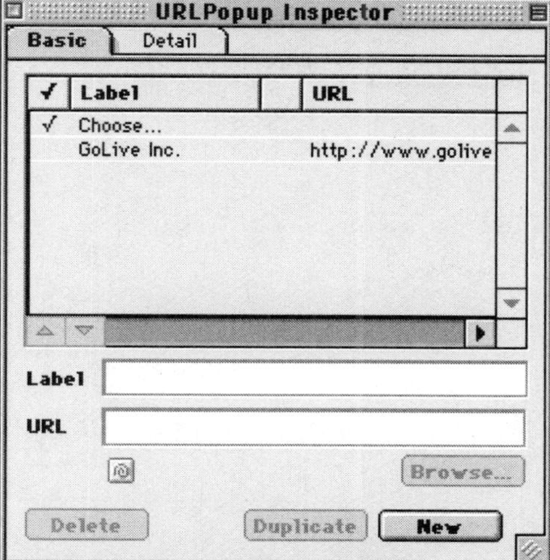

Figure 11.16 The URL popup Inspector.

popup menu at the bottom of the window. You can drag components from the Palette to the document window.

- Components may be different shapes and sizes, but they cannot be displayed on the same horizontal line as another object. For that reason, they are best suited to serve as headers, footers, and other elements that use along the entire width of the page.
- You can edit a component file. The changes you make will be transferred to all files that contain references to it. You will need to re-upload each file that uses the changed components to the Web server before changes take effect.

URL popup menus

URL popup menus are another navigation aid: you can use one to provide visitors a menu of places to go within your site.

To create a URL popup:

1. With a document open, drag the URL Popup tool (**Figure 11.15**) from the Palette to the document window. A small popup box and the URL Popup Inspector appear.
2. In the URL Popup Inspector (**Figure 11.16**), click on the line that says GoLive Inc. (Mac) or Adobe Systems (Windows). (It seems that in this respect, the Windows version is more up-to-date).
3. In the Label field, replace the current text with text of your own, describing the page or site the visitor will see when that item is chosen.

continues on next page

4. Press Tab and type a URL to match the label. You can also Browse or Point & Shoot to fill in the URL.
5. Click New to add another item to the popup.
6. Type a label and URL for the new item.
7. Repeat steps 5 and 6 for each item you want to add.

Figure 11.17 The Inline Action Palette tool.

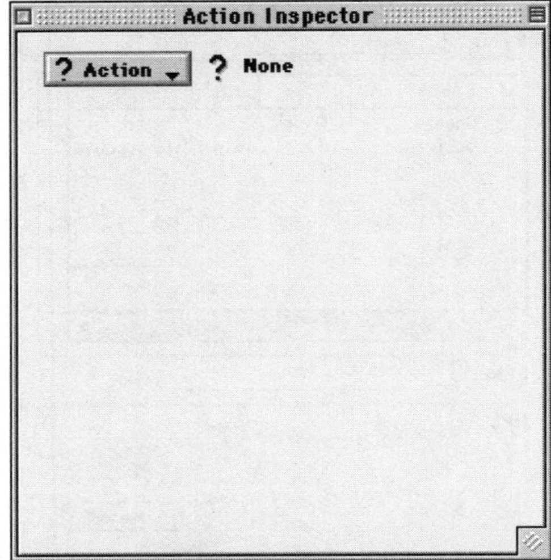

Figure 11.18 The Inline Action Inspector.

Inline and head action items

Adding an action to the head section of an HTML page causes the script to trigger when the page is called by a user's browser. Inline actions, which appear in the body section of an HTML document, serve as placeholders for HTML that an action generates. I cover the full range of GoLive-supported actions in the "Actions" section of this chapter. For now, I'll describe the process of adding inline and head action items to a document.

To add an inline action to the body section:

1. Double-click or drag the Inline Action tool (**Figure 11.17**) from the Palette.
2. In the Inline Action Inspector (**Figure 11.18**), choose an action from the menu. Actions are grouped by type.

Figure 11.19 The Action HeadItem Palette tool.

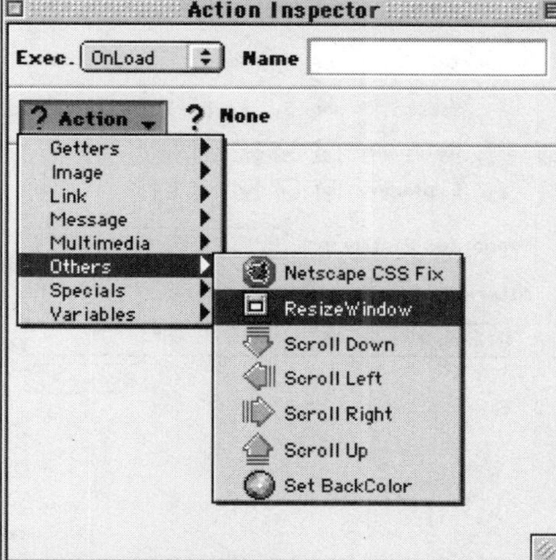

Figure 11.20 The Action HeadItem Inspector.

To add an action headitem:

1. Open a new or existing document.
2. Reveal the document's header by clicking on the small triangle to the left of the page icon, near the top of the document window.
3. Double-click or drag the Action HeadItem tool (**Figure 11.19**) from the Palette to the header pane of the document window. An action item icon appears, and the Action Item Inspector (**Figure 11.20**) becomes visible.
4. Tell the page how to execute the action by choosing from the Exec. Popup menu. (OnUnload means when the window containing the page is closed, or a link is clicked which leads to another page; OnParse executes the Action as soon as its code is read into the browser, which is before the page has finished loading; OnCall means that the Action will not execute until you specifically call it from another Action—probably using the "Call Action" Action.)
5. Choose an action from the menu. Actions are arranged in the functional categories.
6. If necessary, finish configuring the action, using the options that appear in the Action Item Inspector.

Browser Switch item

Adding a Browser Switch item to the header of a document can help you accommodate visitors whose browsers do not support DHTML elements. When a browser switch detects a non-compatible browser, it redirects the user from the current page to one you select.

Like other header action items, a browser switch is invoked before the page loads, speeding the changeover from one page to another. Of course, to use a switch, you need to create a page or pages that exclude DHTML or other 4.0-specific elements that are not supported by older browsers.

To create a browser switch:

1. Open a new or existing document includes DHTML elements.
2. Open the document's header by clicking on the triangle near the top of the document window. The header pane appears.
3. Drag the Browser Switch tool (**Figure 11.21**) from the Palette to the header pane of the document window. A browser switch icon appears, and the Browser Switch Inspector (**Figure 11.22**) becomes visible.
4. If you want GoLive to determine which browsers your page is compatible with, leave Auto checked in the Inspector.
5. Specify a platform (Mac or Windows).
6. To choose specific browsers to support, uncheck Auto and click on the browser versions that you think are compatible with your DHTML page. If a visitor uses a browser version you did not check, he or she will be redirected to a different page.
7. Browse or Point & Shoot to the alternative page, using the Alternative Link field.

Figure 11.21 The URL Popup Palette tool.

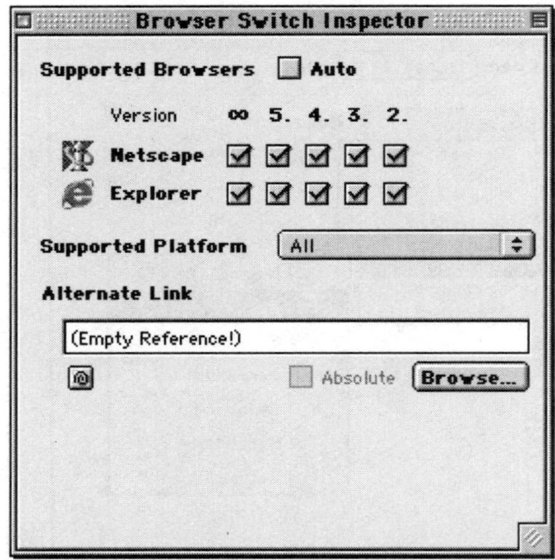

Figure 11.22 The URL popup Inspector.

Actions

Actions are scripted functions that can be executed when a *trigger* is activated. You can use actions to change the appearance of a page or its elements, to open alert windows, play media files, and much more. GoLive includes a large collection of pre-built actions that you can add to pages, animations, text, and images using mouse- and keyboard-related triggers.

You will find action tabs in the Inspector windows associated with several GoLive tools. I've avoided them until this point, because they work pretty much the same in all cases, and this is the best place to describe them. You can also apply actions to animations using the action track in the Timeline editor. In this section, I use the Inspector as the interface to GoLive actions. In Chapter 13, I explain how you can add actions to timelines.

About triggers

An action consists of a trigger and a function. When the trigger is applied, the function you specify is invoked. GoLive provides nine event triggers that invoke actions:

- Mouse click.
- Mouse enter.
- Mouse exit.
- Double click.
- Mouse down.
- Mouse up.
- Key down.
- Key press.
- Key up.

Elements that support actions

You will find support for actions in the Text and Image Inspectors, as well as in the Button Image (mouseover) CyberObject explained earlier in this chapter. The Inline Action and Action HeadItem objects described earlier give you the option of adding actions that are not tied to another HTML element. Just drag them into the body or head section, respectively, and configure them. As discussed earlier, you'll also find support for animation actions in the Timeline editor.

Adding an action

Because the process of adding an action is identical regardless of the specific functions and triggers you use, I'll describe the general procedure, and then move on to specific explanations of what each type of action does and how to use it.

To add an action via the Inspector:

1. Open a document and locate an item that supports actions (text, an image, or a button image, for example). The item you choose must be a hyperlink. To add an action to an image, for example, the image must have a URL associated with it.
2. Click the item you want to activate, revealing its Inspector.
3. Click the Actions tab (**Figure 11.23**). A list of triggers and a pane for new actions appear.
4. Choose a trigger from the list by clicking on it. Let's try Mouse Enter, which will trigger an action when the visitor moves the mouse over the text or image we're working with.
5. Click the Plus button (**Figure 11.24**) to add an action item, which appears in the right pane of the window. The Action popup menu is enabled (**Figure 11.25**).

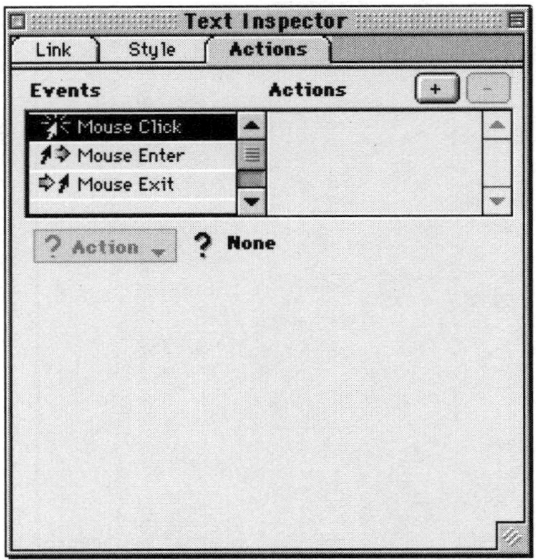

Figure 11.23 The Action tab of the Text Inspector lights up when your cursor is within a text link.

Figure 11.24 Add an action by clicking the plus sign. Delete one by selecting it and clicking the minus.

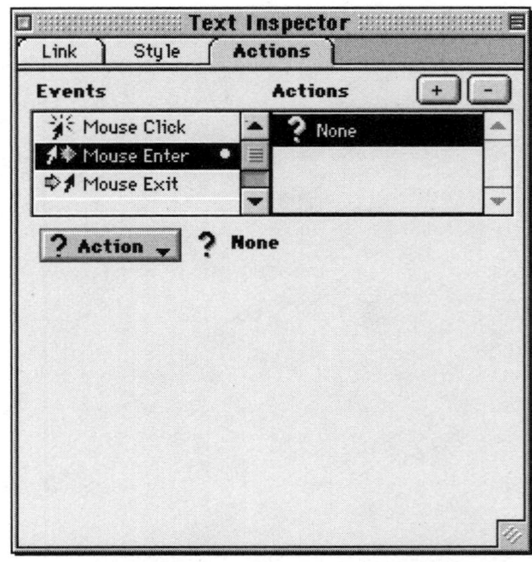

Figure 11.25 You'll see a list of action triggers on the left, and an unspecified action on the right.

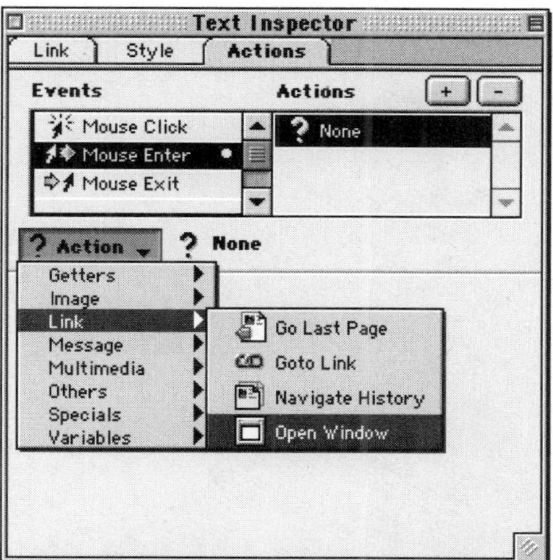

Figure 11.26 Choose from the list of action categories, then pick an action from the submenu.

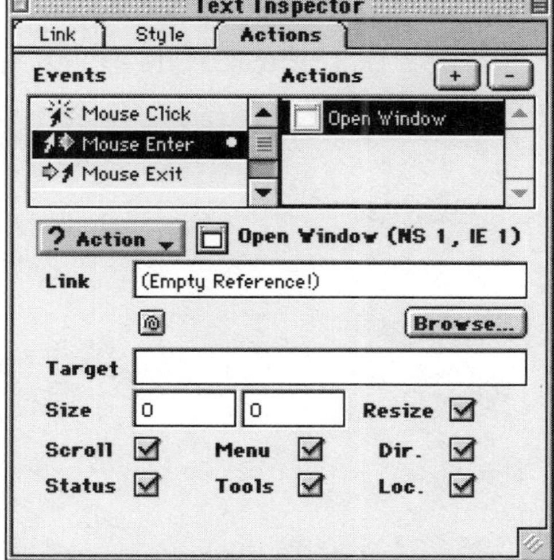

Figure 11.27 Fields specific to the action you choose appear in the bottom half of the Inspector when you've selected an action. Here are settings for an Open Window action.

6. Click on the Actions popup, displaying the categories of actions available.
7. Navigate to the category you want and choose an action. I've chosen Open Window from the Link menu (**Figure 11.26**). When combined with the Mouse Enter trigger I've already set, this action will open a window when a visitor's mouse passes over the link. Now, I need to configure the action. With the action chosen, the Inspector displays configuration options. For the Open Window action, they look like **Figure 11.27**.
8. To create a second action for the text or image you've selected, repeat steps 4 through 7.
9. To delete an action, select it in the Action pane and click the Minus button.

Kinds of actions

The following pages describe the actions GoLive includes. You can create your own actions if you know JavaScript, but using an action that's included with GoLive, or supplied by an independent developer, shields you from any need to know about scripting. In this section, I'll describe the function and configuration required for each of the actions GoLive includes.

As described in the section that deals with adding actions, you begin configuring the action by choosing a linked object and deciding on the trigger you will use. Please review this section before beginning to work with specific actions. The steps used to configure specific actions assume that you've already chosen the HTML element that will have an action attached, assigned a trigger, and created an action item in the Actions pane of the Inspector.

✔ Tips

- Although the general rule of thumb for actions is that your visitor must be using a 4.*x* or later browser, there are some actions that support older browsers. There's a minimum browser listing right next to the Action popup menu in the Action tab of the Inspector:
- The second, and most important, way to ensure browser compatibility is to test each action you create in as many browsers as you can. Testing is also important, because GoLive cannot display all of the results of the actions you create. I recommend that you test each action immediately after creating it in at least one browser (GoLive gives you easy access to browsers from the toolbar, as described in Chapter 1) to be sure that everything works the way it should.

The following actions included with GoLive support a variety of automated events, including many that are related to animating HTML elements. If you are interested in using actions with animation, please read Chapter 13, where I discuss creating animation in detail.

The actions GoLive includes are divided into categories, as follows:

Getter Actions

- *Get Floating Box Position* is a header action that grabs the coordinates of a floating box as it moves across the page as part of animation. You can use this data to invoke another action that locates and acts on the box.
- *Get Form Value* reads the data that a user inputs into a specified form field. The information can be passed to another action or displayed.

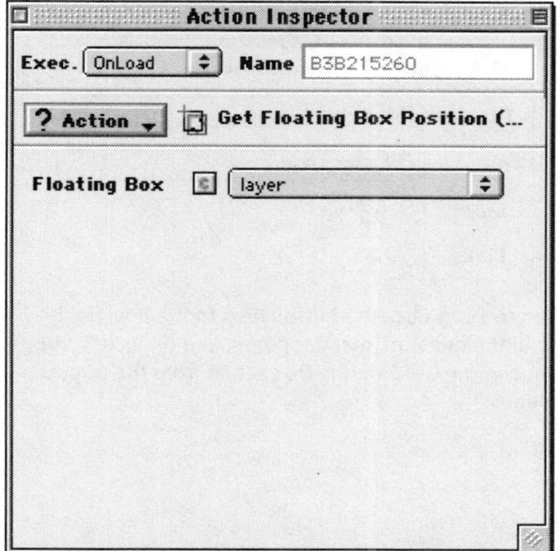

Figure 11.28 Choose a floating box in the Inspector.

To create a Get Floating Box Position action:

1. Create an animation consisting of two floating boxes: one with an animation path and the second with no movement assigned to it.
2. Add an Action HeadItem to the document's header section.
3. Set the Exec. Popup menu to OnCall.
4. When the Name field lights up, give the new action a name.
5. Create a new action trigger, and choose Get Floating Box Position from the Getter Actions menu in the Actions Inspector, or from the Actions tab of the HTML element Inspector you're using (see **Figure 11.28**).
6. Choose a floating box from the popup menu. This is the box whose position will be passed by the action.
7. Add a second HeadItem action to the document's header section.
8. Configure the action by choosing Specials:Idle in the Action Inspector.
9. Uncheck the Exit Idle if Condition Returns True checkbox.
10. Under the Conditional tab, choose a Specials:Timeout action and edit the timeout value.
11. Click the True tab, and choose Multimedia:Move To from the Action popup menu. This action allows you to specify the location to which your floating box will move.
12. Choose the floating box from the popup menu.

continues on next page

13. Click the buttons next to the Pos. field twice, so that the green question mark appears (**Figure 11.29**).
14. From the popup menu, choose the Get Floating Box action you created earlier.
15. Click the False tab.
16. Repeat steps 11-14.

Figure 11.29 Click the button next to the Pos. field until the question mark appears, and (if necessary) choose the Get Floating Box action from the popup menu.

To create a Get Form Value action:

1. Add an action to the header section of a document.
2. Choose Getter:Get Form Value from the Action menu.
3. Choose OnUnload from the Exec. Popup menu.
4. Enter the name of the form from which you want to extract information in the Form field.
5. Enter the name of the form element (the name you've assigned to the element itself, not the element type) in the Element field.
6. Add additional Get Form actions for each form field whose data you want to extract.
7. Create a repository of some kind (probably in another action) for the form data retrieved by the Get Form value.

Image actions

- *Preload Image* is a header action that caches images before an HTML page loads, making it possible for all images that are part of a page to appear simultaneously. Preloading an image also makes mouseovers and animations run more quickly, since their images have previously been cached. You can also use the Button image cyberobject to preload an image.

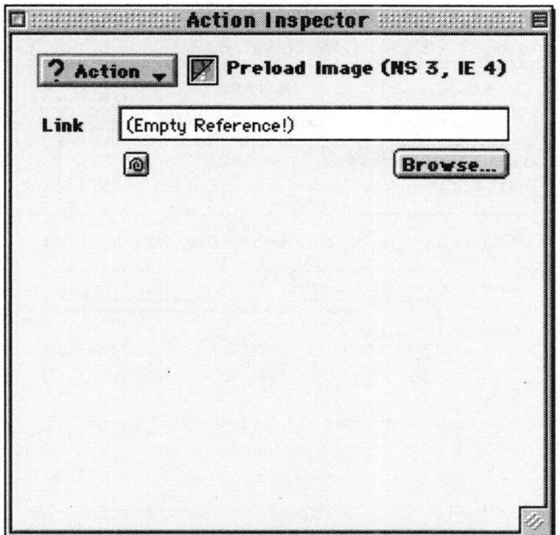

Figure 11.30 Add an image to preload.

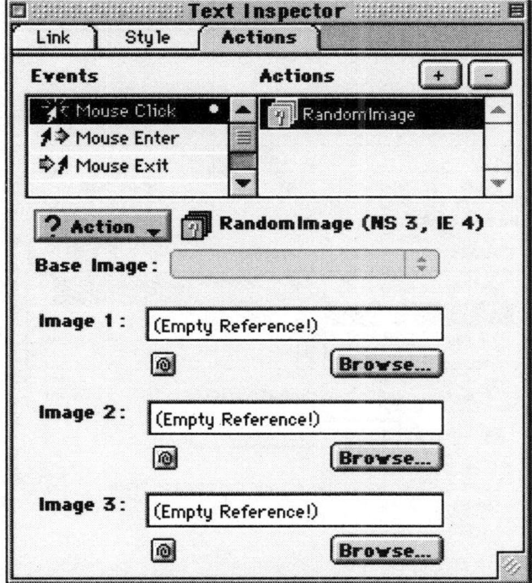

Figure 11.31 Choose several images from which the action will choose one at random.

- *Random Image* replaces the image to which you attach an action with a random image from among several you specify.
- Set Image URL exchanges the current image for another, based on the trigger you specify.

To preload an image:

1. Add an action to the header of a document.
2. In the Action Item Inspector, choose Image: Preload Image from the Actions menu.
3. Use Browse or Point & Shoot to locate an image to preload. See **Figure 11.30**.

To add a random image action:

1. Add a trigger and an action to an image. Be sure that the image is configured with a link.
2. Choose Image:Random Image from the Actions menu. Several image selection fields appear (**Figure 11.31**).
3. Browse or Point & Shoot to locate an image you want to appear randomly when your trigger is activated.
4. Repeat the previous step for up to two more images. Enlarge the Inspector window if needed, to show all three URL fields.

To set an image URL:

1. Choose an image you want to exchange. If it doesn't already have a name, give it one in the Form section of the Spec. tab of the Image Inspector. Be sure not to check the Is Form checkbox.
2. Add an action to linked text or a button image.

continues on next page

3. Choose Image:Set Image URL from the Action menu.
4. Choose the named image from the popup menu.
5. Browse or Point & Shoot to an alternative image to add its URL. The completed Action tab looks like **Figure 11.32**.

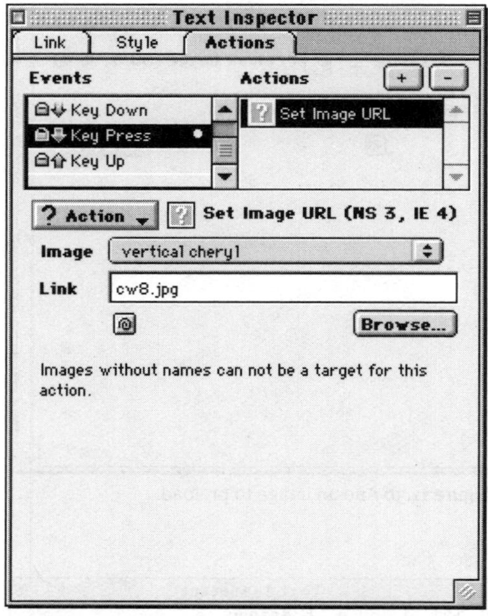

Figure 11.32 A complete Set Image URL action.

Link actions

- *Get Last Page* actions return the visitor to the previously viewed page.
- *Goto Link* actions send a visitor to a URL you select.
- *Navigate History* actions use browser history information (what pages he or she has visited in what order) to take the visitor forward or back by a specific number of pages.
- *Open Window* actions, as the name implies, open a new window when triggered, displaying the link you attach to the action.

To add a Go Last Page or Navigate History action:

1. Create a trigger and action.
2. Choose Link:Go Last Page, or Link:Navigate History from the Actions menu. The Navigate History action appears in **Figure 11.33**. If you're creating a Go Last Page action, you're done.
3. To complete a Navigate History action, type in a number of history items (negative numbers go backward, positive go forward) to move when the action is triggered.

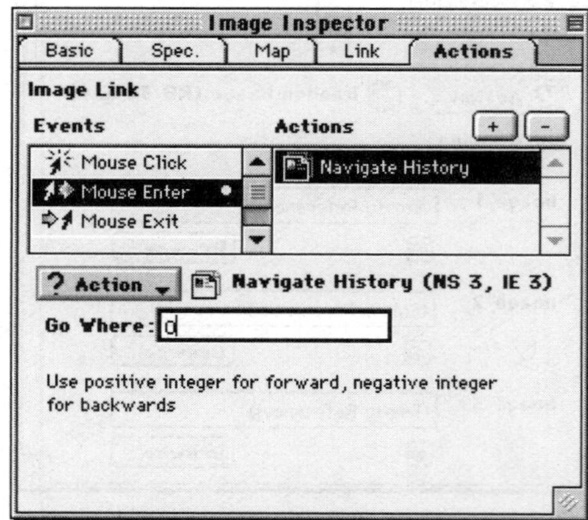

Figure 11.33 A Navigate History action in the Inspector.

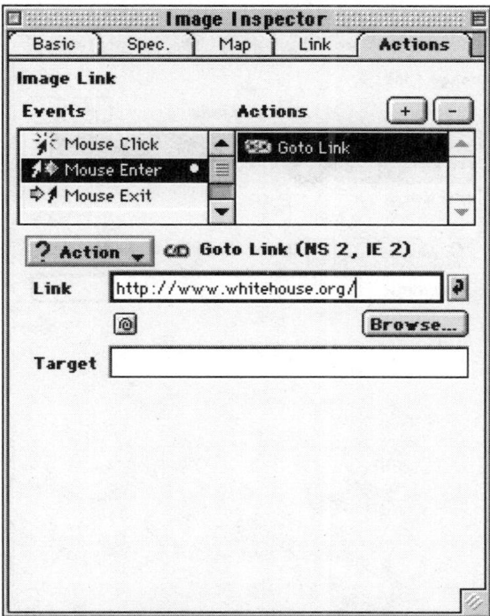

Figure 11.34 A Goto Link action in the Inspector.

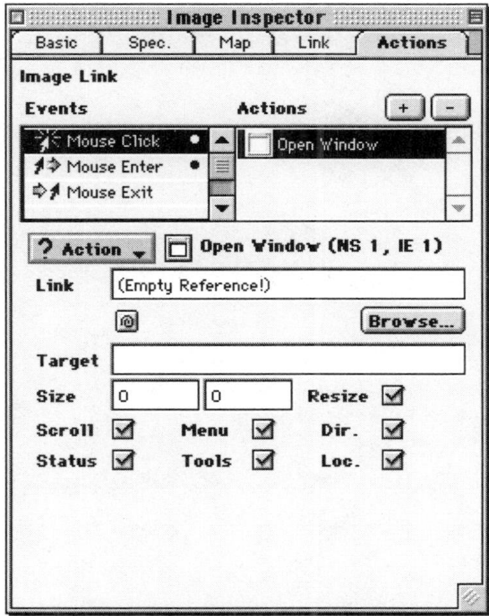

Figure 11.35 An Open Window action in the Inspector.

To create a Goto Link action:

1. Add an action to text or an image.
2. Choose Link:Goto Link from the Actions menu. Goto Link options appear (**Figure 11.34**).
3. Type a remote URL or locate a local file you want to link to.
4. If you want, use the Target field to specify a location where the new page should appear.

✔ Tip

- If it sounds like a Goto Link action does just what a normal hyperlink does, you're right, assuming that you've chosen a mouse click trigger. Using other triggers — like mouse enter, for example — makes things considerably more interesting. Be sure to give your visitors some kind of textual warning that invoking the trigger you set will send them to another page or another site.

To create an Open Window action:

1. Add an action to text or an image.
2. Choose Link:Open Window from the Actions menu. Open Window options appear (**Figure 11.35**).
3. Type, browse, or Point & Shoot to a link that will appear in the new window.
4. If necessary, use the Target field to specify a location where the new page should appear.
5. To control the appearance of the window itself, use the other controls in the Inspector. Start by specifying a size (in pixels) for the new window when it appears onscreen.
6. Click the Resize checkbox to allow the user to resize the new window.

continues on next page

7. Leave any of the six browser display buttons checked to show scroll bars, menus, directory buttons, status indicators, toolbars, and location bars.

Message actions

- *Document Write* works with the Inline Action CyberObject I described earlier in this chapter. Document Write fills the inline placeholder with text or with HTML.
- *Open Alert Window* displays an alert window onscreen when triggered.
- *Set Status* displays a custom message in the status field at the bottom of the browser window.

To create a Document Write action:

1. Add an Inline action to the body section of a document.
2. Choose Message:Document Write from the popup menu.
3. Type some HTML text into the Source field, or click the button to the left of the field until the question mark appears.
4. Choose a remote source—usually another action—from the popup menu.

To create an Open Alert Window action:

1. Create a trigger and action.
2. Choose Message:Open Alert Window from the Actions menu. The Message field appears (**Figure 11.36**).
3. Type the text you want to appear in the alert window.

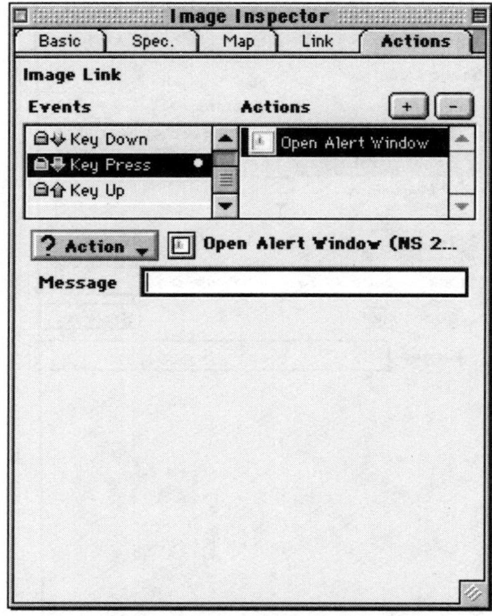

Figure 11.36 An Open Alert Window action in the Inspector.

To create a set status action:

1. Create a trigger and action.
2. Choose Message:Set Status from the Actions menu.
3. Enter the status message you want in the text field that appears.

Multimedia actions

- *Drag Floating Box* allows a visitor to drag content (contained in a floating box) around in the browser window.
- *Flip Move* allows you to move a floating box from a starting point to another position on the page, and back again when triggered a second time.
- *Move By* specifies the vertical and/or horizontal movement of a floating box. When triggered, the box moves according to the measurement in the Move By action and no further.
- *Move To* behaves just like Flip Move, except that it doesn't return the floating box to the original position when triggered again.
- *Play and Stop Scene* actions control the start and stop points of animations created in the Timeline Editor.
- *Play and Stop Sound* actions control the stop and start of sounds.
- *ShowHide* actions control the visibility of a floating box on the page.
- *Stop Complete* stops all animation, including visual and audio playback. It is useful to give visitors a trigger that allows them to stop animation if their Internet connection is slow, or if they simply don't want to bother with it.
- *Wipe Transitions* create a video-like effect that applies to floating boxes as they enter and leave the visitor's view.

To add a drag floating box action:

1. Choose or create a floating box. If the box is empty, add content to it.
2. If you like, rename the box in the Floating Box Inspector. If you don't rename the box, note its default name. You'll be referring to it by name when you create the action.
3. Create a trigger and action.
4. Choose Multimedia:Drag Floating Box from the Actions menu. The Inspector displays a popup containing all floating boxes within the current document (**Figure 11.37**).
5. Choose the box that you want visitors to be able to drag from the menu.

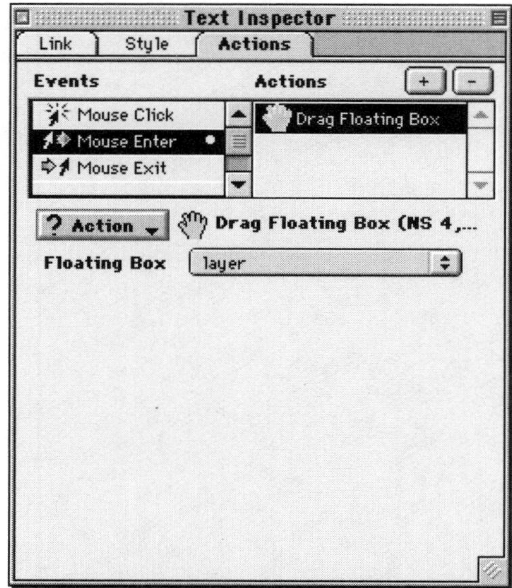

Figure 11.37 A Drag Floating Box action in the Inspector.

To add a flip move action:

1. Within a document that contains at least one floating box, create a trigger and action.
2. Choose Multimedia:Flip Move from the Actions menu. The Inspector displays positioning fields for the action (**Figure 11.38**).
3. Choose a floating box from the popup menu.
4. Click the Get button on the Pos1 line to establish the initial coordinates (in pixels) of the floating box. GoLive fills in the coordinates.
5. Drag the floating box to the position you want to move to, and click Get on the Pos2 line, to fill in the second set of coordinates.
6. Leave the Anim box checked to cause the flip move to work.

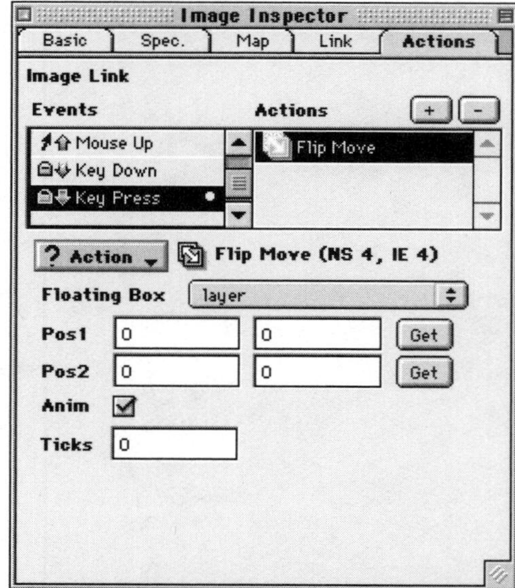

Figure 11.38 A Flip Move action in the Inspector.

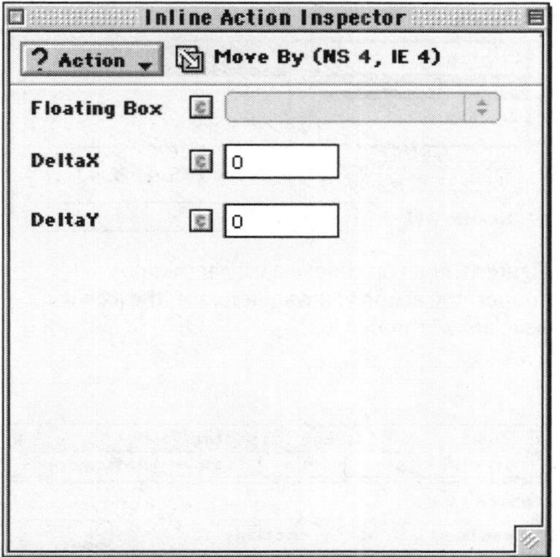

Figure 11.39 A Move By action in the Inspector.

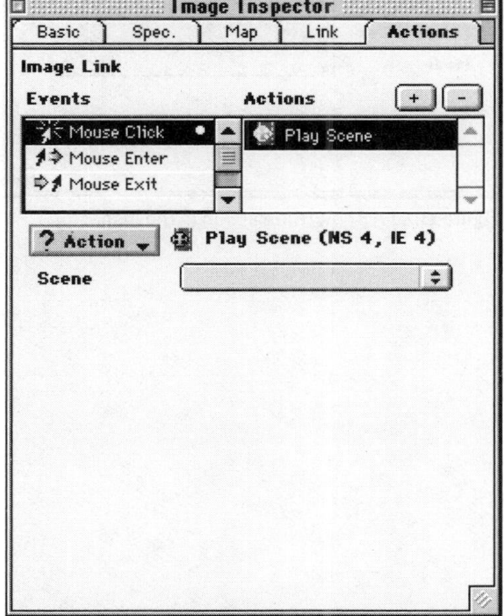

Figure 11.40 A Play Scene action in the Inspector.

✔ Tip

- When you drag the floating box to set its coordinate, you'll lose contact with the Inspector associated with the image or text you're using to trigger the action. Don't worry about that. When you've finished dragging the floating box, click immediately on the text or image, and you'll be returned to the Actions tab. Click Get to set up the flip move, and you're ready to test it.

To create a move to action:

1. Follow steps 1–4 in the Flip Move section, above. In step 2, choose a Move To action.
2. Leave Anim checked.

To create a Move By action:

1. Within a document that contains at least one floating box, create a trigger and action.
2. Choose Multimedia:Move By from the Actions menu (**Figure 11.39**).
3. Choose the floating box to be moved.
4. Enter X and Y coordinates—the number, not the position—which you want the box to move.

To play and stop scenes:

1. Create an animated scene, using the Timeline Editor.
2. Create a mouse trigger and an action.
3. Choose Multimedia:Play Scene from the Actions menu. The result appears in **Figure 11.40**.
4. Choose a scene from the Scene popup menu.

continues on next page

5. To stop the scene, click the "+" button to add a second action to the current trigger.
6. Choose Multimedia:Stop Scene from the Actions menu.

✔ Tip

- Triggers for Play/Stop Scene actions must be mouse events (mouse up, mouse click, mouse enter, etc.). If you choose a non-mouse event, the icon that appears next to the name of the action you select will have an "x" through it. **Figure 11.41** shows an incompatible trigger and action. This applies to any triggers and actions that are incompatible. Use the x as a visual cue that you need to choose a different trigger.

To play and stop sounds:

1. Add a sound to your page using a plugin.
2. Name the plugin in the More tab of the Plugin Inspector.
3. Choose an image, button, or hyperlink and create a trigger and action.
4. Choose Multimedia:Play Sound from the Actions menu.
5. Choose the plugin you named earlier from the popup menu.
6. Click the "+" button to add another action: a Stop Sound action.
7. Choose the plugin name you used before to complete the action.

To add a Show/Hide action:

1. Create a trigger and action.
2. Choose Others:Show/Hide from the Actions menu. The result appears in **Figure 11.42**.
3. Choose a floating box from the Layer popup.

Figure 11.41 If you choose a trigger that doesn't support the action you want it to use, the icon will have an "x" through it.

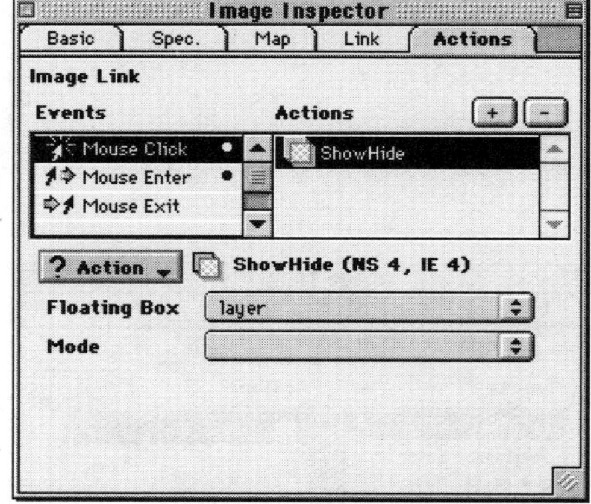

Figure 11.42 A Show/Hide action in the Inspector.

ACTIONS

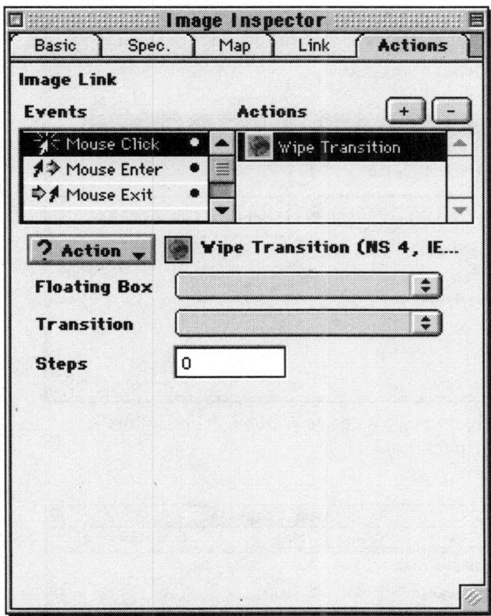

Figure 11.43 A Wipe Transition action in the Inspector.

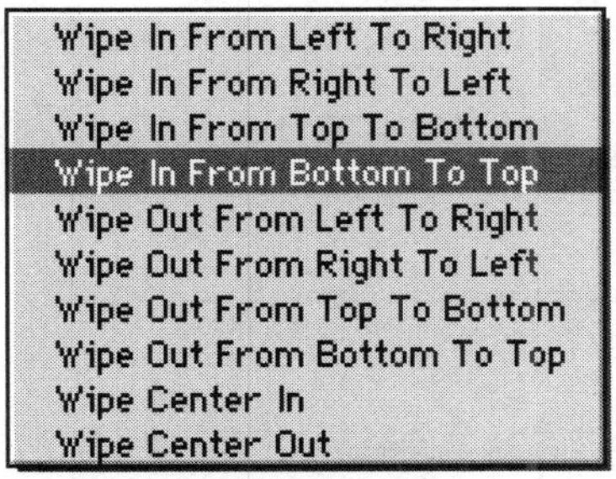

Wipe In From Left To Right
Wipe In From Right To Left
Wipe In From Top To Bottom
Wipe In From Bottom To Top
Wipe Out From Left To Right
Wipe Out From Right To Left
Wipe Out From Top To Bottom
Wipe Out From Bottom To Top
Wipe Center In
Wipe Center Out

Figure 11.44 Choose one of these transition directions.

4. Choose Show, Hide, or Toggle (switch between Show and Hide) from the Mode popup menu.

✔ Tip

- You can use show/hide actions in pairs, creating separate triggers for each position.

To add a stop complete action:

1. Create a trigger and action.
2. Choose Multimedia:Stop Complete from the Actions menu.

To create a wipe transition:

1. With a document including floating box open, choose an item to which you will apply the trigger and action.
2. Create the trigger and action.
3. Choose Multimedia:Wipe Transition from the Actions menu. The result appears in **Figure 11.43**.
4. Choose the floating box you want to wipe from the Floating Box popup.
5. Choose a wipe direction from the menu (**Figure 11.44**).

Other actions

- *Netscape CSS Fix* works around a bug that causes some versions of Netscape Communicator and Navigator 4.0 to lose style sheet and DHTML information when the page is resized.
- *Resize Window* changes the size of the browser window when triggered.
- *Scroll Down, Left, Right or Up* moves the browser display by the number of pixels, and in the direction you set, when triggered.
- *Set BackColor* changes the page's background color.

To add a Netscape CSS fix action:

1. Create a trigger and action.
2. Choose Others:Netscape CSS Fix from the Actions menu.

To add a Resize Window action:

1. Create a trigger and an action.
2. Choose Others:Resize Window from the Actions menu. The result appears in **Figure 11.45**.
3. Enter the Width and Height (in pixels) that you want to apply to the page when this action is triggered.

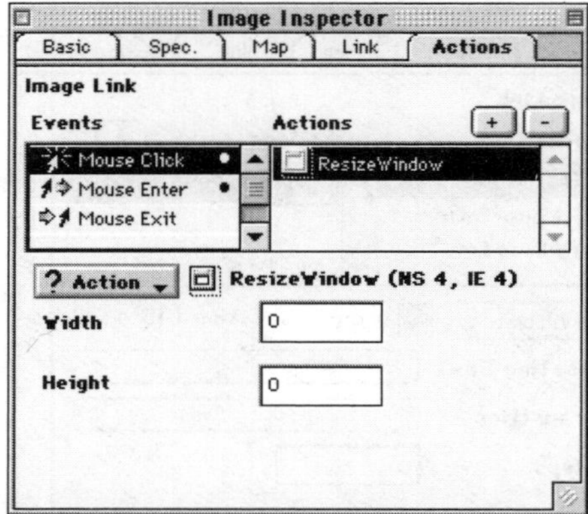

Figure 11.45 A Resize Window action in the Inspector.

To add a scroll action:

1. Create a trigger and action.
2. Choose Others:Scroll Down, Scroll Left, Scroll Right or Scroll Up from the Actions menu. The result appears in **Figure 11.46**.
3. Choose the number of pixels to scroll when the action is triggered.
4. Enter the speed (on a scale of 0–100) to scroll.

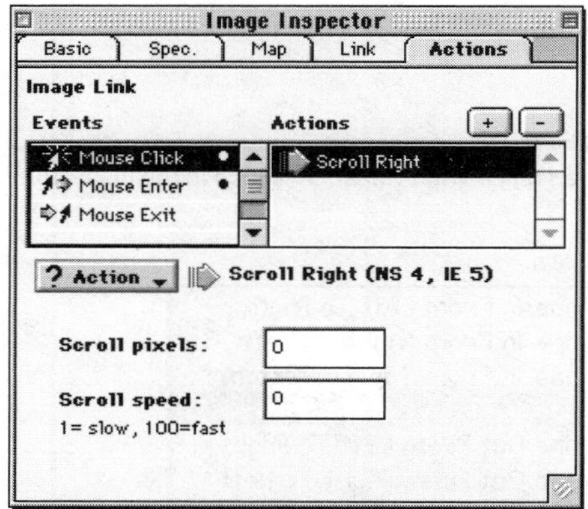

Figure 11.46 A Flip Move action in the Inspector.

To set a Background Color action:

1. Create a trigger and action.
2. Choose Others:Set BackColor from the Actions menu. The result appears in **Figure 11.47**.
3. If it is not available, choose Color Palette from the Windows menu to display it.
4. Choose a color from the Color Palette.
5. Drag from the preview pane of the Color Palette to the Background Color box in the Inspector window.

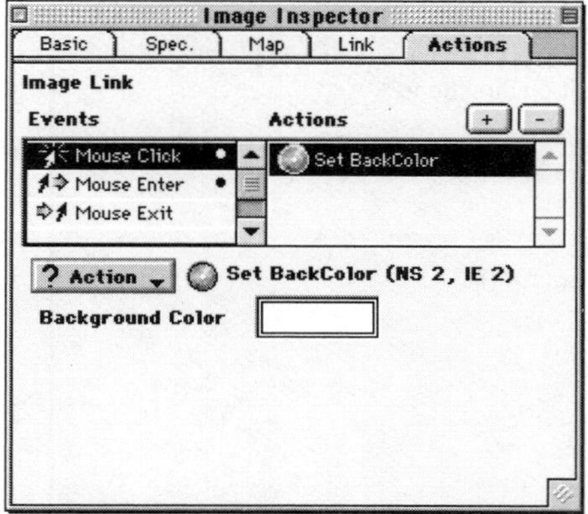

Figure 11.47 A Background Color action in the Inspector.

ACTIONS

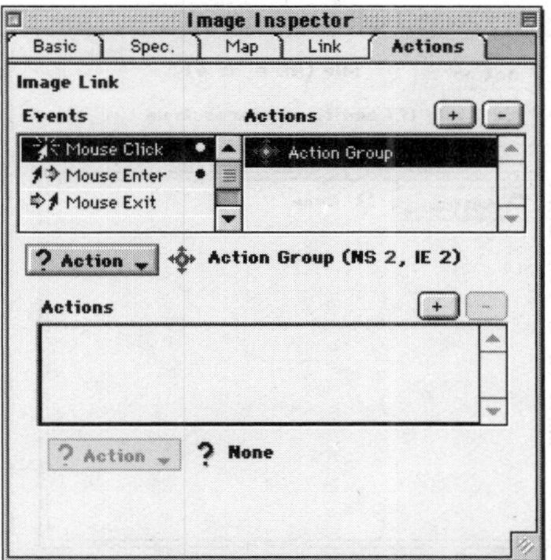

Figure 11.48 An Action Group in the Inspector.

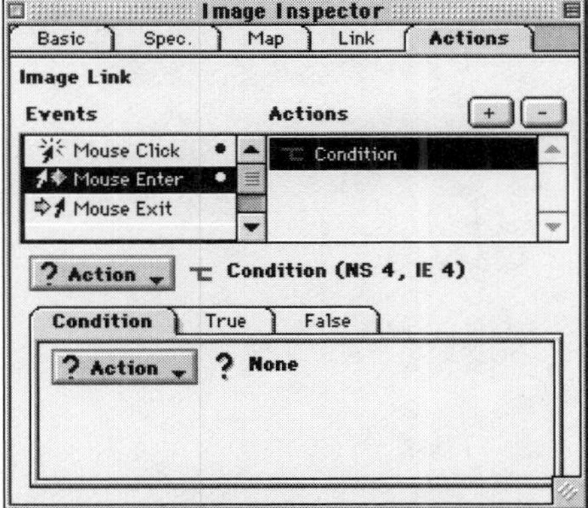

Figure 11.49 [missing caption for 11.49 – coming from author]

Special actions

- *ActionGroup* gathers several actions together to be performed simultaneously.
- *Call Action* calls another Action anywhere on the page. You usually use this Action to call an Action Headitem which you set to execute OnCall.
- *Call Function* calls any custom JavaScript function that you have added to your page.
- *Condition* actions are triggered based on whether conditions (such as other actions) occur. They use the Text Variable, Intersection, and Timeout actions.
- *Idle* actions periodically determine whether a condition has been met. It works with intersection and timeout actions, which yield a true/false result. Idle actions affect the entire page, and should be placed in the header section.

To create an action group:

1. Create a trigger and an action.
2. Choose Specials:ActionGroup from the Actions menu. Result: **Figure 11.48**.
3. Click the "+" button to add actions to your group.
4. Add and configure triggers and actions.

To add a condition action:

1. Create a trigger and action.
2. Choose Specials:Condition from the Actions menu. Result: **Figure 11.49**.
3. Choose Specials:Intersection from the secondary Actions menu to specify the intersection of two floating boxes—whether or not they overlap.
4. Choose two floating boxes within the document whose intersection (or lack thereof) should trigger a conditional action. Or Choose Specials:Timeout to

set a conditional action that will occur when a set amount of time has passed.

5. Set the number of seconds to wait.
6. Click the True or False tab.
7. Configure an action that will occur if your condition is (or is not) met.

To add an idle action:

1. Add an Action HeadItem to the header section of a document.
2. In the Inspector window, choose Specials: Idle from the Actions menu (**Figure 11.50**).
3. Check Exit Idle if Condition Returns True.
4. Choose Specials:Intersection, or Specials: Timeout from the Actions menu on the Condition tab, to specify a condition.
5. Add actions that should be taken if the condition is true or false, under the respective tabs in the Inspector.

To add new actions to GoLive:

1. Quit GoLive.
2. In the Finder (Mac) or Windows Explorer (Windows), navigate to Adobe GoLive: Modules:Jscripts:Actions.
3. Create a new directory in the Actions directory for your new group (optional).
4. Drag the actions you've downloaded or purchased into the Actions directory or the directory you've created.
5. Launch GoLive and verify that your new actions appear in the Actions menu.

   If any new Actions have problems that prevent GoLive from using them, GoLive warns you as soon as it has completely launched. It also creates a text file in the main GoLive folder, detailing the problem. Give this file to the Action's creators.

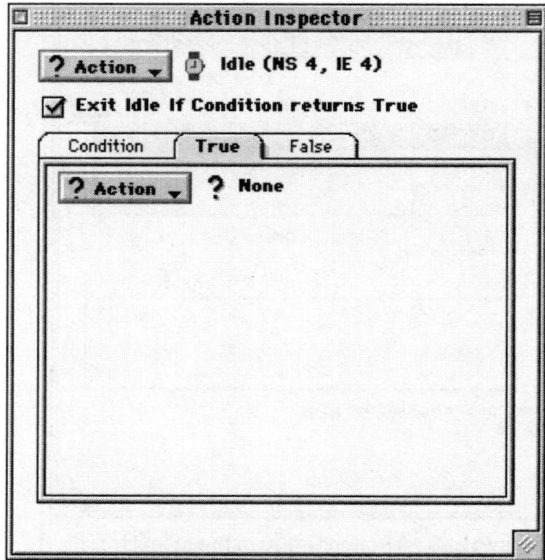

Figure 11.50 An Idle action in the Inspector.

Adding actions to GoLive

You can create your own actions in GoLive, or use actions that are built by others. In addition to the actions I've described in this chapter, Adobe has thoughtfully included an action collection called ActionsPlus.

12

Working with Style Sheets

You can do a lot with basic HTML tags: you can arrange objects and format text, but you can't position text precisely, and you can't always format it exactly as you need to. If you're used to using style sheets in word processing and desktop publishing tools, HTML's limitations can be frustrating.

GoLive includes support for Cascading Style Sheets Level 1 (CSS1), an HTML-standard method of creating formatting instructions and saving them for use with all of your documents. You can use GoLive's familiar tools and fill-in Inspector windows to avoid most of the coding normally associated with creating style sheets.

In this chapter, I cover:

- How style sheets work.
- Types of style sheets.
- Creating style sheets.
- Selectors.
- Adding properties.
- Using style sheets.

How Style Sheets Work

Cascading style sheets consist of files and tags that contain instructions on how to format text on the Web. Style sheets contain individual styles that specify new formatting for an HTML tag throughout a site, or they can alter a single block of text. There are lots of variations, which I describe throughout this chapter.

Like other HTML pages and tags, style sheets require certain syntax to work, and that syntax varies depending on the way the style sheet is intended to work with your document. Similarly, individual styles use syntax to tell a Web browser how to interpret it, and what changes to make in text display and position.

What style sheets are good for

First of all, style sheets allow you to create and save sets of formatting instructions for blocks of text within your Web pages. This makes it easier to establish a consistent design for your pages and to apply it quickly throughout your site without having to remember the parameters you need.

Most importantly, style sheets provide some capabilities that have, up to now, been unavailable to Web authors. You can use them to specify the precise position of text on the page and to set measurements for margins and vertical and horizontal spacing. Without style sheets, the position of your text is subject to the interpretation of each visitor's browser.

Style sheet syntax

It's easiest to think of style sheets and their components as a hierarchy. Style sheets can either be composed of a document, or code that is embedded in the body or header section of a Web page. Each style sheet contains styles, also known as style rules, that specify formatting. Each style is defined by its *selectors, properties,* and *values.*

A selector describes how the style interacts with the documents to which you apply it. Properties identify the type, display, or positioning elements that you want to format with the style. Finally, each property supports *values* that specify the way the element will appear, including relevant measurements.

Style sheets are not composed of HTML tags, though browsers can interpret them, just as they do HTML. Style syntax looks like this:

```
Selector {property:value}
```

As you'll see later in this chapter, there are several types of style sheet selectors. In the following example, the selector is an HTML tag, <H1>, which creates a large heading.

```
H1 {font-family:palatino}
```

A single style may have multiple attributes, as follows:

```
H1 {font-family:palatino;font-size:36pt}
```

Of course, GoLive doesn't require you to type style sheet code. You generate it by using the tools I describe in the next section.

Using CSS1 correctly

Cascading style sheets are part of the HTML 4.0 specification, approved by the World Wide Web Consortium (W3C), the organization that attempts to create and enforce HTML standards. In order for a Web browser to recognize and interpret style sheets properly, it must support CSS1 tags. Even within CSS1, there are a few style elements that version 4.0 browsers don't support. That's because both Netscape and Microsoft have developed their own CSS1 versions. As I proceed through this chapter, I'll note these inconsistencies, so that you can plan for them when constructing your own style sheets.

Types of Style Sheets

All types of style sheets support the same content-formatting options (properties) and most of the same style rules (selectors), but they differ in the way they connect to Web pages. *Internal* style sheets format the content of a single HTML document, whereas *external* style sheets can be used to change the appearance of a group of documents. Within each category are two methods of applying style sheets and styles to text.

Internal style sheets

There are two types of internal style sheets: *embedded* and *inline*. Each is actually part of the HTML page it supports. An embedded style sheet is included in the document's head section. Embedded style sheets apply formatting or positioning properties to all occurrences of an HTML tag within the document. They are contained within the <STLYE></STYLE> tag and use the syntax described above to specify individual styles.

Inline style sheets are included in the body of an HTML document and apply styles to specific tags only. In other words, if you create an inline style to change the color of an <H2> tag to blue, the style rule would appear next to the heading you want to change (in GoLive's Source or Outline view), and would apply only to that instance of the heading. To make all <H2> headings in a document blue, you would need to add an embedded style rule to the header section of the document.

Inline style sheets use class attributes to apply formatting at the location of the HTML tag whose appearance you want to change.

External style sheets

You can use external style sheets to apply styles to one or more documents—your whole Web site, for example. External style sheets can be *linked* and *imported.*

Linked style sheets (using the <LINK> tag in a subject document) are the easiest to understand. All styles for a site can be included in a single style sheet document that you link to each HTML document where its styles should be applied.

Imported style sheets use both internal and external style rules by importing the rules associated with local pages along with global ones that you create within an external style sheet page.

✔ Tip

- GoLive supports imported style sheets, in that it can display them in the style sheet window and preview their results correctly, but you can't use GoLive tools to edit an imported style sheet.

Creating Style Sheets

There are two ways to create a style sheet, and two ways to apply internal and external ones. In this section, I describe how to generate both style sheets and styles. In a subsequent section, I'll explain how to connect internal and external style sheets to HTML documents.

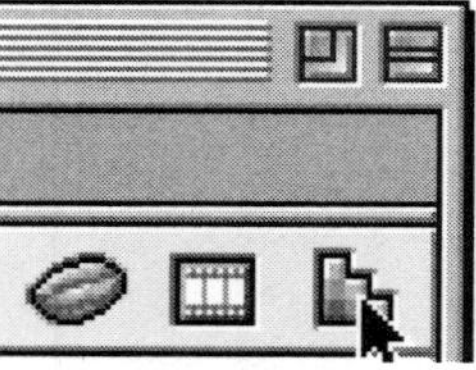

Figure 12.1 Click the Style Sheet button to open the Style Sheet window.

To create an internal style sheet:

With a document open, click the Style Sheet button, located above the main window, at the right edge of the title bar (**Figure 12.1**). A new Style Sheet window appears (**Figure 12.2**).

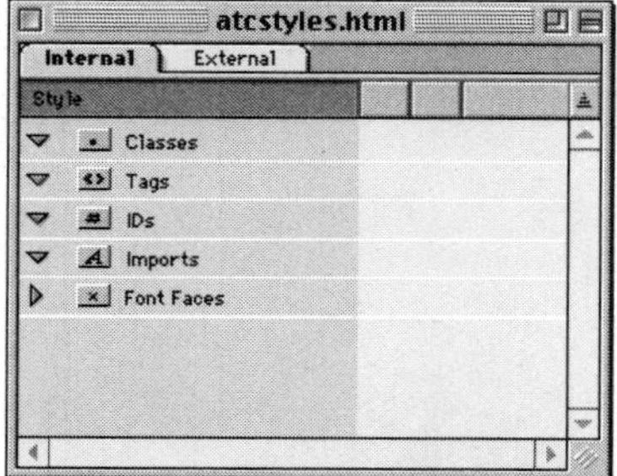

Figure 12.2 The Style Sheet window.

To add a style to a style sheet:

1. With the style sheet file open (the style sheet window should be visible), choose New Class from the toolbar (**Figure 12.3**). A new style appears in the Style Sheet window, under the appropriate heading. You could also have chosen New Tag, or New ID, to create these kinds of style selectors. You'll learn more about selectors in the next section.
2. To begin configuring the style, locate or open the Inspector window, which contains the CSS Selector Inspector (**Figure 12.4**).
3. Name the style. Do not use spaces or underscores in the style name.
4. Click on the other tabs in the CSS Selector Inspector to configure the style's properties. I'll walk you through configuring each tab in the Properties section of this chapter.

Figure 12.3 Choose New Class from the toolbar to add a Class Selector to a style sheet.

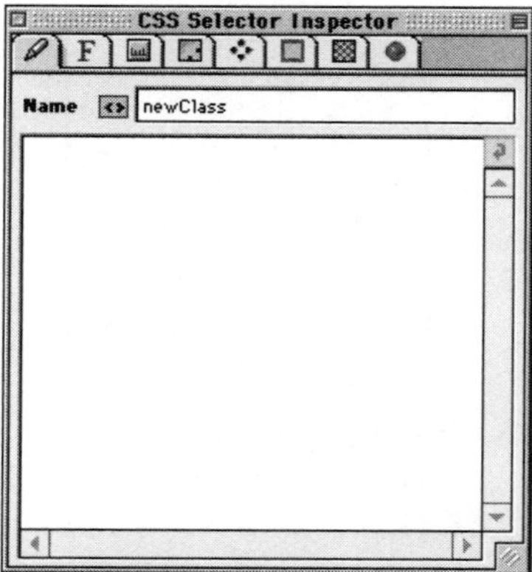

Figure 12.4 The tabs in the CSS Selector Inspector allow you to configure styles.

Figure 12.5 Once you have configured a style, its properties appear in the Inspector.

5. Once you've configured one or two properties, click on the Basic (Pencil) tab (where you named the style) in the Inspector. Notice that your properties appear in the pane below the name of your style (**Figure 12.5**).

To create an external style sheet:

1. Choose New Special:New Stylesheet Document from the File menu. An untitled style sheet window appears.
2. Add styles to the style sheet as described in the previous section, and configure style properties.
3. Save the style sheet to the folder containing your site's Web pages. Notice that the sheet's default name contains the suffix .css. When you rename the sheet, be careful to retain the .css suffix so that the style sheet can be recognized by your visitors' Web browsers.

Selectors

Style sheet selectors tell the style sheet how an individual style will interact with the style sheet and the documents it supports. GoLive recognizes three types of style sheet selectors:

- Tags.
- Classes.
- IDs.

Tag selectors

Tag selectors allow you to apply style rules to any HTML tag within a document. Applying a tag selector tells GoLive (and the browser a visitor uses to view your page) to style all occurrences of the tag according to style properties you specify. You can use tag selectors with all four types of internal and external CSS1 style sheets.

To create a tag selector:

1. Open a new or existing style sheet document, along with a document to which you want to apply a tag selector. Type some text in the document and format the text as a level one heading, using the toolbar.
2. Choose New Tag from the toolbar (**Figure 12.6**). The new tag appears in the Style Sheet window.
3. In the CSS Selector Inspector, type **H1**. Do not include the usual < and > brackets. You can create a tag selector for any HTML tag that uses the <tag> </tag> syntax.
4. Configure the new style's properties under the property tabs of the Inspector window. Notice that the text in your document changes as you specify style options.

Figure 12.6 Choose New Tag from the toolbar to add a tag selector. Add an external style sheet reference by choosing New Item from the toolbar.

Figure 12.7 Choose New Class from the toolbar to add a class selector. Choose the file to refer to with the External Style Sheet Inspector.

Figure 12.8 Choose New ID from the toolbar to add an ID selector.

Class selectors

Unlike tags, class selectors apply style formatting to specific text blocks, rather than to all occurrences of a particular HTML tag. Classes use conditional rules (if x exists and meets these criteria, then the style should be applied). You could, for example, create a class that colors an H2 heading blue, but only when it's also indented from the left margin.

To create a class selector:

1. With a style sheet window open, choose New Class (**Figure 12.7**) from the toolbar.
2. In the CSS Selector Inspector, name the class. You can use any name you like, because classes don't depend on or expect to see an HTML tag as the identifier within the style sheet code.
3. Configure the class style with the Properties tabs of the Inspector.

ID Selectors

ID selectors apply a chosen style to a single text block or element. They don't include conditions for applying a style to tags or to other parts of a document. If you aren't interested in creating an elaborate system of style sheets to manage the formatting of lots of Web pages, ID-based styles are a great way to add a little CSS flare to a page or two. ID selectors are often used to apply styles to floating boxes.

To create an ID selector:

1. With a style sheet window open, choose New ID from the toolbar (**Figure 12.8**).
2. In the CSS Selector Inspector, name the ID. You can use any name you like.
3. Configure the ID style with the properties tabs of the Inspector.

Adding Properties

Throughout this chapter, I've referred to style sheet properties. Properties are the specific formatting elements you use to change the appearance of text with style sheets. All style sheet types and selectors use the same set of properties.

Properties are truly the nuts and bolts of style sheets, because they add formatting capabilities that are otherwise unavailable to Web authors who use standard HTML. For example, using a style sheet property, you can specify that all level 2 headings should be 18 point Helvetica, with 36 points of leading above the heading. Try doing that with basic HTML.

The seven categories of style sheet properties supported by GoLive are:

- Font.
- Text.
- Box.
- Positioning.
- Border.
- Background.
- List.

✔ Tip

- Just because you can create a property doesn't mean that it will work with all 4.0 browsers. Unfortunately, browser vendors are inconsistent about the way they support properties. It's important that you test style sheets with all major browsers before making your pages live.

In this section, I'll describe how to configure style sheet properties. But first I need to explain a couple of unique configuration elements: measurements and color handling.

Measurements

Style sheet properties support a measurement scheme that is different from standard HTML. Although they do support the familiar pixel and percentage measurements, for example, you'll also find that style sheets accept measurements in picas, centimeters, inches, and more.

Units of measure supported by style sheets are:

- *Absolute measurements*: point, pica, millimeter (mm), centimeter (cm), and inch.
- *Relative units*: em, ex, and pixel.
  Em measures the item relative to the height (in points) of the current font.
  Ex measures text relative to the letter X, also in the current font. Pixels are relative to the resolution of the screen.
- *Percent unit:* expresses styled text as a percentage of the default.
- *Keyword units*: ranging from XXSmall to XXLarge measure text, like standard HTML size tags, relative to the default size.

Color

Colors are also handled differently within style sheets than they are in regular HTML. Style sheets support only 16 colors from the W3C RGB color palette. They are named on popup menus within the Properties tabs of the CSS Selector Inspector, or you can drag them from the Color Palette.

To set font properties:

1. Open a style sheet and create a style.

continues on next page

2. In the CSS Selector Inspector, click the Font tab. It appears in **Figure 12.9**.
3. Choose a font color (if you want to change it) from the popup menu, or drag a color from the Color Palette. GoLive will interpret the color you choose from the Color Palette to conform to the 16-color palette.
4. Type a number in the Font Size field and choose a unit of measure from the popup.
5. Type a Line Height and choose an option from the popup, using the one of the same measurement units. Line Height is referred to as *leading* in the print publishing world.
6. To apply a new typeface, choose a font family from the popup at the bottom of the Inspector window (**Figure 12.10**), or click New to add a new family.
7. Choose font style, and/or decoration options in the Inspector.
8. To change the font's weight, choose a number from 100 to 900 from the popup. Choosing Normal applies a weight of 400, while Bold equals a weight of 700. Font weights are absolute, but the Bolder and Lighter options are relative to the default, or to any existing style from which this new style inherits properties.

To set text properties:

1. Click the Text tab in the CSS Selector Inspector. It appears in **Figure 12.11**.
2. Edit Text Indent, Letter Spacing, and Word Spacing the same way you chose numerical font properties, as described above.
3. Choose an option from the Vertical Alignment popup to relate the styled text to the rest of the text on the page.

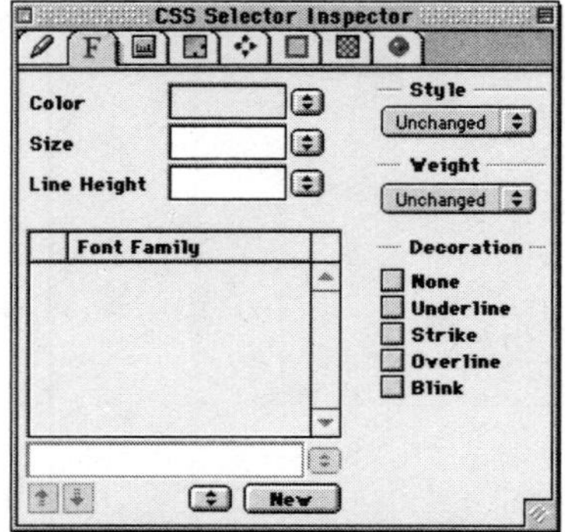

Figure 12.9 The Font Properties tab of the CSS Selector Inspector.

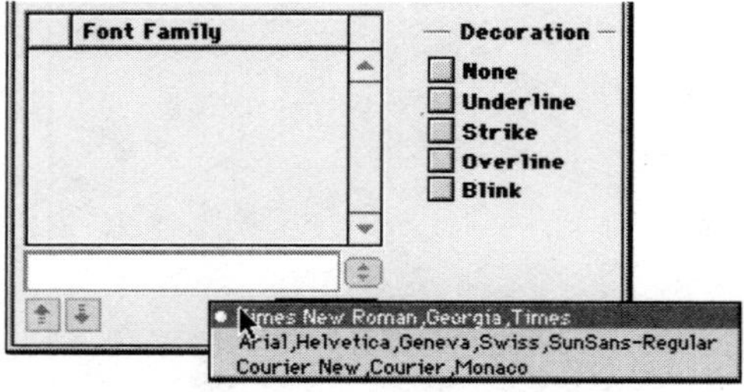

Figure 12.10 Choose a font family from the popup menu.

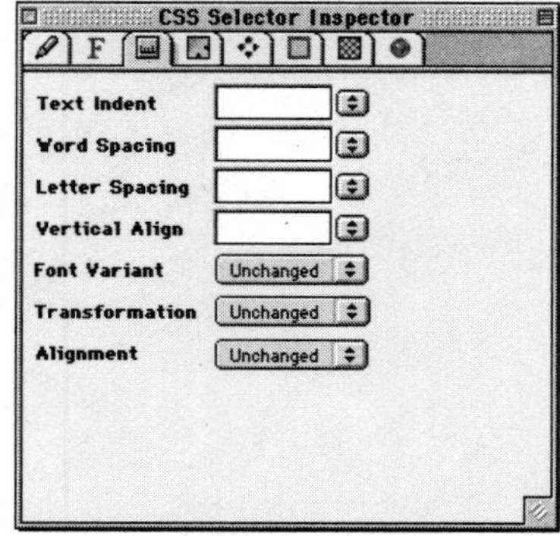

Figure 12.11 The Text Properties tab of the CSS Selector Inspector.

ADDING PROPERTIES

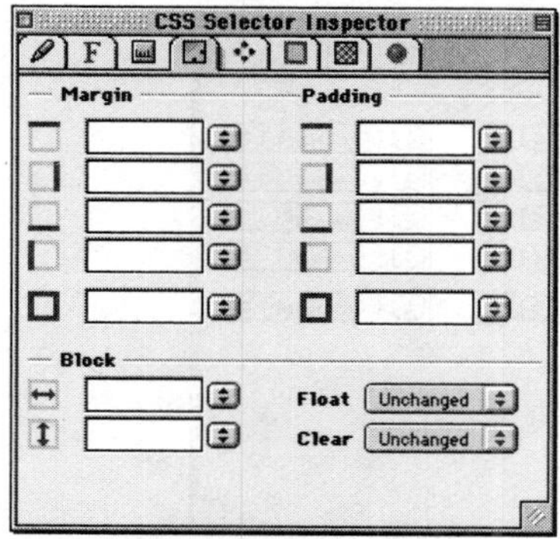

Figure 12.12 The Box Properties tab of the CSS Selector Inspector.

4. Use the Font Variant and Transformation options to further customize the text within your style. Both allow you to change the case of styled text.
5. Like standard HTML alignment options, the Alignment popup under the Text Properties tab aligns text to the page horizontally.

To set box properties:

1. Click the Box tab in the CSS Selector Inspector. It appears in **Figure 12.12**. The "box" defines the area of the document controlled by the style you are creating.

   If you don't change box properties, the boundary is the text itself. If you do, there will be space between styled text and other elements of the page.
2. Choose margins for the box to create it. You only need to choose margins for those boundaries you want to extend.
3. Choose padding to create space between the styled text and the margin you've created.
4. You can use the Block option (horizontal and/or vertical) to define width and height of the box. This property is most useful when you need to include an image within the styled box.

To set border properties:

1. Click the Border tab in the CSS Selector Inspector. It appears in **Figure 12.13**. Unlike the box properties we created earlier, which create an invisible boundary around the element you are styling, border properties specify a visible border for the styled element.
2. Choose left, right, top, and/or bottom border thickness by typing values and using the popup menus to choose a measuring unit.
3. Choose colors for borders from the popup or with the Color Palette.
4. Choose the type of border (solid, dotted, etc.) from the popup menus.
5. If you want a four-sided border where each side has the same thickness, color, and line style, use the box field and popup menu (**Figure 12.14**).

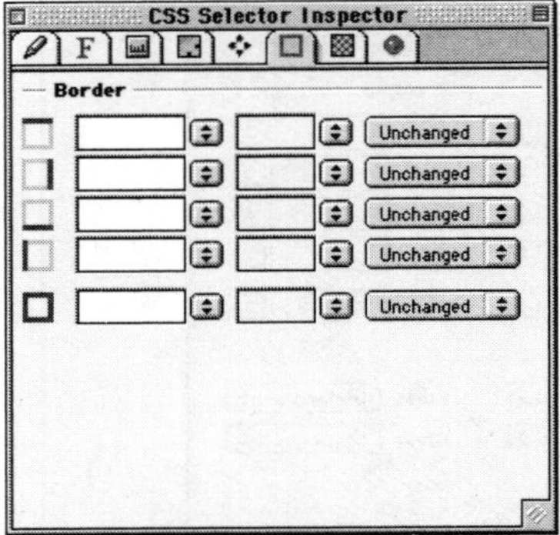

Figure 12.13 The Border Properties tab of the CSS Selector Inspector.

Figure 12.14 Make the border uniform on all sides with the box options in the border tab of the Inspector.

To set background properties:

1. Click on the Background properties tab in the CSS Selector Inspector. It appears in **Figure 12.15**. Use these options to add a background color or image to the box that surrounds your styled text.
2. Click the checkbox, then the Browse button (or use Point & Shoot) to locate a file you would like to use as a background image.
3. Choose a Repeat option to tile the background image within the box. Repeat X tiles the image horizontally; Repeat Y tiles it vertically.
4. Choose an Attach option to specify whether or not a background image should scroll as a visitor scrolls within the browser window.

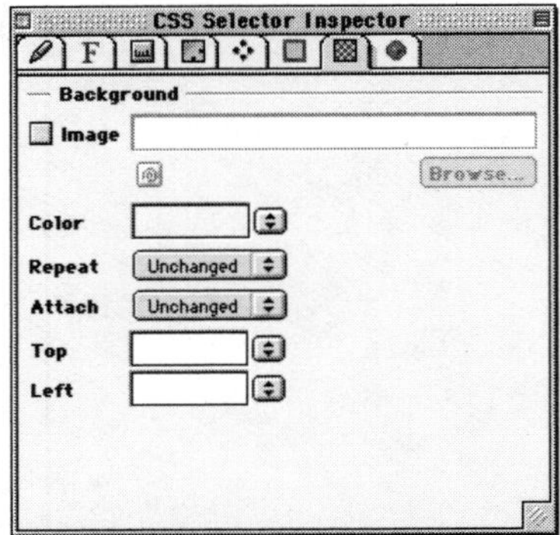

Figure 12.15 The Background Properties tab of the CSS Selector Inspector.

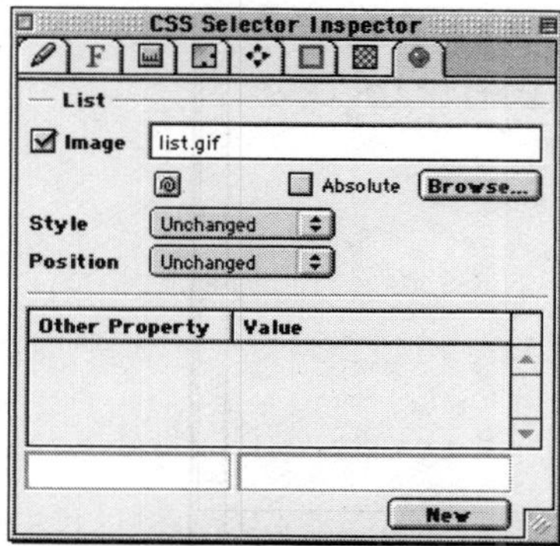

Figure 12.16 The List Properties tab of the CSS Selector Inspector.

5. Choose Top and Left measurements to position a background image relative to the box in which it is located.

6. To create a colored background, choose a color from the Color Palette or the popup menu.

To set list properties:

1. Click the List tab in the CSS Selector Inspector. It appears in **Figure 12.16**. List properties allow you to customize bullets or other list item markers that appear within HTML lists.

2. Click the image checkbox and locate an image to use as an alternative list item marker.

3. From the Style popup, choose an HTML list style to use.

4. From the Position popup, chose Inside (to set the list item marker and subsequent lines of text flush) or Outside (to set the list item marker apart from the remaining lines of text).

Using Style Sheets

When I defined the two general types of style sheets (internal and external) and the four ways of applying them, I noted that *attaching* styles to one or more HTML documents differentiates style sheets in GoLive much more than *creating* them does. As promised, here's the scoop on adding the styles you've created to HTML pages.

First I explain how to apply internal style sheets, in the form of classes and IDs, and then move to linking and importing external styles.

Applying classes

Unlike tag styles, which apply automatically to all matching HTML tags in a document, classes—which apply to conditional instances of text—must be specifically connected to relevant text.

To apply class styles to text:

1. Create and configure a class-based style in a document to which you want to add the style.
2. Click on some text to display the Text Inspector.
3. Click the Style tab to display classes available to this document.
4. Choose the way you want to apply the style by clicking in the appropriate column, next to the style you're working with (**Figure 12.17**). A checkbox appears beside the option you choose. (See **Table 12.1** for style type definitions).

Applying IDs

Unlike most operations in GoLive, applying an ID style requires you to edit HTML code. You'll need to locate the text you want to style, modify the existing formatting slightly, and add the ID tag. Here we go!

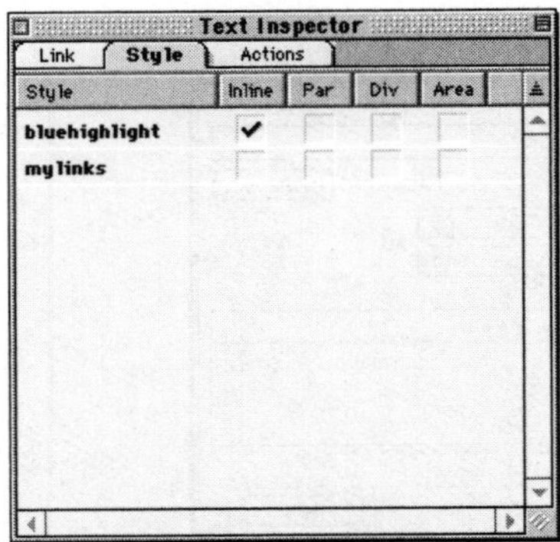

Figure 12.17 Apply an inline style by clicking in the Inline column, next to the style you want to use. A checkbox appears.

Table 12.1

Style Type Definitions

STYLE TYPE	DOES THIS
Inline	Styles a selected text block with an inline class
Par	Styles a full paragraph
Div	Styles selected text and separates it from other elements on the page, allowing you to align it independently.
Area	Applies a class to the entire body section of the current HTML page

USING STYLE SHEETS

To apply an ID selector:

1. With an ID created and configured, click on the Source tab in the document window to display the Source view.
2. Locate the text you want to format with an ID.
3. To apply an ID to all text enclosed within HTML tags, insert the ID selector within the start tag of your text block, by adding **ID=idname**. Here are two examples:

   Original code:

   ```
   <H2>One Day Sale!</H2>
   <P>All bicycles 50 percent off,
   → today only.</p>
   ```

   With IDs added:

   ```
   <H2 ID="salebanner">One Day
   → Sale!</H2>
   <P ID="redandlarge">All bicycles 50
   → percent off, today only.</P>
   ```

1. To apply an ID only to a portion of a text that falls within tags, use this syntax:

   ```
   <P>All bicycles <SPAN ID=
   → "salebanner">50 percent</SPAN>
   → off, today only.</P>
   ```

2. Verify your work by returning to the layout view, or, better yet, checking out your new ID styles in a CSS-capable browser.

Referring to external style sheets

Like ordinary hyperlinks, external style sheets are referenced in an HTML page with links between two documents.

To refer to an external style sheet:

1. Open a GoLive document to which you want to add external style sheet references.
2. Open the style sheet (for this page) by clicking the Style Sheet button.

continues on next page

3. In the Style Sheet window, click the External tab.
4. Choose New Item from the toolbar (**Figure 12.18**). An empty reference appears in the External tab of the Style Sheet window.
5. Click in the Inspector window, which has changed to become the External Style Sheet Inspector.
6. Click the Browse button (or use Point & Shoot) to locate a document containing styles you want to use in the current document.

   or

   With the Site window visible, locate the .css document and drag it onto the page icon at the top left edge (near the page title) of the document window.

   The finished Inspector appears in **Figure 12.19**. Meanwhile, the Style Sheet window now includes the name of the document, a checkmark indicating that the link is valid, and the URL (**Figure 12.20**). The document is updated automatically to reflect the newly linked style or styles.
7. If the current document refers to multiple style sheets, use the up and down arrows to move the current style sheet up or down in the cascading order.
8. To take a look at the external style sheet, click Open in the External Style Sheet Inspector.

Figure 12.18 Add an external style by clicking New Item in the toolbar.

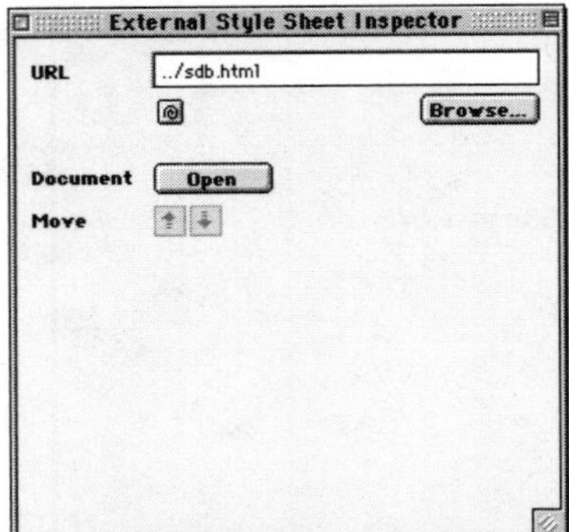

Figure 12.19 Choose an external style sheet in the Style Sheet Inspector.

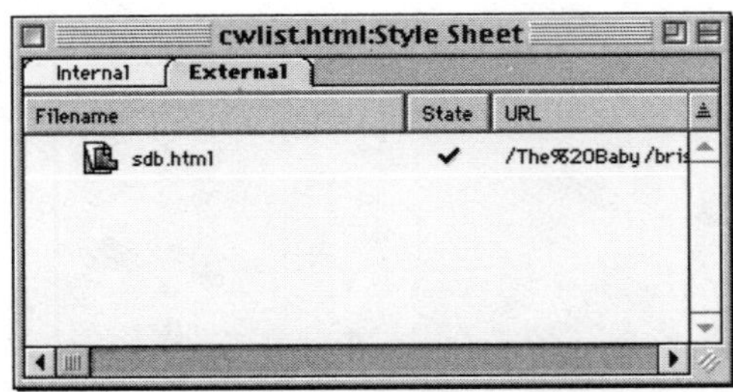

Figure 12.20 This external reference has been linked to a style sheet.

13

ANIMATION

I've described how you can use GoLive's dynamic HTML tools to position text and objects, and how actions can add interactivity to a page. Now, for the final piece of the DHTML puzzle: animation, the ability to cause objects to look as if they're moving within a Web page.

DHTML animation allows you to move layers (floating boxes, in GoLive-speak), change their dimensions and visibility, and rearrange them relative to one another by altering their stacking order.

In this chapter I cover:

- Animation prerequisites.
- Creating a basic animation.
- Adding actions to animation.

Animation Prerequisites

You create DHTML animation by filling floating boxes with content and then specifying a path along which the floating box will move on the page—by creating a *timeline*. Timelines use JavaScript to control the movement and appearance of layers (floating boxes) on the page. You can add bells and whistles to animated content with JavaScript actions that control the way animated objects move, or how they interact with other items on the page.

The tools you use to build animation should be familiar to you, if you've read Chapters 10 and 11 in this book. Chapter 10 introduced the floating box, the structure within which all animated objects reside, and describes how to configure and stack multiple boxes. Chapter 11 describes how to use JavaScript actions to bring interactivity to the page, and includes details about all of the actions included with GoLive.

We'll add a bit more background in this chapter, and then we'll begin to animate some objects.

✔ Tip

- Because animation depends on DHTML to simulate the movement of objects, only 4.0 or later browsers can display animated content.

Figure 13.1 The Timeline Editor button.

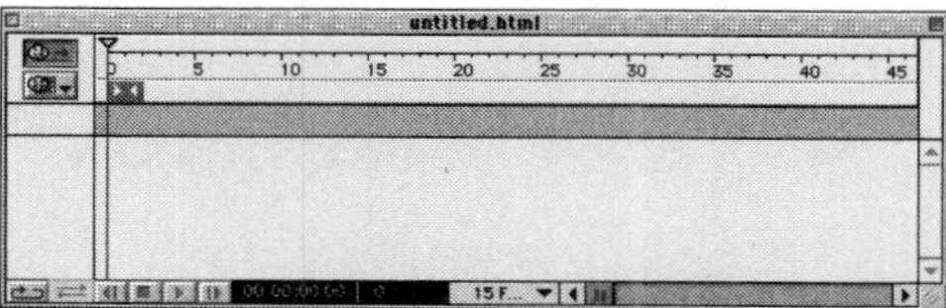

Figure 13.2 A new Timeline Editor window.

The Timeline Editor

Animations come to life in the Timeline Editor, where you specify when and how layers move, and attach actions to them.

To open the Timeline Editor:

1. Open a GoLive document.
2. Click the Timeline Editor button at the top of the document window **(Figure 13.1)** to view the editor window (**Figure 13.2**).

Control of animation is centered in the Timeline Editor. You manage not only the timing of the animation, but also its relationship to other animation on the same page; the keyframes that signal the beginning of an animation, or a change in one; and actions that trigger the animation's playback. All animation elements (scenes) on a single Web page are controlled from a single Timeline Editor window, which bares the name of the host page. The Timeline Editor is also where you apply and control actions—JavaScripts that control behavior of floating boxes.

Preparing to Animate

Before you can animate, you must first create and configure the objects that are to be animated, along with the floating box that will contain the animated content.

To prepare objects for animation:

1. Choose an object you want to animate. If you will be animating an image, prepare it by saving it as a Transparent GIF or Interlaced GIF. These formats remove the image's background, so that it appears transparent when placed on your page. You can use shareware tools such as GIFConverter or GraphicConverter to do this.
2. If your animation will include multiple versions of the same object that change as you animate them, duplicate the original object and make the changes to the image that will appear as the animated image comes into view.

To add a floating box:

1. Open a new or existing GoLive document in the Layout view.
2. Double-click or drag the Floating Box tool from the Palette's Basic tab into the document window.
3. Add the image you created earlier to the document by dragging an image placeholder into the floating box. Locate the image with Point & Shoot or by browsing to the file you want.

   You can also add existing page content to the floating box by dragging it from elsewhere on the page.

4. If you want to include a second object in this animated frame, drag that object into the floating box, too. Do not use this step if your animation will cause a second object to replace the first. This step should only be used to create a single animated frame. You can add text or a second image to the floating box.

5. When you're finished adding items to the floating box, resize it so that the box fits tightly around the object or objects inside.

6. Name the floating box in the Floating Box Inspector.

7. Choose a background color for the floating box as you wish.

✔ Tip

- You can configure the floating box, just as you can other GoLive objects, with the Inspector. For our purposes, the floating box is ready for a simple animation. If you want to learn more about configuring floating boxes, see Chapter 10.

Building a Simple Animation

Now, we're ready to create a simple animation, in which one floating box and its contents will move across the page.

To animate the floating box:

1. Select the floating box you created earlier.
2. Open the Timeline Editor by clicking the Timeline Editor button at the upper-right corner of the document window's title bar. The Timeline Editor window appears.
3. The Timeline Editor contains a single keyframe, which indicates the starting point for the timeline. Create a new *key frame*—a marker that indicates a change in the animation playback range—by Command-clicking (Mac) or Control-clicking (Windows) in the timeline's time track, as shown in **Figure 13.3**. Your new keyframe marks the animation's endpoint. In the document window, drag the floating box to the location where you want it to appear at the end of the animation.
4. If you have not already positioned the floating box in the document window, click the keyframe at the beginning of the time track in the Timeline Editor and drag the floating box to the desired starting point in the document window.
5. To set the box's ultimate location—where it will be when the animation is completed —click the second keyframe and then drag the floating box to your chosen location.
6. Click the Play button at the bottom of the Timeline Editor (**Figure 13.4**) to preview your animation. You can use the other tape recorder-style buttons to move forward, backward in your animation, or to view it in a loop.

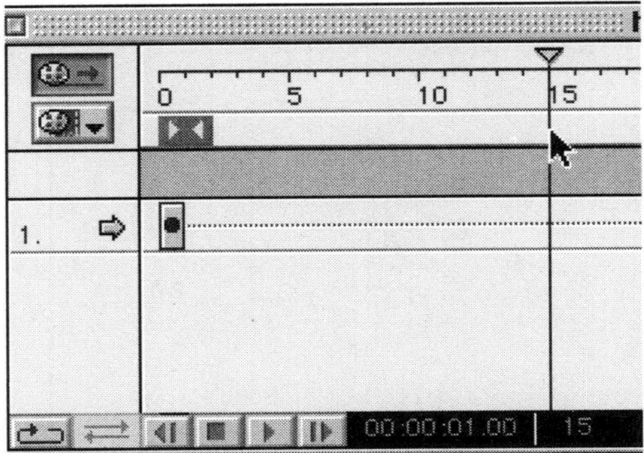

Figure 13.3 Command-click (Mac) or Control-click (Windows) on the Timeline Editor's Time track to create a new keyframe. The keyframe will appear on the keyframe track. Note that there is already a keyframe at the beginning of the keyframe track.

Figure 13.4 Click Play to preview your animation.

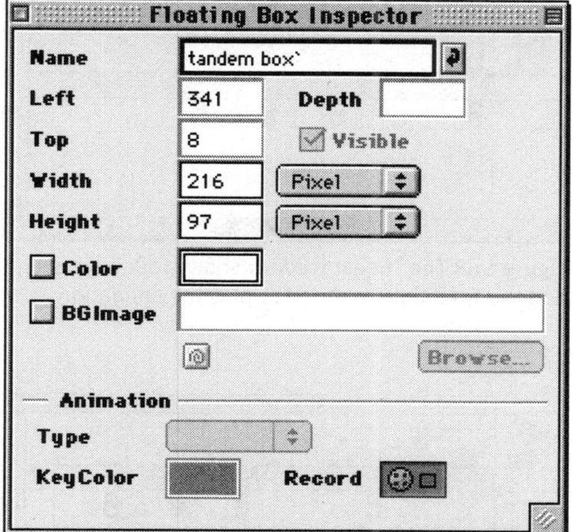

Figure 13.5 Click the Record button in the Floating Box Inspector to create animation as you drag a floating box across the document window.

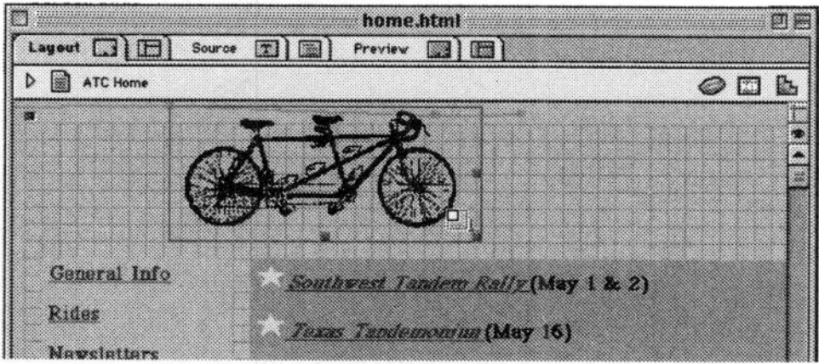

Figure 13.6 Here is the simple animation. It moves the tandem bicycle from left to right, above the text.

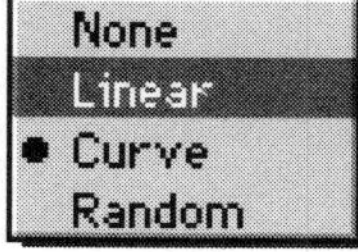

Figure 13.7 Choose the path from the Type menu in the Floating Box Inspector.

✔ Tip

- You can also animate a floating box by using the Record feature of the Floating Box Inspector. With the Timeline Editor visible, select the floating box, which should be located at its origin on the page. Click the Record button in the Floating Box Inspector (**Figure 13.5**). Drag the box across the screen. When you reach your destination, click Record again to end the animation. Preview the animation by clicking Play. Your animation moves across the screen (**Figure 13.6**).

To vary the animation's path:

1. With the floating box in its original position (click on the first keyframe), add a new keyframe between the two existing ones. To make more room, first drag the second keyframe to the right.
2. Select the floating box and drag it to a location that is not on the original path you created—below and to the right of the origin, for example.
3. Click Play. The animated object moves from the origin to the new location to its final destination.
4. Add more keyframes to create additional points along the animation path.
5. Play back the result to see how you like the way the animation moves.
6. To specify the type of path the object should take between two keyframes, select the final keyframe in the animation, and drag the floating box past the right edge of the document window (or set a Left value beyond your window's width in the Floating Box Inspector). Then choose a path from the Type menu, under the Animation label, in the Floating Box Inspector (**Figure 13.7**).

Adjusting the timeline

I decided to move my bike across the page in four steps, dropping it down from the top, then moving further across, and then back up to the top. To do this, I used four keyframes. The trouble is that the animation looks jerky if I don't place the keyframes at reasonable intervals (to control the speed) and use appropriate animation paths (to control the motion of the bike).

To tweak the timeline:

1. With a multi-point animation path set up, look at the Timeline Editor. Mine shows that I'm using four keyframes in 22 frames. The animation takes 1.07 seconds, at 15 frames per second (**Figure 13.8**).
2. Consider the total length of the animation. In my case, stretching it out to a full two seconds seems like a good idea. Move the last keyframe along the time track until it reaches the 30-frame mark. That's 30 frames at 15 frames per second, for a total of 2 seconds of animation. When I move the final keyframe, the others move to the right, proportionate to their original positions.
3. Move other frames within the timeline to space them evenly.

   Since I am using four points in this animation, I want them to occur at equal intervals so that the movement will appear smooth.
4. To help space items precisely, click and drag the ruler (**Figure 13.9**) to the position you want and note the frame number in the bar at the bottom of the screen.
5. When you have reached the frame you want, drag a keyframe to the ruler.

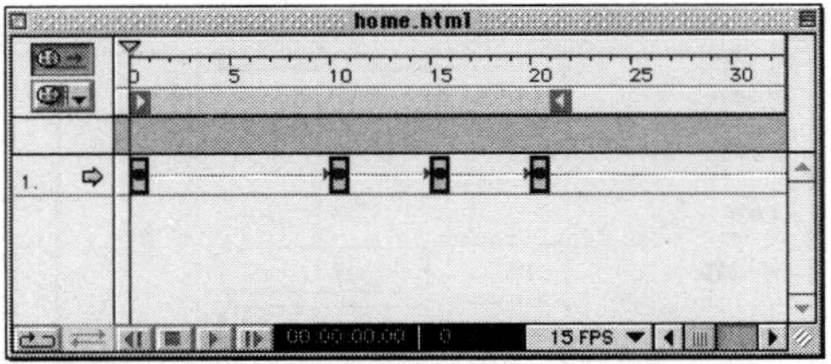

Figure 13.8 The Timeline Editor shows four keyframes and the Total time required to play the animation.

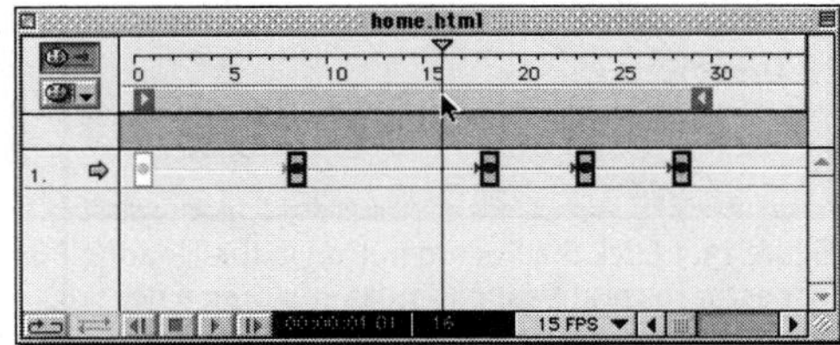

Figure 13.9 Use the ruler to position keyframes and to determine your frame count.

Building a Simple Animation

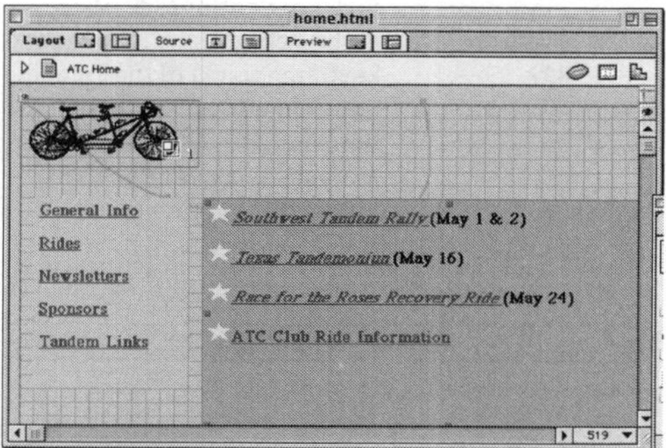

Figure 13.10 My bicycle animation moves along these wobbly lines.

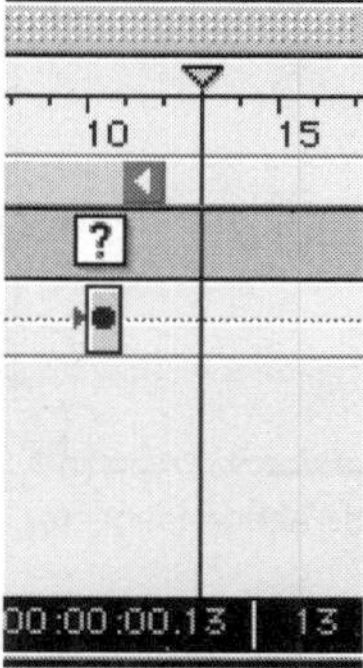

Figure 13.11 The first and second points visited by the animated floating box are connected with a linear path.

6. With keyframes spaced properly, click the Play button to see how the animation is shaping up. Mine is still jerky, because the path (**Figure 13.10**) leaves a lot to be desired.
7. If you like where the paths go, but not how they get there, click on the first keyframe and then Shift-click on the second. Choose a path from the Floating Box Inspector and note the change in the document window (**Figure 13.11**).
8. Changing one path's course may upset the next one a bit. Click the third keyframe to select it and to move the floating box there.
9. Drag the floating box a bit to line it up with the second keyframe location.
10. Click the first keyframe and then Play to see how your animation looks.
11. Make final adjustments and save your work.

Adding Actions to an Animation

You can add any of the actions described in the Actions section of this chapter to an animation timeline. In fact, you can create an action in the Timeline Editor, rather than using the Action tab of the Inspector.

To add an action to a timeline:

1. With the Timeline Editor open, Command-click (Mac) or Control-click (Windows) on the Action Track . An action icon appears, in the form of a question mark (**Figure 13.12**).
2. Click on the action icon to display the Action Inspector.
3. Choose an action (**Figure 13.13**) and configure it. The action item in the timeline changes to reflect your configuration.
4. If necessary, move the action item to the location in the timeline where you want the action to be invoked.

✔ Tip

- Many actions included with GoLive are specific to animation, and plenty of others affect the display of floating boxes, whether animated or not. For more information about configuring and using actions, see Chapter 11.

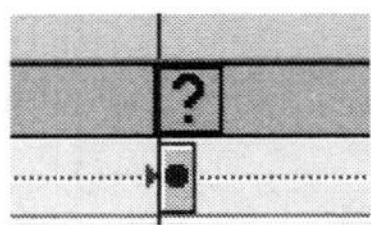

Figure 13.12 Command-click (Mac) or Control-click (Windows) in the Action Track (above the keyframe track) of the Timeline Editor to add an action to the timeline. The action icon appears as a question mark until you configure it.

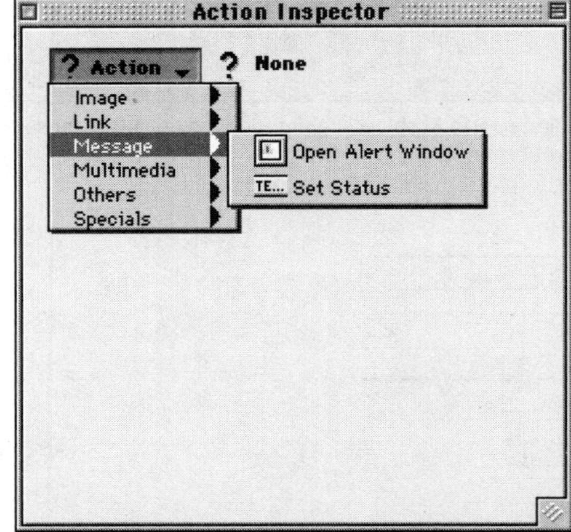

Figure 13.13 Choose an action in the Action Inspector.

WORKING WITH TAGS

As appealing as visual page design is, there are times when it is necessary (and even helpful) to work with HTML directly.

GoLive includes two HTML editing views: the Outline View and the Source View. Although not as intuitive as the Layout View, the Outline View does present HTML pages in hierarchical, organized terms. The Source View breaks down all barriers between the Web page author and the HTML underlying the page.

Once you've got your first taste of Web page coding, you'll be ready for a look at some specialized HTML tags that can add information about your document, such as header tags. You can work with and add your own HTML tags in the Web Database, a tool that helps you and GoLive keep up with the ever-changing HTML standard. Finally, GoLive supports the inclusion of "foreign code"—XML and ASP—in HTML documents.

In this chapter, I cover:

- Using the Outline View.
- Working with the Source View.
- Using header tags.
- Using the Web Database.
- Adding "foreign" code.

Using the Outline View

Think of the Outline View as a bridge between WYSIWYG Web page development and the dark recesses of the HTML language. Like the layout environment, the Outline View can display images and text. And Web page elements (headers, headings, and body elements) appear within an easy-to-understand hierarchical window.

The Outline View displays a hierarchical version of your Web page with HTML tags around the text and graphic elements. **Figure 14.1** shows a Web page in the Layout View and a portion of the same page in the Outline View.

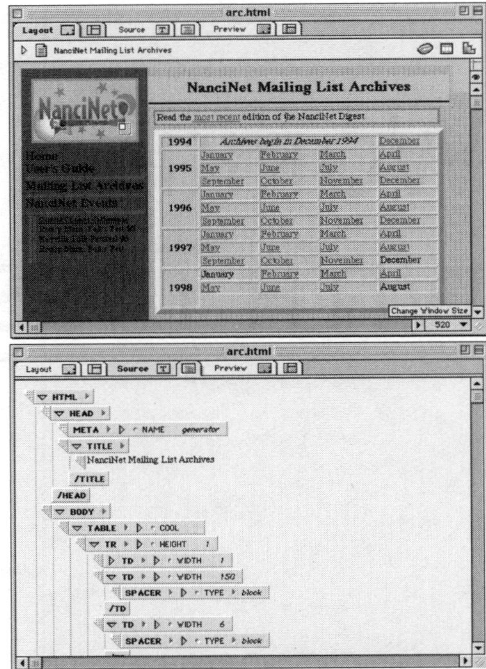

Figure 14.1 Here is a Web page in the Layout View and the same page in the Outline View.

To view a document in the Outline View:

1. Open a GoLive document.
2. In the document window, click the Outline tab (**Figure 14.2**) to switch to the Outline View. The page's outline appears.

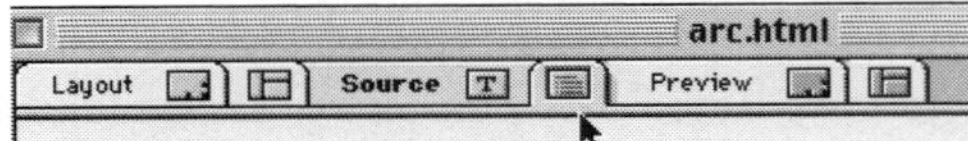

Figure 14.2 Click the Outline tab to view a page in the Outline View.

To view the outline of a new page:

1. Open a new document.
2. Click the Outline tab to view the outline (**Figure 14.3**). Even without text or images, the empty page already has an outline, containing the required structure for the page.

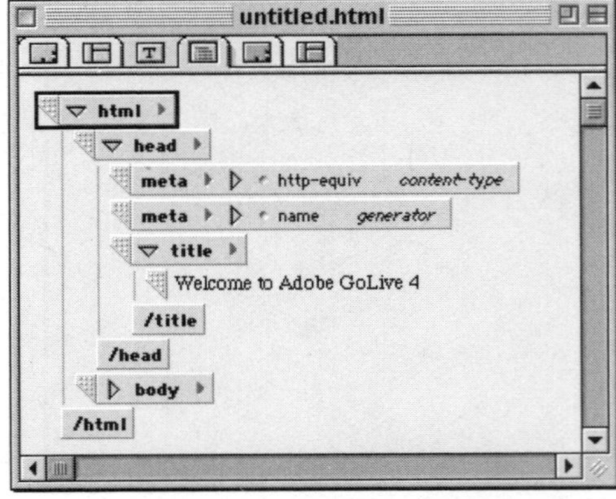

Figure 14.3 A new page as it appears in the Outline View.

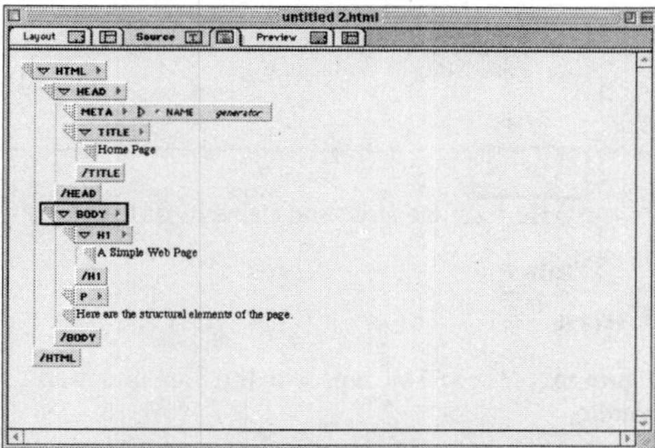

Figure 14.4 This basic outline shows structural and control elements.

Anatomy of an outline

The outline that appears when you view a new GoLive document contains all the essential elements of an HTML page. In the Outline View, they are displayed the way the HTML language expects them to be when a page is translated for viewing on the Web. The HTML tags are arranged hierarchically. Several required elements (HTML, HEAD, and BODY) lead the hierarchy and, like many tags must also be *closed* at the end of the outline, or they will not work properly.

Boxes within the outline represent HTML tags and Web page content. Tag contents appear in subordinate (child) lines within the outline. Tag lines also contain the structural, control, and display attributes of HTML tags. These appear when you expand the outline. In addition to Web page text, you can view images and other objects, just as you can in the Layout view. **Figure 14.4** shows a basic Web page with labels indicating the components described in the next section.

Structural attributes

The Outline View uses three structural components:

- *Boxes* indicate HTML tags. These outline elements' "children"—lower-level items in the hierarchy—contain both content (images and text) and attributes used to display the content properly.
- *Indents* indicate an item's position within the HTML hierarchy. <P> (paragraph) tags appear under and to the right of the <BODY> tag, because paragraphs are contained within the BODY element. The same goes for BODY tags themselves, which are contained within the HTML tag.
- *Vertical* lines between tags indicate that the tags are paired open and close tags, as in <I> and </I>.

Controls

HTML tag entries contain tools that let you manipulate the tag within the outline. These tag entries are:

- *The drag-and-drop handle* moves a tag when you click and drag the handle through the outline.
- *The collapse/expand triangle,* when clicked, shows or hides content and settings for an HTML tag.
- *The show/hide attributes triangle,* to the right of an HTML tag, shows or hides attributes associated with the tag. In some cases, clicking on the triangle displays a popup menu from which you can choose display attributes.
- *The HTML tag name* is itself a control. Command-clicking it displays a popup menu of other HTML tags that you can replace it with if you choose.

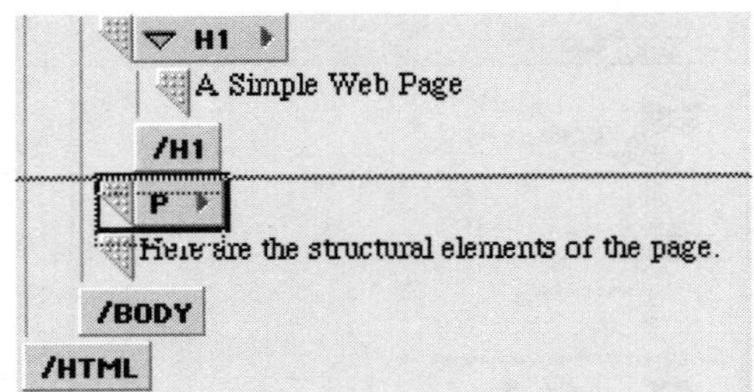

Figure 14.5 Move HTML tags with the drag and drop handle.

Editing in the Outline View

The tools to add or rearrange items in the Layout View (Palette, drag-and-drop, toolbar) are available in the Outline View.

To drag and drop within an outline:

1. In the Outline View, click and drag the drag-and-drop handle (to the left of an HTML tag) up or down. As you drag, a box representing the line you're moving and its content and attributes moves across the screen (**Figure 14.5**). A horizontal line appears as you drag over other tags to indicate where the item will be displayed when you complete the drag.
2. Release the button when you reach the location where the tag is to appear.
3. Click the Layout or Preview tab to examine the change you've made.

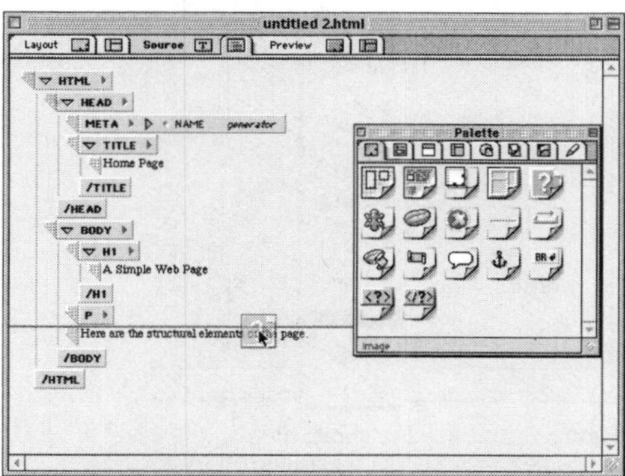

Figure 14.6 Drag a tool from the Palette to the Outline View to add a new tag.

Figure 14.7 In the Outline View, choose New HTML Tag from the toolbar.

Figure 14.8 This is an undefined HTML tag in the Outline View.

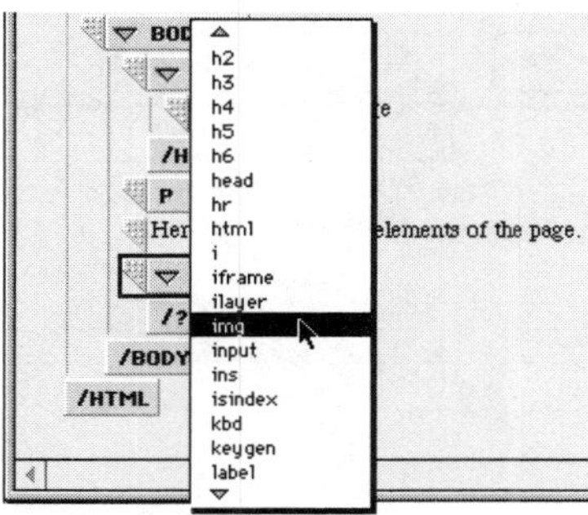

Figure 14.9 Command-click (Mac) or Control-click (Windows) to view the menu of available tag types.

To add tags with Palette tools:

1. With the Outline View visible in the document window, select a tool from the Basic tab or the Forms tab of the palette and drag it into the document window. A horizontal line indicates where the tag is as you move the tool through the window (**Figure 14.6**).
2. Let go of the mouse button when you reach the desired location for your tag. Empty tag attributes appear.

✔ Tips

- Unlike the Layout View, dragging a Palette tool to the Outline View does not display an Inspector window. If you want to use the Inspector to configure a new tag, return to the Layout View after you add the tag and click the object. Otherwise, use the HTML tag attributes described in this chapter to configure it.
- You can add any body or form tag to the Outline View, with one exception: you cannot add a Layout Text Box. The Layout Text box is not actually an HTML tag but a GoLive layout convention.

To add tags with the outline toolbar:

1. Click at the location in the outline where you want a new HTML tag to appear.
2. Choose New HTML Tag (Mac) or New Tag Item (Windows) from the toolbar (**Figure 14.7**). The tag appears in the Outline View (**Figure 14.8**).
3. Command-click (Mac) or control-click (Windows) the mouse button on the new tag to view the Tag Type popup menu (**Figure 14.9**).

continues on next page

4. Choose the type of tag you want from the menu. The tag appears onscreen.

5. Click and hold the mouse button on the new tag's show/hide attributes triangle to view a list of attributes that match the tag you've created (**Figure 14.10**).

6. Choose an attribute. In many cases, choosing an attribute brings up another show/hide triangle, allowing you to choose more attributes by clicking and selecting them from a menu. **Figure 14.11** shows an attribute that adds a specific image to the IMG tag.

✔ Tips

- If you are creating a tag that has lots of available attributes, such as an IMG tag, it's usually easier to add the tag in the Layout View and use the Inspector to configure it.
- Using a Palette tool to add a tag is also simpler than creating each attribute from scratch because the tool brings basic attributes along when you add it to an outline. **Figure 14.12** shows the result of dragging an IMG (image) tag from the Palette.
- On the other hand, some tags support browser-specific attributes. These are not available through the Inspector windows, but you will find them in the tag's attributes menu in the Outline View.

To add text to an outline:

1. In the Outline View, place the cursor where you want new text to appear.

2. Choose New HTML Text (Mac) or New Text Item (Windows) from the toolbar (**Figure 14.13**). A text box appears (**Figure 14.14**).

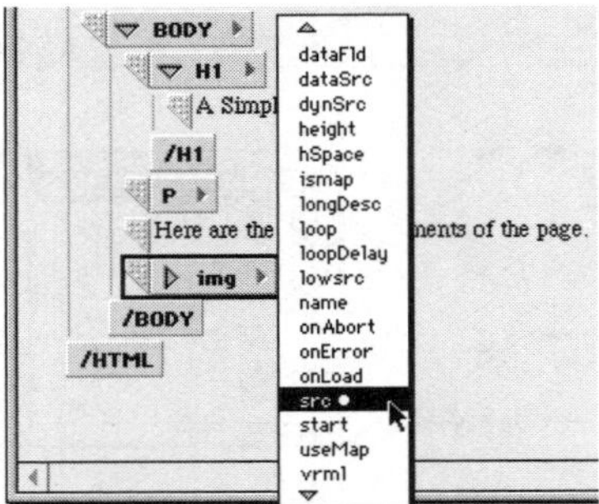

Figure 14.10 Click the show/hide attributes triangle to view tag attributes.

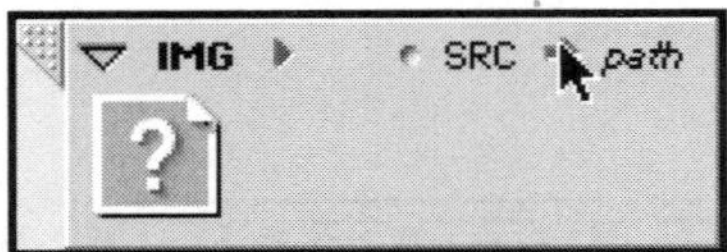

Figure 14.11 This IMG tag includes an SRC attribute, and a pointer that allows you to set a path to a specific image.

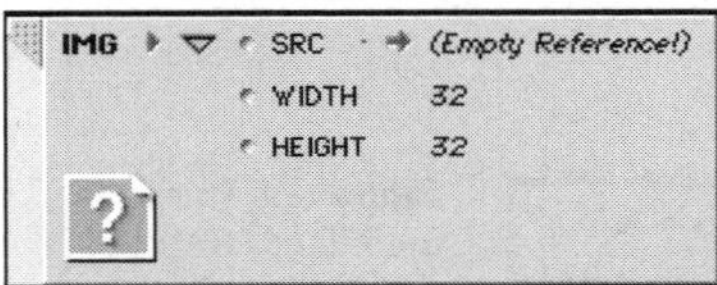

Figure 14.12 An image tag with some basic attributes configured.

Figure 14.13 Chose New HTML Text (Mac) or New Text Item (Windows) from the toolbar.

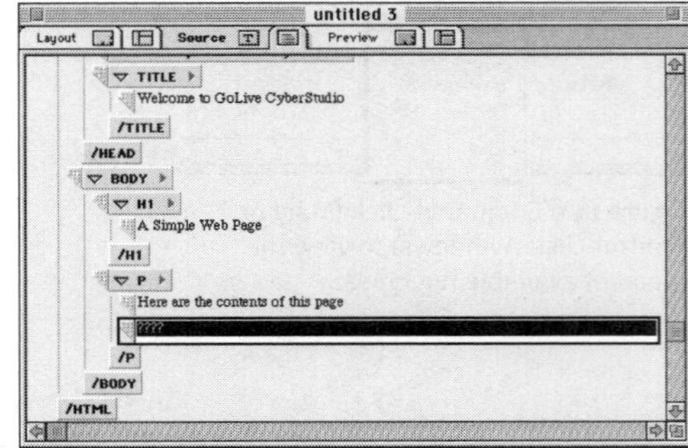

Figure 14.14 Type some text into the empty outline item.

Figure 14.15 Choose New HTML Comment (Mac) or New Comment (Windows) from the toolbar.

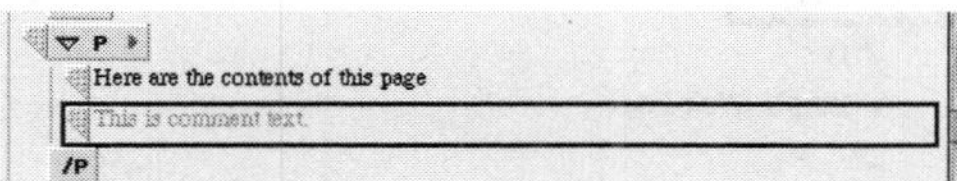

Figure 14.16 You can view HTML comments in the Outline or Source views, but not Layout or Preview.

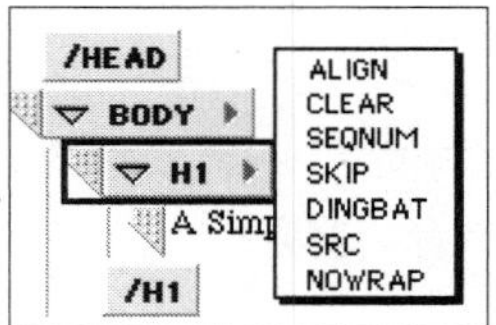

Figure 14.17 Click on the show/hide attribute triangle to pick an attribute.

3. Type the text over the selected question marks. When you preview your page, the text you typed will conform to the HTML tag surrounding it.

To add HTML comments:

1. In the Outline View, place your cursor at a location where you would like to insert an HTML comment. A comment is a note to you or to someone else working on the Web page. It will not be visible to those who visit your Web site.
2. Choose New HTML Comment (Mac) or New Comment (Windows) from the toolbar (**Figure 14.15**). A blank text box appears in the outline.
3. Type your comment. HTML comments do not appear on the page when you preview it or upload it to the Web. Within the Outline and Source Views, they appear in a different color than HTML toolbar text (**Figure 14.16**).

✔ Tip

- You can also add comments by dragging the Comment tool from the Palette to the Outline View or Layout View.

To add attributes to an HTML tag:

1. In the Outline View, click an HTML tag to select it.
2. Click and hold the show/hide attributes triangle to view the popup menu containing all attributes supported by this tag (see **Figure 14.17**).
3. Choose an attribute.
4. Type a number, choose a color, or make any other selections appropriate for the attribute you've chosen.
5. Repeat steps 2-4 to add more attributes.

To toggle the binary format:

1. Click on a binary HTML tag. Binary tags are those that enclose content with opening and ending tags—<H1>Heading</H1>, for example.
2. Choose Toggle Binary from the Edit menu (see **Figure 14.18**). By default, the Outline View displays both halves of a binary HTML tag (e.g. <H1> and </H1>). The binary toggle hides the closing tag, making it easier to navigate the outline. **Figures 14.19** and **14.20** show the same section of an outline with the toggle on and off. Note the toggle changes only the currently selected tag.

Figure 14.18 Choose Toggle Binary from the toolbar.

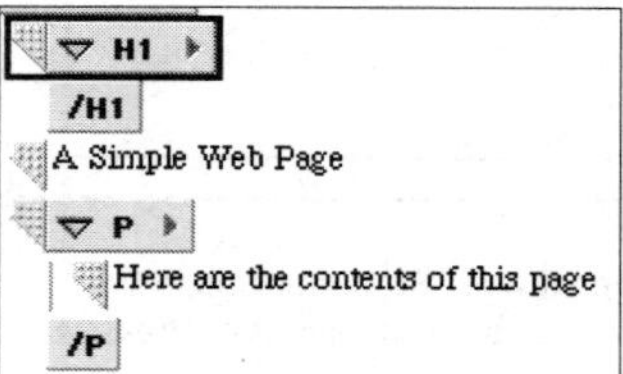

Figure 14.19 The complete binary tag for <H1> is visible.

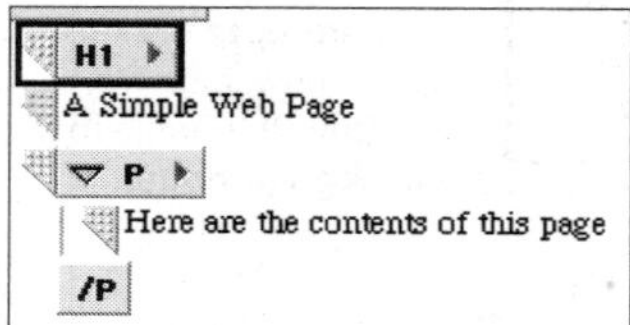

Figure 14.20 The closing binary tag for </H1> is hidden.

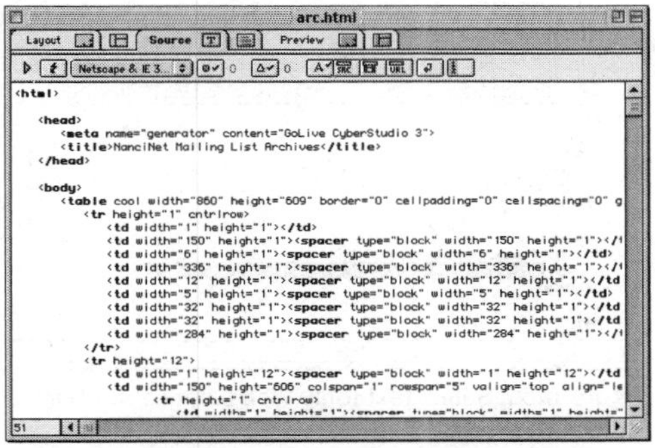

Figure 14.21 The document displayed in Figure 14.1 appears here in Source View.

Figure 14.22 Switch to the Source View by clicking the Source tab in the document window.

```
<html>

  <head>
    <meta name="generator" content="GoLive CyberStudio :
    <title>Home Page</title>
  </head>

  <body>
    <h1>A Simple Web Page</h1>
    <p>Here are the structural elements of the page.
  </body>

</html>
```

Figure 14.23 A simple HTML page as it appears in the Source View.

Using the Source View

Although most Web page design happens in the Layout View, and the Outline View offers a convenient way to examine HTML structure, the Source View provides an unvarnished view of the code and content that makes up a Web page. In the Source View, there is nothing between you and the code that tells a browser how to display your Web page.

The Source View is a text editor, where you can see and edit all of the tags, attributes, paths, and text that form the HTML page. **Figure 14.21** shows a Web page in the Source View. You can type directly into the Source View, move around with the cursor, and cut and paste text. Like other GoLive views, the Source View supports drag-and-drop editing and allows you to use Palette tools to add content.

To view a document in the Source View:

1. Open a GoLive document.
2. Click the Source tab (**Figure 14.22**) to switch to the Source View. The view changes to show the HTML underlying the page.

Examining the Source View

When you look at an HTML page in the Source View, you see the same HTML tags that appear in the Outline View. **Figure 14.23** shows a basic Web page with only two lines of text. The rest of the tags here represent the HTML hierarchy.

All text within <> brackets (and colored differently than the page's content) represent HTML tags. Most lines are indented according to the tags' places within the HTML hierarchy. Those indents don't appear on your Web page, however—they are created merely to remind you where you are on the page. You can change the way the Source View displays HTML with Source Preferences, discussed later in this chapter.

You can type new text or tags into the Source View, and you can format text in the Source View using either menus or the toolbar. In addition to the standard text formatting toolbar, the Source View includes an inline toolbar for setting Source View-specific options.

To type text in the Source View:

1. Click where you want to add text in the Source View.
2. Type the text.
3. Add HTML tags around the text if necessary.

✔ Tip

- When you type more than a line's worth of text, GoLive wraps to the next line, just as many word-processing applications do. But the wrap you see in the Source View is not identical to what you see in a Web browser. If you want to control exactly where lines of text break, you should either create a
 (line break) tag at the end of each line or use the <p></p> tag pair to create a paragraph, which includes a line break at the end.

To format text using the toolbar:

1. Select some text in the Source View (**Figure 14.24**).
2. Click the Bold button on the toolbar. Bold tags appear around the selected text (**Figure 14.25**).

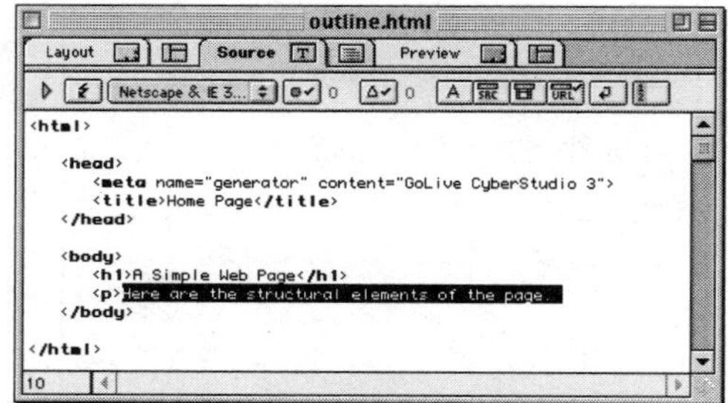

Figure 14.24 Select text (only Web page content) in the Source View.

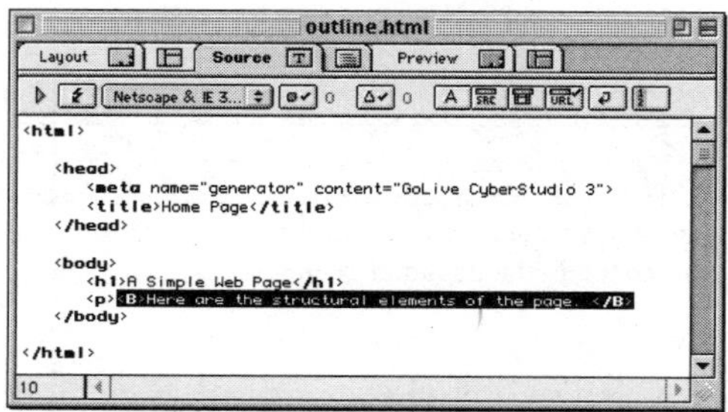

Figure 14.25 Formatting tags appear around the text after you select them from the toolbar. Notice that the new formatting tags are selected along with the text.

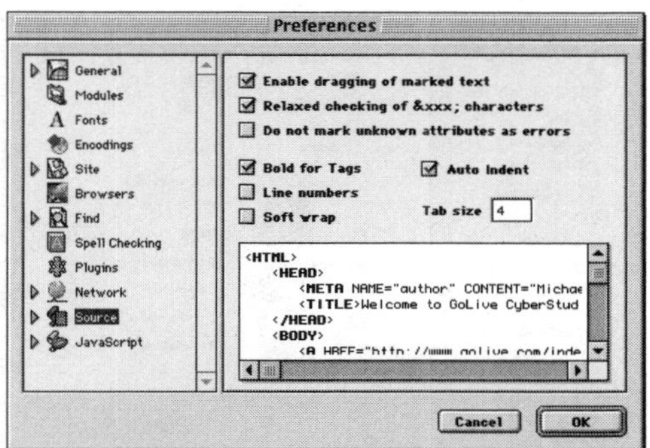

Figure 14.26 The General Source preferences window.

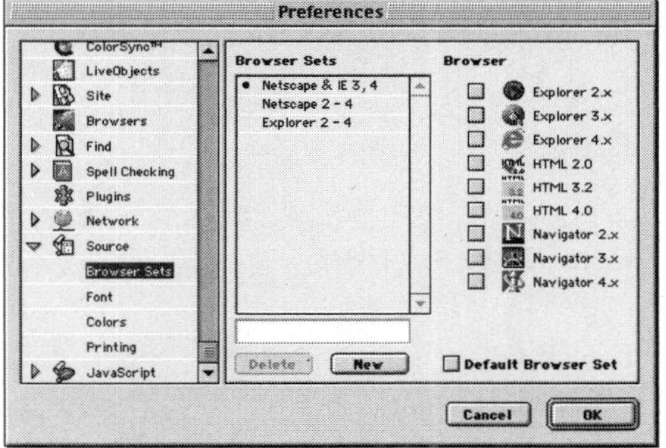

Figure 14.27 Choose a new browser set if you want to be sure that your pages conform to a particular browser's rules.

✔ Tips

- You can use all menu and toolbar formatting tools to add HTML tags to text. You can see the results when you look at a page in the Layout or Preview Views.
- Format an entire paragraph by triple-clicking to select it. Then choose a formatting tool to add tags.

To set Source View preferences:

1. Choose Preferences from the Edit menu.
2. Click the Source icon (**Figure 14.26**). Scroll through the window if necessary
3. In the General Source Preferences window, deselect "Enable dragging of marked text" if you want to disable drag and drop in the Source View.
4. Disable "Relaxed checking of &xxx; characters" to give GoLive permission to ignore some questionable characters when you check the page's syntax.
5. Use "Do not mark unknown attributes as errors" if you add new HTML tags or other unknown items to your pages.
6. Use the Bold Tags, Auto Indent, and other formatting options to customize the appearance of the text in the Source view. The example in the lower half of the window shows how text will look with the options you choose.

To choose browser sets:

1. Click the triangle (Mac) or plus sign (Windows) next to the Source icon, to view more Source prefs.
2. Click the Browser Sets label. Browser sets (**Figure 14.27**) tell the Source View whether or not to recognize tags associated with a particular browser.

continues on next page

3. Choose a new browser if you want GoLive's syntax checker to match your tags with additional browsers.

4. When you click on a browser on the left, GoLive checks the appropriate boxes on the right.

5. You can add a browser by clicking New, naming the new browser set, and checking off HTML standards to apply.

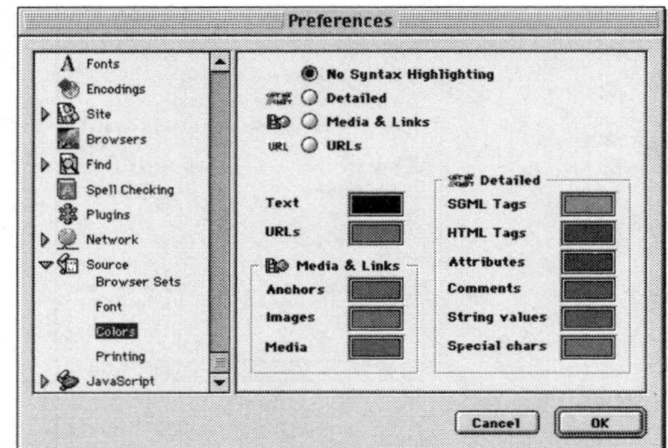

Figure 14.28 Syntax highlighting preferences let you color text and tags in the Source View.

To set font preferences for the Source View:

1. Under the Source Preferences icon, click the Font label.

2. Select a typeface, size, and style for text within the Source View. This typeface appears within the Source View only, not on the pages you publish on the Web. You can see how your choice will look in the Preferences window.

To set color and printing preferences:

1. Choose the Colors item under Source preferences. The result appears in **Figure 14.28**.

2. Use the "Detailed," "Media & Links," or "URLs" button to support different levels of text coloring within the Source View. Leave "No Syntax Highlighting" selected if you don't want to see colored links, tags, or text.

3. If you want to change the displayed colors of tags or text, use the Color Palette to apply a new color to each type of text, tag, or attribute.

4. If you intend to print your Source View pages, click Printing under Source Preferences.

Figure 14.29 The Source View toolbar provides access to syntax highlighting options.

Figure 14.30 Click the Syntax button on the Source View toolbar to check for tagging errors in your document.

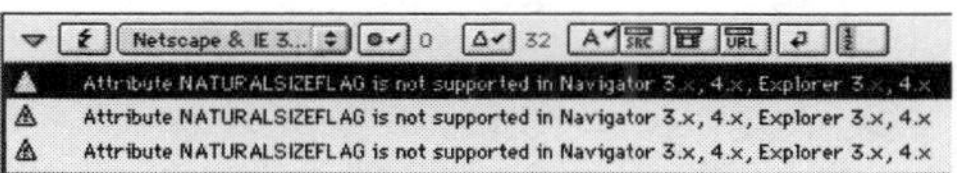

Figure 14.31 Syntax errors found in the Source view look like this and appear in a pane above your HTML document.

5. Choose syntax colors and fonts for printing if you would like to use colors and fonts different from those you use to display the page onscreen.

The Source View toolbar

In addition to the formatting toolbar that occupies its own window above your GoLive documents, the Source View includes its own toolbar, designed to help you find and fix problems. The toolbar (**Figure 14.29**) works with the preferences you set in the previous section to give you quick access to syntax highlighting and error-checking options.

To check HTML syntax:

1. With a document open in the Source View, click the Check Syntax button (**Figure 14.30**) on the Source View toolbar. GoLive opens a pane above the HTML code, displaying any syntax errors (**Figure 14.31**).
2. Click on an error message to see the problem highlighted in the document.
3. Fix or delete the subject tag, and the error message disappears.

continues on next page

✔ Tips

- You've already seen that you can set syntax highlighting levels in the Preferences window. You can also change them from the Source View toolbar. The buttons shown in **Figure 14.32** allow you to turn highlighting off and specify whether you'd like to see detailed highlights, media, and links, or just URLs.
- When you instruct GoLive to check HTML syntax, it does so according to the current browser set. As we discussed earlier, you can use a browser set to ensure that the tags you use comply with the specs for one or more browsers. To select a new browser set, simply choose it from the popup menu on the Source View toolbar (**Figure 14.33**).

Figure 14.32 Choose the level of syntax highlighting you wish to see in the Source View by toggling these toolbar buttons.

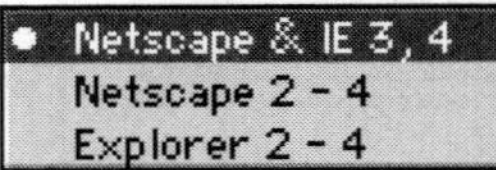

Figure 14.33 Choose browser sets from the popup menu on the Source View toolbar.

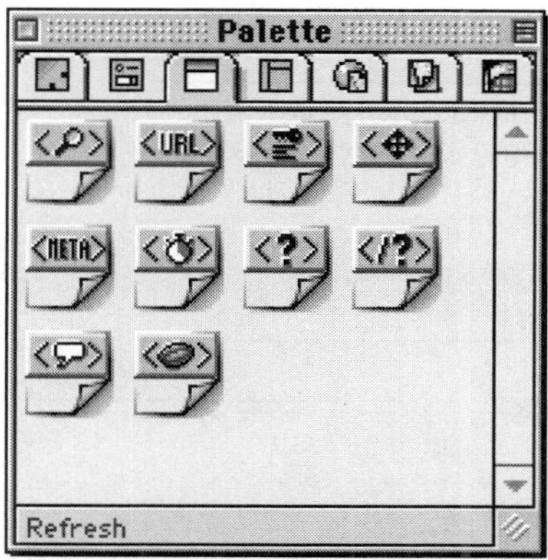

Figure 14.34 The Palette's Header tab contains a tool for each kind of header tag.

Header Elements

HTML pages have two main parts: the body (signified by enclosing <BODY> and </BODY> tags), and the header (signified by <HEAD> and </HEAD> tags). All the text and graphics that make up the page appear between body tags and are edited in GoLive's Layout View. Header tags, although they usually don't contain visible page elements, can store lots of information about the page that visitors to your site can use when searching for your site. More importantly, header tags provide you a means of controlling the display and other properties of Web pages. Headers can vary the behavior of a page based on the user's browser, for example. Many headers also contain scripts that execute when the page is loaded.

The most basic header tag is the <TITLE> tag, which specifies the name your page has when added to a Web browser's bookmarks list. You fill in the title tag when you replace the words "Welcome to GoLive" at the top of the document window with your title.

Other header tags are optional and must be entered in the Layout, Source or Outline views. In this section, I describe header tags available from the GoLive Palette, and explain how to add and configure them.

Adding headers

Like other HTML elements, header tags can be added to a Web page from the Palette's Header tab (**Figure 14.34**). To add header tags this way, you must drag Palette tools to the header area in the Layout View. You can easily configure each header's attributes and content within an Inspector window specific to that header. If you prefer, and if you are familiar with HTML, you can use the Outline or Source Views for editing, but—unless you prefer to type raw HTML—you'll want to create the headers in the Layout View.

✔ Tip

- Don't confuse *headers* (which appear within the <HEAD> and </HEAD> tags, above the Web page's body) with headings, which use <H1>, <H2>, and so forth. *Headings* format text within the page, and appear between the <BODY> and </BODY> tags. GoLive makes this HTML distinction a bit of a challenge by referring in the toolbar to headings as headers—but they really are headings.

To add a header to a Web page:

1. Open a new or existing GoLive document to the Layout View.
2. Click on the small triangle in the title bar of the document window (**Figure 14.35**). The header pane appears (**Figure 14.36**).
3. Drag a tool from the Header tab of the Palette into the header pane of the document window (**Figure 14.37**).
4. Click on the new tag to display its Inspector window.

Isindex headers

The Isindex header adds a search field to the Web page, allowing visitors to search a site by entering a text query. In most cases, it's more desirable to use a form (see Chapter 7) as an interface for site searching. Whether you use a form or Isindex header element, you will need to connect the page to a CGI application, which actually performs the search.

To set up an Isindex header:

1. Drag the Isindex Palette tool to the header pane (**Figure 14.38a**).

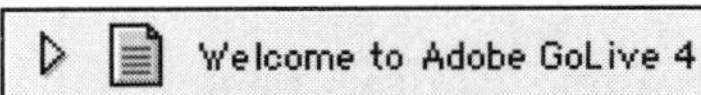

Figure 14.35 Click the triangle next to the page title to open the header pane.

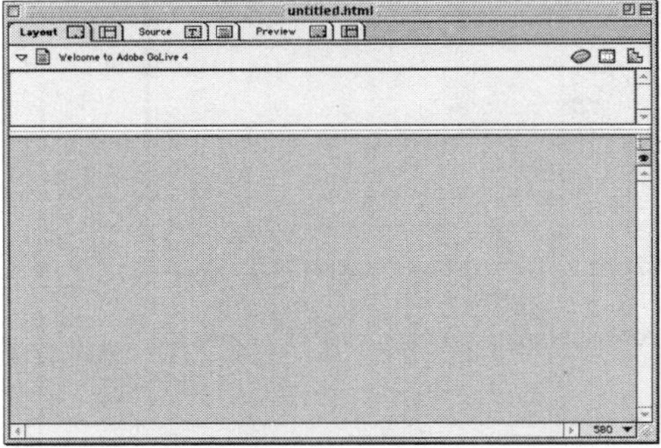

Figure 14.36 The header pane appears at the top of the document window.

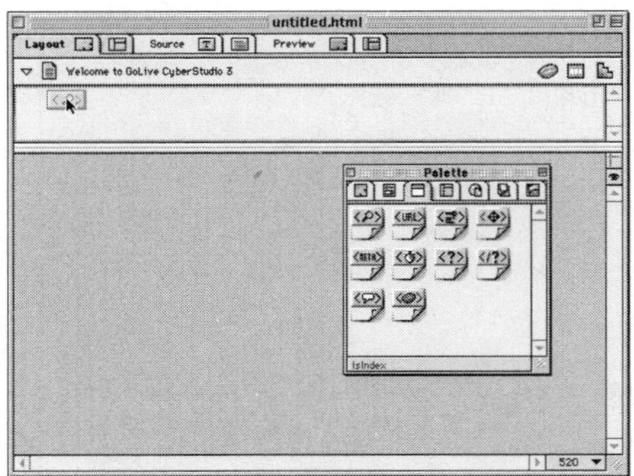

Figure 14.37 Drag a header tag from the Palette to the header section of a page to add a header tag.

Figure 14.38a The Isindex palette tool and header tag.

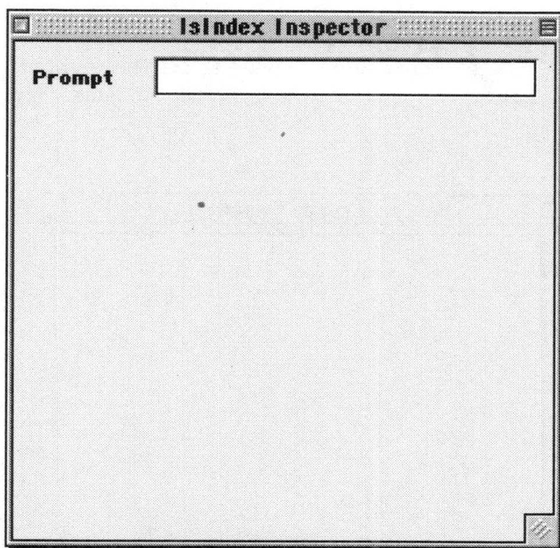

Figure 14.38b The Isindex Inspector window.

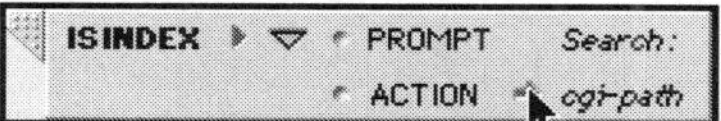

Figure 14.39 In the Outline View, configure the Isindex header's ACTION attribute to connect to a server CGI.

Figure 14.40a The Base palette tool and header tag.

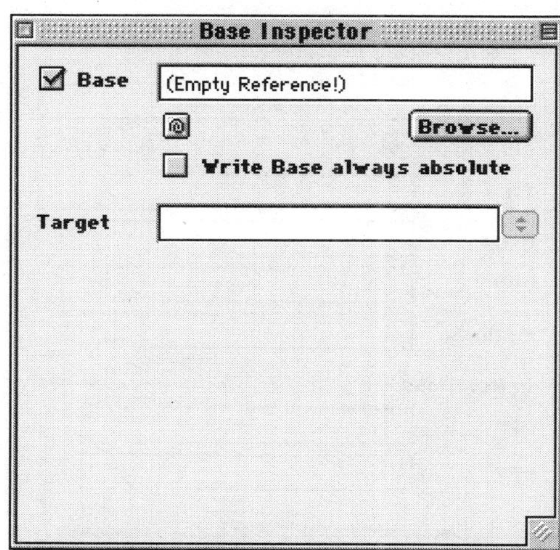

Figure 14.40b The Base Inspector.

2. Click to display the Isindex Inspector window (**Figure 14.38b**).
3. In the Prompt field, type the text you want to appear adjacent to the search field.

✔ Tip

- When you are ready to upload this Web page to your server, you need to connect the Isindex header to a CGI application. To do this, switch to the Outline View and locate the Isindex header. Click the collapse/expand triangle. In the ACTION attribute, click the arrow (**Figure 14.39**) and choose a CGI file or type the URL in the dialog box.

Base headers

The Base header allows you to specify an absolute URL for Web pages within your site, making it possible for you to use relative URLs within the site. Of course, you don't have to use a base header to do this. Most Web servers will correctly resolve relative URLs when the linked files are stored within the same site. Though it is included in the GoLive Palette, the Base header tag is not really compatible with the software. Avoid it.

To set up a Base header:

1. Drag the Base Palette tool to the header pane (**Figure 14.40a**).
2. Click to display the Base Inspector window (**Figure 14.40b**).
3. Click Browse or use Point & Shoot to locate a base document.
4. Choose "Write Base always absolute" to use an absolute, rather than a relative, path to locate the base document.

Keywords headers

The Keywords header allows you to insert keywords into your document that Web crawlers and search engines can use to categorize and add your page to their databases.

To set up a Keywords header:

1. Drag the Keywords Palette tool to the header pane (**Figure 14.41a**).
2. Click to display the Keywords Inspector window (**Figure 14.41b**).
3. Click in the keyword field near the bottom of the Keywords Inspector window.
4. Type a keyword and press Add. The keyword appears in the upper field.
5. Repeat for each keyword you want to add.

✔ Tip

- Here's another way to add a keyword. Within a GoLive document, use the mouse to select a word you would like to use as a keyword and choose Add to Keywords from the Special menu. GoLive creates a keyword header (if one doesn't already exist) and adds your keyword. Avoid this tag. Leading browsers don't yet support it.

Figure 14.41a The Keyword palette tool and header tag.

Figure 14.41b The Keyword Inspector.

Link headers

The Link header adds a link between one page and others within your site, making it easier to organize a group of pages.

To set up a Link header:

1. Drag the Link Palette tool to the header pane (**Figure 14.42a**).
2. Click to display the Link Inspector window (**Figure 14.42b**).
3. Type, browse, or Point & Shoot to a URL you want to link to this page. Press Tab.

Figure 14.42a The Link palette tool and header tag.

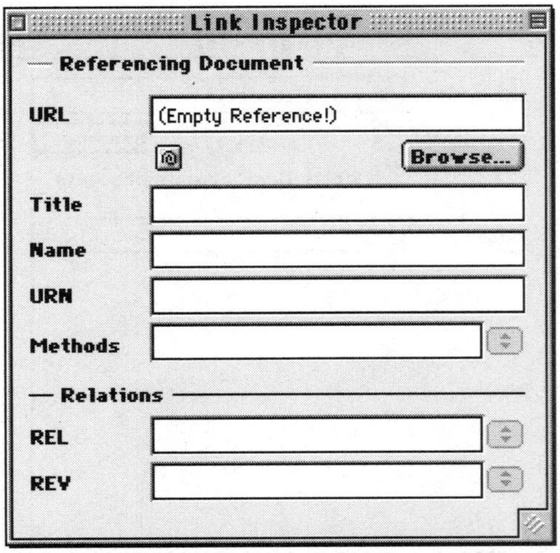

Figure 14.42b The Link Inspector.

HEADER ELEMENTS

Figure 14.43a The Meta palette tool and header tag.

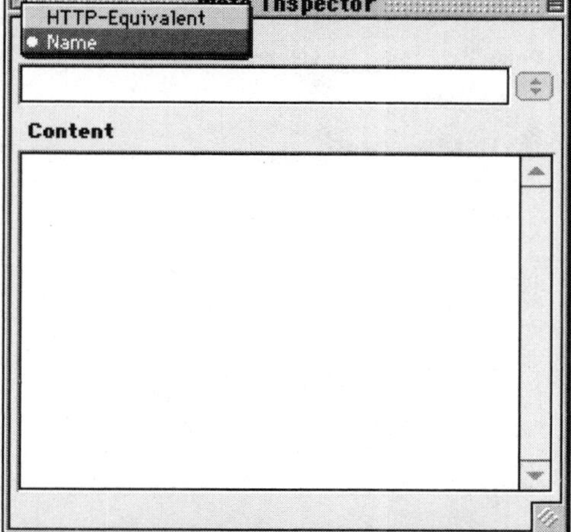

Figure 14.43b The Meta Inspector.

4. Enter the related page's title in the Title field. Press Tab.
5. If you're linking to an anchor, type it in the Name field.
6. Leave the URN and Methods fields blank unless you use these attributes. Most Web authors don't.
7. In the REL field, type the relationship of your page to the linked page that follows, i.e. if the page you're working on is a subsidiary of the page to which you're linking. Press Tab.
8. Type the reverse relationship in the REV field.

Meta headers

Meta headers supply information about the document to Web page visitors. When a visitor chooses Document Info within his or her Web browser, the browser displays the contents of the page's Meta headers. Meta headers usually tell the user something about the page, its author, the associated Web site, or the software used to create it.

By default, GoLive includes the Meta headers for file format, character set, and file creator in each document you create. You can also add your own Meta headers, or even alter those created by GoLive.

To set up a Meta header:

1. Drag the Meta Palette tool to the header pane (**Figure 14.43a**).
2. Click to display the Meta Inspector window (**Figure 14.43b**).

continues on next page

3. Choose HTTP Equivalent or Name from the popup menu. HTTP Equivalent tags tell the Web server to act on the HTTP request entered in the Content field below. A Name Meta tag sends the tag's contents as text.
4. Type a name for the HTTP header or for the text element you want to enter.
5. In the Content field, type the meta tag content that you want to appear to site visitors.

Refresh headers

The Refresh header updates a Web page at intervals you set. This header is useful when you're creating pages with live or near-live elements and want them to reload without user intervention.

To set up a Refresh header:

1. Drag the Refresh Palette tool to the header pane (**Figure 14.44a**).
2. Click to display the Refresh Inspector window (**Figure 14.44b**).
3. Choose the delay interval in seconds. Press Tab.
4. Click "This Document" to apply the refresh rate to the page you're working with. Otherwise, you can choose URL if you want the browser to replace your page with a new page. If you choose URL, use the Browse button or Point & Shoot to locate a URL.

✔ Tip

- You can create a slide show affect by adding multiple Refresh tags and pointing them to different URLs.

Figure 14.44a The Refresh palette tool and header tag.

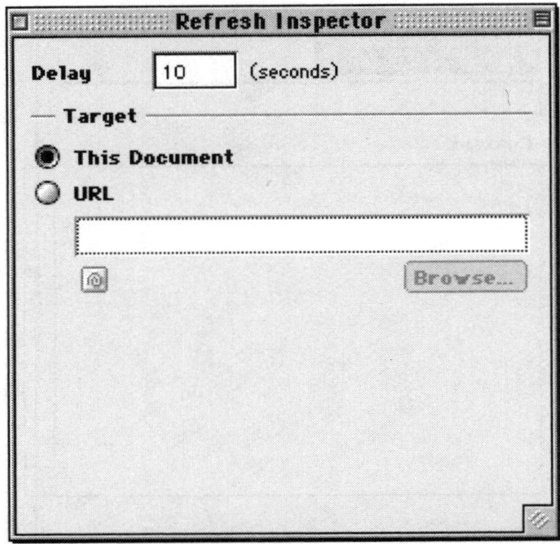

Figure 14.44b The Refresh Inspector.

Figure 14.45a The tag palette tool and header tag.

Figure 14.45b The tag Inspector.

Figure 14.45c The Endtag palette tool and header tag.

Adding unknown headers

As the HTML standard develops, new tags become available to Web developers. You can add a header tag that is currently unknown to GoLive with the Tag and Endtag Palette tools.

To set up an unknown header:

1. Drag the Tag Palette tool to the header pane to open an unknown tag (**Figure 14.45a**).
2. Click to display the Tag Inspector window (**Figure 14.45b**).
3. Type a name for your new tag in the Tagname field.
4. Click New to add an attribute to the new tag. The new attribute box is selected when you click.
5. Type a name for the attribute. Press Tab.
6. Type a value for the attribute.
7. Repeat steps 4-6 to add additional attributes.
8. Drag the Endtag Palette tool to the header pane to complete the new tag (**Figure 14.45c**).
9. In the Endtag Inspector window, type a name for the endtag that matches the opening tag.

Comment headers

Comment headers add a non-displaying comment to your Web page header.

Figure 14.46a The Comment palette tool and header tag.

To set up a Comment header:

1. Drag the Comment Palette tool to the header pane (**Figure 14.46a**).
2. Click to display the Comment Inspector window (**Figure 14.46b**).
3. Type a comment in the Inspector window.

Figure 14.46b The Comment Inspector.

Script headers

The Script header adds a pointer to a JavaScript, allowing the script to execute when a visitor opens a Web page.

Figure 14.47a The Script header palette tool and header tag.

To set up a Script header:

1. Drag the Script Palette tool to the header (**Figure 14.47a**).
2. Click to display the Head Script Inspector window (**Figure 14.47b**).
3. Type a name for the script. The language field is filled out for you.
4. Locate a script with the Browse button or Point & Shoot.
5. To edit or create a script, click Edit. The JavaScript interface appears. (For details on editing JavaScript, see Chapter 10.)

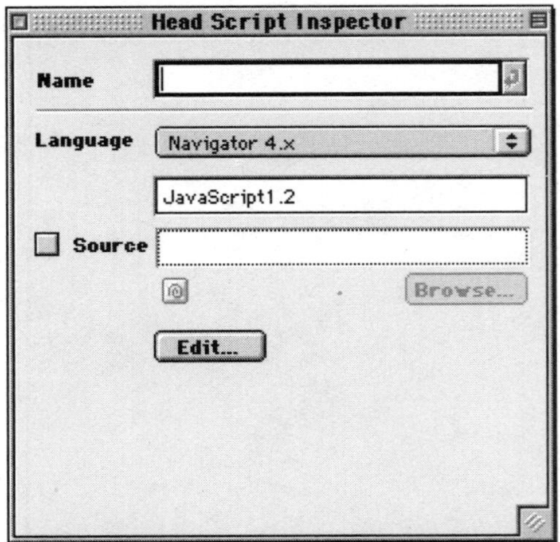

Figure 14.47b The Script header Inspector.

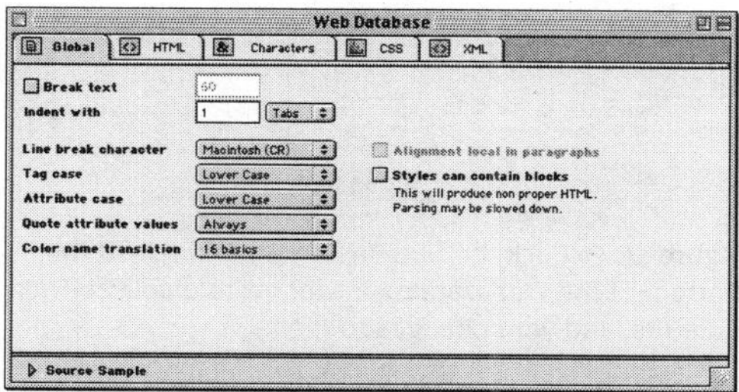

Figure 14.48 The Global tab of the Web database lets you customize the default HTML framework for Web page.

The Web Database

All of the tags, characters, and styles you use to construct your Web pages are stored in GoLive's Web database. When you work with tags in the Outline View, GoLive uses the Web database to specify these tags and their attributes. The software's syntax- and error-checking tools depend on the database to check the validity of tags entered or edited by hand in the Source View. You can use the database to look up tags and attributes and to add new ones. As HTML evolves, new tags and attributes are likely to come into common use. With the database, you can keep GoLive up-to-date.

Like many other GoLive tools, the Web database appears as a tabbed window. Individual items, when clicked, display a context-sensitive Inspector window.

The Web Database's contents are available under five tabs. They are:

- The Global tab.
- The HTML tab.
- The Chars tab.
- The CSS tab.
- The XML tab.

To open the Web database:

Choose Web Database from the Special menu.

The Global tab

The Web Database's Global tab (**Figure 14.48**) is really an extension of the Source preference you've already set. Like those options, the global items in the Web Database allow you to customize the look and behavior of your HTML code. Here, you can choose text wrap, tab, and line break options, as well as case and color naming preferences.

To see how your choices will look, click the Source Sample triangle at the bottom of the window. The resulting pane updates as you change options, above (**Figure 14.49**).

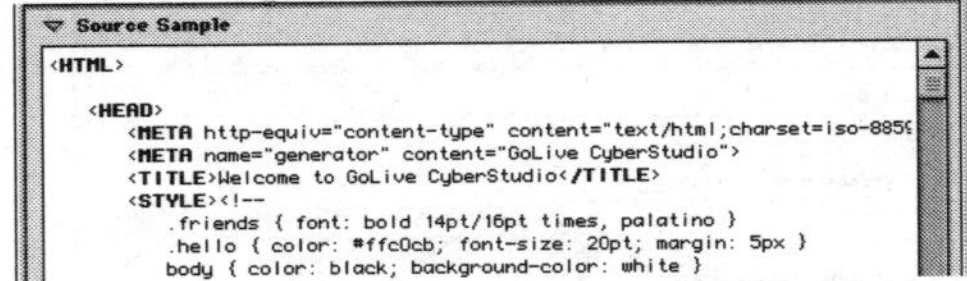

Figure 14.49 Click the Source Sample triangle at the bottom of the Web Database window to display HTML defaults, and your changes to them.

The HTML tab

The HTML tab is the heart of the Web Database because it contains all of the tags that GoLive (and the current HTML standards) recognize and use. Tags are grouped together under logical headings. Each tag listing includes a short description that explains the tag further. Clicking on a tag displays a related Inspector window.

To locate existing tags:

1. In the Web Database window, click the HTML tab.
2. Locate a tag category, such as Table. Scroll through the tag categories if necessary. Categories contain individual tags, which in turn contain attributes.
3. Click the triangle (Mac) or plus sign (Windows) to open the tag category, revealing individual tags and attributes.
4. Click the desired tag. A WebDB Inspector, complete with information specific to the tag you selected, comes to life (**Figure 14.50**).
5. Note the Inspector settings for the tag you're working with. The settings tell you what the tag is (Tag Name, Comment) how the tag appears (Structure), what it includes (Content) and whether or not it needs an End tag to complete it.
6. Click the Output tab in the Inspector to see how the tag will appear, relative to other items on the page.
7. Click the Version tab. GoLive displays a list of browsers with those that support the tag checked (see **Figure 14.51**).

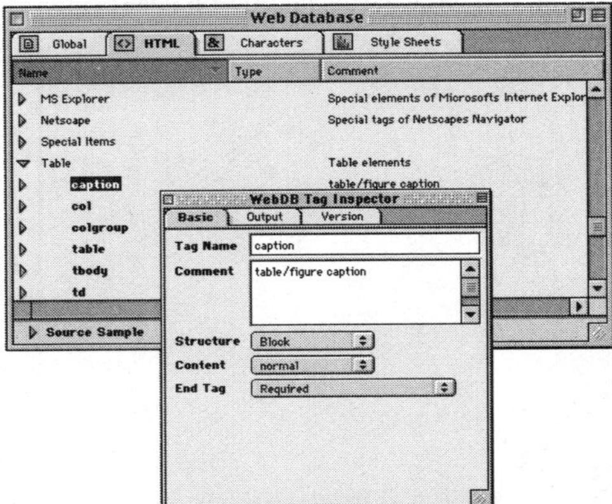

Figure 14.50 Selecting a tag in the Web Database brings up a corresponding Inspector window.

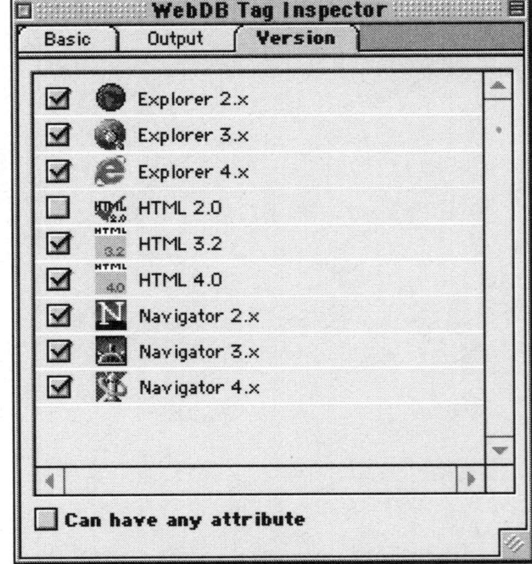

Figure 14.51 Click the Inspector's Version tab to see which HTML standards and browsers support it.

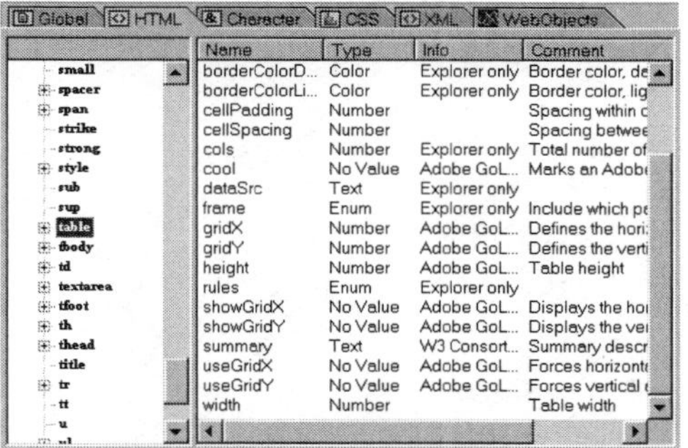

Figure 14.52 In the Windows versions of GoLive, the Web Database lists some tags under categories, but leaves most at the root of the HTML window. These versions also use Windows Explorer's two-pane display approach.

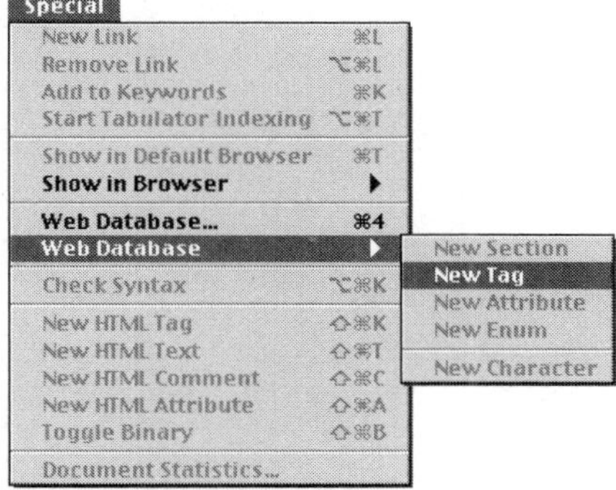

Figure 14.53 Choose New Tag to add a tag to the Web Database.

8. If you chose a tag with a triangle (Mac) or plus sign (Windows) next to its name in the Web Database (table caption is a good example), expand the tag to display the tag's attributes. These are the same attributes you can edit in the Inspector when you add a tag to your Web page with a Palette tool.
9. Keep clicking to expand the tag and its attributes fully.

✔ Tips

- Unfortunately for Windows-based Web authors, the Mac and Windows versions of the Web Database differ from one another. While the Mac version encloses most available tags in categories, making them easy to locate, the Windows version keeps many individual tags at the root level of the window. **Figure 14.52** shows the HTML tab under Windows.
- Take a look at the various options in the Inspector. Though the Structure, Content, and Endtag popups can be edited, for example, it's almost always a bad idea to change the default options of existing tags. The Web Database stores tags and their configurations according to HTML standards, and altering a tag could cause serious problems if you're not sure you know what you're doing.

To add a new tag to the database:

1. With the Web Database's HTML tab showing, click once on a category label (one of the tag headings in the window) into which your new tag would logically fit.
2. Choose New Tag from the Web Database submenu, of the Special menu (**Figure 14.53**). A new tag label appears in the Web Database, and the WebDB tag inspector appears.

continues on next page

3. Name the tag in the Inspector window. Use the actual text of the tag as it will appear in your HTML code.
4. Describe your new tag in the comment field.
5. Configure the tag by choosing Structure and Content parameters from the popup menus in the Basic tab.
6. Make choices about the tag's appearance, relative to other items on the page, under the Output tab.
7. Finally, assign the tag to browsers that support it under the Version tab.

✔ Tips

- Adding a browser or HTML standard in the Version tab doesn't mean that your new tag will be supported by that version of HTML. It's just a reference. Before you use the Web Database to add new tags to your pages, check an HTML reference book or Web site for detailed information about new tags, their attributes, and which browsers support them.
- The items in the Web Database menu are also available from the context-sensitive toolbar at the top of the screen.

Tag attributes

You can add attributes to existing tags or to those you've just created. Attributes allow a Web author to configure features of a tag, such as its alignment, value, font, and so on.

To add an attribute:

1. Select a tag in the Web Database window.
2. Choose New Attribute from the toolbar or from the Web Database submenu of the Special menu.

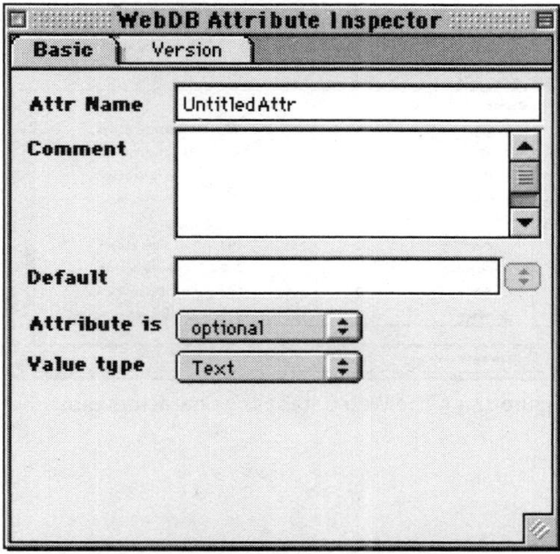

Figure 14.54 The Attribute Inspector window.

3. Like the WebDB Tag Inspector, the Attribute Inspector provides fields for naming and describing the attribute (**Figure 14.54**).
4. You can also choose a default condition for the attributes tag when the attribute is not specified. For instance, if you add an alignment attribute, you might choose to make the default alignment left.
5. Use the Attribute Is item to tell the database whether the attribute is optional within its tag or required.
6. Choose a value from the Value Type popup.
7. Click the Version tab to identify browsers and HTML standards that support the attribute. It is possible for a tag to be supported by a particular browser while an attribute is not.

Enumerations

Some tag attributes include options. An alignment attribute, for example, includes an option to align the attribute to the left, right, or center. That group of options is called an *enumeration*.

To add an enumeration:

1. In the HTML tab of the Web Database, click on an attribute belonging to an HTML tag. The attribute you choose must have an Enum. value type selected.
2. Choose Web Database:New Enum from the Special menu or choose Add Enum from the toolbar. The WebDB Enum Inspector appears.
3. Type a name for the enumeration in the Name field under the Enums heading.
4. Under the Versions tab, choose an HTML standard supported by the enumeration.

The Characters tab

While HTML language displays alphanumeric characters just as they are typed, a number of non-alphanumeric characters require that you surround them with HTML tags. To display a special character, you must surround it with an ampersand (&) and a semicolon (;) like this:

```
<H1>M&ouml;ntag</H1>
```

uml indicates that the accented o in *Montag* should have an umlaut over it.

The Special Characters tab stores the HTML name of the character, a description of the character, and the code needed to generate it on a Web page.

Special characters are displayed under the Characters tab in three sections:

- *Basics*: includes punctuation marks, such as quotation marks, colons, etc.
- *Characters*: accented letters and other characters that are not part of the ASCII character set.
- *General Punctuation*: includes dashes and spaces

Basics characters include the ampersand, the greater than sign, and the quotation mark. Most alphanumeric characters (many of them with accent marks used in languages other than English) are stored under the Characters section, while the General Punctuation section includes several en dashes, em dashes, and a non-breaking space character.

To view a character:

1. In the Web Database window, click the Characters tab. It looks like **Figure 14.55**.

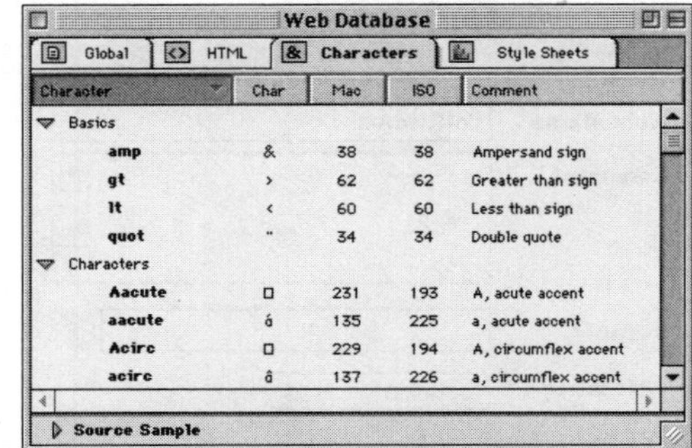

Figure 14.55 The Web Database's Characters tab.

✔ Warnings

- Like HTML tags, characters you add to the Web Database will not necessarily be supported by HTML. The character must have an ISO code and byte code, and it must be supported by browsers.
- You can edit Special Characters, but changing an existing character's codes will make it inoperable, and may cause errors in your Web page.

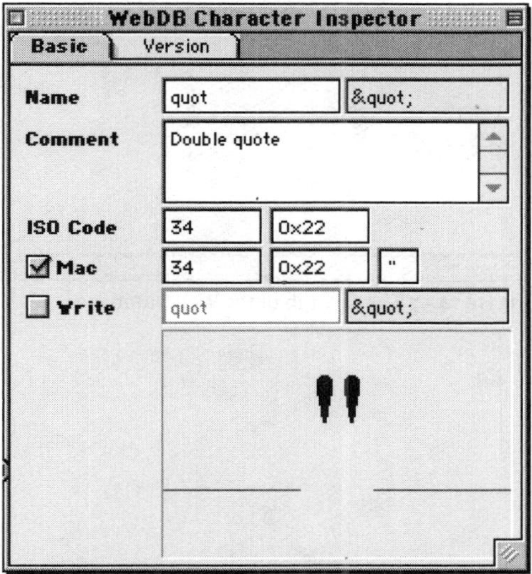

Figure 14.56 The WebDB Character Inspector shows attributes and a sample for a quotation mark.

2. Locate the quot item under the Basics heading and click on it. The Inspector window now displays the WebDB Characters Inspector (see **Figure 14.56**).

   The Inspector displays the name, code, and description of the character. In addition, you'll find the ISO and byte codes that identify the character within the HTML standard, and the Mac code that identifies the character to the Mac OS, if it is specific to the Mac. (The Mac code option is available in both Macintosh and Windows versions of GoLive). The Write option (unchecked in this example) can write the contents of the nearby text box to the HTML code, rather than the name of the special character being defined. Finally, the lower pane of the Inspector shows how the character looks when displayed in a browser.

To add a new character:

1. Decide which section your new character best fits in and click on the section heading.
2. Choose New Character from the Web Database submenu of the Special menu, or choose new Character from the toolbar.
3. Give the character an HTML name; the HTML code will be filled in automatically.
4. Type a descriptive name for the character.
5. Determine the correct ISO code, byte code, and (if applicable) Mac OS code for the character.
6. Click on the Versions tab to specify HTML versions and browsers that support the character.

continues on next page

The CSS tab

The CSS tab aids you in displaying cascading style sheet content in GoLive. It isn't intended to provide an editable style sheet. With the CSS tab, you can select style sheet display methods that correspond to several popular Web browsers. GoLive uses the default style sheet you select to preview style sheet content in the Layout View Controller. When you use the controller to preview style sheet content, GoLive will approximate the fonts, text properties, and positioning when you preview your pages. Changing the default style sheet in the CSS tab allows you to see how styled content will look in various browsers.

The CSS tab also includes a few options that control how style sheets are created.

To set style sheet options:

1. Open the Web Database and click the CSS tab (see **Figure 14.57**).
2. Unless you want to disable style sheets in GoLive, leave the Use Style Sheets checkbox checked.
3. Choose a default unit of measure from the popup menu. This unit will apply to all style sheets applied in GoLive, unless you choose to override the default in a specific case.
4. Choose an Output option to control how the style sheet code appears in the Source View. By default, the code display is compact; the successive menue options display the CSS code in the Source View with more white space between words and lines.
5. Leave the Indent checkbox alone if you want the style sheet code to be indented from the left margin.

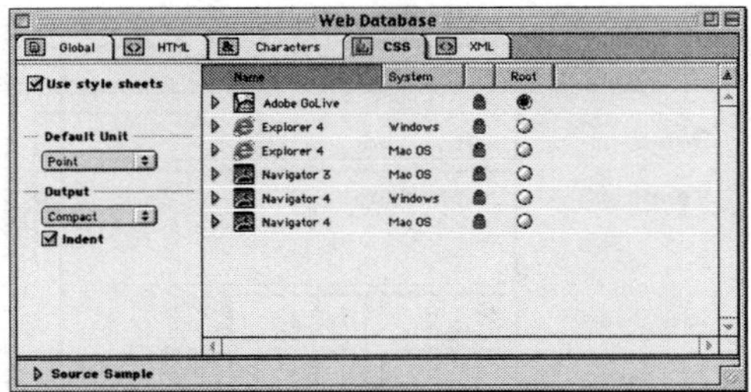

Figure 14.57 The CSS tab of the Web Database.

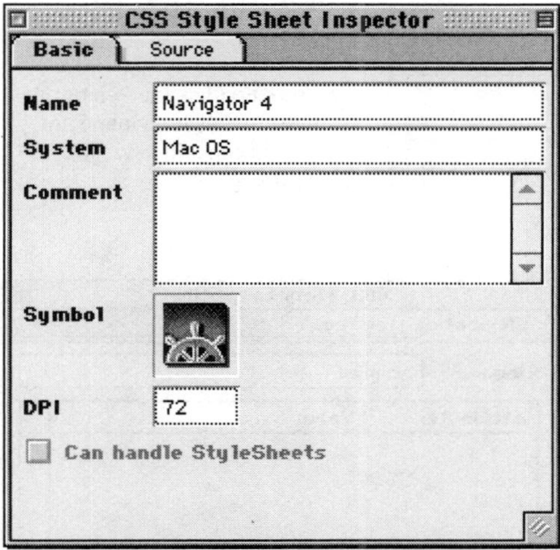

Figure 14.58 The CSS Style Sheet Inspector window.

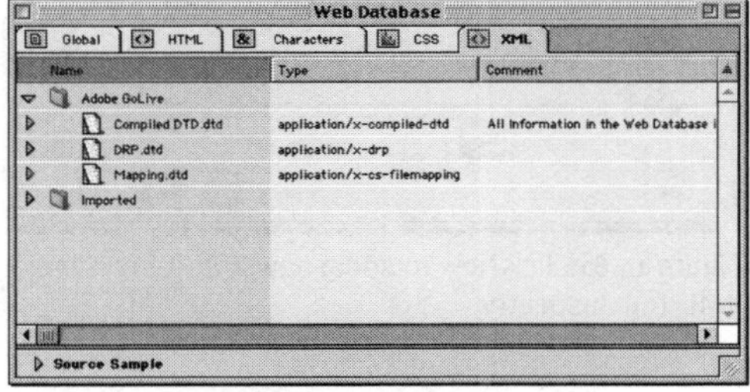

Figure 14.59 The XML tab of the Web Database.

To choose a default style sheet:

1. In the CSS tab, choose a browser from the list in the right side of the Style Sheet tab, and click on its heading. The CSS Style Sheet Inspector displays details about the browser, its platform, and the screen resolution it uses.
2. Click the Source tab to see the style sheets supported by the browser. You can view the style sheets individually in the Web Database by expanding the heading.
3. In the CSS tab, click the Root button (Mac) or the checkbox next to the browser name (Windows) to select the current browser as the default style sheet.

The XML tab

GoLive recognizes and reads XML, the simplified dialect of the SGML language. XML can be used to structure information on the Web. The XML tab of the Web database (**Figure 14.59**) displays the XML structures supported by GoLive.

In the current version of GoLive, you can view XML tags and their attributes, but you can't add your own.

Foreign Code

Tags that are not part of the HTML specification are referred to as *foreign code*. GoLive supports the inclusion of foreign code within a Web page. You can edit foreign code in the Source or Outline views.

GoLive supports foreign code types including XML and Microsoft's ASP (Application Server Pages) spec. GoLive can read XML documents, just as it does HTML pages. You can view and edit XML files in the Source or Outline view. XML files have the .xml suffix.

You can view or import ASP code into GoLive documents, and edit them manually in the Source View. GoLive does not make changes to the code, and you can't use its graphical tools to preview pages that include it.

To view an XML document in GoLive:

1. Double-click a file with the XML suffix

   or

   Drag an XML file onto the GoLive application. GoLive opens to the Layout View, showing a collapsed version of the XML file.
2. Click the Pen button **(Figure 14.60)** in the upper right corner of the document window. The XML Item Inspector **(Figure 14.61)** appears.
3. Click New to add a new XML element and value.
4. Switch to the Outline View to examine the attributes of the XML file.
5. Edit the file's attributes just as you would an HTML document.

Figure 14.60 Click the Pen button to view the XML Item Inspector, where you can add new XML elements.

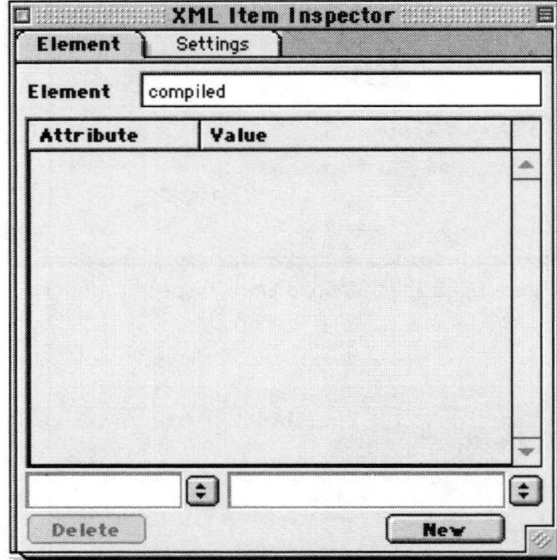

Figure 14.61 Click New to add a new XML item in the XML Item Inspector.

✔ Tip

- XML authoring is beyond the scope of this book. Fortunately, there are lots of XML resources on the Web that can help you learn and use it to structure information on the Web. Start at http://www.w3.org/XML/, the World Wide Web Consortium's XML reference site. Other sites include XML.com (http://www.xml.com), The XML Zone (http://www.xml-zone.com/), and XMLepahnt (http://www.xmlephant.com/).

15

BUILDING SITES

A Web site is the sum of its parts: HTML pages, images, and multimedia files. Juggling a large number of site elements and organizing Web content so that it is easy for users to work with make site management a necessity for most modern Webmasters.

To manage a Web site with GoLive, you need to create a *site*. Sites are collections of files and resources that you can view, manipulate, and publish on the Web. Within a site, you can store the pages and media files you create, links to external resources—such as other sites and e-mail addresses—and font and color information. Once you have created a site, you can organize it by adding and rearranging files. With GoLive, you can also get a bird's eye view of the entire site with the Site and Link Views. Next, check the site and its pages for errors, and fix them on the spot. When you're ready to put the site on the Web, you can use GoLive tools to publish it.

In this chapter, I cover:

- Using site tools.
- Building sites.
- Fine-tuning preferences.
- Adding resources to a site.

Using Site Tools

You build GoLive sites with several tools, commands, and preferences. I cover each one as I work through the process of creating and maintaining a site, but here's an overview.

The Site window

The Site window is where the action is. You add, rearrange, and link files from here. Under its five tabs, you store files, external URLs, colors, and font sets. There's also a tab providing a graphical view of the site. More on that later.

The Site window looks and works much like the Mac Finder or Windows Explorer. You can view and sort files and folders and move items between folders within the site. In the Macintosh version of GoLive, you can drag items into and out of the site window from the Finder. The Mac and Windows site windows look a bit different from one another (**Figure 15.1**). For the most part, though, they work identically.

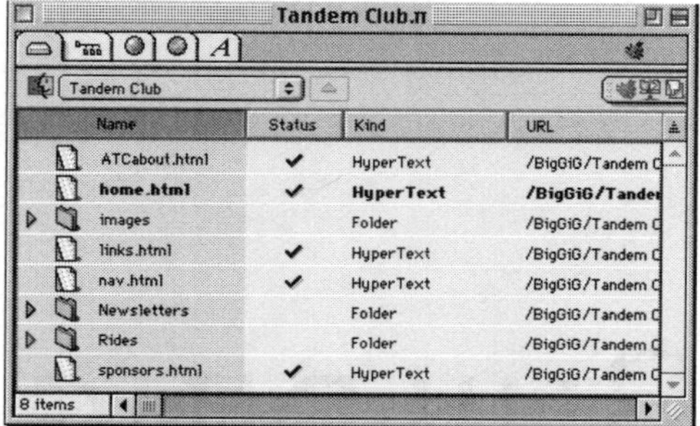

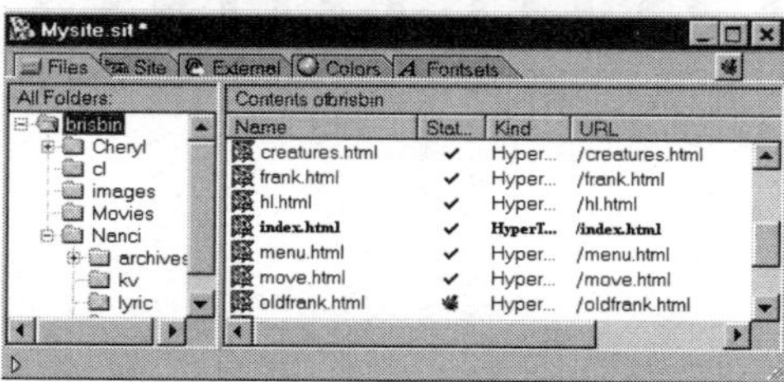

Figure 15.1 The Site window displays files and folders that make up a GoLive site. (Mac version at top, Windows below.)

The Site tab of the Palette

The Site tab contains tools that you can use to add elements to the site by dragging them into the Site window (**Figure 15.2**). Most of them support the addition of new pages or other items to a GoLive site.

Figure 15.2 The Site tab of the Palette.

The toolbar

With a GoLive site open, the context-sensitive toolbar adds several site management items (**Figure 15.3**). You can create new folders, update a site's links, check and change preferences, and locate files.

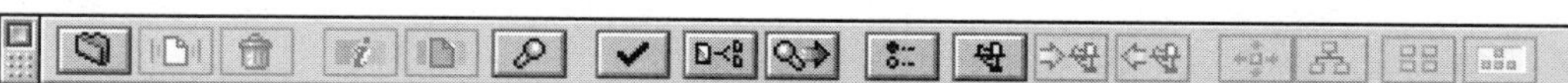

Figure 15.3 The toolbar contains site management tools when a GoLive site is open.

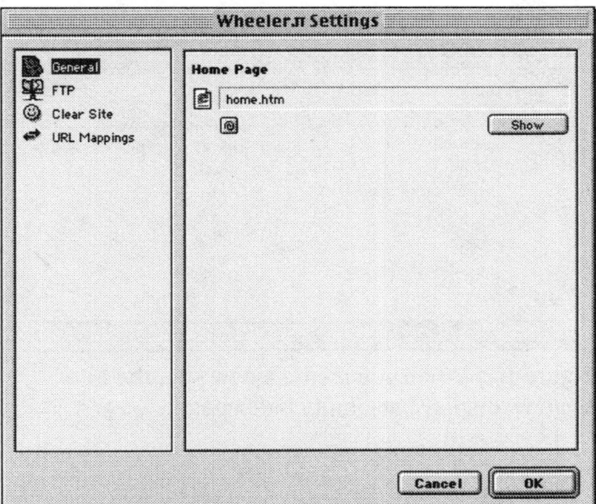

Figure 15.4 The Site Settings window (not a part of the Preferences window) contains settings for uploading and mapping your site.

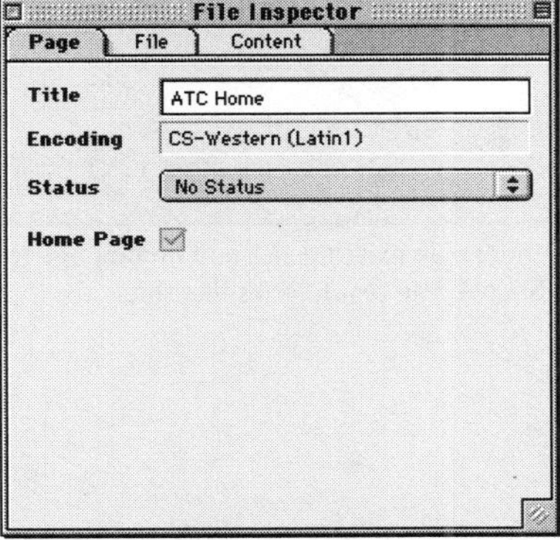

Figure 15.5 Configure the characteristics of individual site files in the File Inspector.

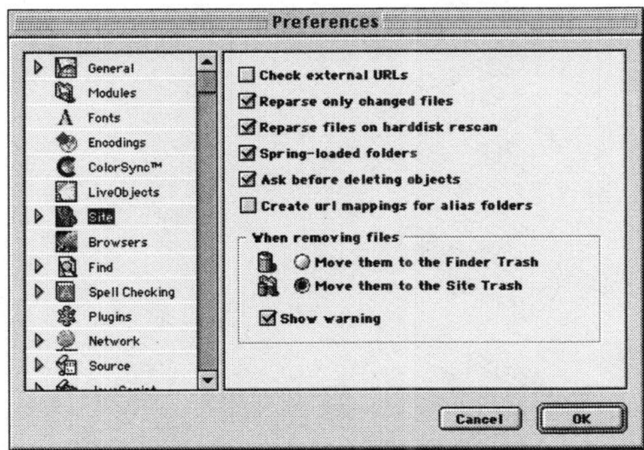

Figure 15.6 The Site Preferences pane of the Preferences window.

Site settings

You can edit site-wide parameters with the Site Settings window. Most of the options relate to publishing your site on a remote Web server (see **Figure 15.4**).

File inspector

Each site file has its own Inspector window that allows you to configure and view options specific to that file (**Figure 15.5**). These properties are specific to the file's relationship with the site—for example, you don't use the File Inspector to align or resize image files.

The Site menu

Most of the commands on the Site menu involve adding site elements or making global changes and verifications. You can also reach the Site View and Link View, which I discuss in the next chapter.

Site preferences

You'll find options for publishing your site and adding new files to the site (**Figure 15.6**).

To locate Site Preferences, choose Preferences from the Edit menu and click the triangle next to the Site label to view all of your options.

Site and Link Views

The Site and Link Views provide a graphical look at the contents of your site. Where the Site window offers a view of the files and resources themselves, the Site View shows the relationships between HTML files. Those relationships are defined by links. The Link View takes the display one step further, showing all links coming to and from a page. I'll cover the Site View and Link View in the next chapter, when I discuss organizing and managing sites and their contents.

Building Sites

To begin a GoLive site, you first create the site file and then add HTML and media files to it. Along the way, you can set preferences that affect the way site elements are added and manipulated.

There are three ways to start your site:

- Create a blank site.
- Import an existing site that is stored on a local hard disk.
- Import a site that is stored on a server, using FTP.

To create a blank site:

1. Choose New Site:Blank from the File menu.
2. Choose a location for your site. Leave the Create Folder checkbox selected to have GoLive create a folder that contains the Site file and the other components of the site. You don't need to use the New Folder button.
3. Name your site and click Choose. The Site window (**Figure 15.7**) and Site Inspector windows appear.

A new blank site includes one HTML file: index.html. This blank file is the home page for the new site.

To import a local site:

1. Select New Site:Import from Folder from the File menu.
2. In the dialog, click Browse and locate the folder containing the site you want to import.
3. Back in the Import Site Folder dialog, choose the site's home page. When you're ready to import the site, the window should look like **Figure 15.8**.

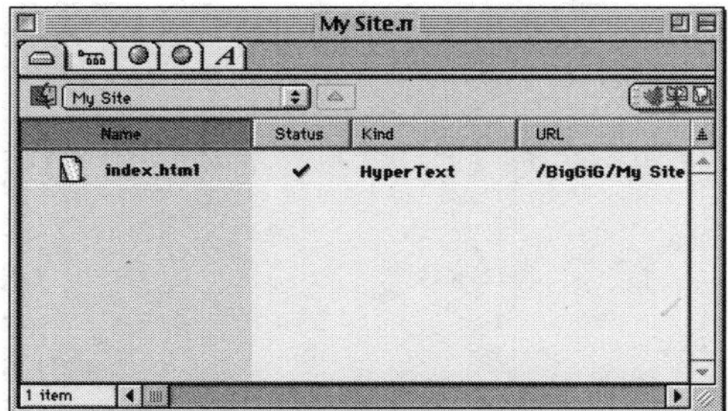

Figure 15.7 When you create a new site, the Site window displays an empty index page.

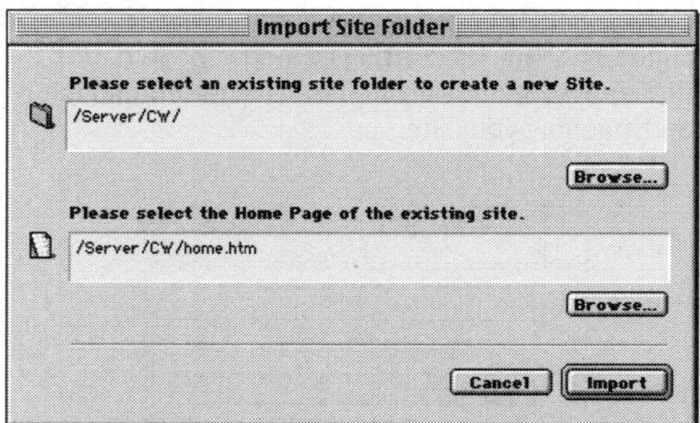

Figure 15.8 Choose an existing site and home page to import into GoLive. The result looks like this.

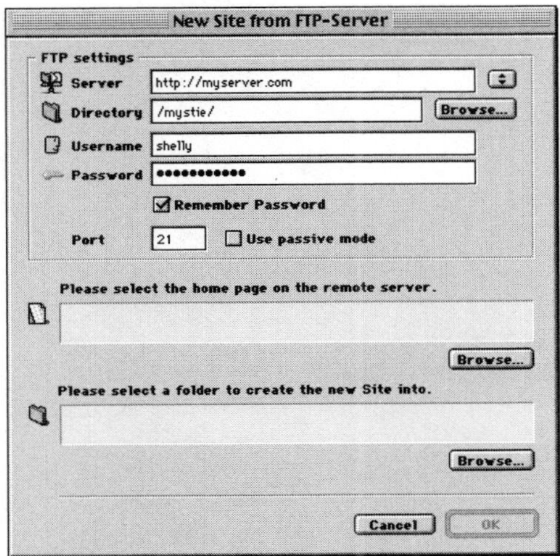

Figure 15.9 Configure your connection to the FTP server that contains a site you want to import.

4. Click OK to begin importing your site into GoLive. When the site has been imported, its contents appear in the Site window.

✔ Tip

- You can also import a site by dragging and dropping a site folder and/or home page into the Import Site Folder window.

To import a site using FTP:

1. Select New Site:Import Site from FTP from the File menu.
2. In the New Site from FTP-Server window (**Figure 15.9**), type the server URL and directory path in the appropriate fields. If you're not sure of the directory path, leave it blank and click the Browse button and navigate to your directory. GoLive will fill in the correct path for you—which may be blank (empty, null).
3. Enter a username and password in the appropriate fields.
4. Locate the home page of the site to be imported by clicking Browse under the appropriate label.
5. Choose a folder on your hard disk to accept the imported files.
6. Click OK to begin the import. When the import is complete, the Site window appears, containing the newly imported site.

Adding Files

You can add items to your new (or newly imported) site in several ways. When you add files, GoLive checks to see whether they contain hyperlinks and tries to reconcile them with other files in the site. If you have instructed GoLive to check external URLs, GoLive will connect to the Internet and attempt to verify that the links in your new files are good. There are three ways to add resources to your site:

- Create new files as you work.
- Use the Add Files command to import files and folders.
- Add files with drag-and-drop (Mac).

To create new files within your site:

1. Open a site.
2. Choose New from the File menu to create a new document.
3. Add text, images, or other content to the page.
4. Save the document to your site folder. The new file appears in the Site window.

To add files from the Site menu:

1. Open a new or existing site.
2. Choose Add Files from the Site menu.
3. In the dialog box that appears, locate a file or folder that you would like to add to your site.
4. Select each file or folder you want to add to the site and click Add. To add all files in the current folder, click Add All.

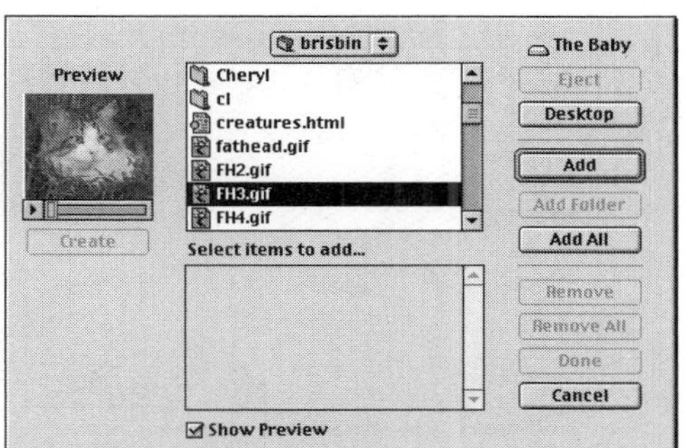

Figure 15.10 Preview image files by clicking on them in the Add Files dialog box.

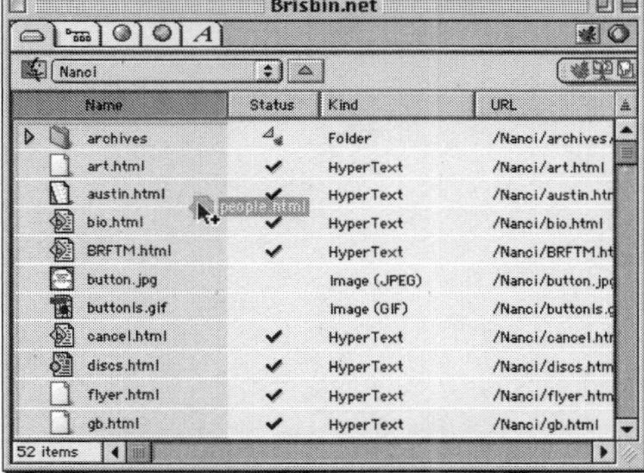

Figure 15.11 Drag a file or folder from the Macintosh Finder into the Site window to add the item to a GoLive site.

✔ Tips

- You can use the Add Files command to bring a complete Web site into a GoLive site file, or to add individual files and folders to an existing site.
- If you select a GIF file from the Add Files dialog box, GoLive displays a preview of the image. If you select a JPEG file, you can see a preview by clicking the Create button (**Figure 15.10**).

Ⓜ To add files to a site with drag-and-drop:

1. Open a site.
2. In the Finder, locate the folder containing the files you want to add to the site and open it.
3. In the Site window, be sure that the Files tab is visible.
4. In the Finder, drag the files you want to add (or the whole folder, if you like) into the Site window (**Figure 15.11**) and let go of the mouse button. GoLive examines the files you've added, copies them to the site's folder, and adds them to the site's database.

✔ Tip

- If you begin dragging a folder or file to the Site window and realize that the Files tab is not visible, you can drag the file or folder over the Files tab to bring it to the front. With that done, drop down into the window and let go of the mouse to complete the addition to your site.

Adding Non-file Resources to a Site

In addition to locally stored HTML files and graphics, GoLive sites can store pointers to external resources, and references to custom colors and font sets. Once included in a site, these resources can be added to pages with Point & Shoot. Like files, external resources can be examined and edited with the Inspector.

You can import groups of external resources or add them one at a time. There are two ways to import multiple URLs: add files to a site, or import resources from bookmark or address book files. You add single external resources much the way you would a new file. I cover this adding process in the next section.

Importing external resources

If you are creating a site from scratch using GoLive (rather than updating an existing one) you may not have external URLs or e-mail addresses stored in your site. However, you may have bookmark files or address books that include this kind of information, with no way other than cutting and pasting to add them to a new Web site. GoLive allows you to import bookmark files and address or nickname files. When you are ready, you can use Point & Shoot linking to add URLs and addresses to a page within your site.

To import bookmarks or addresses:

1. In the Site window, click on the External tab to select it.
2. Choose Import File from the Site menu.
3. In the dialog box that appears (**Figure 15.12**), locate a URL or address file in one of the supported formats: bookmarks (Netscape Navigator), favorites (Internet Explorer), addressbook (Navigator), or nicknames (Eudora).

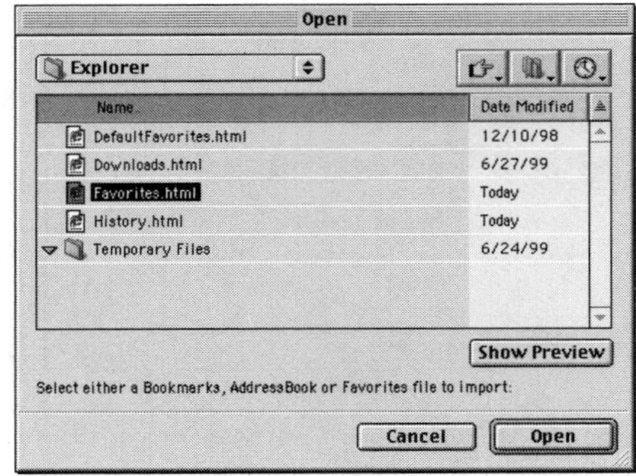

Figure 15.12 Choose a file from which to import bookmarks or addresses.

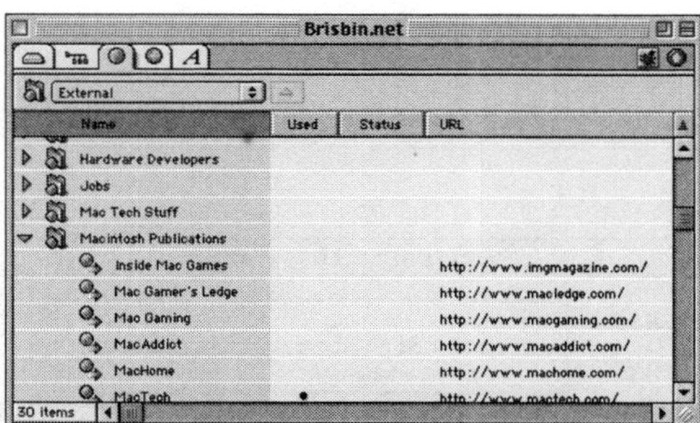

Figure 15.13 URLs imported into a GoLive site appear in the same folder structure that the original favorites or bookmark file does.

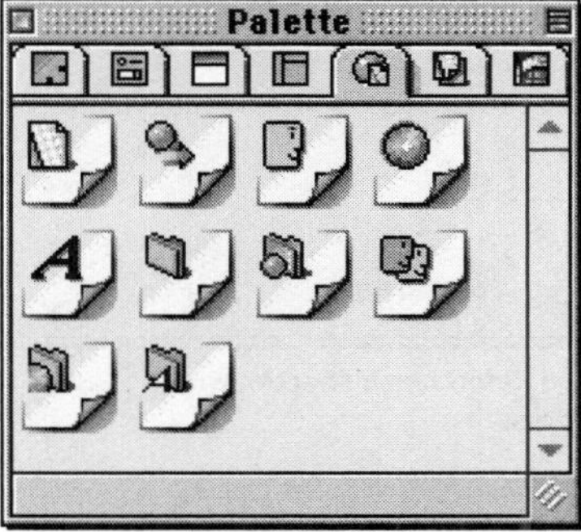

Figure 15.14 The Site tab of the Palette.

Figure 15.15 The URL palette tool.

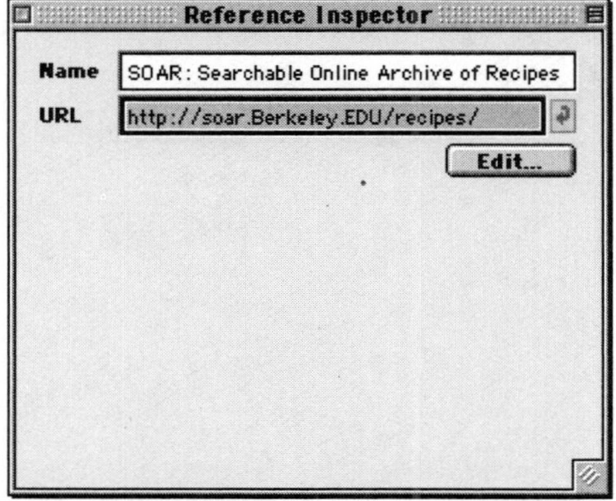

Figure 15.16 Edit a URL in the Reference Inspector.

4. Click Open. If you have selected the "Check external URLs" checkbox in the Preferences window, GoLive will connect to the Internet and try to verify the URLs in your bookmarks or favorites file. When verification is complete, the new items appear under the External tab (**Figure 15.13**).
5. Click the triangle (Mac) or plus sign (Windows) to the left of the new Group icon to display its contents. If your bookmark or favorites file contains folders, GoLive preserves them when you import the file into a site.

To add a single URL:

1. Click the External tab of the Site window.
2. Click the Site tab in the Palette (**Figure 15.14**).
3. Double-click or drag the URL tool (**Figure 15.15**) from the Palette into the Site window. An untitled URL appears under the External tab in the Site window, and the Reference Inspector appears.
4. If you want to store the URL in an existing folder, drag it over the folder's name.
5. Type a name for the URL in the Name field and press Tab.
6. Type the full URL (including http://) into the URL field. The finished URL appears in **Figure 15.16**.

✔ Tip

- Another way to add a new URL to a GoLive site is to drag it from a Web browser. In the browser, select the URL and drag it into the External tab of the Site window.

To add a new address:

1. Double-click the Address tag (**Figure 15.17**) or drag it from the Palette into the Site window. The Reference Inspector appears.
2. Type a name for the address in the Name field and press Tab.
3. Type the e-mail address into the Address field. The finished address appears in **Figure 15.18**.

Figure 15.17 The Address palette tool.

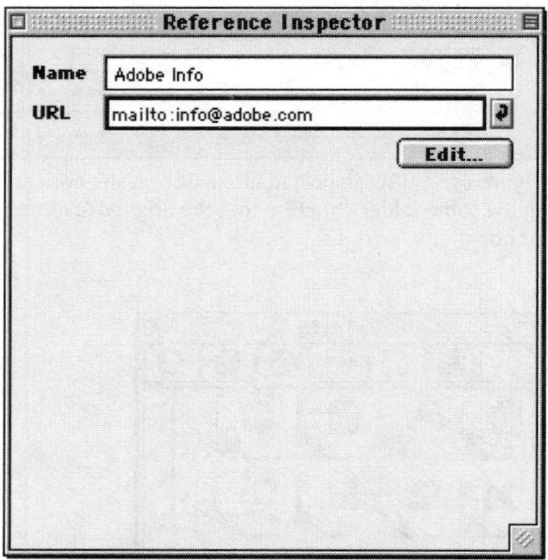

Figure 15.18 The Reference Inspector, with a completed address.

✔ Tips

- GoLive helps you enter addresses by filling out the portion of the URL for you (when addresses are used as links, these links are URLs). Type `info@adobe.com`, and GoLive completes the URL by adding "`mailto:`".
- Unlike URLs, e-mail addresses cannot be verified by selecting the Check External URLs preference. GoLive will indicate an error in an e-mail address only if it has incorrect syntax.

Adding site colors

You can store colors within a site, much as you do files and external resources. You'll find this option useful if you have created a custom color in the Color Palette, and for upholding a sitewide color scheme. Like other site objects, colors can be added to a Web page with drag-and-drop or Point & Shoot.

Figure 15.19 Click the Colors tab in the Site window to view site colors.

To add colors to a site:

1. In the Site window, click the Color tab (**Figure 15.19**).
2. Double-click the Color tool (**Figure 15.20**) or drag it from the Palette to the Site window. An untitled color appears in the Site window.

Figure 15.20 The Site Color palette tool.

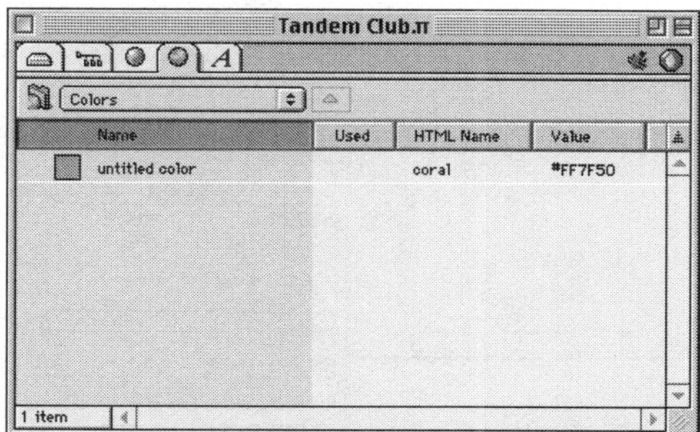

Figure 15.21 Create new site colors by dragging them from the Preview pane of the Color Palette to the Site window's Colors tab.

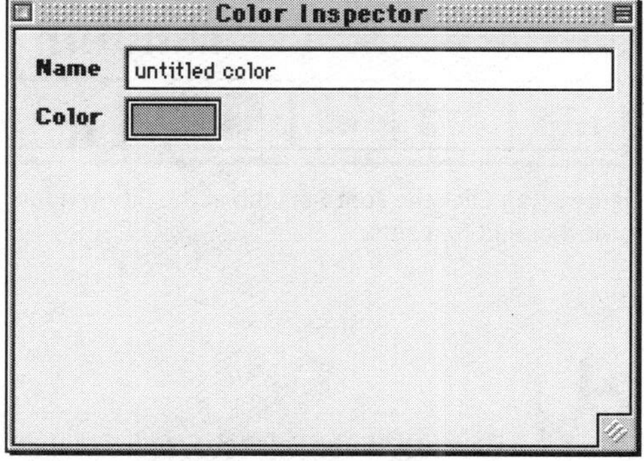

Figure 15.22 You can name and view a new color in the Reference Inspector.

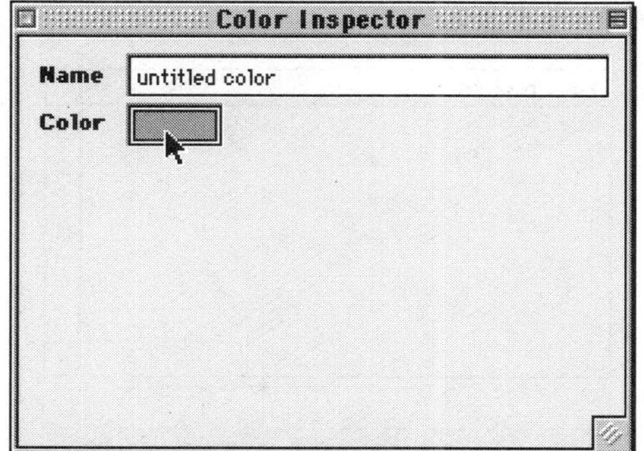

Figure 15.23 Open the Color Palette from the Color box in the Inspector window.

3. Double-click the new color. The Color Palette window opens.
4. Choose a color from one of the Color Palette tabs. (For more information about creating and customizing colors, see Chapter 4.) The color appears in the Preview Pane.
5. Click in the Preview Pane and drag to the color box next to the new color you created. When you release the mouse button, the color appears in the Site window (**Figure 15.21**).
6. With the new color selected, click the Inspector window, which now displays the Color Inspector (**Figure 15.22**)

   or

   Click on the color's name (untitled) in the Site window to make the name editable.
7. Give the color a descriptive name and press Return to confirm the name.

✔ Tips

- You can also add site colors by first creating them in the Color Palette and then dragging from the Preview pane to the Colors tab of the Site window.
- When you add a new color, GoLive examines it to determine if it is Web-safe—one of the 216 colors supported by all Web browsers and computer platforms. If not, a bullet appears in the Web Safe column. It's a good idea to choose a Web Safe color instead.

To replace an existing site color:

1. In the Site window's Color tab, click the color you want to change.
2. In the Color Inspector, click the Color box (**Figure 15.23**). The Color Palette opens or comes to the front if already open.

continues on next page

3. Choose a new color.

4. Drag the new color from the Preview pane to a color icon in the Site window (**Figure 15.24**). The color changes along with its HTML Name and Value. The color is now Web safe.

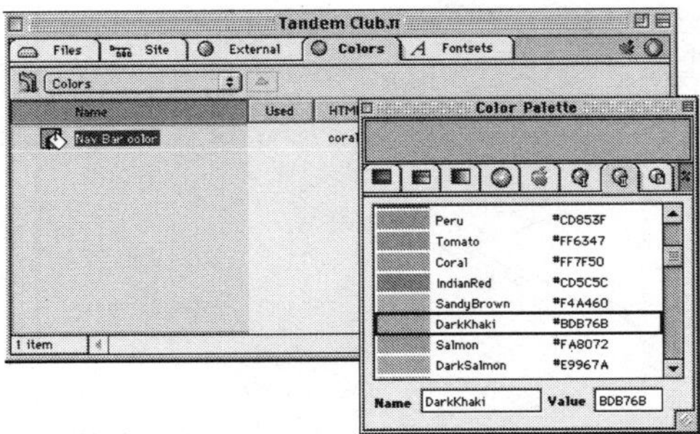

Figure 15.24 Dragging a color from the Color Palette to the Color tab of the Site window creates a new site color.

Adding font sets

Font sets allow you to save and use fonts with your Web site. Without them, you're limited to the typeface supported by your site visitors' Web browsers. You can store font sets as part of a site, just as you do custom colors. You can only use fonts that are installed on your computer.

To add a font set to a site:

1. In the Site window, click the Font Sets tab (**Figure 15.25**).

Figure 15.25 Click the Font Sets tab in the Site window to view or add font sets.

2. From the Palette's Site tab, double-click or drag the Font Set tool to the Site window (**Figure 15.26**). An empty font set item appears.

Figure 15.26 The Palette's Font Set tool.

3. In the Font Set Inspector (**Figure 15.27**), name the font set.

4. Click New. The field near the bottom of the Inspector lights up, along with a menu to its right. Click and hold the menu to view a list of available fonts.

5. Choose a font from the list.

6. If you want to add more fonts to the set, repeat steps 4 and 5.

Figure 15.27 Name and configure new font sets in the Font Set Inspector.

To use a font from an existing document:

1. Open a GoLive document that contains custom fonts. The document need not be part of a site, but be sure that a site is also open.

2. In the Site window, click the Font Sets tab.

3. In the document window, select some text that uses the font you wish to add to the site.
4. Drag the text into the Site window. A set appears in the Site window, and the Inspector changes to display the Font Set Inspector.
5. Type a name for the font set in the Font Set Inspector and press Return to confirm the name of your font set. The font used in this set appears in the Font Set Inspector.

✔ Tips

- You can copy font sets or colors between sites. With two sites open, click on a font set or color in the Site window and choose Copy from the Edit menu. In the destination site paste the font set or color into the Site window's Font Sets or Colors tab.
- For details about how to safely add font sets that will be recognized by most browsers, see Chapter 4, "Working with Text."
- Any time you add an item to a site via the Site window, GoLive determines whether or not the item is currently in use within the site. For example, if you copy a font set used within the site in the way I described above, the Used bullet will appear in the Font Sets window.

Fine-Tuning Preferences

The Preferences and Site settings windows include options that change the way you interact with your site. I've covered some of these options in the course of adding files and resources, and I'll cover another batch when I discuss publishing Web sites in Chapter 17. For now, though, there are a few settings you may find useful as you work on your site.

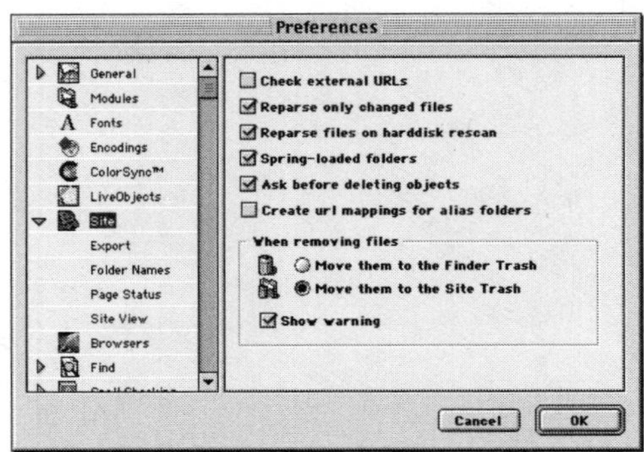

Figure 15.28 Site options in the Preferences window.

To set site preferences:

1. Choose Preferences from the Edit menu.
2. Click the Site icon to display site-related options (**Figure 15.28**).
3. Click the "Check external URLs" check-box to have GoLive validate remote links within your site as they are added.
4. When GoLive opens a site file, it checks the site's links. Leave "Reparse only changed files" checked to have GoLive verify only links in files that have changed since the last time the site was saved.
5. Spring-loaded folders in a site file behave just like folders on the desktop of a Macintosh. If you drag an item onto a folder and hold down the mouse for a moment, the folder opens. Note that although the Windows version of GoLive includes a spring-loaded folder option, this option does not work.
6. Leave "Ask before deleting objects" checked to receive a warning when you remove a file from a site.
7. Choose to send deleted files to the Site Trash folder (a folder stored within the GoLive site hierarchy) or to the computer's Trash/Recycle bin.
8. Click OK to finish setting preferences.

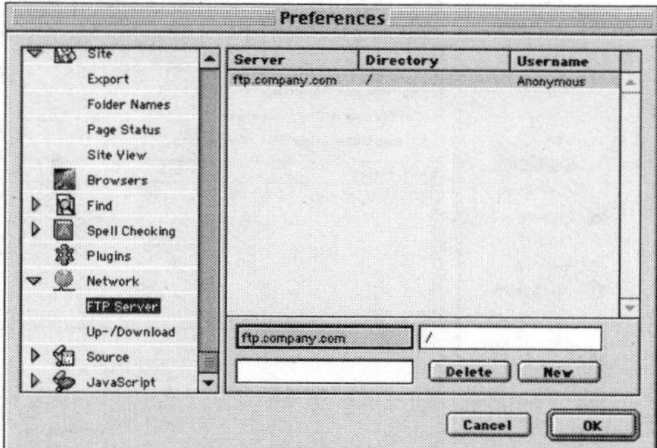

Figure 15.29 Add to the list of servers your site can reach in the FTP Server preferences window.

To prepare for uploading to multiple servers:

1. In the Preferences window, click the triangle (Mac) or the plus sign (Windows) to the left of the Network label. Scroll through the Preferences window if necessary to reach it.
2. Click the FTP Server label (**Figure 15.29**).
3. Click New to begin setting up access to a new server. A placeholder URL appears in the Server field.
4. In the server field, type the URL of a Web server, including the complete path to your Web site directory.
5. Press Return.
6. Repeat steps 3-5 for each server you want to add.
7. When you are finished adding servers, click OK to close the Preferences window.

✔ Tip

- In order for the multi-server feature to work properly, you need to create a separate folder for files that will be published on the secondary server. You will need to relocate any files that will be stored on the primary server to another part of the site's hierarchy.

To filter URLs:

1. In the Preferences window, expand the General label and then click the URL Handling item. URL filters allow you to store non-HTML files within your site without incurring GoLive error indicators.

continues on next page

2. Click the New button to create a URL filter (**Figure 15.30**).
3. Type **cgi-bin** in the URL filter field. Many CGI (Common Gateway Interface) applications use files and folders whose names include "cgi-bin." These files are not HTML or multimedia files, so they generate errors when they are included in a GoLive site. A cgi-bin URL filter allows these non-standard filenames to be used without generating errors. You can create additional filters to bypass other unusual filenames.
4. When you have finished creating filters, click OK.

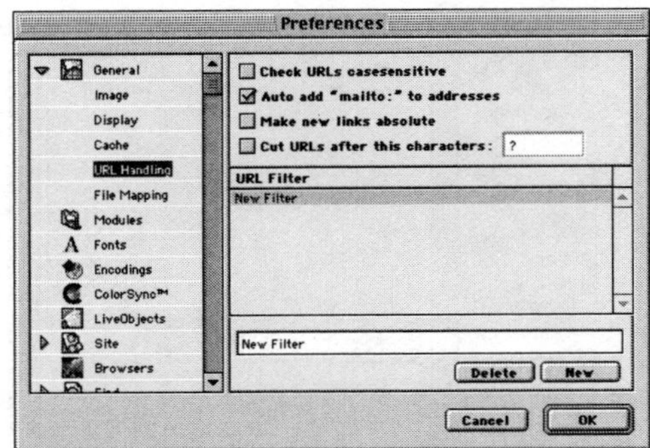

Figure 15.30 Create URL filters to allow non-HTML or media files to reside within the GoLive site hierarchy.

16

MANAGING SITES

The real value of site management tools lies not only in creating a well-organized site, but also in maintaining it. Large sites often become unmanageable because of the vast number of links and confusing hierarchical relationships. Adding, deleting, and moving files tends to introduce errors. And things change on the Web; over time, remote links get broken.

GoLive's site management tools allow you to take a visual and logical look at your site and find and correct errors efficiently.

In this chapter, I cover:

- Working with site objects.
- The Site View.
- Working with links.
- Designing sites with generic pages.
- Troubleshooting sites.

Working with Site Objects

Files, URLs, e-mail addresses, colors, and font sets are all objects within a GoLive site. Each type of object can be configured, renamed, and moved, just as items within a document can be. Also like layout objects, site objects can be configured within the Inspector window.

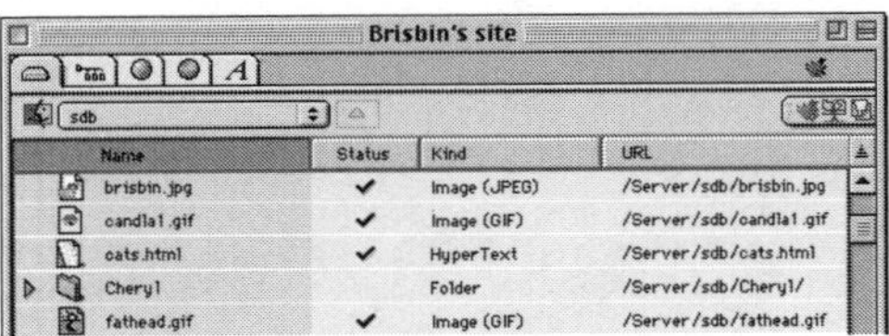

Figure 16.1 The Site window's Files tab looks and acts much like a Finder (Mac) or Windows Explorer (Windows) window.

Managing site files

Unlike layout objects—text frames, images, and multimedia, for example—site files are all configured using the same Inspector window.

Because the Site window is a window to the actual files that make up a site, you can perform some site management tasks in the Finder (Mac) or Windows Explorer (Windows), if you prefer. Like these operating system-based file managers, the Site window is organized into files and folders (GoLive calls them groups, but they look and act just like folders or directories). You can also use the Site window's Files tab to view file attributes (type and location on disk) and to sort files by their labels. Finally, you can open and rename files, just as you do in the Finder or in Windows Explorer.

To use OS-like file management options:

1. Open a GoLive site file, and make sure that the Site window's Files tab is visible.
2. Examine the column under the Kind label of the Site window. If the column is empty, you'll need to set File Mapping Preferences, as described in Chapter 3. If the column contains labels such as hypertext, image (GIF), etc., you already have file mapping preferences set, and you can use the Kind column to identify your site's files. **Figure 16.1** shows a portion of my Site window, with files mapped.

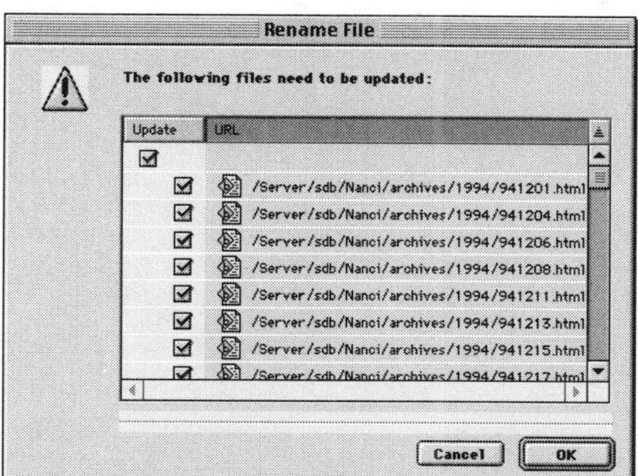

Figure 16.2 When you rename a file, GoLive searches for files containing links to the changed file.

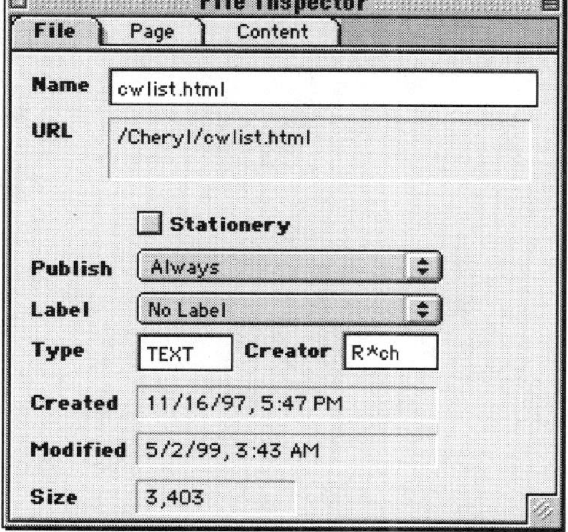

Figure 16.3 The File Inspector appears when you select a file within the Site window.

3. Click once on the Kind column label. The column is sorted by object type.
4. Click on the Name label to restore alphabetical order. You can use the Ascending/Descending arrow at the right of the window to sort items in the reverse order.

To rename a file in the Site window:

1. Click on a file name in the Site window. The selected file name should now be surrounded with a text frame.
2. Type a new name, overwriting the old one. Don't forget to preserve the file's extension (.html, .gif, etc.).
3. Press Return to confirm the name. If the file is linked to others in your site, GoLive will search for URLs that need to be changed and present you with a window containing files that should be updated (**Figure 16.2**).

To rename a file with the Inspector:

1. With a site open, click on an HTML or media file. The File Inspector appears (**Figure 16.3**).
2. To change the name of the file, type a new name in the Name field. Don't forget to keep the file extension.
3. In the dialog box that appears, click OK to confirm the name change.

To move a file within a site:

1. Locate a file you want to move. Drag it into the folder you want to move it to. GoLive displays the Update window and asks if you would like to update the file's URL and its connection to other files in your site.
2. Click OK to update the site.

✔ Tips

- You can change URLs and e-mail addresses, too. Using the Finder/Windows Explorer metaphor, you can change the name but not the address or URL itself. Changing the name within the site will not update your Web page.
- To edit a URL or address, select the item in the External tab of the Site window and edit the URL in the Inspector. When you're done, GoLive will present the usual Update window and give you the chance to correct references to the URL within your pages. To verify that your new URL is good, you'll need to connect to the Internet and make sure that the Check External URLs preference (discussed in Chapter 15) is checked.
- You can choose to change only selected occurrences of a filename or URL. In the Update window, all links have checkmarks next to them. Uncheck any link you want to leave alone.

To change a file's status:

1. Select a file by clicking on its icon in the Site window.
2. If the Page tab is not already selected in the File Inspector, click on it.
3. Click and hold the Status popup menu to display available choices. If you have not set status options in the Preferences window, the menu is empty.

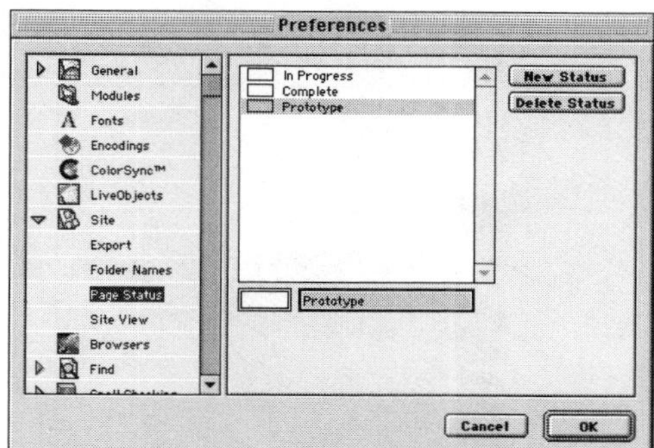

Figure 16.4 Create new Status options in the Page Status area of the Preferences window.

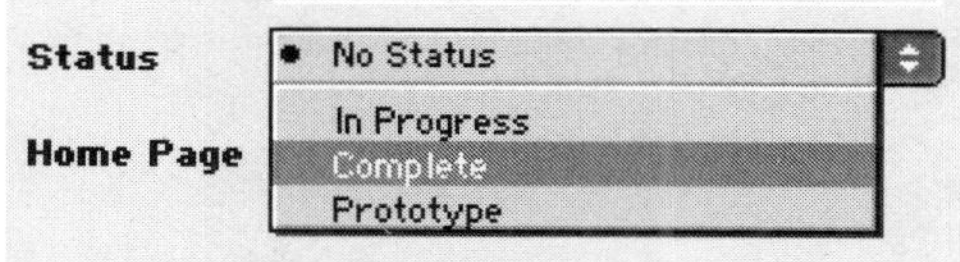

Figure 16.5 The File Inspector's Page Status popup contains items you create in the Preferences window.

To set status preferences:

1. Choose Preferences from the Edit menu.
2. Click on the Site triangle (Mac) or plus sign (Windows) to display Site Preferences.
3. Click the Page Status item tab to display the Status window.
4. Click New status to create a status option.
5. Type a status option, e.g. **complete**, **in progress**, etc.
6. To add more status options (**Figure 16.4**), click New status and type the text you would like to appear in the Status popup menu of the File Inspector. When you're finished, click OK to close the Preferences window.
7. In the File Inspector, click the Status popup menu. Several options are now available (**Figure 16.5**).

To add file management features to files within a site:

1. To apply a colored label, select a site object and click the Inspector to bring it forward.
2. In the File tab, use the Label popup menu to choose a label and associated color as specified by the Finder.
3. Click the Stationery checkbox if you want to use the site file as a template.
4. To change the file's publishing status, which tells GoLive whether to export the file for uploading to a Web server, choose an option from the Publish popup menu.

continues on next page

✔ Tip

- You can alter the label and publishing status of files and of folders. To change the status of a complete folder, select it and click on the appropriate popup menu. All files within the folder will be changed accordingly.

To preview a site file's contents:

With a site file selected, click on the Content tab of the Inspector. A thumbnail representation of your HTML file or image appears (**Figure 16.6**).

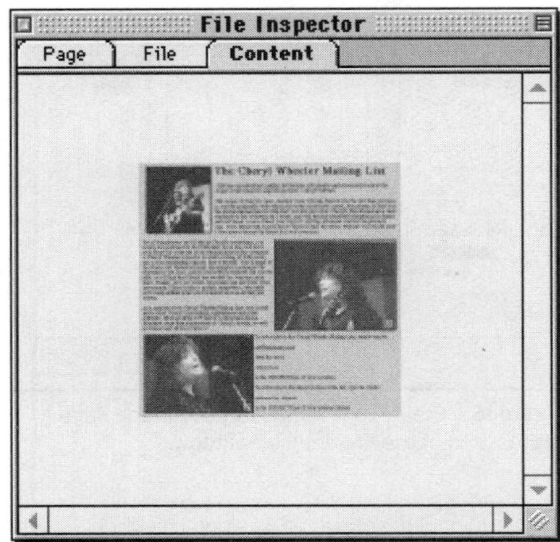

Figure 16.6 An HTML page, previewed in the Content tab of the File Inspector.

✔ Tips

- Ⓜ In order to display the contents of an HTML file in the File Inspector, the file must have been saved with GoLive. To learn how to change the file's creator, see the next step-by-step section. Any Web-compatible image can be displayed in the File Inspector.
- You can add a previewed image to a document from the File Inspector by clicking on the image in the Inspector's Content tab and dragging it into the document window (**Figure 16.7**).
- You can play multimedia files in the Content tab, just as you can play them in the document window. GoLive provides built-in support for QuickTime and QuickTime VR files. Other multimedia formats will play if the appropriate plug-ins are present. For a complete discussion of plugins, see Chapter 9.
- You can drag-and-drop images or multimedia files to the document window. You can't place HTML thumbnails within a document.

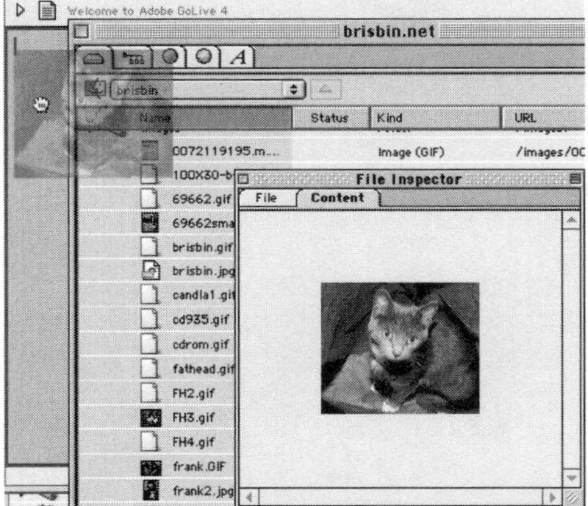

Figure 16.7 Drag and drop an image from the Content tab of the File Inspector to the document window.

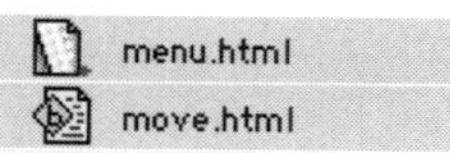

Figure 16.8 The file called menu.html was created with GoLive. The file move.html was created by BBEdit, an HTML editor. By changing the Creator of the file, you can make move.html a GoLive file, too.

Figure 16.9 The New Folder tool.

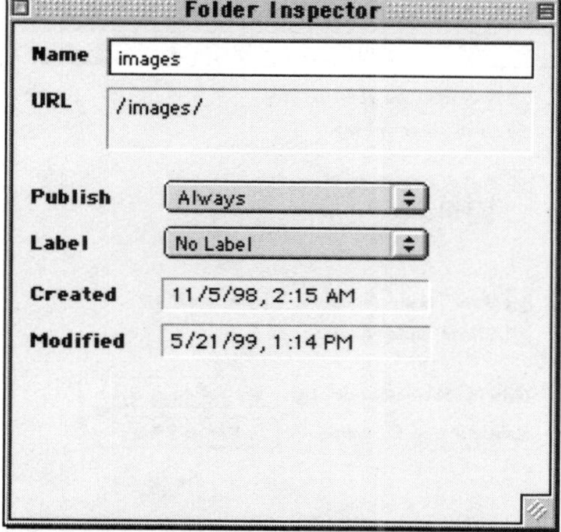

Figure 16.10 The Folder Inspector.

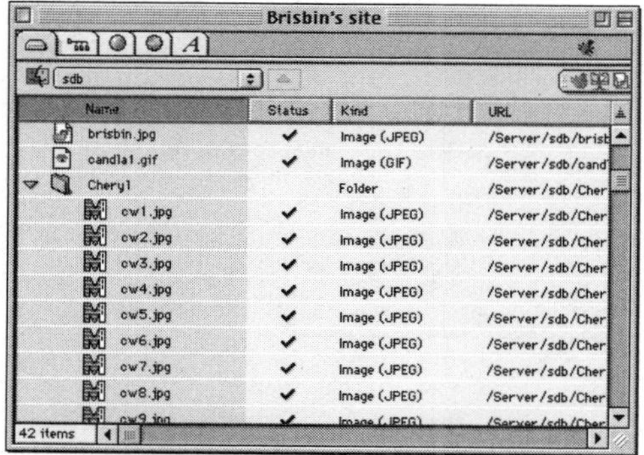

Figure 16.11 Open a folder by clicking the triangle (Mac) or plus sign (Windows).

Ⓜ To change a file's creator to GoLive:

1. In the Site window, select an HTML file that was created with an application other than GoLive.
2. Under the File tab of the File Inspector, change the entry in the Creator field to GoMk.
3. If the Type field contains an entry other than TEXT, change it as well.
4. Return to the Site window. The file's icon has changed to that of GoLive (**Figure 16.8**), and the page preview appears in the Content tab of the File Inspector.

Using site folders

If you have a large Web site, managing lots of site files can be a challenge. GoLive recognizes and uses your site's imported folder hierarchy. You can also add Site Groups to organize files logically. You can create groups that store pages, media files, URLs and addresses.

To create a site folder:

1. With a site open, click on the Files tab to open it.
2. Choose the Site tab from the Palette.
3. Drag the Folder tool (**Figure 16.9**) from the Palette to the Site window. An untitled folder appears in the Site window.
4. Click on the Inspector window to display the Folder Inspector (**Figure 16.10**).
5. Type a name for the folder.
6. In the Site window, add HTML files to your new folder by dragging them onto the folder's icon.
7. View the contents of your folder by clicking on the triangle (Mac) or plus sign (Windows) to the left of the Folder icon (**Figure 16.11**).

The Site View

Think of the Site View as a bird's eye view of your Web site. Starting with your home page, the Site View displays miniature representations of each page in the site and the links that connect them to one another. The home page is the *parent* page for the entire site. Each linked page is a *child* of the home page and a *sibling* to other pages. The Site View displays links to and from each page and draws lines between parent and child pages.

To examine a site with the Site View:

1. Open a site.
2. Click the Site tab in the Site window. The Site View (**Figure 16.12**) and the Site View Controller appear.
3. Click the Site View Controller to bring it forward (**Figure 16.13**).
4. If the Site View Controller's Navigation Hierarchy button is selected, click the Link Hierarchy button instead, to display the actual links that exist between files in your site.
5. Leave Auto Arrange Icons checked, to keep an orderly Site view.
6. To vary the view of a large site (making it easier to find things and less space consuming), check Stagger Items.
7. Leave "Use Hide and Show" Live Buttons to have GoLive display triangles at each page icon to allow you to expand or collapse the page. The triangles appear when you move the mouse over the page, as shown in **Figure 16.14**.
8. Click the Filter tab of the Site View Controller to tell GoLive which objects to display in the Site View. By default, only HTML files are visible. This is the simplest

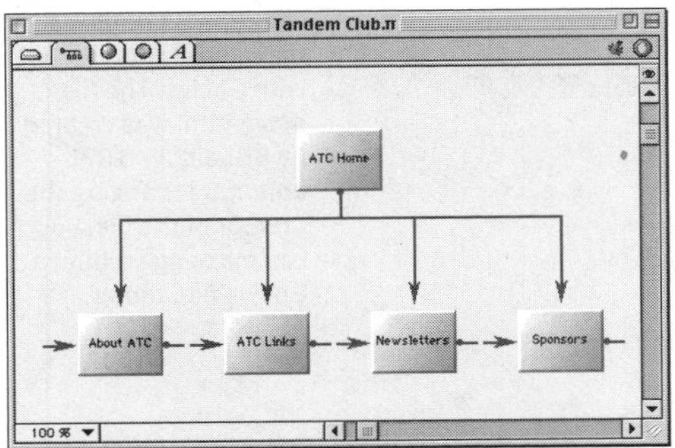

Figure 16.12 The Site view shows a hierarchical view of your Web site.

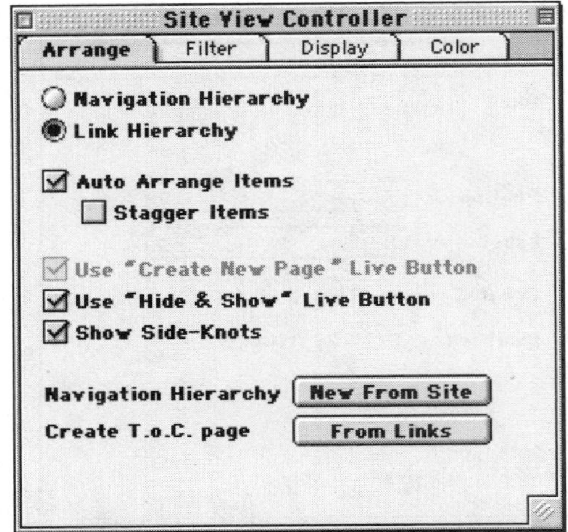

Figure 16.13 The Site View Controller.

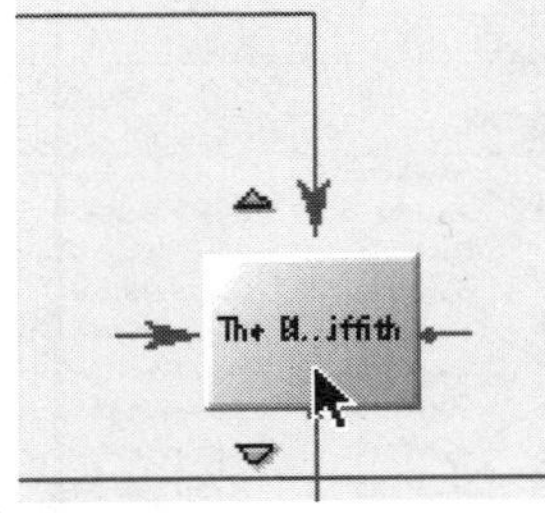
Figure 16.14 You can expand or collapse items that have child or parent items, respectively, by moving the mouse over the item to be changed and clicking the appropriate triangle.

THE SITE VIEW

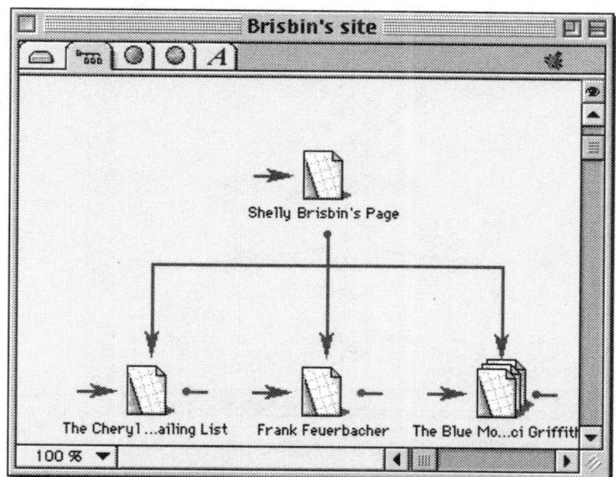

Figure 16.15 The Site View, with icons representing each page.

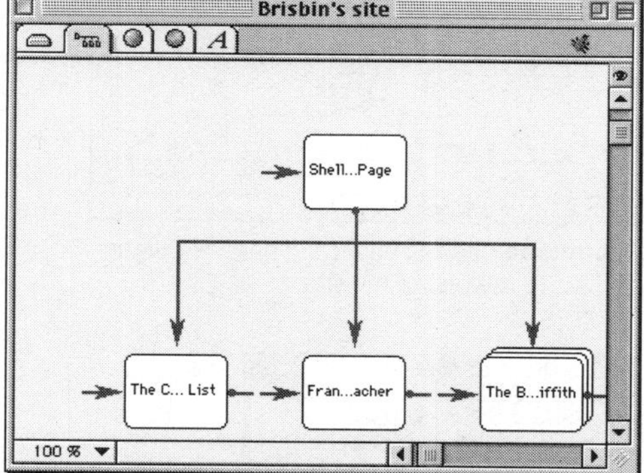

Figure 16.16 The Site View, with TV screens (they look more like boxes with rounded corners to me) representing each page.

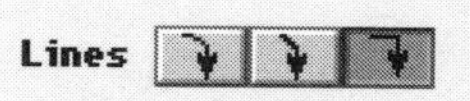

Figure 16.17 The Lines buttons in the Site View Controller.

arrangement for large sites. If you need to see images, URLs, or addressees that are stored within your site folder, consider using the Link View (described in the next section).

9. If you want to see items that are not linked to the rest of the site (directly, or through a link hierarchy) click the "If Unreadable" checkbox.

To change the appearance of the Site View:

1. Click the Display tab in the Site View Controller.
2. You can choose to display pages using the default frames, icons (**Figure 16.15**), thumbnails, or TV Screen (**Figure 16.16**).
3. You can also control the spacing of pages and the size of frames from the Filter tab.
4. Use the buttons near the bottom of the Site View Controller (**Figure 16.17**) to alter the angle at which lines between pages are displayed in the Site View.
5. Click on the Color tab of the Site View Controller. Here, you can choose colors for Navigation Curves, Link Curves, Background, and Text.
6. To apply a color, open the Color Palette and choose the color you want.
7. Click and drag from the Color Palette's preview pane to the appropriate field in the Site View Controller.
8. Make a choice from the Item Color buttons, to tell GoLive whether to use GoLive status colors or Finder labels to determine the color of site items. You can also choose monochrome if you prefer.

continues on next page

If you click on your home page in the Site View, the links between it and the other pages in your site light up (**Figure 16.18**), and the Site View Controller is replaced by the Inspector for the file you selected. Clicking on other files within the site highlights their path to the home page and to other files in the hierarchy (**Figure 16.19**).

To use the Site Outline view:

1. With the Site View visible, click the Display tab in the Site Controller (**Figure 16.20**).
2. Click the Outline button, near the bottom of the Inspector. The Site View now displays the Outline, which is collapsed.
3. Click the triangle (Mac) or plus sign (Windows) to expand the outline from the index.html page. Instead of a folder hierarchy, the outline view displays the site from the index page downward. Pages with links have triangles next to them. Click them to see the linked files (**Figure 16.21**).

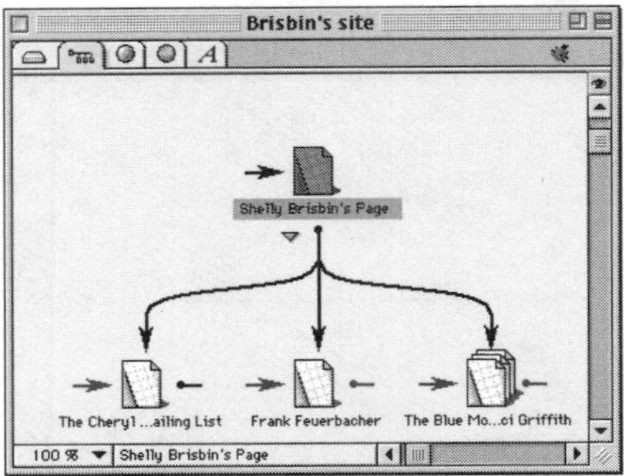

Figure 16.18 Selecting the home page lights up links to other parts of your site.

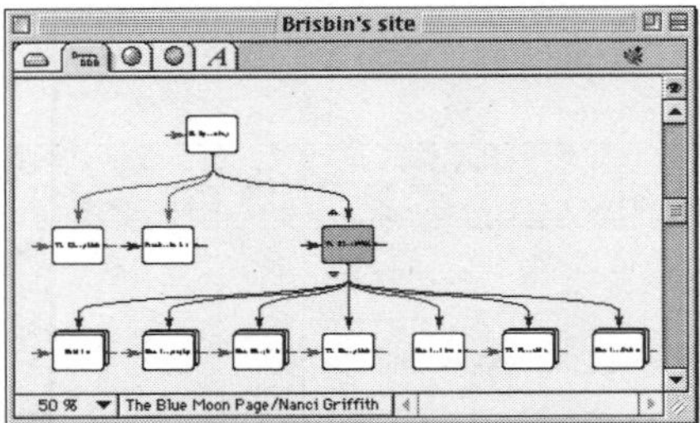

Figure 16.19 Clicking on a child page highlights its links to the rest of the site.

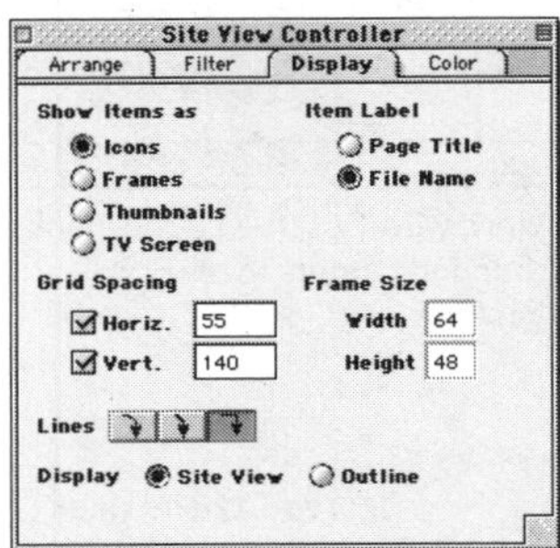

Figure 16.20 Click the Outline button in the Site Controller.

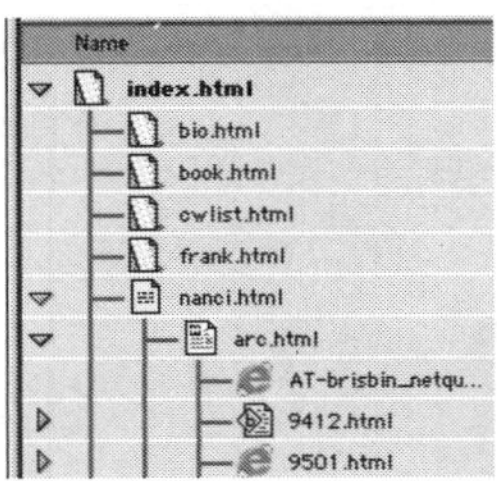

Figure 16.21 The Outline Site View shows a hierarchy of linked files.

Figure 16.22 View the Site Navigator by clicking the Open Site Navigator from the toolbar.

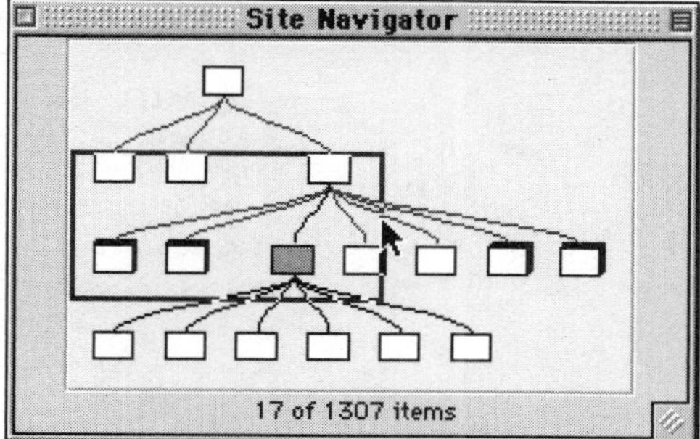

Figure 16.23 The Site Navigator displays a reduced version of the Site View. Drag the rectangle to locate the portion of the Site View you want to work with. The Site View shifts as you drag.

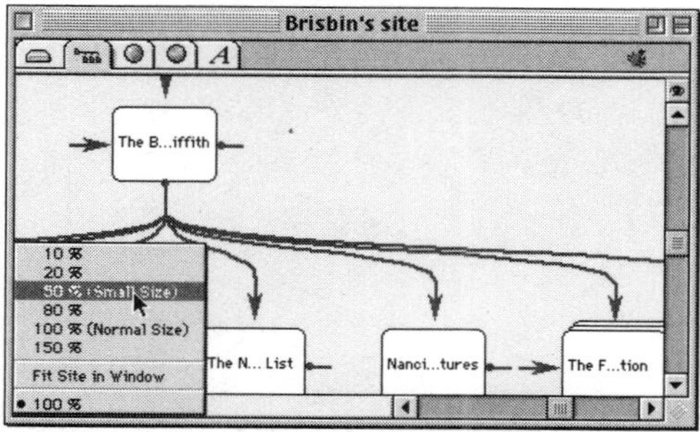

Figure 16.24 The Site View's Zoom menu allows you to view more or less of the site.

Navigating within the Site View

You can use the Site View's tools to help you move around a large site, change your location within the site, or zoom in and out to see more or less of it.

To locate a specific portion of your site in the Site View:

1. With the Site View visible, choose Open Site Navigator from the toolbar (**Figure 16.22**). The Navigator appears (**Figure 16.23**), and the cursor is now a hand.
2. Drag the box around the Navigator window and notice that the Site View changes to display full-size versions of the items in the navigator box.

To zoom the Site View:

◆ Click the Zoom popup menu at the bottom left of the Site View (**Figure 16.24**) and choose 50%. The Site View displays more of your site. You can also enlarge the view.

✔ Tips

- Of course, you can also see more of your site by using the familiar Grow box or Zoom box to change the size of the Site View window.
- Using the triangles found around items with parent or child relationships (as described in a previous section of this chapter) are also a great way to customize your view. You'll be able to tell when a set of links is collapsed by the stacked pages or icons in the Site View.

Working with Links

When you're ready to move from a high-level, file-centric view of your site to a link-centric one, you'll also move from the Site View to the Link Inspector to do your work. Despite its name, the Link Inspector is not an Inspector at all, at least in the way that GoLive defines the word. The Link Inspector is actually an alternative view of a single page, from the point of view of the links it contains, and the links that lead to it.

With the Link Inspector, you can follow links throughout your site, and make sure that all the links actually reach their intended pages.

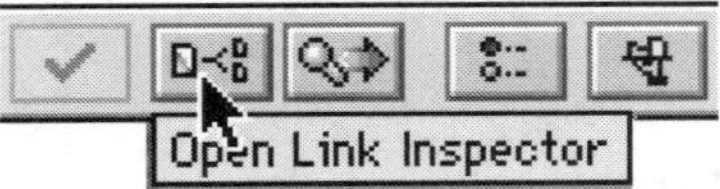

Figure 16.25 Choose Open Link Inspector from the toolbar.

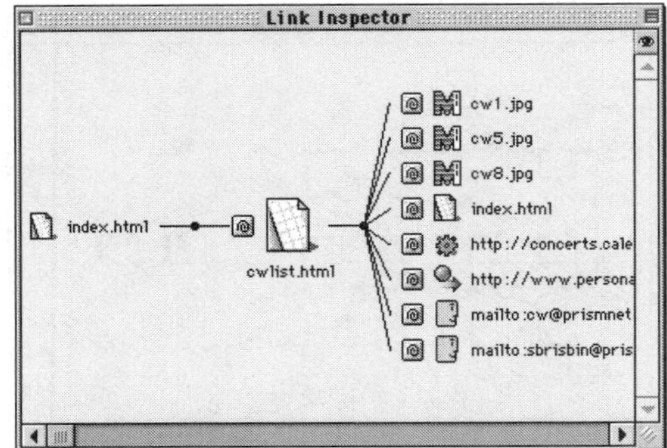

Figure 16.26 The Link Inspector shows links leading to and from the selected file.

To view a page in the Link Inspector:

1. With the Site View visible, select a page.
2. Choose View Link Inspector from the toolbar (**Figure 16.25**). If you've checked the Show Side-Knots option in the Site View Controller, you can bring up the Link Inspector by moving the mouse over a "side-knot" and clicking on it. Either way, the page's Link Inspector appears (**Figure 16.26**).
3. If you need to, resize the Link Inspector so that you can see complete filenames and/or URLs.

   Notice that the Link Inspector shows both files and URL links found on this page, all on the right side of the window. On the left side is the page from which this page links—in this case, the home page of the site.

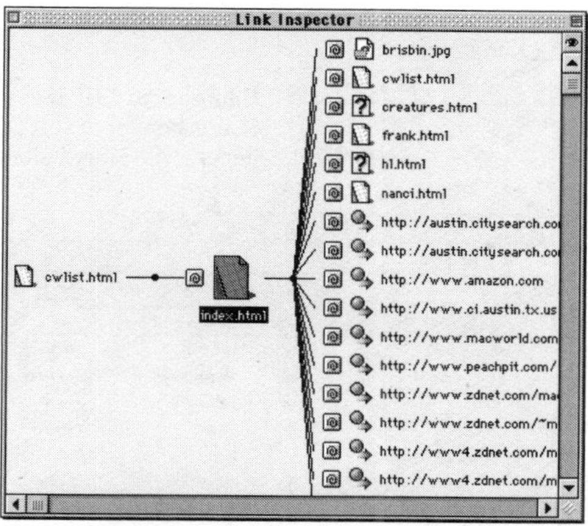

Figure 16.27 Click on the item on the left side of the window to move it to the center of the display and show all of its links.

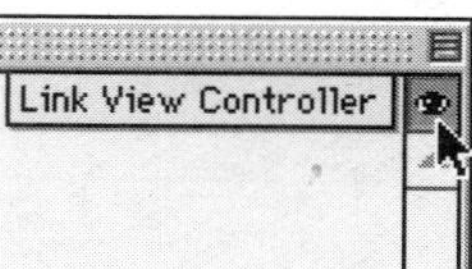

Figure 16.28 In the Link Inspector, click the eye icon to view the Link Inspector.

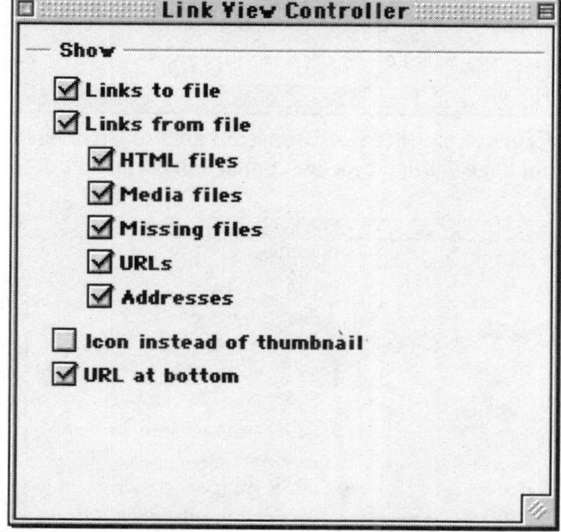

Figure 16.29 The Link View Controller.

4. Click on any link to bring it to the center of the Link Inspector. If you click on the index.html link at left, it moves to the center, and all of its links appear on the right. The original page I inspected, cwlist.html, has moved to the left (**Figure 16.27**).

✔ Tip

- When you click on an icon in the Link View, the item's Inspector appears, allowing you to edit the resource's configuration.

To customize the Link Inspector:

1. In the Link Inspector, click the "eye" button (**Figure 16.28**) at the upper right-hand corner of the window. The Link Inspector Controller appears (**Figure 16.29**).
2. Choose whether or not to display inbound links.
3. Choose which outbound links to display.

Troubleshooting Sites

Earlier in this chapter, I explained how to update your site by changing file names and how to keep it organized by examining your site with the Site and Link Views. Changing things, though, can introduce errors. GoLive includes several tools for finding and fixing errors.

Identifying errors in the Site window:

1. Open a site.
2. In the Site window, click on the Status header (**Figure 16.30**) to sort files and objects by their status within the site. GoLive sorts files with no errors to the top of the list.
3. To bring broken files to the top of the window, click the Ascending/Descending arrow, located at the upper right corner .

The Site window in **Figure 16.31** shows three of the possible Status indicators. They are as follows:

- A *checkmark* indicates that the file contains no errors and that all the files or URLs it points to are where they should be.
- A *bug* indicates that the file contains broken links.
- A *warning icon* indicates that the file is pending and has not yet been given a URL.

GoLive uses two other error indicators: one appears in the External tab of the Site window (**Figure 16.32**), and the other appears in the Link Inspector (**Figure 16.33**).

These indicators are as follows:

- A *Stop icon* indicates that the link is broken, or cannot be verified.
- A *question mark* instead of a file icon indicates that there is no physical file corresponding to the site object.

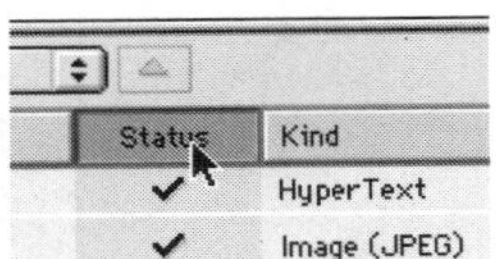

Figure 16.30 Click the Status header to sort items in the Site window.

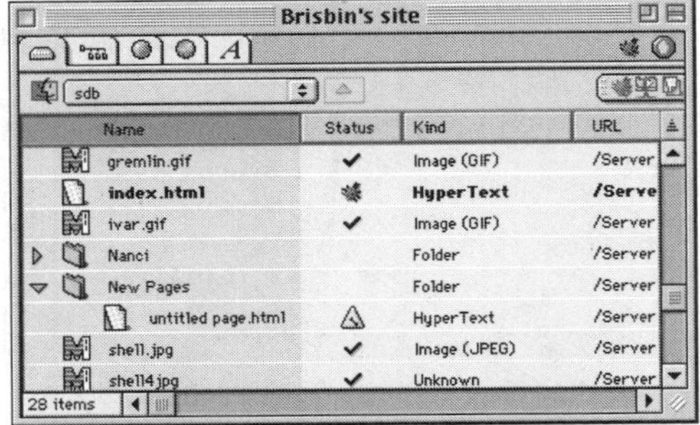

Figure 16.31 Click the Status header to sort items in the Site window.

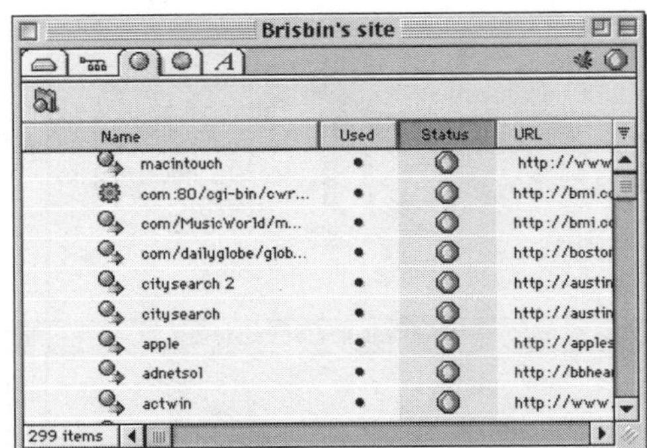

Figure 16.32 URLs with Stop icons are broken or have not been verified by a live connection to the Internet.

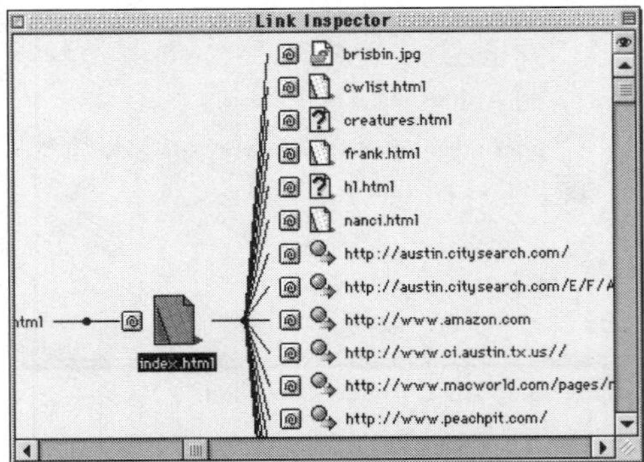

Figure 16.33 A page icon with a question mark indicates that there is a link to a page that isn't stored within your site.

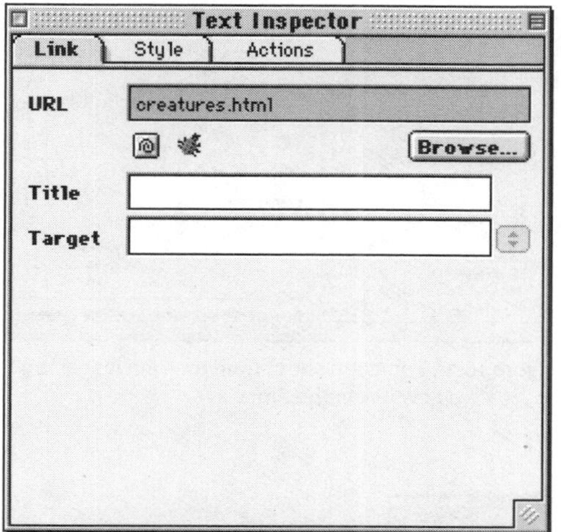

Figure 16.34 The Text Inspector points out a broken link.

✔ Tips

- When files with broken links are present within a site, the bug and/or stop icons appear at the upper right corner of the Site window, as shown back in **Figure 16.32**.
- To verify links to remote URLs, you must have the "Check external URLs" checkbox selected in the Site Preferences window. You must also be connected to the Internet. For more on Site Preferences, see Chapter 15.
- E-mail addresses do not display status indicators because there isn't a simple way to verify them.

To check pages for errors:

1. Locate items in the Site window with a "bug" icon in the Status column.
2. Double-click the file to open it.
3. Look for any obvious problems: missing images, for example. If you find a broken image link, click on it to display the Inspector and try to fix the problem by locating the file that should be linked.
4. Choose Show Link Warnings from the Edit menu.
5. Links that are broken are highlighted on the page. Click on a broken link and use the Inspector to fix it. Inspector windows representing broken links include the bug icon and a grayed-out URL, as shown in **Figure 16.34**.
6. When you've fixed all the links on the page, save and close the file. The Site window should now display a checkmark in the Status column for the file you've worked on.

Another way to quickly fix page links is to use the Link Inspector and Point & Shoot.

To repair links with the Link Inspector:

1. Click on a file with a bug in the Status column.
2. Open the Link Inspector.
3. Look for missing file symbols (a page with a question mark) in the Link Inspector. Note the file name.
4. With the "buggy" file still selected, so that its Link Inspector is visible, scroll through the Site window until you find the file you want to point the broken link to.
5. In the Link Inspector, click on the Point & Shoot icon next to the broken file and drag the mouse onto the new file, as shown in **Figure 16.35**.

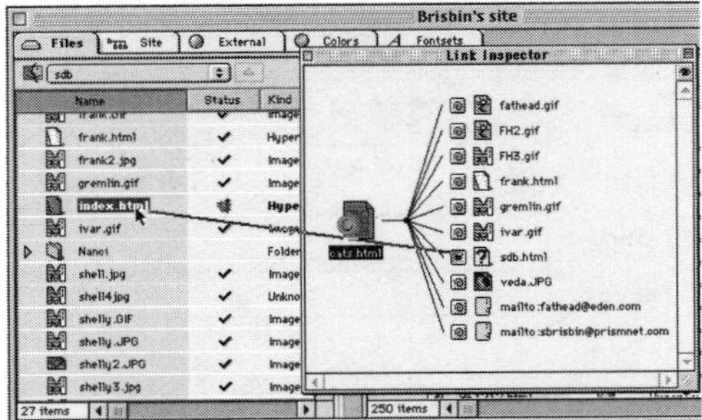

Figure 16.35 Point and shoot from the Link Inspector to create a new link in the Site view.

Figure 16.36 The button opens the Site window's second pane.

To check a site for errors:

1. Click the icon bar at the upper right corner of the Site window (**Figure 16.36**). The Site window splits into two panes.
2. Click on the Errors tab in the right pane. The result looks like **Figure 16.37**.

   The Errors tab displays missing files: those that are linked to by other pages in the site but can't be found within the site folder. These files may have been deleted entirely, or may have had their names changed, possibly because the site has been edited by multiple people.
3. Click on a missing file. The Error Inspector (**Figure 16.38**) displays the URL for the missing file. This information may give you a clue to its actual whereabouts.
4. If you can't resolve the broken link with its URL, choose Open Link Inspector from the toolbar. The missing link appears on the right, and the file or files

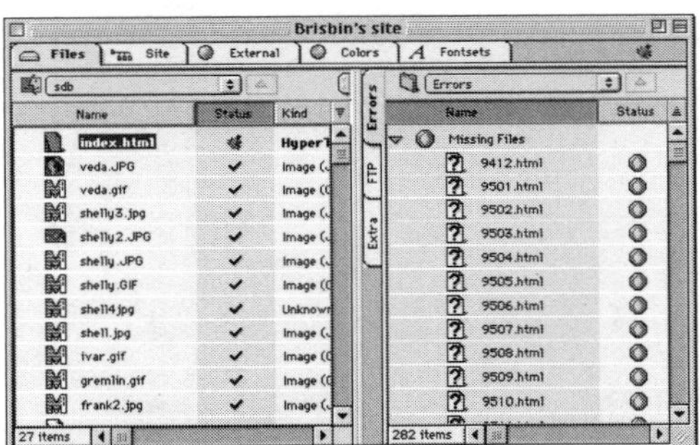

Figure 16.37 Here's the Site window's right pane with missing files visible.

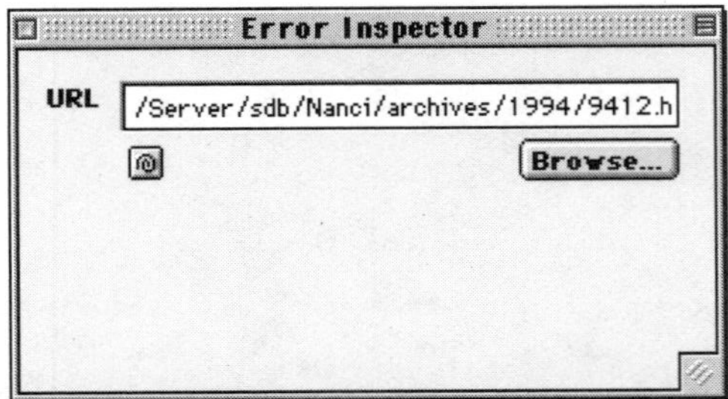

Figure 16.38 Click on a missing file to bring up the Error Inspector.

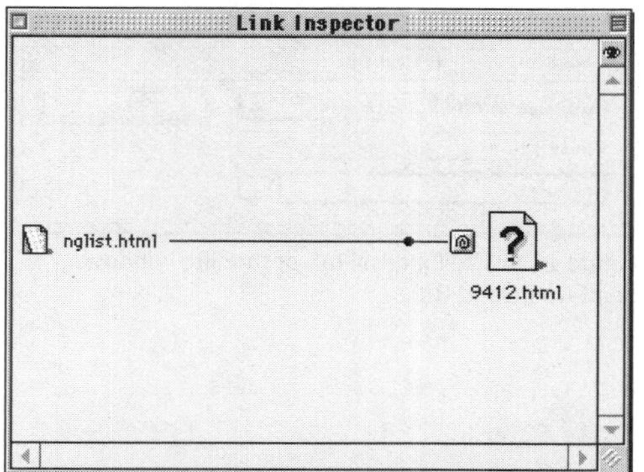

Figure 16.39 The Link Inspector shows the missing link (right) and the file or files that use it.

Figure 16.40 The Find dialog box.

that use it appear on the left (**Figure 16.39**). Now you know which pages in your site use the missing file, and you can decide whether to solve the problem by eliminating the link, by recreating the file, or by leaving no stone unturned to find the original.

Following are some options.

If you think the file has been misplaced within the site:

1. Click Find Files in Site (**Figure 16.40**) from the toolbar. The Find dialog box appears, displaying the Find File tab.
2. Type all or part of the name of the file you want to look for.
3. Click Find.
4. If GoLive finds the file, it will be highlighted in the Site window. If the file has been moved to the wrong folder, you can drag it back into its original location within the site. In that case, an Update References dialog will appear.
5. Click OK to update the site.

If you think the file has been renamed:

1. In the Link Inspector, note the files to which the missing file should be connected. Write the file names down or print the Link Inspector window.
2. Search the site manually, or with the Find command, for files that may be the one you're looking for.
3. When you locate the file you want, restore its original name, in which case all of the links will be repaired. Or open the file and add links according to the list you made from the Link Inspector.

continues on next page

To locate and repair URLs:

1. Be sure that the "Check external URLs" option is checked in the Site Preferences window.
2. If you're not already online, connect to the Internet.
3. Click Update Site from the toolbar. GoLive checks all the links and URLs in your site.
4. Click on the External tab in the Site window.
5. Click the Status label to sort URLs by their Status.
6. If necessary, bring invalid URLs to the top by clicking the Ascending/Descending arrow at the right of the Site window. **Figure 16.41** shows several invalid URLs.
7. Click on a URL and open its Inspector, or view the URL in the Site window's URL column.
8. Examine the URL for any obvious problems.
9. Open the Link Inspector. The Link Inspector will show you which files within your site link to the URL.
10. If all the information you've gathered leads you to believe that the URL should be valid, copy the URL from the Inspector and paste it into your Web browser.
11. Connect to the Web and check the URL.
12. If the URL does not work, delete it from your site and remove or replace any links to it.

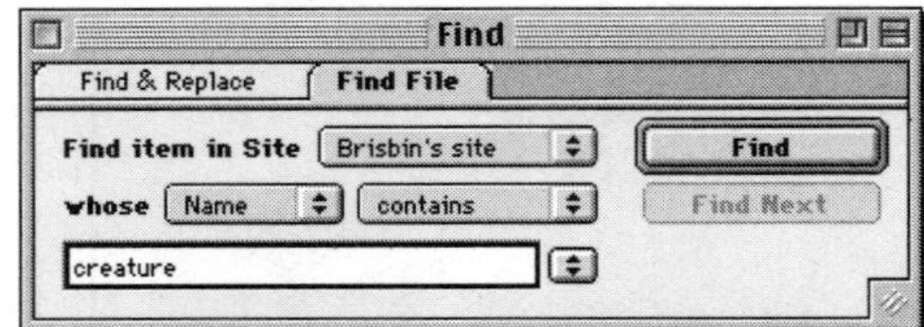

Figure 16.41 The External tab of the Site window displays invalid URLs.

PUBLISHING YOUR SITE

17

After the text is typed, the images placed, the links connected, and errors checked, it's time to put your site on the Web. If your Web server is located in your own office, this may simply be a matter of copying folders to the server machine. If you use an Internet Service Provider (ISP), you'll need to use FTP to transfer your files to a remote server.

Wherever your Web site lives, GoLive can help you get everything in order for the big upload.

In this chapter, I cover:

- Built-in FTP.
- Stand-alone FTP.

Exporting a Site: Three Ways to Publish

GoLive provides three ways to move a site from your computer to the Web:

- Built-in FTP.
- Stand-alone FTP.
- Site export.

Two of these methods (built-in FTP and site export) include features that help you choose the specific files you want to copy to a Web server. Stand-alone FTP doesn't hold your hand as you get ready to publish your site, but it does allow you to perform custom upload, and to download files from an FTP server.

The two FTP publishing methods actually copy your files to a Web server, whereas site export simply copies them to a folder for uploading by any application or method you choose.

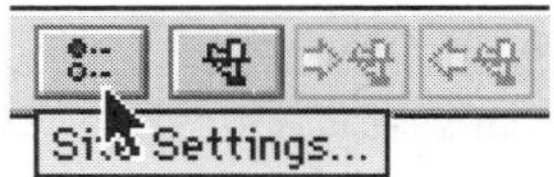

Figure 17.1 Choose Site Settings from the toolbar.

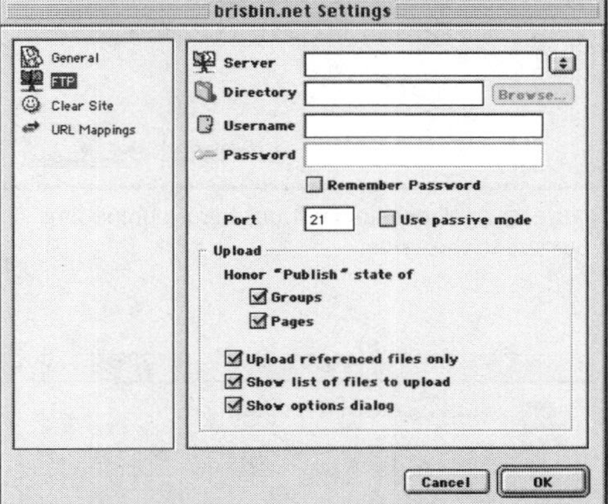

Figure 17.2 Set up access to your Web server from the FTP pane of the Site Settings window.

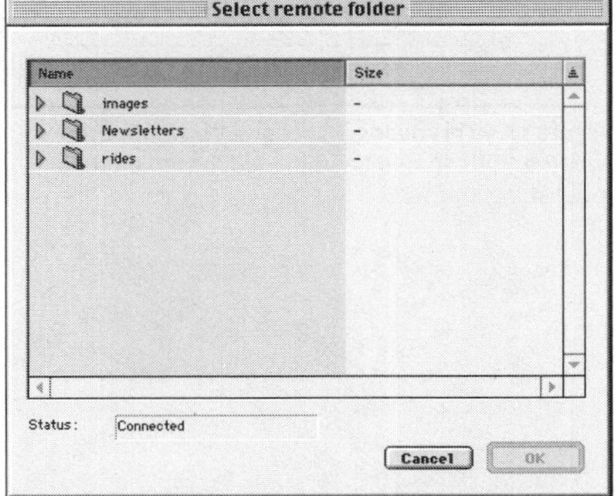

Figure 17.3 A directory window displays the contents of your FTP server.

Built-in FTP

GoLive includes an FTP feature that can copy your complete site to a single Web server. To use it, you'll need to configure Site Settings for uploading and choose which files, and under what circumstances, you want published.

To configure built-in FTP:

1. Open a site that is ready to be uploaded to a Web server.
2. Choose Site Settings (**Figure 17.1**).
3. In the Site Settings window, click the FTP item on the left side of the window. The result appears in **Figure 17.2**.
4. Type the domain name of your server, such as **ftp.myserver.com**, in the Server field, and the name of the directory you want to upload to, such as **/directory/**, in the directory field.
5. Type your user name in the field.
6. Type your password.
7. If you're not sure of the directory path to your site on the Web server, click Browse. GoLive connects to the server.
8. After connecting to the Internet, GoLive will display your server's directories in a window that looks like **Figure 17.3**.
9. To choose a subdirectory, click on it. If the directory you want is below one that is currently displayed, click on its triangle (Mac) or plus sign (Windows) to open it, and locate the one you want.
10. With a directory selected, click OK. The Directory field contains the path to your upload destination.

continues on next page

11. In the FTP Site Settings window, choose whether to use the publish status of groups (folders) and/or pages to determine which files will be uploaded to the Web server. If you leave the boxes checked, only files that are labeled Publish (all are by default) will be uploaded.
12. Leaving the "Upload referenced files only" option checked tells GoLive to ignore unused files within your site.
13. The "Show list" and "Show Options" checkboxes provide a final chance for you to override publishing settings before files are transferred to the server.

✔ Tip

- If you have trouble connecting to a server, check your connection settings with your system administrator or Webmaster. Even if you have the server, directory, user name, and password right, you may find that you need to change the port number and/or click the Passive mode checkbox. Passive mode connections are often used when FTP servers are protected by security firewalls.

To upload your site:

1. Choose Connect to Server from the Site menu or from the toolbar.
2. When the connection is complete, choose Upload to Server from the Site menu.
3. If you chose to view options before publishing the site, a dialog box (**Figure 17.4**) appears, asking whether you want to publish the site according to the parameters you've set. Click OK to proceed, or change options now.
4. A final dialog box (**Figure 17.5**) lists the files to be uploaded. If you want to eliminate specific files from the upload, uncheck them.

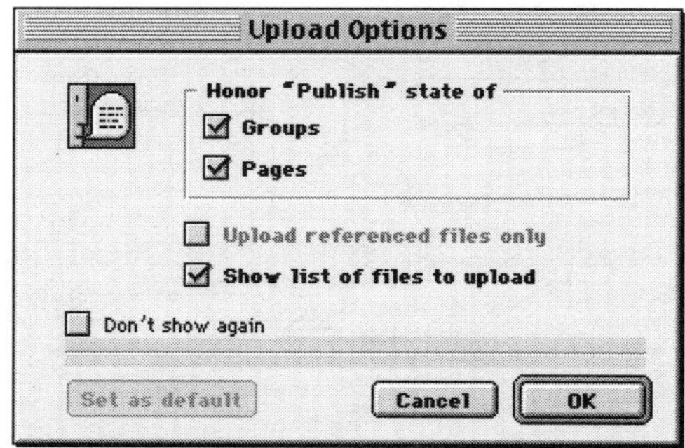

Figure 17.4 Choose final options before uploading your site to the server.

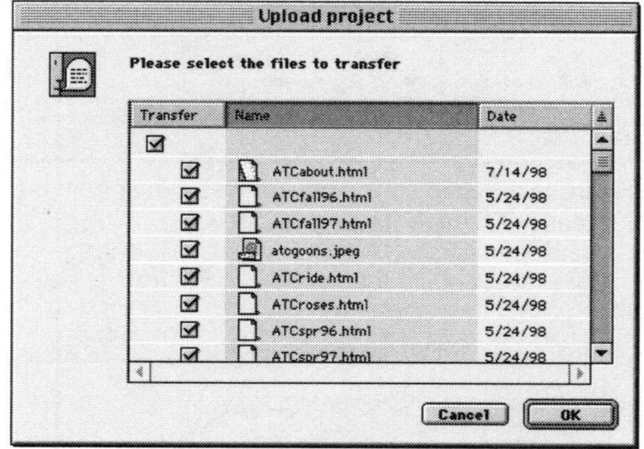

Figure 17.5 This dialog box allows you to determine whether files should be uploaded, based on their publishing status.

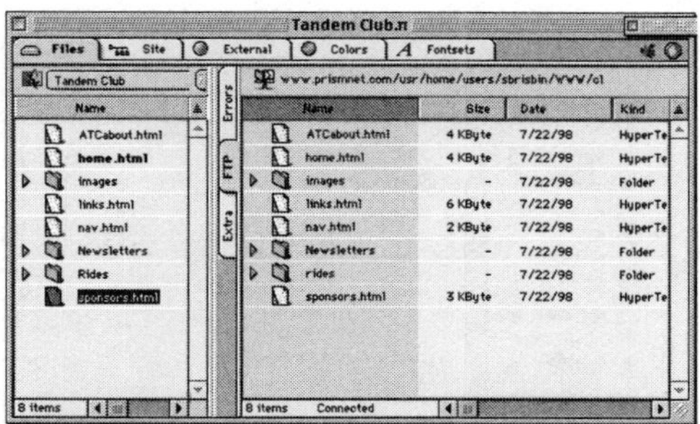

Figure 17.6 The Site window lets you know which files were actually uploaded to the server.

5. Click OK to begin uploading. A status window shows the upload's progress.

   When all files are uploaded, the right-hand pane of the Site window displays them.

6. If the pane is not visible, open it by clicking the button above and to the right of the label bar in the Site window. Then, click FTP to see the results of your upload (**Figure 17.6**).

✔ Tips

- GoLive's indication that you are connected to the server once you click Connect is a bit subtle. Look in the bottom right side of the Site window for the word "Connected."
- When you disconnect from the server, the list of uploaded files on the right side of the Site window goes away, leaving an empty pane. If you want to work with the list of uploaded files (to compare it to the original list, sort it, etc.) do so before breaking your connection to the server.
- You can keep your GoLive site in sync with the directory on your FTP server with the Download from Server menu item. Connect to the server as described on the previous page, and choose Download from Server from the Site menu. GoLive compares the files in your site folder to those stored on the server. If newer files are found on the server, GoLive downloads them to their proper location in your site, replacing the older versions.

To upload new or changed files to the FTP server:

1. Connect to the FTP server as you did in the preceding section.
2. Choose Upload to Server from the Site menu. GoLive compares your site with the files on the server and uploads the new or changed ones.

Stand-Alone FTP

Just like any FTP client (you may have used Fetch, Anarchie, WSFTP, CuteFTP, or a Web browser to exchange files with an FTP server), GoLive can upload and download files on your terms, one file at a time, or a whole site's worth. The stand-alone FTP tool is designed to let you pick and choose files to copy, and to give you a clear picture of the directory structure available on your FTP server. Like other FTP tools, it can also be used to grab any file stored on a remote server, whether or not it's related to your Web site.

To configure the FTP tool:

1. Choose Preferences from the Edit menu.
2. Click on the Network label. Network preferences appear in **Figure 17.7**.
3. Ⓜ If you use Internet Config to set up your access to Internet tools, click Use Always to apply your current Internet Config settings, or Open Internet Config to confirm or create settings.
4. If the FTP or HTTP server you will use to upload your files uses a proxy server, or requires passive mode access for security reasons, click the appropriate checkboxes and set the proxies up using information provided by your network administrator or ISP.
5. Click the triangle (Mac) or plus sign (Windows) to the left of the Network label to view more preferences and open FTP Server preferences by clicking on the label.
6. Click New to add a server.
7. Fields for server name, directory path, and user name appear. Enter the information according to the format shown in **Figure 17.8**.
8. To add another server, repeat steps 7 and 8.

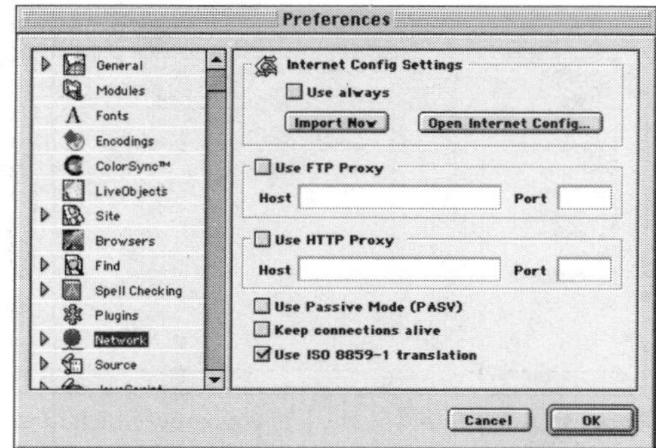

Figure 17.7 The FTP pane of the Preferences window.

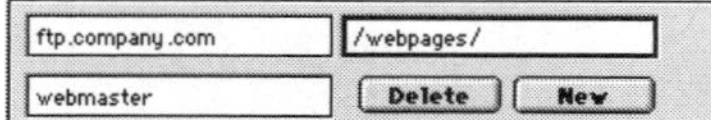

Figure 17.8 Add a new server to the list of FTP servers.

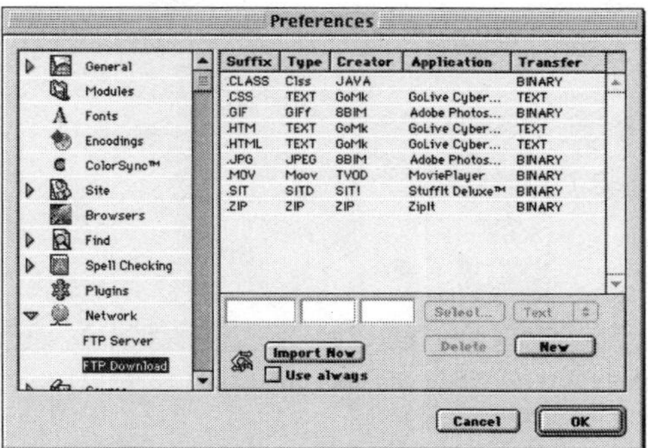

Figure 17.9 View or add file mapping suffixes in the Up/Download preferences pane.

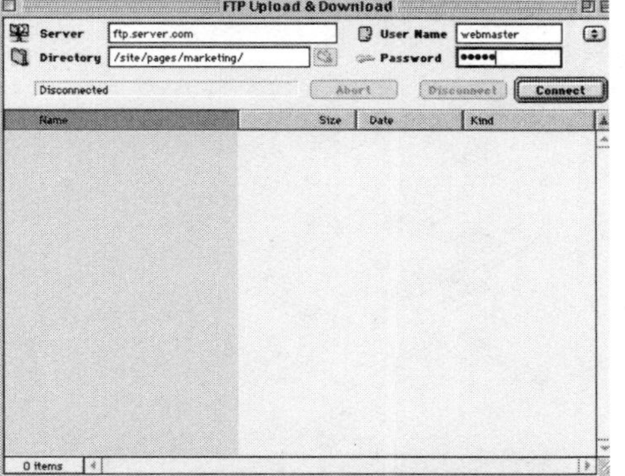

Figure 17.10 The FTP Upload and Download window provides another place to set up an FTP server.

Figure 17.11 Choose an FTP Server from the popup menu.

✔ Tips

- If you've already configured a server connection using the Site window's FTP tool, those settings appear in the FTP Server window, and will show up when we move to the FTP upload/download window.
- Ⓜ If you chose to use Internet Config options with GoLive, you've already provided instructions on how the Mac should deal with files you download. Internet Config matches a downloaded file's suffix (.zip, .sit, .mov, .html, etc.) with a Mac application and file type, so that you can open the file under Mac OS. GoLive also includes some built-in file mapping, and you can add new mappings by hand in the FTP Download window (**Figure 17.9**). The best way to ensure consistent file mapping on your Mac is to use Internet Config and choose the Use Always checkbox in this window.

To use stand-alone FTP:

1. With GoLive open (you can be working within a site file or not), choose FTP Upload & Download from the File menu. The Upload/Download window appears (**Figure 17.10**).
2. If you have already set up one or more FTP servers, the fields at the top of the window will be filled in. To choose a new server, enter a set of parameters or choose a server from the popup menu at the upper right corner of the window (**Figure 17.11**).

continues on next page

3. Click Connect. GoLive will attempt to open an Internet connection, via PPP or over your LAN connection, and will open the FTP server when it succeeds. The server's directories and files appear (**Figure 17.12**).
4. Navigate through the window just as you would in the Finder or Windows Explorer, or in a GoLive site.
5. To upload a file or folder, drag it from the Finder or from the Site window into the server window, onto the appropriate directory label. The FTP tool copies the file or files.
6. To download a file from the server, drag it from the server window into a Finder window.
7. When you've finished working with this server, click the Disconnect button. If you're connected to the Internet via a dial-up connection, you will need to disconnect the phone call separately.

✔ Tips

- You can also download items by double-clicking them in the FTP server window. When you do, you'll be presented with a standard Save dialog. Navigate to the folder you'd like to use, and GoLive will copy the file or directory.
- You can use the labels at the top of the FTP Upload and Download window to sort server directories and files, just as you would in the Finder or the GoLive site window.

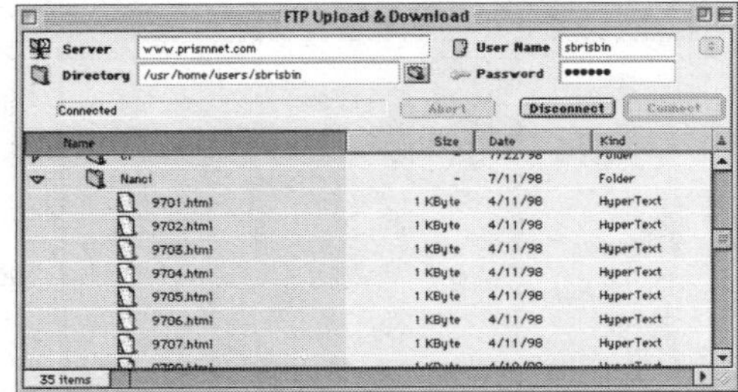

Figure 17.12 When you are connected to a server, its contents appear here.

Using Web download

GoLive can grab and download a Web page, including the HTML file itself, along with linked images or media files.

To download a page:

1. Choose Web Download from the File menu.
2. Type the site's URL of the page you want into the dialog box.
3. Click Save As.
4. GoLive asks where you want to save the index page. If you're connected to the Internet, downloading begins, and a status box keeps you updated on the download's progress. If you're not connected, GoLive attempts to make a connection and then downloads the page.

Exporting a Site

If you're not quite ready to upload your site, or if you need to prepare it according to a structure established by your Webmaster or service provider, you can use the Export Site command as the first step to publication.

Although most people won't find the export option easier than either FTP choice, there are a few circumstances in which it could be useful. If, for example, your Web server is a Mac or PC on your network, you can export a site and drag it into the proper directory on the server. You can also specify publishing options, like requiring that an exported site include only files that are being used within the site, or that include a Publish flag.

To export a site:

1. With the Site window open, choose Export Site from the Site menu. The Export Site Options window appears (**Figure 17.13**).
2. Choose whether you want the site to be exported "As in site" (using the folder structure you created within the Site window), "Separate pages and media" (creates one folder each for HTML pages and media files), or "Flat" (puts all site files in a single folder). If you choose to separate files, or to export the site flat, GoLive recreates the site's links to accommodate the new folder structure.
3. Leaving the Honor Publish State boxes checked will cause all files and/or groups (folders) with a Publish flag to be exported with your site. By default, GoLive sets files to be published, so that no files will be left out unless you have changed their publishing status.

Figure 17.13 The Export Site Options window.

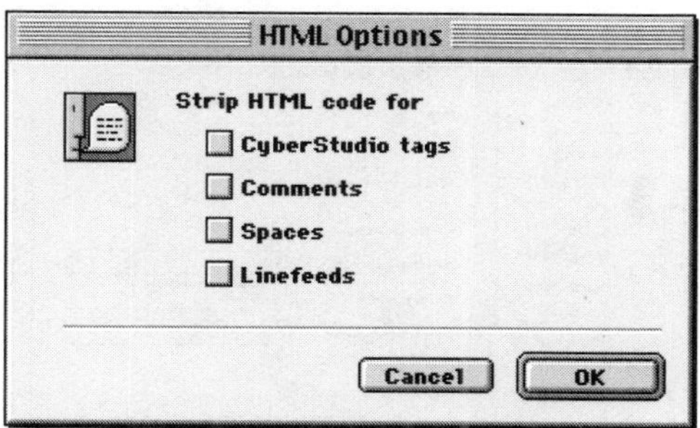

Figure 17.14 Strip excess HTML tags in the HTML Options window.

4. If you do uncheck a publish checkbox, the "Export only referenced files" box lights up, allowing you to make that choice by clicking on the checkbox.
5. Leave "Export referenced files that are not part of the site" checked if your site links to files that are not part of the site.
6. Click the More button if you want to clean up your HTML code for export. **Figure 17.14** displays HTML Options.
7. Click a checkbox to eliminate extra HTML information; Stripping GoLive tags eliminates some GoLive-specific code and prevents GoLive from downloading and editing plugin- and animation-related features of your page. Comments, spaces, and linefeeds increase the size of the page, and they can make it appear cluttered.
8. Click OK to return to the export Options window, and click OK again to export the site.
9. When GoLive presents a dialog box, find a location for the newly exported site and click OK. GoLive creates a folder for the site and copies your site's contents to the folder. When the process is complete, a window appears to tell you what was transferred, including the number of unreferenced files, if any, that are part of the exported site. You can now copy the exported site to a server volume or use FTP to upload it to a remote Internet site.

continues on next page

✔ Tips

- When you export a site with separate folders for media and HTML files, GoLive creates folders called Pages and Media by default. You can use different names by setting them in the Preferences window before you export your site. Under the Site Preferences label, choose the Folder Names option and name your folders under the Export Folder Names heading (**Figure 17.15**).
- A few old GoLive item names from previous versions have made their way into GoLive 4: if you see the word *group* where you think it should say *folder*, your intuition is right. Similarly, older versions of GoLive referred to *sites* as *projects*, and this term has survived in a few preferences windows.

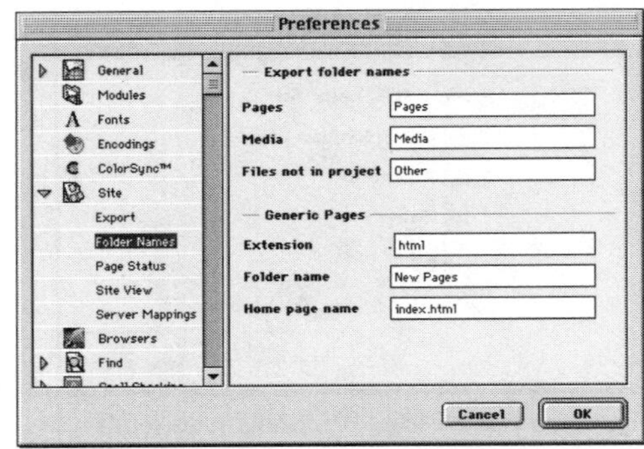

Figure 17.15 Rename export folders in the Folder Names section of the Preferences window.

INDEX

D

E

F

G

H

INDEX

INDEX

INDEX

U

V

W

X

Z

TK 5105.8885 .A34 B74 1999